"Hoi, Wotcher Doin' 'Ere?"

Great grandads Fish and Chip Shop – J.W. Insole (Wet, Smoked and Fried)
Est. mid to late 1880s. Demolished 1927/8

WAPPING DOCKLAND MEMORIES

of

John Insole

1931 - 1945

"Hoi, Wotcher Doin' 'Ere?"

Sister Lily and me, Caught at a more angelic moment.
I would not smile ' for the birdie'. Hermitage, 1932

Contents

The rights of John Insole to be identified as the author of this work has been asserted in accordance with the Copyright, Designs and Patents Act, 1988

ISBN 978-1-915787-00-2

Printed by Biddles Books Limited,
King's Lynn, Norfolk

Dedications

To Lily in Memorial
1928 – 2013

Also especially to my wife Margaret and family, Peter Susan and Gill.
Who have withstood my frequent bouts of enthusiasms, depressions
and frustration with patience and encouragement in equal doses.

Not least the extraordinary environment and the vibrant community
of Wapping people. Which together enriched my memories.

Acknowledgements

Suzane Williams. 'Quick brown fox' Cambridge. For her contribution of transcribing on to digital file 63,440 words from my original untidy manuscript. Who unfortunately could not continue due to ill health;

Linda Lait 'Office Assist' Sudbury Suffolk who completed her valued contribution of 97,500 words to finalise the completed digital file;

Kathy Cohen who finally proof-read to 'print ready' the whole… Thereby rescuing me from a disorganised depth of despair;

Tamsin Bookey, Heritage Manager and the team at Tower Hamlets Library and history Archive. For their valued help and interest;

Ray Newton and Helen Keep. Trustees Wapping History Trust for their encouragement and interest;

Nigel Mitchell of Biddles Book Printers Norfolk. Who demonstrated an extreme level of patience with my digital incompetence;

Peter Insole (son) who organised artwork and photo illustrations, scanning to digital file;

Paul Missen (Son-in-Law) Photographing and scanning all my original artwork to digital file;

Susan Insole (daughter) who created the artwork for the front cover, derived from my own descriptions and sketches;

Gill Missen (daughter) who had (and still does) supported me/us with enthusiasm and encouraging comment to keep going through Covid lockdowns and shielding and other ongoing age and health issues, principally cancer;

Josh Hurrell (Family Member) who completed layout of book cover and title design;

Lucy Menzies. Her book 'Father Wainright, a Record' 1947 (out of print). Copyright holders: St Peters Church, Wapping Lane

Finally myself and a small pat on the back for my abiding stock of everlasting Wapping memories, including my own artwork sketched from memory. Which made possible and created this memoir.

Chapter 1

First Impressions

I always hesitate whenever I am asked the question: "Whereabouts in London do you come from?"

It's not because I am embarrassed to answer that causes the hesitation. It has always been a matter of some pride with me that my London origins might seem to some to be rather confusing and obscure. As far as I am prepared to go at this particular time is that I was actually born in 1931 somewhere on what was then a brand-spanking new council housing estate in Dagenham, Essex, but for some inexplicable and difficult to understand reason, before I had reached the age of a single solitary year, and not yet positively aware of my individual existence, never mind my actual location in the scheme of things, Mum and Dad and sister Lily, who was in a better position than I was to know what was what, because she was three year older and that much wiser than me, decided to move back homeward to Wapping, the very heart of London's extensive dockland area. In fact, it couldn't be more central than its postal district: E1W.

It's all very well to speak nostalgically about the Isle-of-Dogs, Surrey docks and other later developments beyond the City of London's boundaries, Wapping's place, being directly situated close up to the city's ancient wall, was the first and natural choice to expand the growing sea borne trade. Bearing in mind that the curious never ask me where I was born, assuming that London's designation is enough for anyone, I tend to ignore the otherwise interesting fact that I was

1

born in Dagenham, Essex, which was not London at all. So, with that, I shall pass it over as being an indication that I want to be taken seriously…observing the niceties of correctness and veracity.

I concede the point though that my enquirers generally take the view that my birthplace was London, and a simple 'yes' would have been enough to confirm it. However, having been asked the question so many times, I had come to expect some strange reactions to my reply: "I come from Wapping". This startling revelation more often than not causes my questioner to look at me with something bordering on the incredulous. The look always accompanied by a momentary pause, as if they are trying to work it out in their minds.

I know from long experience what usually follows: "Wapping… where on earth is that?"

Long explanations are usually necessary. So, I suppose I ought not to take anything for granted and that you may not know exactly where or what Wapping is all about and repeat the explanations.

Of course, present company excepted, there are always the 'clever clogs' who claim extensive knowledge of London's equally extensive geography. But even these 'smarties' are inclined to display some mystification by intimating that although he or she had certainly "heard of it", it generally transpired that 'heard of it' is about the extent of their knowledge. Insisting that they most certainly 'knew of it' offering me the consolation of a profound nod of the head, whilst searching in the depths of their minds for some vague recollection, "Oh yes…it's in the East End…isn't it?" Others with a more facetious turn of mind regard my reply as something of a good 'leg pull'. "Oh yes…that's a whopping good un' that is". This is only for starters. It usually proceeds from the ridiculous to the positively moronic without any further help from me…so you see…that is why I always hesitate!

2

Well anyway, to cut a long tedious story down to manageable proportions, I had arrived at the mellowing middle portion of my first year having somewhat survived under great difficulties in that otherwise salubrious part of Essex, otherwise known as either Becontree or more generally, Dagenham. I say, 'somewhat survived' because according to the best reports available to me now of this interesting time, it was discovered that the salubrious airs of Dagenham did not exactly suit my tendency to be 'chesty'. The best medical advice available at the time suggested that we move... nowhere in particular was suggested... anywhere would do, anywhere else rather than Dagenham. I now suspect that medical science being what it was at the time, that there was no other cure available.

I had probably caused various and many Hippocratic heads to be scratched and over-exercised for a solution to my bronchial problems. The collective opinion came up with the obvious conclusion that the best remedy was for us to quit Dagenham for more conducive airs. Anyway, such a move would solve their diagnostic dilemma, so long as we went as far away as possible and out of their sphere of medical influence. Naturally, Dad being a Wapping born and bred man, the obvious solution for him was to move back homeward.

In any case, every Wapping born and bred knew that Wapping was the healthiest place on earth. Everyone knew that it was 'where seven winds met', so 'Big Gran Insole' said.

I puzzled for years over this marvel of geographical wonders. I thought that perhaps it was rather like Grandma's cure for a cold. Lemon an' honey, hot. As she told me "Lemon t' cut it, an' honey t' cure it". Perhaps the mix of seven winds was something like that? Until I realised (much later as it happens) docks...of course it should have been obvious. In the days before steam ships...sails. Sailing ships need wind, and ships came into the London Docks from every quarter of the Seven Seas. Therefore, there had to be seven winds to bring them home. The only problem I saw with this was that winds from some quarters must be decidedly unhealthy... but then, lemon juice is bitter and the honey sweet, mixed all together the perfect cure for chesty bronchial conditions. Provided the proverbial London fogs were ignored.

The other knotty problem that exercised my mind for years was how Dad and Mum and sister Lily had come to live in Dagenham in the first place, when Wapping had obviously offered so much?

During the late twenties, the London County Council (LCC) had adopted the belated promise to create a 'land fit for heroes' and had embarked on a programme of extensive slum clearance, which on reflection might have had more to do with increasing industrial growth than with a promise made to the heroes (most of whom had been slaughtered in foreign fields anyway). Building the vast council housing estates of Becontree and Dagenham to house the dispossessed... Mum and Dad and sister Lily were caught up in the rush (well the trickle) of those who were actually willing to be dispossessed and reluctantly accepted the offer to become a country esquire and lady of a dwelling euphemistically described as a 'cottage' in the green fields of faraway Essex. The only trouble with this was that in the building of the estate the green fields mysteriously disappeared under endless acres of concrete, roads, and equally endless rows of terraced houses, each one looking exactly like its neighbour's, but then, the upside of all this must have done some good. In the fullness of time, I was born... these things I am told are quite natural in country places but things, as I have said, didn't quite go as planned.

At the time of the family's trek homeward back to Wapping, my opinion was never asked for. In any case, my horizons were limited by the urgent necessities of the moment, these being what they normally are in one so young, I doubt that I could have expressed an opinion other than to let someone know I was either hungry, uncomfortable, wet or all three together, these needs being satisfactorily provided for. I suppose I must have been reasonably content with my circumstance and location. If I had known though, at the time, discoveries in the fullness of time and experience, how much Wapping was going to mean for me, I have no doubt at all what my opinion would have been.

The LCC having gone to all the trouble and expense to provide us with a two bedroomed house, and luxury of luxuries, a bathroom and indoor toilet of our very own, could not and certainly would not, provide us with council accommodation in Wapping. The policy had been to move people out of the area. There was no other alternative but to find private accommodation...oh dearie me!

Obviously, there were no great opportunities of choice in the matter. The wonder of it all is that a move back was ever contemplated at all.

Chapter 2

A Brief but Very Necessary Geography Lesson and a Little History Thrown In

Wapping is situated just east of the City of London and shares a common boundary with that historic square mile. In ancient times the city was surrounded by the city wall, a stone and brick rubble-filled construction built by the Romans, its remnants can still be seen to this day in places.

Tradition has it that London was a fortified settlement long before the Romans came. A perfectly reasonable assumption bearing in mind that Britain was not as Roman historians would have us believe, populated by hordes of uncivilised woad-painted barbarians, but on the contrary, a nation, or more properly a group of nations, who were individually well organised by civic administrations, capable of expressing themselves through channels of art, religion, and culture. It is also reasonable to assume that if such a fortified settlement existed it would be an important settlement, since London is sited at the ancient limit of the navigable River Thames, and the first easily fordable place fifty miles from the sea. There is also a school of thought which maintains that the very name of London itself comes from Roman pre-history. The Romans merely latinised the name to Londinium.

It is easy to understand that whoever held the fort, held the power. It would have been well defended. The Romans knew this only too well and quickly replaced the ditch and palisade embankment fortifications with their more secure wall, probably extending them in the process. The wall encircled the garrison on three sides: to the east, to the west and the north, and the Thames served as a barrier to the south. Londinium became a very important garrison, for one thing the Thames was Britain's prime river, for another London was sited almost at the centre of their campaigns of conquest, set nicely between the warring kingdoms who were taking it into their heads to resist the invasion of their territories. In fact, the timetable for the conquest was completely upset, it took fifty years to finally subdue the contrary islanders. So much for woad-painted, flint axe bearing barbarians… even then only as far north as the Scots Borders. It can even be said that the northern Celtish Welsh and the Picts and Scots were never really brought to the Roman heel. Neither would it be going too far to suggest that throughout the four hundred years of the Roman occupation, the province of 'Pax Britannica' was always a 'Painium in the posterium' for them.

For this reason alone, the Londinium garrison was extremely important strategically. Stores and the sea-sick legions could be brought up river right into the enemy camp, as it were. It was also an easily defended base from which to launch their campaigns of 'pacification' into the deeply wooded interior. However, in spite of London's importance strategically, it was never considered as the capital city of the province. The Romans liked their creature comforts too much for that.

London wasn't quite the place we see today. What the Roman's saw were the sparsely populated tracts of black muddy marshland of the wide Thames Valley, shrouded for most of the year with a lowering mist of damp decay, dark moisture dripping forests reaching down from the wide river valley hills to its reed bogged margins and a year of short summers and long dark winter months wreathed in spirit lowering fogs of clinging vapours. The legionary troops didn't matter too much, but who could blame the generals for wanting the capital elsewhere.

Over the four centuries of the Occupation, London's military role became less important. Young Paulus either managed to get a hundred sesterces to buy himself out, or he died of pneumonia waiting for it (actually I think he went on to become an Emperor, or something). Economics became the main pre-occupation of the port. Although the main principle of the garrison remained, it was still a fortress set against the sullen populace, and the precedent was set for the next nineteen hundred years.

When the Romans finally left these shores, with a final shout of 'whoopee' from the lower ranks who saw the prospect of drying out under a Mediterranean sun, the abandoned city of Londinium was left to the predations of various mini kingdoms each trying to fill the vacuum left by the departed legions... Briton's history descended into the so-called 'Dark Ages', marked principally by the coming to these shores by the Saxons and the Danes.

Sometime during the seventh century, Saxon settlers came to the marshes to the east of the city wall and established their farms. The marsh came to be called 'Stepney' named after the Saxon chieftain 'Stybba', the landing place of Stybba, or Stybbanhyth.

The Saxons sorted out the indigenous locals in time, took possession of the abandoned city, refurbished the ancient walls, built churches on the sites of the abandoned Roman temples, and introduced institutions more in keeping with a well defensible city, still very important as a fortress and enough to make any aggressor realise that any aggression was doomed to bash itself out against the ancient ramparts. There was no way to breach the wall, no way to lay siege and starve out the defenders. If ever there was a jewel in the crown of a monarch it was London.

With this sort of supremacy thrust upon it by the legacy of the Romans, and by virtue of its position, London continued to hold the bulk of the nation's trade. How much trade there was there is no way of knowing. All that can be said is that the Saxon kingdom of Britain became the richest nation of Europe. A real foretaste of what was to come in later centuries. London was to continue in this favourable state until the next major event in its history - William, that intrepid conqueror and Harold, and the Saxon king's demise at Hastings.

Eventually, William having done his conquering and taken possession of London, realised that the populous was none too keen on his feudalistic ideas and were kicking up a 'shindig' from time to time, caused to be built the Tower to the east of the old city wall, overlooking the Stybbanhyth Saxon marsh farms.

Wapping's name itself is reputed to be of Saxon origins. Wapp was either, it is said, an original itinerant coloniser's name or alternatively it is suggested 'Wapp' could be translated as 'place of the mud'. Wapping as it came to be known was certainly that - nothing less than a tidal flat, flooded at every high tide.

William, as history will confirm me, managed to hold on, decided to wrest the best possible return on his investment of conquest. The doling out of large lumps of prime Saxon properties to his henchmen, the building of the Tower together with about ten thousand other castles and fortresses, must have cost him (or most likely the dispossessed Saxon landowners) quite a bit. In the style of monarchic monopoly of the times, his investment had to increase at least a million-fold to have been worthwhile. He made sure that trade grew with his now open provinces, producing a lively export and import situation. His coffers filled to bursting. He had grabbed the richest nation of Europe and was determined on making it richer still.

It was never my intention to enter into a detailed account of how London became a busy maritime port and the largest of the big league of international trade and commerce, nor of London as the greatest trading institution the world has ever known. It has been rightly said that at one period: "All the world's trade found its way to London".

Therefore I shall take the liberty of jumping over the next five centuries after William and take it for granted that he continued to enjoy the prosperity of the port, and simply acknowledge that it is more than likely that he gave it its initial boost. It wasn't until the Elizabethan age of global discoveries and maritime enterprise that really began the process of Empire building and world domination of trade, a situation that generated a huge problem. The upper Thames at London bordered on the chaotic with hundreds of vessels arriving daily. It was said that it was possible to walk from bank to bank within the city walls and not get one's feet wet. Countless vessels lay at anchor in the Pool for weeks on end waiting to discharge their cargoes. Most times the ships had to be unloaded mid-stream, first into 'lighters' (hence the name, it made the vessel lighter). To ease the problem, a few berths were provided on the Southwark side of the river, but the South side and Southwark wasn't the City of London but a city in its own right, which meant that London's merchants lost control of the goods landed. There was, however, another alternative. Downstream beyond the city wall towards the east and the sea, onto the tidal flats of Wapping.

This wasn't altogether an inspirational idea because these activities had been going on for centuries, probably since Roman times or earlier. Evidence for this has been the discovery of ancient timber jetties some of them hundreds of yards from the present river frontage. It made good sense to increase the number of berths there, at first the only facilities provided were riverside jetties and these stretched down river a mile or so from the city wall and the Tower.

The major problem with this solution was that tolls and import duties had always been a jealously guarded prerogative of the Crown, and these dues fell directly into the Royal coffers. The Royal Exchequer wasn't about to surrender this privilege. By tradition, these dues were levied at the jetties within the city walls. A decree was issued that all vessels that carried duty traffic still had to discharge their cargoes within the city bounds. Even so, there was still an enormous volume of dutiless traffic. Wapping's jetties were fully occupied constantly... Thus, it was that Wapping's role in the building of Britain's dominance in global trade began long before such places as Liverpool, Bristol, Southampton were little more than seaside village harbours (with a few notable exceptions), London had become Britain's principal port. Wapping's part in this extraordinary process was extremely vital and deserves better recognition than is usually reserved for it.

Over the next few centuries trade continued to grow, and the vessels carrying it grew in size too. By the end of the seventeen hundreds, it became clear to the city merchants that deep water berths were becoming urgent. The Thames being a tidal river caused problems with larger ships settling onto the mud at jetties, added to which were the problems of security. It has been estimated that two percent of every cargo that arrived in the port was lost to thieves. Indeed, it wasn't unknown for whole cargoes to disappear altogether along with all the removable parts of the vessel itself. Added to which the landed goods were subjected to the predations of organised gangs of plunderers. Nothing was safe either ashore or afloat. Every effort to stem the losses failed. The merchants and city bankers responded by setting up the Thames Marine Force at Wapping Old Stairs in 1798. By then of course the river front, the 'Lower Pool' at Wapping, was a thriving riverside dock. Wapping itself was also a haven for the roving bands of Fagin-like thieves.

Following this enterprising development of a water borne police force, discovering that it hadn't made so much as a dent in the ranks of the river pirates, it was realised that the only alternative was to petition Parliament for permission to construct enclosed and secure deep water docks in Wapping. Permission being granted, the dock building was to eventually transform Wapping, an event that should have destroyed the old and replaced it with something new. Prior to the dock building of 1800-20, for nearly seven centuries the area close up to the city wall and the Tower was extremely crowded and indeed the marsh beyond.

St Katherine's was thickly tenanted by hutments of the most primitive sort... the homes of the poorest of the poor, the destitute and the desperate.

St Katherine's took its name from a hospice that had been founded by Queen Matilda in 1125 to serve the poor and destitute. There were plenty of candidates for its ministration where it stood. The marsh had long been settled beginning with the Saxons, certainly, as a farming community. The land though being unfit for anything other than grazing. The low marsh however, came by degrees an ideal dumping ground for the city's rubbish along with the dumping ground for the city's unwanted wasted humans.

Queen Matilda must have been daily reminded of the vile sight of the stinking marsh and its hordes of wretched people. A view from the Tower's ramparts would have assured her of that. Teeming acres of coarse rotten dwellings erected on a site no better than an evil smelling marsh, the residents themselves no better off than the cattle that once grazed the spot.

The only certain means of sustenance was the easy pickings of river piracy, theft and vice, a mass of seething activity filling the marsh close to the river from the city wall and the Tower moat to the tiny hamlet of Wapping Village itself, no more than three quarters of a mile away to the east. Most of the activity was a constant battle fought by the residents for the means of survival and practically all of that effort by the foulest means, an occupation that was never carried out undercover or shrouded in darkness, the people were far too desperate for that, but rather carried out in the full light of day. Neither was there the slightest trace of conscience lurking in the breasts of the roving bands of murderous cut-throats, cut-purses, pick-pockets, and petty thieves... all perpetrated openly. For who was to stop them?

Parliament having at last agreed to the plan to enclose Wapping, at the same time suggested that various other sites further down river should also be developed, the Isle-of-Dogs, for instance. It was a much bigger area, and, finally, it was also virtually uninhabited except for a few farming communities. There was considerable opposition from the city merchants to this suggestion because any increase of influence further away from the centre of the city meant that they ultimately lost control of it. In the end expediency overcame the objections and the powerful East and West India Companies developed and opened their deep water docks there. Because of the complicated problems of the congested population close up to the city boundaries, and the demolishing and re-siting of the ancient St Katherine's hospice, the dock which took its name was not completed until 1827, quickly followed by Wapping Basin and the larger London Dock complex later. St Katherine's Dock was built within yards of the city wall and the Tower moat.

If the creation of the dock did nothing else, it most certainly cleared the area of the terrifying slum dwellings... It is recorded that 23,000 people were displaced. One wonders though, what happened to them? It can only be assumed now that the majority had to move on and set up their 'rookeries' elsewhere. It was also just as likely that their style of living was not greatly changed. There must also have been many who did manage to find regular work in building the new docks... For the rest... things had not changed dramatically, they were still the sweepings of the city's mean alleys. Their natural survival talents had not diminished with the building of the new dock building. There hadn't been any need to change their ways. They were still caught in the same dire straits of poverty that had beset their fathers and their fathers before them. For them there was no other way, no other redress but to steal and cheat.

They were the young orphan and teenage 'mudlarks' who made sure that there was something to scavenge at low tide by tipping coal, and anything else that came to hand off unattended barges and lighters. 'Dredger men' who stole unguarded cargoes from the quayside while ostensibly 'dredging', 'scuffle hunters' who masqueraded as regular labourers, diverting attention by starting mock fights and carrying off goods in the confusion. 'Night plunderers' who robbed moored vessels and lighters in darkness, 'sweeping boys' who offered to sweep empty holds and cleaned out the cabin while they were about it. 'Trinket sellers' who came to barter as the ship prepared to sail out and robbed as the vessel left port. 'Light horsemen' who claimed the right to spillages, but managed to increase the sweepings of spilled tea, coffee, spices, and sugar, 'lighter men' who stole a percentage of every cargo, and sometimes whole cargoes by off-loading them into stolen lighters in broad daylight. River pirates who raided moored vessels in the Pool, overcoming the watch either by bribery, or complicity or outright violence or just roving bands of 'muggers' and 'pick-pockets' hustling the city crowds, burglars, tricksters and doubtless murderers too.

They had been the dispersed people of St Katherine's and the marsh slums of Wapping whose activities did not disappear with their mean dwellings. All too many had found it necessary to continue in their mean way of life, finding equally mean dwellings wherever they could. They would generally set up their 'rookeries' in such places as Shadwell, Ratcliff and Limehouse. Others clung tenaciously to whatever bits of the old Wapping that weres left to them. Neither should it be denied that in the enthusiasm for the dock development, a lot of dwelling improvements were put in hand. New 'improved' tenement buildings euphemistically called 'improved workers' dwellings' were erected, together with streets of two-up, two-down back-to-back houses crammed into whatever available space was left - all to house the expected hordes of muscle, the men to work the docks. Some areas were set aside for the better off - artisans and such, skilled craftsmen, dock superintendents and the like. Large family town houses were built for them. Trees planted; a small recreation ground set out. In all, the intention was to create a better class of area for the better off... Hey ho! Whatever happened to the dream?

The hordes did arrive, drawn by the offer of decent regular paid labour, including many hundreds of Irish 'Navigators' who came to dig the dock basins, and dug themselves in so deep that they couldn't dig themselves out again, so decided to stay where they were and help to work the finished dock. Those and the indigenous that remained in Wapping, soon learned that 'enclosed dock' meant exactly what it said. The massive walls built to keep them out also had the effect of locking them in. Added to which it did not take long for the separate companies operating the docks to realise that there was a mutual advantage in linking the various basins of Hermitage Basin with the advancing construction of the massive undertaking of the London Dock development, including Shadwell and Wapping Basins, together by lock and canal. As a result, not only were the people trapped within the dock walls, but they also found themselves marooned on a manmade island. There was finally no way to get in or out of Wapping 'tween-d-bridges' of St Katherine's, Hermitage and Wapping Basin entrance locks without crossing a bridge or taking a long hazardous swim to the south bank of the river and Bermondsey. A factor which, ancient history apart, was enough to shape the destiny of Wapping for the next one hundred and fifty years of the dock's existence. Isolated from the rest of London and the East End, the people of Wapping became insular, isolated and inward looking, and finally possessive of their island home.

Chapter 3

Hermitage

Having kicked the dust and mud of Dagenham off our feet, we had come to live in Hermitage. There was absolutely no chance of finding alternative council accommodation in Wapping but somehow, private accommodation had been found in Hermitage Wall, a turning off the High Street close to the Wapping Basin entrance at Pier Head. On reflection, the wonder of finding anything at all after the clearances must have been because nobody wanted a top floor couple of rooms at No. 74 Hermitage Wall.

This part of Wapping is situated close up to the Tower of London and St Katherine's Dock, tight up to Wapping Basin and London Dock, squeezed between the river and the 'Dock Wall', the Wapping Basin entrance known as 'Pier Head'. Hermitage Wall was all of 125 yards long and five yards wide, a side street leading out of Wapping High Street.

The designation 'High Street' must surely bring to mind a picture of a street where one might expect to find the usual amenities of a typical village situation. The shops, a parish church, pub and post office and the like. Not so. Wapping High Street. It ran for three quarters of a mile or thereabouts within yards of the river frontage, but for practically its whole length it snaked like a narrow canyon, the walls of which were the high wharfs on each side of it. Criss-crossed by steel girdered walkways. Looking up, all one saw was a narrow strip of sky over which clouds raced like horses jumping over a ditch. The canyon walls on the river front side of the street were here and there broken by dark narrow passages, set between the wharf walls. These damp flag-stoned tunnels led to stairs to the river and the shoreways.

The original purpose of these stairs was to provide access and public rights of way to the river. This was very important in the days when the river was used more as a public highway. It was also a means of livelihood for many of the locals. In the years prior to the 1800s and even after the Dock enclosures, groups of wherries, skiffs, etc, would be seen gathered at the stairs of the causeways. Some plied their trade as river taxis ferrying passengers up and down and across the river, carrying small loads of goods. 'Bum-boats' plying from ship to ship lying in the Pool, selling to ship bound seamen goods of all descriptions, but mainly beer and spirits.

Crowds of mudlarks. Those mucky scroungers - often orphans or abandoned children beach combing for anything of saleable value, firewood, coal, shreds of discarded cloth of any kind. Fish and vegetable merchants selling their wares to the locals. And of course, the bands of thieves waiting and watching for an easy picking from unguarded jetties and moored vessels... the 'bounty hunters', every one of them legitimate or otherwise.

Over the years though, this right of way had slowly been relinquished. Finally, the wharf owners saw their chance to close most of them off with the plausible excuse that as children had certainly been drowned from time to time, then needs must. The real reason I suspect was that it was more to do with security for the unguarded jetties and moored vessels than for any real concern for the safety of the locals. With gates erected across them, the last public service that they provided were tantalising glimpses of the river, and on a clear day a narrow sighting of the far bank and the mysterious country 'over-the-water' - Bermondsey.

Leading out of the High Street, Hermitage Wall at the 'Pier Head' entrance to Wapping Basin sloped slightly downhill, flanking the dock wall on its right hand side, twenty or so feet high or thereabouts, the wall was built of dirtyish red-yellow bricks, euphemistically called 'London Whites'. But over the years the wall had become grimed with smoke and dirt and covered with a kind of smoke blistered decay.

On the left hand corner out of the High Street, a corner 'sweet and baccy' shop, and proceeding downhill eight or so Georgian three storeyed narrow terraced town houses built in the same kind of bricks as the wall… equally matching its smoke dirtied hue.

At the bottom of the slope the wall and the street turned sharp left forming a right angle. From the High Street it looked as though the street was a cul-de-sac. This was 'our end' of Hermitage Wall, the street though continued on for a few hundred yards until it re-joined the High Street at the Hermitage Dock entrance. Leading off from it in a kind of herring bone fashion, little streets and alleys crammed full of houses, just like our own. At its further end, where it joined the High Street it included the backs of 'Royal Jubilee' buildings. This grand sounding name might be a bit misleading, for there was certainly nothing 'Royal' about them to justify the description… a dark brooding block of flats, four or five storeys high, composed entirely of two or three-roomed flats held together, it seemed to me, by dark concrete stairways and rickety iron balconies at their rear. These tiny flats had as their tenants, families for the most part generally of extraordinary largeness (in numbers that is, not stature).

Jubilee buildings were completely devoid of adequate light, it would have been a rare occasion when sunlight broke through to the tiny courtyards at its rear, let alone its windows at its High Street frontage. They faced the 'Colonial' Wharves in the High Street and were completely dwarfed by them. Built in 1890, originally to house the workforce who operated Tower Bridge… That idea though was speedily abandoned (the 'workforce' must have known something about what was on offer), and the flats were ultimately let out to all comers. I have it on reasonably good authority that the block had been built entirely with second-hand materials... the wonder is that it managed to stand up at all.

The flats' amenities were nicely described for me by my Brother-in-Law Jack (Ward) who's family and he had been ex-tenants. "Out on the balconies...", he said "...each flat had its own toilet. It used to be beside the coal-hole, if you were in there an' you sneezed you came out coal black." Not only that..." he said, "... if you happened to poke the fire, you'd poke next door's as well." "Come to that..." he added "... if next door had their chimney swept, the soot 'ould come down ours. As for bathing...", he said "... do you remember how we used to keep those old tin baths out on the balconies? You could always tell when it was Friday night because they all disappeared indoors. The dads always had theirs first, and us kids 'ould get in the same water afterwards. A few kettles of hot water to warm it up. You didn't half have a scummy old bath if you were the last one in. But it all worked, didn't it? We managed. Everybody was friendly... nobody locked any doors... we had nothing to pinch anyway." He never mentioned Mum's bath. I expect she had the scummiest bath of all. Last, when all were washed and abed.

Jubilee buildings were finally pulled down in the 1950s. I expect they just fell down because they refused to stand up unassisted any longer. As for the rest of Hermitage Wall, a walk through it presented an amazing tapestry of what living in Hermitage meant. Come to that, what living in Wapping as a whole was all about. It certainly contained all that was worst, and at the same time all that was best. There were a few shops squeezed between houses, factories, and small depots of one sort or another. A domino manufacturer, egg distributor, a wine store, tin box maker, marine chandlers, and many other similar undertakings. A shop-cum-dairy. The dairyman kept his horse and float in the backyard. As for the shops, it is a wonder to me now that their proprietors made a living, judging by the look of the premises. Not very well I should think. Mr Leonard's 'fruit and veg', five pounds of 'whites' (spuds) a tanner (2½ pence); a pennyworth of 'pot herbs' (onion, carrot, and swede to make a stew in the pot). He also sold quarters of coal. If you couldn't afford a quarter, he'd sell you a stone (14 pounds). If you were really 'skint', half a bucket full in exchange for a couple of spare pence.

A baker's shop, Bill Martin's 'bag wash' and Mrs Hawkins' news, baccy and sweet shop. Alleys and courts offering glimpses of ramshackle buildings used for 'goodness knows what'. A jumble of the fairly new-built (if a hundred years old can be described as new?) and the positively tumbledown. New and old shrouded under a permanent blanket of perma-dust. And of course, the people. No Hermitage and Wapping tapestry would be complete without, especially the unforgettable local characters. Mrs Thompson who kept the all night coffee stall at the Irongate Wharf by the Tower entrance out of St Katherine's Way. Shamus O'Brien, who sang at the top of his voice wherever he went, as the locals remarked, "He were the only bloke in Wapping what dinnant need a megaphone to be heard in Brighton." Shamus also worked for Stepney Council, he was a sewer man and claimed that he would sooner "Wade in it down below, rather than have it chucked at me up above." There were many more like them. For the rest of us, houses shared with chickens and rabbits in the backyards, cats, and dogs in the living rooms. There had even been a goat kept as a pet indoors. One family kept a goose that was more like a guard dog. It would chase those it didn't take a fancy to up the street. A costermonger who kept his donkey in his backyard and there was no other way to get to it except through the house.

Hermitage Wall, just like Hermitage as a whole, was only partly residential, or, it should be said 'residential in parts'. Its inhabitants had to share what little space there was with chain makers, sack makers, marine engineers, depots and docks, wharves, and warehouses. The whole area of Hermitage could not have exceeded 45-50 acres, squeezed as it was between the dock walls of St Katherine's, Hermitage Basin, the London Docks, Wapping Basin, and the river. It was home though for probably more than a thousand souls. I think that three quarters of those were children!

The whole area was almost devoid of contrasting colours, time and grime seemed to have reduced everything to the same indescribable hue as the 'Wall'. The only splashes of murky colour to be seen seemed to be the universal reddish-maroon paint on dock gates, wharf platforms and the cast iron window frames and loopholes, the standard colour for private companies and the dock authorities alike.

The houses of Hermitage were built in the early 1800s-30s, for a richer sort of tenant than us, dock officials, ships officers and the like. These worthies though, had long since deserted the claustrophobic aspects of an industrialising Wapping of those early years of the dock development for more salubrious and sunnier surroundings, the houses given over at last to the likes of we, mostly not as tenants of a whole house, as of yore, but under the good old tried and tested system of 'front pair', 'first floor backs', or 'attic singles', or at worst for some, the 'airy basement'. Not a kitchen or a bathroom to be found in any one of the delightful tenancies. A black iron gas cooker tucked into a corner, the ubiquitous tin bath hung on a nail in the backyards, keeping company with the usual 'shared' outside loo.

Our house, No. 74 Hermitage Wall, the last in the terraced row facing the dock wall, was of three storeys and the typical 'airy basement'. It seemed so narrow to me. The street door, an ancient Georgian type with a semi-circular fan light over it. The paintwork had not seen fresh paint for countless years, so its blackness could only have been the collection of the same countless years of soot deposits and perma-dust. It opened into a dark narrow passage that smelt of wet and rotting timbers, mysterious doors led off from it, I never remember them ever being opened. It led straight through the house passing on its way through a dingy scullery, the walls of which were dark green painted, peeling and time-worn dirty. In one corner a shallow brown earthenware butler's sink with a cold tap over it, which was held insecurely to a rusty nail with an equally rusty twisted wire. A small window that was minus a few panes of glass, those remaining thick with dirt and dusty cobwebs. In another corner a brick built copper in which Mum and the other tenants boiled their wash. I used to like feeding the little fire under it with bits of wood to make it boil. Mum would say, "Just a little at a time to keep it going." She knew from experience, that I tended to cram the fuel into the fire if I was not watched, with the result that the boiling soap-sudsy water would lift the copper's wooden lid and suddenly burst out all over the place, but this usually quietened the fire down anyway with a frightening hiss accompanied with a shower of ash descending all over the place… including me!

The passage passed on through the back of the house to a tiny piece of overshadowed openness that had some time in the distant past pretended to be a garden but had somehow degenerated in its sober old age into a backyard and had abandoned the earlier deceit. When the 'front' door was left open there was an unrestricted view of the 'privy' at the back wall of the yard. The lavatory was the only one and shared by all the tenants in the house. I remember once when playing in the street, seeing one of my peers, who evidently had few inhibitions about the matter in hand, nor any thoughts about the impropriety of the private business he was attending to, pants down and seated contentedly on the long wooden bench-like seat, legs swinging and oblivious to all but the contemplation of the other natural things that happened to be represented by a few grey plants of dubious species, struggling to survive in one small patch of soot pretending to be soil. They must have been weeds of a more hardy sort. For one thing, nobody would have had the audacity, much less the expectation to plant proper garden flowers. Our backyard-cum-garden did at least boast a tree. A mature London plane tree, which in the proper seasons managed to produce a reasonable show of leaves and an abundant shower of yellow balls of fluffy seeds at the right season.

As far as I remember it was *the* only tree in the whole neighbourhood of Hermitage. On reflection there wasn't much in the way of vegetation at all, apart from a few optimistic window boxes here and there, or a few pots perched precariously on windowsills showing early evidence that something had begun well enough but had given up the struggle after one or two yellow leaves had sampled the air... duty done, and promptly expired, but then, nature will not be ultimately defeated. There was one very notable exception. Opposite to 'our' house in the angle of the 'wall' stood a gas streetlamp. Above it draped over the 'wall' was a vigorous crop of ivy. At night when the lamp was lit, it turned from the drab grey-green of the day and glowed like pure gold. I watched as clouds of moths circled and danced, caught in the glowing gaslight.

We occupied the top floor of No. 74. Euphemistically described as a 'flat' if one could dare to call it such? It consisted of three small rooms and a stairs landing which was used as a kitchen. On it stood our black iron gas cooker with a shiny brass plate on the oven door - 'Commercial Gas Co Ltd'. Mum kept it polished and the stove black-leaded. A daily chore. Tins of 'Zebo' black-lead and special brushes that were almost as shiny as the cooker and beside it a brown earthenware shallow sink, but it wasn't plumbed. A bucket behind a curtain collected the waste. Mum had to carry it downstairs to empty it in the yard. It would be easy to understand that more harassed mums in similar circumstances, might just think that as there was a long haul downstairs carrying an overflowing slop bucket and a long climb back up again, she might also just notice that there wasn't anyone about below and the open window was convenient. I prefer not to believe that there were reports of sudden and unexpected showers of rain, or sightings of sodden garments put out to dry in the smoke… and not on a Monday wash day either!

A small room at the back of the house overlooking the 'yards' was our living room, the two at the front were bedrooms. I think that the two had once been a single but had been divided into two cubicles. Lily and I shared one of them. As far as I can remember there was just one other tenant on the second floor, a Mr, and Mrs Owl. The ground floor was unlet, as was the 'airy' basement. This probably had everything to do with the interesting fact that every time a Thames high tide came in the 'airy' cellar flooded. There are limits to everyone's requirements for accommodation, regular flooding is definitely one of them. The 'airy' was one thing, as far as it went even for the ground floor it would definitely have been too much to have the residue of the Thames sloshing about a couple of feet beneath the floor and the feet of the bed. This of course, explained the mystery of the closed doors and why the under stairs door to the cellar 'airy' was permanently nailed shut and padlocked. The flooding could be seen from the street. The 'airy' had a grill light on the pavement. We kids thought it was exciting watching the black oily looking water slowly rising, all of us hoping that it would flow out into the street, but it never did and our disappointment as it stopped rising, sinking back again to eventually disappear altogether leaving behind it yet another layer of black slimy mud.

Dad explained it to me. That the house had been built at the bottom of the slope at 'our' end of the street, probably in an old filled in water channel when Wapping, and especially Hermitage, was still a flood plain marsh. In the end the interest waned somewhat, and the flooding was relegated to being merely a part of Wapping's natural existence except when a sparrow fell in, or when rats were seen swimming. I imagine that they must have been of the sewer variety, I cannot think why ordinary rats would want to go swimming in our flooded 'airy'.

There were plenty of rats about though, there wasn't any shortage of sustenance for them. The docks and the wharves must have been crawling alive with them. With such an abundance of provisions for them, it is a wonder to me that any sensible rat would want to wander but they did. Perhaps 'the grass' might have looked a little greener the other side of the 'wall'. They must have discovered their mistake when they visited us.

In my cot at nights, I remember Dad banging on the floor and the ceilings with the poker to frighten them away. He always told Lily and me that they were only pigeons "And you're not frightened of pigeons are you?" We weren't deceived. Even I knew that pigeons didn't squeak and scuttle about like that. The infestation of pests of any sort was nothing to do with Wapping people being dirty or negligent, nor from any lack of domestic cleanliness. Of course, there were a few families who had succumbed to the impossible struggle against poverty and its inevitable squalor, there always will be. Apart from the generally poor environment, large families and poverty did the rest.

The sort of houses in Hermitage, considering their age and neglected condition, were a constant source of pest infestation. The risk of fleas and bed bugs were endemic. People were always diligent about any crawling insect. I can see Mum now, darting across the room, slipper in hand to crush the life out of anything crawling up the wall whether it was obnoxious or not. As it was succinctly put locally: "If yer squashis it an' it turns out red, i'twere a bed bug". In which case it meant an immediate turning over of the mattresses and bed clothes just to make sure that it was an isolated case. Even if nothing was found it always meant a liberal sprinkling and a thorough wash down with turps. If the infestation was really bad, the local council's sanitary man would come (known locally as 'Dan the sanitary man'). He would close up the premises to fumigate it with an evil smelling sulphurous kind of candle. The houses stank of them for weeks afterwards. Punishment enough for any negligent mum, never mind the shame that came with it.

A thoughtful scratch of the head by any child could always guarantee to produce a scourging, lasting, it always seemed to me, to be hours of torment under the painful pulling of a fine-toothed nit comb. I contrived to do my scratching when I thought I wasn't being observed. The nit comb ritual for me was excruciating but Mum would brook no nonsense, nor any delay. A newspaper spread onto the table my head hanging over it, fists clenched tight in anticipation as the sharp-toothed nit comb gouged into my scalp. Not once, but over and over again. If anything did fall out, even if it was only one of my precious hair buds, it was carefully placed between thumbnails and crushed. Whether anything was found or not, a thorough hair washing of the most vigorous head-shaking variety always followed and all because I scratched my head at an unguarded moment. Oh yes. Wapping mums were as clean and as fastidious as far as circumstances would allow.

There were probably more scrub brushes per capita in Wapping than anywhere else in the UK. Neither was it a case of a bristle surplus gathering dust in some forgotten corner. Wapping housewives used them at every conceivable opportunity. Even the smallest member of the community who was foolish enough to stand still longer than a few seconds would come in for a liberal dose of 'elbo' and finish up red-raw and smelling sweetly of carbolic soap. The only remedy was to keep moving and at least twenty yards away from a threatening sack-apron and a scrubbing brush.

The pavements came in for a   daily ritualistic treatment as well, producing bright semi-circular pavement areas around each doorstep, finished off with a whitened step and woe betide anyone careless enough to step on it… there were a few unsolved murders!

Mum, who originally came from Bermondsey, arranged our domestic comforts very well indeed. We weren't any different from our neighbours, certainly where accommodation was concerned. Dad was working regularly, albeit relatively poorly paid, for an engineering firm in Dagenham, probably the main reason why Dagenham had been an attractive proposition for housing in the first place. At least he was in regular work, something that most Wapping dock workers could only hope for. For them it was practically all 'casual' and very few or no guarantees that there would be any work at all.

The general consensus of opinion was that we were relatively 'well off'. It is true that we were well fed and well supplied with normal daily needs but then so were all Wapping kids. Wapping parents thought the world of them, not only their own children, but any child, whoever they were, wherever they came from in Wapping. It was the only qualification required. Well remembered visits to friends were always finalised with a feed of thick slices of bread spread with dripping or marge, sprinkled with sugar, butter if they had any, and if you were very lucky it might be jam as well. Often it would be 'lumps' of rice pudding. My friend 'whistling' Bobby Coombs' mum was particularly famous for it, not the milky sort of genteel tables, but the sort you could cut with a knife, sprinkled over and baked with grated nutmeg. It wasn't that we actually needed feeding, the underlying instinct was that the kids got enough of what they needed, grub was stuffed into you wherever you went. Nobody took offence at this, whether kids needed feeding or not they got it… frequently a clean-up into the bargain, solely on the basis of, "We can't send yer 'ome mucky kin we?"

However, it soon became evident to me that the difference between ours and my friends' possessions was sometimes obvious. Our furniture was certainly old and mostly second-hand but good by general Wapping standards. I noticed too that many of my peers had to sleep four and five to a bed, 'sardines', some at the top and some at the bottom… male and female all in together from tots to teens and for bed covers had to make up with old coats. After all, I did have my own cot and Lily had her own bed. Nothing else in the room, but the floor was covered with a square of printed 'oilcloth' (lino) and a tiny mat. Always sparklingly clean, the oilcloth pattern well-nigh scrubbed away... Didn't we know it if we made a mess.

The living room had the obligatory pine kitchen table and a few odd kitchen chairs, an enormous sideboard, dark polished with an oval mirror in its backboard but the one item of furniture very special to me was Dad's chair, a high-backed armchair with side wings. It stood beside the fireplace. During the days when Dad was at work and Lily was at school, and Mum, well, I had no idea where she may have been or not been, I seemed to find myself alone most of the time (I'm sure that can't really be the case, it is just how I recollect it now). The chair became all sorts of things to me. It might be a ship. The next, it was a lorry or a cart, a whole procession of required, imagined, or desired things. In it I could be a magician performing all kinds of wonders. In it I could be invisible, or change myself into anything I wanted to be, or imagined I was. I could fly up to the sun and the moon or go down into the locks with the divers I had watched as they descended into the dark muddy water of the dock entrance to Wapping Basin from the Pier Head bridge over the lock.

Mum was always careful that we got all the right things to keep us healthy. Cod liver oil and malt to fill us out, and California syrup of figs to empty us out. I liked the cod liver oil and malt the best. Once when finding myself alone as usual, the winged armchair became a ladder to reach the malt jar on the mantelpiece. Unfortunately, the jar parted company with me on the way down. Worse, the lid parted company with the jar, 'plop' into the seat of the winged armchair. The red stain on my bottom disappeared within a few days. The brown stain on the chair's cushion remained forever to remind me. Never mind, I thought. It became my badge of possession. Dad just laughed.

This was something that I could not have explained to anyone, including Lily. In any case she seemed to me at the time to be above all that sort of thing. She was never slow to point out to me any evidence of silliness on my part. I had no alternative but to accept her verdicts and opinions. She was three years older than me. I kept my own counsel though. I had to look to myself to improve myself. After all, she did go to school and I thought that she ought to be in a far better position to know what was right, and what was most probably wrong.

When she was at school, or on some other mysterious excursions into goodness only knew what unknowable territories, with goodness only knew what friends, I could only wonder. She was, however, my mentor and my guardian. She was my boss it seemed to me most of the time. Where Mum was at these times I have no idea. Probably out 'scrubbing' somebody else's house? She did say later in life, that she "would scrub house from top to bottom for one and six" (7½ pence).

I don't know whether she meant that she would or that she did, all I know is she was absent enough to have scrubbed all the houses in Hermitage. She also later told me that the housekeeping budget was a shilling a day (5 pence), or 12 old pennies, sixpence a day for meat (2½ pence), when we had it, a penny for 'pot herbs' (½ penny), potatoes were two pence, and a penny (old money), for the gas meter to cook it with. So, one and six would have gone a long way. We never went hungry.

Chapter 4

The Wonderful World of Wapping Kids

Considering the vast numbers of children in and around Hermitage, the wonder is that it didn't erupt into open warfare. Apart from the occasional 'incidents' common to all children everywhere, like boyhood fisticuffs over some relatively serious matter soon forgotten, and girlish squabbles over trivial matters never forgotten, in some strange manner the social aspects of our young untried world was well ordered, and fairly civilised. No tidal waves of serious discord seemed to ruffle the calm waters. A minor ripple now and again, caused by the inadvertent trespass onto some clan's declared and recognised territories; arguments between the various gangs whose main interest seemed to be to lord it over everyone else. Mind you, they also seemed to have other objectives which mysteriously materialised like mushrooms and faded away just as quickly. For instance, groups of card players, suddenly there would be an explosion of card players all engaged in the same activity.

The moment some new interest appeared; the old card groupings dissolved to form the new ones. The real problems came at the dissolution of the 'old' order and before things settled down into the new temporary patterns with groups of confused card players wandering about, not knowing what to do with their spare time and unoccupied energies. For those like me, who were too young to enter into the thing of the moment, we were never too troubled with the otherwise oppressive aspect of our surroundings. Our minds were never stultified by claustrophobia. There was always something going on, always something exciting happening… Like the day of the secret panel.

A few houses just up the street from ours, once in its heyday, had a splendid, panelled stairway all the way up. The woodwork however had seen better days and displayed the marks of countless generations of aspiring Hermitage wood carvers. Some of these were reasonably nicely executed. Initials finely entwined into intricate designs, cut with a sharp new penknife or such like, but mostly looking as though done with the excessive use of a blunt axe. One day, when things had come to that pass after strenuous activity and everybody collapsed with fatigue, a young carver who had found himself in that state of indecision because the card playing season had come to an end and nothing had taken its place as yet, resolved to add his name for the sake of his posterity to the stairs panelling, applied his knife and inadvertently discovered a great mystery. He had found a loose panel and when prized open revealed… Ah well!

The news was shouted up and down the street, droves of disengaged kids came from all directions to see this new wonder. I certainly wasn't going to miss out on this and added my diminutive stature to the general rush. However, the narrow passage and the stairs had not been designed to accommodate the hordes who were trying to find viewing space. Nobody had the slightest regard for the smallest member of the curious - me. I found myself being stood on and generally crushed in the chaos developing on the stairs.

Now the 'carver's' mum whose name had to be 'Rosie' was also a dab hand with a broom. In more peaceful times she was more often seen 'swippin' d' stairs an' passige', stirring up a cloud of dust flying out of the front door and horror of horrors, we had desecrated her sacred whitened doorstep. We all stood transfixed by the terrifying sight of 'Rosie' and her broom, sleeves rolled up and armed with that terrific broom. There was a sudden silence broken only when Rosie bellowed,

"Hoi... wots dis den? Oi, git out on it th' lot on yer!" Panic set in. Those at the top of the stairs trying desperately to get down, those at the bottom still moving with the original momentum in the rush to get up. Me in the middle not being able to get up or down, was firmly squeezed between the two opposing sides, silently enduring. It is always the silent majority who gets stamped on.

Now it so happened that about a hundred of us felt that we had some territorial right to be there, as we all lived at 'our' end of Hermitage Wall, so we sat tight. In a voice squeaky with nervousness, our young carver appealed to his mum's sense of wonder, "Look Mum, look what we's farnd", putting his head into the dark cavity as he said it. Rosie's interest and her curiosity was aroused. "Well, I'll be blowed. I'll be blowed". One of the departing crowd suddenly found the courage to take his life in his own hands. "Cor blimey Rosie, git yer broom art, tain't arf dusty in dere".

Long after the throng had left, the privileged few who could remain by virtue of territorial right were able to view the discovery to our hearts' contents. It was dark in there. It was whispered that this was a great secret of olden days, heeding the warnings that it was filled by ghostly occupants, dusty skeletons guarding the hidden treasures, and blood thirsty pirates who had hidden it. This was the entrance to dismal dungeons and dark tunnels that led all the way to the Tower.

We were enthralled, grouped around the dark hole. It was dark enough on the staircase landing as it was, letting our minds wander through a veritable fairyland of make believe but there is always a spoilsport. He soon revealed himself with a sudden leap and a shout. "Look art... I seed der ghost". This caused the girls to flee screaming down the stairs. I forgot my sex temporarily and fled unashamedly with the girls.

It is marvellous what that dark sealed up cupboard did for our imaginations. The panel was nailed up again, but the stories and the terror stayed with me for long afterwards. Nothing would induce me to climb those stairs alone again, nor would I have liked to live in that house. I became convinced that those rats in the roof were really lost in the secret tunnels that surely honeycombed all the houses in the street.

The sealed up cupboard (so it was generally thought) was evidence that it was originally intended as a hideaway for contraband and stolen goods. Smuggling and theft had always been a feature of the docks, no less so in the 1800s than in the 1930s. Anyway, we kids constantly heard stories about secret tunnels, "All the way to the Tower". We knew about stealing from the docks and were obsessed with the ideas of tunnels and hideaways. We were always on the lookout for evidence of such things. Even the adults were convinced of such things.

I personally have on recorded tape that some, even to this day, firmly believed in the existence of tunnels. A lady of advanced seniority spoke to me and claimed with all sincerity that her cousin's cousin (twice removed) had actually been into one, reputed to lead all the way to somewhere or other (it may well have been the 'Tower'. Where else, one might ask?) "But...", she said, "... it had collapsed, and they couldn't get very far into it".

Logically, I suppose, the fact that smuggling and river piracy was such a well-known and accepted pastime of Wapping folk, tales of contraband and hideaways were always topical gossip, so for us kids it didn't take much evidence to prove the existence of such things and if they didn't exist we didn't need any evidence, we were quite capable of inventing it ourselves.

Children being children the world over, we knew how to amuse ourselves. If there wasn't a suitable toy available to match the game, any old piece of rubbish and plenty of imagination filled the gaps. No Wapping kid had a super abundance of toys. Even a lowly ball was a prized possession and gave its owner the right to demand leadership over the games played with it. Imagination played the greater part of any game that was undertaken. I can vouch for the fact that imagination was left far behind in an exercise of reality most of the time, a real preparation for adulthood in Wapping, with no nonsense ideas creeping in to fog the issues.

It is a very natural feature in the minds of the young to sort out the facts from the fictions, Wapping kids sorted them out very quickly indeed, and if they couldn't sort them out for themselves, older brothers and sisters would soon put it right. We all lived too close together to be deceived by silly notions although I have to admit to various silly notions of my own.

The 'Wall'

One of my notions was the conclusion I came to about the 'Wall'. In this particular case my imagination ran rampant in my mind, because it is what I wanted to believe, in spite of Lily's and my friends ridicule. One has to understand to begin with what the 'Wall' meant in the psychology of Wapping people, to even begin to understand something of my own particular fantasies.

Its construction in the early 1800s was a vast undertaking. Conceived by the architect of Dartmoor Prison, its presence was meant to convey to the locals that its intention was to surround the whole of Wapping's activity of Empire building with a total fortress-like protection, and to let them know that their part in it was not to be trusted. As it happened, not unsurprisingly, its actual effect was more than this. Not only did it imprison everything within its circle, but also everybody outside that lived within its shadow.

It strode throughout the length and breadth of Wapping, marking its very boundaries, allowing the minimum of living space within its bends and turns for free space, for habitations and the movement of the people. Its overpowering presence together with the massive riverside wharves, narrow cobbled streets, bridges over the locks and canals linking the dock basins, the close-packed housing, only reflected the prison mentality of the wall's designer.

We kids had few doubts, any more than our parents and adults in general did about the meaning of the 'Wall', but that didn't stop me fantasising about it. For me, it belonged to the realms of Dad's armchair. I was convinced that it was as old as time itself. As old as the Tower, and Dad had impressed me totally with the scale of its age as compared to anything else around us including myself. Even I could have seen that the wall would not have got as dirty as it was if it had been new.

In my imagination I had soldiers marching along the top, clad in armour and armed with bows and arrows. Cannons ready to boom. I had things happening on the inside of the wall that were best hidden from view, things we ought not to know or think about - people getting their heads chopped off, horrible stinking dungeons, screaming sufferers writhing at the stake, and all the horrors of the torture chamber. Dad had fuelled the fantasy by telling me stories about the Tower. I absorbed the mention of the gallows that had stood on Tower Hill. Felt the sharp axe on my neck and the threat of the Tower's bastions. Dad told me these things and I firmly believed that it was all still happening then. The 'Wall' was utterly and totally an extension of these tales in my mind. Oddly enough, for some inexplicable reason, they still do, insofar as the images of the docks, the walls and warehouses, the Tower and Tower Bridge get rolled together in my mind as a single entity, if for nothing else, more significant than a continuity of Wapping's history as a whole.

Our bedroom window on the third floor of 'our house' came just level with the top of the 'Wall', and I often watched the superstructures of ocean-going ships passing through the Pier Head entrance lock into Wapping Basin and the London Dock complex. I distinctly remember too seeing the masts and spars, sails furled of tall ships passing through the lock. There were still some clipper type sailing vessels as late as the early thirties coming into the dock.

Along the length of 'our end' of the street, about a foot or so above the pavement were small ventilation grills. I always wanted to find one that opened all the way through so that I could see the 'other' side of the 'Wall', but they didn't. There was always a movement of warm air through them though, loaded with a musty and damp smell of decay, laced with spiciness. At one time it might be oranges, then at another liquorice or lemons. I actually knew that they were only ventilation grills, but this did not spoil my fantasies that they were really ways into secret dungeons. I was often seen kneeling, whispering words of comfort to the unfortunate prisoners. I suppose I must have been odd and over-imaginative. More often than not, I terrorised myself.

There was never a shortage of children around us, and to a casual observer Wapping's future would have seemed well assured. The consequences of such numbers ought to have produced a sort of chaotic anarchy rampant amongst the kids, but it didn't. It should have ended in the total annihilation of separate identities. In some natural and mysterious way there was an unwritten code of conduct. A sort of constitution that none of us dared to break. No child was ever instructed by older brothers or sisters in the intricacies which governed our society. There was never any need for instruction. One was born with the knowledge just as birds are born with the knowledge of nest building.

Each street, alley or court or part of a street was a well-defined territory. These were the exclusive reserves of those who lived in them. There wasn't much intercourse between the various groups, the games played in them, the occasional exciting events were theirs and theirs alone. No one dared to venture into or interfere with whatever was in progress, although one could watch from the side-lines. Sometimes one would be permitted to join in with them but only if you were in the company of one of the tribal residents and only then if you were required to make the numbers up and that your mentor was prepared to vouch for you. "S'all right, Johnnie's wiv me", and even then, only if you were willing to be the missing goalpost, or more particularly if you were the possessor of a ball.

Children had to meet at school and friendships were formed, this was perfectly acceptable during school times and for out of territorial excursions. At the end of the day though, personal preferences polarised back into the normal recognised tribal pattern. Mind you, it may have had very little to do with inborn instincts but more to do with the undeniable facts of life in tribal areas, that irate mums like 'Rosie' and her formidable broom, were often seen guarding the precious whitened doorstep at street doors, or at upstairs windows yelling at a noisy crowd: "Clear orf, the lot on yers! Git rarnd yer owen plices an' create!" The kids got the message and with the passage of time in the process of natural selection a Wapping species of child-folk was created known as 'Littleuns Separatus'.

Lily, however, seemed to have escaped this natural net somehow. Perhaps it was because she was born in Bermondsey and hadn't been exposed from pre-birth and from birth to these powerful influences that had shaped clamouring hordes into reasonably well-defined Wapping mini-societies. However, she had an indisputable passport and moved freely from group to group at will. I think that it may have had something to do with the fact that she was a rare combination of several things. For one thing she was in some respects tomboyish in a feminine sense and that she was also a tough nut to crack, and for another, she was popular with the boys in a natural feminine way (this didn't always go down too well with the girls). To top it all, Lily was a determined bossy-boots used to getting her own way. She was just too tough and untouchable for them to tackle and get away with it. In her shadow I became untouchable too. I was always in her shadow and never bothered.

Just around the corner from 'our end' was a triangled area, strangely called 'The Square'. On one side houses just like ours, on the short side, Thomas Allen's transport depot was situated… the third side, a continuation of the 'Wall'. The wall here was pierced by gated 'loop-holes'. They were for loading and unloading carts and lorries. They weren't very high as loop-holes went, being perhaps eight to ten feet high from the pavement. They were wonderfully convenient though for the kids when the docks were not working and became lofty castles to be won or defended. They weren't so easily accessible but the use of a piece of rope and a few eroded bricks as toe-holds provided the means. I have never been famous for my stature, in fairness though I was perhaps somewhere in the region of my third birthday, I found myself deposited on one of these loop-holes. How? I have no idea, other than the recollection of choking rope and scuffed knees and a distinct memory of the terror that blotted out all other details of my elevation in life.

I had been elected to be the prize to be won. My opinion in the matter was not asked for, and I clamoured to be released. The game degenerated downwards at about the same rate as my distress rose. Everybody but me had decided that it would add realism to the business if I took the role of prisoner rather than a prize, because it had obviously occurred to them that it was quite in order to let prisoners alone to rot at their leisure. In the meantime, Lily, who I suspect had been party to the whole proceedings in the first place, had dashed home to call out the reinforcements and to report to headquarters in the shape of Dad. Lily was a marvellous protector, and I was her big responsibility. Normally she was quite capable of guarding my interests, this unavoidable 'retreat' could not have been an easy decision for her to have to make. One had to fight one's own battles in Hermitage… and win them. The extra reinforcements arrived. The hordes retreated to a safe distance to watch the proceedings but poised ready to disappear into the honeycomb of streets and alleys if things got nasty.

Dad looked up to me marooned on my lofty perch. "How did you get up there?" he asked. I couldn't tell him. Neither could I tell him how I was ever likely to get down again. A voice from about forty feet away from across the other side of the square, "I know mister rinsole, 'e flied up there jest like a sparrer". Dad just laughed. I couldn't quite appreciate the joke; all I know is that the descent was just as terrifying as the ascent.

During the workdays, the square was always crowded with horses and carts, or big lorries loading or unloading at the loop-holes. Thomas Allen's, were, I believe, one of the main dock hauliers and a large part of their operations were carried out by horse and cart. Guinness imported most of their stout through the London Dock and Allen's carried most of it to depots and bottling plants elsewhere in London. The drivers knew of Dad's talents as an engineer and asked him to make them clever syphons to extract the stout 'perks' from the barrels. Every driver had to have one. Dad admits to having forgotten how many he made. "No idea…" he said, "… what they were used for", but the household never seemed to be short of frothing jugs of stout.

The Tommy Allen horses were stabled on the upper floor of their depot. They were taken up to their night stalls by means of a sloping ramp at the rear of our backyard. In my cot at nights, I could hear them stamping and snorting and early in the mornings being taken out to be harnessed into the shafts of the carts, the rattle of chains and brass fittings, steel-shod hooves ringing on the granite cobbled street. The shouts of "Whoa dere. Come on hup dere". Hup… hup… whoa".

In the next street (Samson Street) was a blacksmith farrier. He probably shod all of Thomas Allen's horses. His 'smithy' was in a little side alley. The horses waiting to be shod he tethered to the alley wall. The farrier looked even bigger to me than he might otherwise, because he wore an even bigger leather apron down to his feet revealing rust-stained wooden soled clogs. I worried about the horses, they were big cart haulers, Suffolk Punches I believe, but then everything looked huge to me since I was about as high as the average cart horse's knee joint. I wouldn't be convinced that the farrier wasn't hurting them, cutting their hooves with a big knife and the file. The blows of the hammer and the nails… Maybe I thought it was because they were so big that they didn't feel any pain. I didn't mind watching him make the shoes, the showers of sparks, the forge glowing and the anvil ringing but when it came to the shoeing, the clouds of smoke and the smell of the burning hoof… I was none too sure.

Just around the corner from out of Great Hermitage Street into the High Street, were the spice mills. The mill stones were in the basement cellar. At the pavement level were windows that opened inwards. The rich spicy smells that floated out of the open windows into the street were wonderful. If I was allowed to linger, I would kneel on the pavement watching the milling and savouring the perfume of freshly milled spices. The lights in the cellar, each with a halo of fine spice dust dancing around them, cast dull yellowy light. The mill workers' aprons, caps, faces and arms powdered with brown ground spices; stacked to one side were jute sacks filled with nutmegs, cloves, cinnamon, and ginger; paper sacks filled with the milled spices. The stones, probably six feet in diameter, stood upright in pairs. When working they trundled round on their stone beds milling the spices.. .the slow grinding rumble as they turned and ground. Lily always had great difficulty in dragging me away. As a child I never had any difficulty in understanding the nursery rhyme 'Sugar and spice and all things nice, that's what little girls are made of'. A visit to the spice mill's windows was all the evidence I needed. Not when they were milling pepper though.

Lily always had some important mission elsewhere, and never let me dally for too long anywhere. She was always off somewhere for reasons that I could never fathom. Sometimes it was into the depths of Hermitage only to find ourselves in strange quarters, never quieter quarters! Such a place did not exist in Hermitage. There was always a crowd of noisy kids engaged in all sorts of noisy games or just idle mischief. The boys seemed to spend most of their time rolling in the streets or gutters, pummelling the life out of each other, or climbing dangerously on tottery walls, shinning up lamp posts, or balancing precariously on viciously spiked 'airy' railings.

The girls totally oblivious to their shows of derring-do, busy making homes and houses with bits of old sheets tied to the 'airy' railings, older bits of decayed carpets, quarrelling over where the table ought to be. There was no table, just a scrappy bit of tatty board picked up from somewhere. It would be discarded at the end of the game to be found later by some other group and used for another purpose. We might on the other hand be going on an errand. I liked going to Mrs Hawkins' shop, it was a sweets, news and baccy shop and they sold comics but also sold various other necessities in a general way. An enamelled sign outside declared the legend 'Aspro' and a full range of other medical supplies were to be had inside. I liked Hawkins' shop. There was a hand-printed notice pinned to the counter about, or just a little above my eye level. I had to know what it said. Lily spelt it out hesitatingly for me. "Papers delivered daily, paid weekly". Mrs Hawkins was hoping that a 'flush' customer would ask for his papers to be delivered daily with the milk so that he could enjoy his tea an' toast and have a good read at the same time.

Mrs Hawkins leaned over the counter and looked down at me and asked, "Good mornin' sir, will yer 'ave th' Times or the Daily Mirrer?" Did we beat a hasty retreat, or face it out? I thought it best to tell her, "My dad gets his paper at the station in the mornin". "Oh", said she, "'E don' get it 'ere den do 'e?" and burst out laughing. "Just yer wait till I tells yer mum". 'Now', I thought, 'I'm really in trouble'.

Close by Mrs Hawkins, was Bill Martin's 'bag wash shop'. Practically every housewife had 'bag wash'. It was usually one of the boys' jobs to take the jute sack of soiled washing, to be collected the next day. Easy enough when the clothes were dry, not so easy though when it came home soaking wet.

On our way homeward from Mrs Hawkins' emporium, a boy of our acquaintance had been sent for the washing and was arguing with Mr Martin. "I ain't takin' it" complained the lad. Now, Mr Martin who felt that he had completed his part of the transaction with the handing over of the nine pence fee, was of a different opinion. "An' I sez yer ain't leavin' it 'ere nor neither". The sack of wet washing now weighed about three-hundred weight compared to the ten pounds dry yesterday... the boy in tearful reproach reminded Bill. "I's kint carry it". "An' I sez, yer can't leave it 'ere nor neither". With that Bill disappeared into the depths of his soap-sudsy smelling bare board floored shop. The boy now realising that there was nothing else for it but to drag the wet bag of washing behind him along the pavement as best he could. I expect that the bag wash arrived home dirtier than when it had been sent. That is if the wet sack survived the journey. Some of the washing may not have arrived safely back home at all.

When these things palled, and out of sheer boredom, we might go round to the park. More often than not we only found our way there by accident, merely passing through on our way to somewhere else.

The 'park' wasn't very big. However, it was the largest 'reasonably' open space in Wapping, considering that it was enclosed on all sides, two of which consisted of the ubiquitous and ever present 'wall', Tench Street and its facing row of tall terraced Georgian houses, Greenbank on another, graced in a small way by St John's Parish Church and St Patrick's Roman Catholic Chapel. How it got the name of Greenbank must be one of the great mysteries of history, for as far as I remember, or anyone else I expect, there was never any green to be seen, much less anything resembling an embankment but if dad was right he said that it had once been a green bank on the Thames side and vessels once berthed there. It was at least 75 yards from the shoreways and the riverside. Very possibly he was right.

The 'park' was almost entirely surrounded by plane trees, tall, terraced houses and of course the 'wall'. It had one or two smallish, grassed areas upon which one was forbidden to step, one or two flower beds in which the plants were forbidden to flourish and a tiny bandstand, everything railed off. All there was for recreation were the black gritty asphalt pathways.

A small children's play area, swings, and roundabout, covered with a red dusty clay surface and if one played there one was likely to return home a delicate shade of dusty pink.

It wasn't very popular, better to play in the streets and go home a natural shade of Wapping dirt. So, we only arrived in the 'park' when there was absolutely nothing else to do. We could though always go there to annoy the grumpy old 'park-keeper' who from his little shed would shout and blow his whistle. "Hoi, git orf d' grass!", or for some other grievous sin deliberately perpetrated just to annoy him. Long experience though, had taught him that he never left the fortress security of his little wooden shed for any pretext other than the most dire necessity. Fifty kids just looking for mischief was taking his sanity into areas of high risk.

If we got tired of these innocent pursuits, we could always go to the foreshore, or, as they were more generally properly known as 'The shoreways'. When the tide was low these were wide stony expanses and thick black oozy mud. Strings of moored lighters settled onto them, pressing down, and squeezing pools of water around themselves, as if they still floated. The shoreways could be reached by stairs to the river that were still open and became mucky playgrounds for the children. It was forbidden territory for most children whose parents were well aware of the dangers of the river. The swift flowing tides, moored vessels, lighters, and jetties of concrete platforms supported by pitch-blackened heavy wooden piers, making deep caverns beneath them. Death to the unwary caught by a swift incoming or ebbing tide.

It was impossible to return home without bringing the evidence of transgression with us. However, the fear of retribution didn't always deter us, and we would venture onto the stone causeways at the bottom of the stairs… Bolder spirits than we would pass us by, to wallow to their heart's content.

It wasn't uncommon to see the sodden corpses of drowned rats, cats, and dogs, left on the shoreways or floating by on a retreating tide. I even remember a drowned sheep once. Mixed in with all sorts of rubbish, flotsam and jetsam together with hundreds of unidentifiable objects that had fallen or had been deliberately thrown from wharf jetties, bridges and passing vessels. The river was a convenient dumping ground for rubbish of the most obnoxious kind. The Thames water was filthy at the time. I don't particularly remember the word 'sewage' mentioned, but even in the thirties the practice of discharging raw sewage into the river continued as in the days of yore. Even so, boys would swim in it. It was well-known that one did not take in a mouthful of this disgusting brew. Nor was the risk of poisoning the only danger. The swift tides and a constant traffic of vessels up and down river. Moored lighters packed in strings and groups, to get swept in amongst them rarely resulted in a survival. The luckless or unwary swimmer would be sucked down and under them with the inevitable consequence. There were also the wharf jetties to get trapped under. There were plenty of drownings to be sure but boys being what they are, accepted the risks as a challenge.

For us beachcombing kids there was lots of excitement too, plenty to see, plenty of things to find. Old coins and other interesting things (even to this present day the London 'shoreways' are a rich and productive source of archaeology. Even in the early thirties I found a mid-seventeen hundreds half penny piece, but it was bartered ultimately for a comic or some other bauble that took my fancy. There were always lots of interesting things going on and tons of scope for all sorts of mischief. Quite apart from getting filthy in the process, everything left high and dry on the shoreways had to be examined, one never knew what seemed to be rubbish would turn out to be absolute treasure, or the next piece, or the next.

I was often tempted to join the happy band of latter-day mudlarks. Quite apart from the threatened consequences of such a venture, I didn't think that the prospect of wading up to my neck in thick black sticky mud to be worth the effort. I was content just to watch from the safety of the stairs causeway. Anyway, my tardiness was usually accepted on the grounds of my tiny stature coupled with my lack of years. I was lumped together with the girls as part of an audience to be impressed by the boys of 'otherwise' tender years manliness and superiority. For some reason though, I had to be shown all their finds. Once I was told, "Dere's drarndid sailers art dere...I ain't seed 'em mesel' but me dad 'as". That put the seal of certainty onto the story. If his dad had seen drowned sailors then who was I to dispute it? I wouldn't have wanted to see a drowned sailor. The dead sheep was bad enough. I wondered if drowned sailors smelt as bad as that too?

It was only from the shoreways that much of the river could be seen. In spite of the fact that it was only within yards of the High Street, it was so completely hidden by the high wharves that it might as well have not been there at all. I loved being on the 'shoreways', here I could sit on the stairs and enjoy the river sights and sounds and such wonderful sights they were. Surely they would have been a joy to any youngster? Ships stood against jetties, some of them rusty old tramp steamers looking like fat dirty grey and rust coloured hens sitting on nests of black mud; others, big ocean-goers, crisp and bright with fresh paint. They leaned against the thick wooden pilings of the jetties; forests of supports driven into the foreshore forming dark sinister caverns beneath their heavy concrete decks. Tall cranes stood above the vessels like long-legged waterfowls, long-necked like grey herons their hooked cables dipped into the ships' holds heaving out sacks, crates, boxes and bales, barrels and all the varied shapes and sizes of merchant goods from goodness only knew what foreign port. A crane paused as I watched, its load hoisted high, for a fleeting second before the crane turned and its load disappeared into an open 'loop-hole' high in the wharf. Lighters moored close to the ships' sides like chicks clustered around the hen, cargoes being loaded into them for destinations elsewhere.

All the while tugs dashed up and down river towing behind themselves strings of lighters gathered at their sterns. Some loaded so heavily that their decks were awash, others empty, stood high out of the water, the tugs' sirens piped, ships' sirens boomed in answer. Gulls screamed; men shouted. Black-hulled, sprits'l sailed, Thames barges tacked up and down river, their red sails swollen in the breeze.

Blue clouds of pigeons rose up, wheeled, and settled, pecked at spilled grains, rose up and settled again. Black low funnelled colliers' hulls deep laden churned upriver. Empty colliers high out of the water, their propellers thrashing half exposed. Big ocean-going merchant vessels manoeuvring and nosing into dock entrances, fussed by tugs pushing and pulling their helpless charges. Smokeless funnels. Bells clanging. Chains rattling and a cable's shriek as its wet coils screamed against a lock bollard.

Dirty vessels rust ridden and paintless, funnels belching black tarry smoke, and the sights, the sounds, and the smells… A fast changing panorama of a busy riverside dock, and never a whisper reached the High Street barcly a few dozen feet away…

Not that the High Street was quiet, just as cargoes were gorged into the wharves at the river's edge, so they were disgorged into carts and lorries at their rear. From high up loop-holes fitted with rope hoists, similar sacks, bales, crates, boxes, and barrels swooped down on the rope hoists as if they were in freefall, to stop suddenly and jerkily a foot or so above the cart, and for the next few seconds descend almost imperceptibly to come to rest precisely where it needed to be placed.

A constant traffic in each direction filled the High Street. Loaded vehicles and unloaded, noisy lorries, very often steam driven with hard solid rubber tyres and a length of chain clanking along behind to earth the static electricity, trailing smoke and sparks as they went. Horse drawn carts, big, covered waggons with tarpaulin curtains and heavy chained tail-boards at their rear. Boys hanging on under the tail-board out of sight of the carter stole rides dragging their steel tipped heels along the granite cobbled street to make the sparks fly. Steel tyred wheels grating on the cobbles, the horses' hooves threw up showers of sparks. I often saw puffs of smoke where the horses trod. Stationary carts waiting for a load, horses stamping impatiently, muzzles deep in nose-bags snorting clouds of chaff. Brass buckles, thick leather straps attached to chains on the cart shafts rattled to every movement of the horse, bright yellow streams in the gutters as the horses peed where they stood. Shouting men, and the clamour of an industry at full pitch. These were the sights and the sounds of Wapping High Street.

It may be a matter of speculation on just how much we Wapping kids were deprived of things to do and to think about compared to country kids. True, our country cousins were reckoned to live in healthier surroundings with heaps of freshness to fill themselves with. It is also true that they came home from play in a different sort of dirty condition. Wapping dirt could never be compared with a country lane kind of dirt. But then scuffed knees, torn trousers and snagged skirts are still all of the things pertaining to children anywhere, whether they are torn, scuffed, or snagged by blackthorn or broken glass.

For us though, if there were no fields and woods to search, we had the streets filled with wonder, courts, and alleys brim-full of character and characters. If there was no ploughing and the harvest, we had a constant stream of a thousand harvests from the world over daily passing our doors. Ships and the docks to see. Horses and carts and lorries, tug-boats, ships, cranes, and jetties. The Shoreways, Tower of London, Tower Bridge. The river swinging bridges and cantilever bridges, lock gates. Ships coming in and going out. Big ships and little grubby tramps.

I dare say that we had a thousand things to do, and a thousand more ways to get into mischief. We would have missed out on all these things wouldn't we? I certainly wouldn't have wanted to miss them for all the world to play in.

Chapter 5

Broadening Horizons

By the time I had reached the grand old age of two full years, I discovered that my days of idleness were over. Whatever Wapping and the miraculous winds were supposed to do for my lungs, it didn't. The healing qualities of those beneficial airs had not yet worked their wonders on me but then, good medicine is not necessarily fast medicine. To help it along a bit I had spent quite a lot of my spare time in Wapping's little cottage hospital. St George's in the east. I wondered what St George was doing in the east when his hospital was in Wapping? In fact, I spent so much of my time there that I, along with the hospital staff, began to question whether I lived anywhere else. I was prone to return there pretty often. On one well remembered occasion it was minutes between discharge and re-admittance. I was being carried down from the ward by my favourite nurse, when my curiosity about the workings of the lift got the better of me. I managed to insert my hand in the wrong place at the wrong time just as the safety gate was closing. I found myself back in the ward again with nothing more serious than a few cuts, abrasions, and ugly bruises but it was apparently a good enough excuse to stay a little longer. Apparently, I took it all quite manfully however, it was mainly because of my bronchial condition, plus one or two scrapes with imminent death due to bouts of Scarlet Fever, that seemed to re-occur at regular intervals, but not always. For instance, one of my delights was... (well to tell now would spoil the tale).

I was rushed to hospital yet again because this time somebody noticed that there was blood in my urine. "This really could be serious this time" everybody said. I spent the next week leisurely watching specimens of my urine drying in little laboratory bottles lined up on a windowsill. It went from bright red at the beginning of the week to pinker, then to brighter pink, then finally to its usual normal tint. Everybody was baffled as to the cause of this strange medical phenomenon... until that is, Grandma Insole came up with the solution. She had discovered that about two pounds of pickled beetroot had vanished from her store cupboard, vinegar, and all. Knowing about my partiality for this particular delicacy, the red pee was instantly explained, and I was as just instantly discharged under a cloud of shame that my robbery of Gran's store of pickles had been discovered and my guilty secret was out. I could have told from the beginning that it was beetroot however, I will not admit to drinking the vinegar. That was disposed of down the kitchen sink. I thought I was covering my tracks.

After this latest confrontation with extinction, the doctors of St George's thought it was about time they had a rest from my troubles. In the time-honoured fashion they jointly conspired to get me out of harm's way (and to give them a breathing space and time in which to recover) by recommending that I spend some time recuperating at a remedial nursery designed with youngsters like me in mind.

Wapping was provided with the very place they had in mind, a daily nursery that also did duty as a clinic for those who had had an unfortunate brush with one of the 'Nitty Noras'... The indomitable school nurses who visited local schools to examine the kids heads for lice amongst more alarming things like rickets, general malnutrition, sores and bruises, bad eyesight, and deafness. On the whole a wonderful institution but rather downgraded to some extent by the overwhelming factor of nits, as nine hundred and ninety nine percent of those who turned up at the clinics did so to get their heads seen to, but not on a permanent and daily basis like me and my supposed problems. I really have no idea what they really were, apart from those I have already suggested.

The nursery was situated on the Pier Head lock entrance to Wapping Basin, conveniently no more than a minute's walk from 74 Hermitage Wall. It used to be the dock Superintendent's (master's) house. A beautiful Georgian mansion with rooms that seemed enormous to me, which of course, compared to our own cramped rooms, they were. The high windows giving wonderful views of the river up to the lower Pool of Tower Bridge and downriver to the bend of the river into Limehouse Reach.

The house was at the end of a short row of similar but not so grand terraced houses along the quayside of the lock entrance, fronted by a narrow cobbled access roadway leading out of the High Street, no more than fifty yards or so from the top of Hermitage Wall. Its columned porch entrance looked so grand and impressive to me, leading into a vast hallway graced with a wide staircase to the upper floors. At the corner of the house stood a semi-circular turret facing the river. I was very impressed.

I soon realised that the regime functioned on orderly lines. None of the free-for-all running noisy mayhem of our normal street society. There were proper times for each activity, times to play, times to be examined by the attending doctors, times to sit quietly listening to stories and simple educational activities. I remember things like tying shoelaces, putting wooden puzzles together and the like, and the times for rest and sleep. I remember these times with some irritation, curtains drawn and the low beds and the insistence to sleep when all I wanted to do was the opposite. The nursery furniture was of great interest to me, semi-circular banana-like shaped tables and tiny chairs, some with arms and some without, all painted in bright colours: reds, blues, and yellows. I claimed my own particular favourite, and woe betide anyone else who sat on it. The regime was so well organised that when the order was given to set out the tables and chairs for a particular purpose, the children performed the setting out themselves. When the order came, I was otherwise engaged and therefore at a disadvantage. "Where is my chair?" I thought. I spotted the desired object through the legs of a grand piano. I had to get to it fast before somebody else took a fancy to it. I dived under the grand piano and grabbed it. I can still feel the triumph as I walked to my place carrying it upright, which just goes to prove how little I was... or, how big the piano was?

Connected to the house was a kind of summer house built onto the quayside facing the river. It looked down onto Wapping Old Stairs of ancient repute and notoriety. Living as close to the river as we did, and yet not seeing much of it except from the stairs passages and cluttered causeways or narrow glimpses from lock bridges, it was a rare treat to be allowed into the summer house a few at a time. Being merely a few yards from the Wapping Basin lock entrance, we had a grandstand view of ships entering or leaving the dock. All this, as if it were not enough, and the general river activities. Sometimes we had our afternoon rests there... no hope of rest for anyone, including me!

I was offered a telescope once and told where to look by my favourite nurse. I don't remember her name. All of sixteen or seventeen I suspect. As I had decided to marry her I tried to be as helpful as possible, I couldn't see a thing, but pretended that I could. That was the day that the press came. I had no idea what they wanted my photograph for, but all was explained when I was shown the newspaper the next day with my picture in it. I felt very important and grown up. Lily didn't comment!. (Daily 'Herald' and the 'Sunday Chronical', June 1933)

The day came though when I had to reluctantly say a goodbye forever to my favourite nurse, and the remedial clinic. It was time for me to move on to higher things. There has to be progress in any walk of life and as distasteful as this necessity was for me, I just had to accept that the hour had come for me to experience the sharper side of an adult-like world. The next stage was to be pre-school nursery, and time to become acquainted with things like letters and numbers.

The move wasn't very far where distance was concerned. Again, no more than a hundred yards or so from Hermitage Wall, even so, I realised that my horizons were broadening. There was no knowing where all this progress was going to end. Just around the corner from Hermitage Wall into the High Street, and over the Pier Head swing bridge, was Scandrett Street, a little non-entity street whose main reason for its existence seemed to be to connect the High Street with Greenbank and Tench Street. Almost a street that had been overlooked and had existed unchanged for at least a hundred and fifty years.

Within it was St John's, the parish church of Wapping. On the opposite way, a tiny pocket handkerchief sized church yard tucked into a bend in the dock wall. It was the only graveyard in Wapping. Very much overgrown and disused, soot blackened gravestones lurked in amongst the tangled undergrowth. A dark brooding kind of place, further shaded and darkened by the deep shadows cast by Oliver's Wharf, large plane trees and the ever present dock wall. It was protected by a low brick wall surmounted by heavy wrought iron spiked railings which, from my tiny point of view, might have been at least ten feet high. Two massive stone capped gate posts supported high ornate iron gates which were permanently locked and further secured by a heavy rusty chain and padlock. I wondered whether the intention was to keep people out or the unfortunate residents in? Personally, I preferred the former. There were too many ghosts wandering around in sealed up landing cupboards in my imagination already.

St John's church was a large brick and stone edifice with a high tower capped by an ornate dome. The tower had a clock, with a black face and golden numerals, facing the river. Curved stone steps led up to the portico's main entrance, a high limestone door-case with time-blackened oak panelled door. Attached to the church in Scandrett Street was a range of buildings dating mostly from the seventeen hundreds, they housed the secular activities of the church. One of the buildings had been a day school financed originally under the terms of a generous will. It had been the first regular charity school in Wapping. By the thirties however, education had been largely taken over by the London County Council. However, some of the original functions had been retained and it had become a pre-school nursery, presumably funded by the legacy.

The church and its buildings date from the mid-seventeen hundreds. Built just at the time when docking and ship-borne trade began to spread out from the confines of the city boundaries. This part of Wapping in those days was considered to be the ultimate 'posh' end of Wapping. The houses typically had been built for the professional and artisan class of dock managers etc. In the best tradition of building for the 'better-off', thought had been given to the style of the area. Trees had been planted, and the park set out. The church had to be of the very best that money would provide.

According to tradition, an ancient Saxon church of St John had been demolished and the new church built on the same site. Yet, not more than a few hundred yards away from these trappings of wealth was the most appalling poverty of the most evil kind. Not only did the dock development require artisans and tradesmen, managers, and merchants, it also needed an un-numbered host of raw muscle to hoist and pull, dig, and lift, to sweat and to bleed, and to do so for a mere pittance of a few pennies. Housed in the most unbelievable squalor, crowded together in dingy sunless alleys and courts, stinking of 'night soil' and non-existent drainage, or proper water supply. The stench of it all and the obvious dangers to themselves and their property must have been too much in the end for them. They soon left Wapping for more healthy and safer pastures in the rapidly developing suburbs, but they left their grand church and their dead behind them, covered, and recorded by expensive tombstones, and they locked the graveyard against the poor.

The schoolhouse in Scandrett Street was a large ground floor schoolroom which opened off from the street and a similar upper room for older boys and girls. The ground floor was used for titches such as me. Built at a time when odd additions to a structure took no account of their utilitarian purpose but included, I suspect, to impress a wondering and subscribing public. Over the doors and windows were added plaster scrolls and knotty bits and pieces painted cream, their presence did more for the outward observer than it did for the inside aspect.

The schoolroom on the ground floor level, dark and low ceilinged, one had to step down into it from the pavement. The windows high up and totally inadequate to light the interior, green painted walls of indeterminate hue, did nothing to brighten things up but the schoolroom did boast what I thought to be grown up desks. There was even a blackboard on a easel in a corner. I wasn't bothered by the overall dinginess; I was far more impressed by a few leaves brushing against a high up rear window. I knew seeing these that there must be a garden at the back of the school. I also suspected that it was just as overgrown and as darkly secret as the graveyard opposite. A lot of my time was spent watching the leaves trace semi-circles on the dusty panes of the window. My imagination created strange and mysterious things, fairies, and hobgoblins that I had seen in my picture books. Sometimes the leaves became little faces peering in at me when I wasn't looking.

The school had a tiny play area that was no bigger than twice the size of an average Hermitage backyard. From it a narrow concrete path set between the main building and a high brick wall led to a single lavatory, the sole (as far as I remember) sanitary arrangement for male and female alike. I didn't notice the inadequacy. I don't think any of my peers did either. Many of them didn't even bother to shut the door.

Between the nursery school and the church, the main building was used for other church activities but also, originally as a day school, presumably it had been for older boys and girls. It had a carved wooden portico around the main doors, surmounted by two splendid niches, complete with two very lifelike statues representing a boy and a girl, presumably to complement the improving merits of the church's educational motives. To me, they appeared too angelic, and pink faced to represent anything other than the pink faced scallywags like us, admittedly hidden under a mask of Hermitage Wapping dust… anyway, they did wonders for my imagination. I was absolutely convinced that they were really alive and only stood in their niches during the day quite still and patiently until dark when they came down and went to bed like everybody else. Whenever I passed by, I always spoke to them, little bits of local gossip I thought they would like to know… not out loud mind you, I didn't want Lily to think that I was stupid.

Chapter 6

Tower Beach and Other Outings

When Lily was not otherwise engaged at school, at weekends or on some other mission, she frequently took me on various outings. She was quite an accomplished traveller, both within the confines of Wapping and outside of it. One often repeated excursion was to the Tower and Tower beach.

Wappingite kids never ever thought of the Tower as having anything to do with the city. As far as we were concerned, it was definitely a part of Wapping and belonged exclusively to us. It was plain to all of us that the main gateway on to the Wharf (the Irongate) out of St Katherine's Way was the main gate. It wasn't, but it was imposing enough to be the main entrance. We had heard unconfirmed rumours that there was another gate somewhere on Tower Hill, but it was only a rumour. In any case, even if there was a gate, it could only have been the back gate 'out' of the Tower. Our own gate, which was exclusive to us and for our own convenience, was so obviously the way in and as we always came out by the same means there was no need for any other gate. Surely that was a reasonable conclusion for anyone who might think otherwise.

The 'Irongate' is a high, wide gated archway under the Tower Bridge approach road. During the Tower opening times, it was in those days manned by those imposing Yeoman Warders dressed in their Elizabethan style uniforms. They are traditionally called the 'Beefeaters'. They had a guardroom under the archway, in which against one wall was a rack of long pikes resplendently decorated with red ropes and tassels, emblazoned with the Royal Arms in gold, ready to hand to repel the aggressive and the unwanted.

Passing through the archway from out of the dark canyon-like St Katherine's Way, which threaded its way between the Irongate wharves and warehouses on the riverside, and the securely walled and enclosed St Katherine's dock complex on the other, I was always overawed by the grand aspect of the Tower Wharf and the Tower, the first sight of the majestic walls and curtain towers of what must be the most significant national monument in the British Isles. It bears the bulk of post-Norman history within its sombre and brooding confines. It's very stones are saturated with a powerful force of menace radiating outwards. Even I, young as I was, 'felt' the oppressive and threatening strength of its presence. Dad had more than impressed me with his own enthusiasm in telling me stories of Kings and Queens. The deep dungeons like the 'Little Ease' so called because within it there was nowhere to lay in comfort, sit or stand. About the prisoners thrown into 'The Pit' to be eaten alive by rats. Queenly heads chopped off on 'Tower Green' with a big executioner's axe. The gallows on Tower Hill. Beheadings and quarterings. People burned at the stake. Traitors' Gate, murdered princes... how could I have failed to be impressed and overawed. My mind ran riot over it all. In my mind's eye I saw the blood and the rolling heads, suffocating princes, rats and torture chambers, and horrible dungeons. Such terrors haunted my daydreams.

He also told me that Kings and Queens once lived in the Tower many years ago in a palace built onto the eastern side of the Tower, but it no longer exists... in fact, built beyond the ancient Roman city wall which marked the city boundaries encroaching onto the marsh of Wapping itself. Just think of the consequences that could have led to. A Britannic monarch having to admit: "Our palace is in Wapping". It doesn't have quite the same ring as Westminster or London or Hampton Court. It might have been 'Wapping chimes', 'City of

Wapping' or 'Wapping Court'. Fortunately, the Crown chose to ignore simple matters of geography.

In the thirties, huge bronze and iron cannons stood on the wharf overlooking the river. Trophies of umpteen battles and general warfare. Dutch, Spanish, French and from every corner of the globe, wherever we managed to get mixed up in the quest for conquest. Ornately beautified, as if to conceal their warfare purpose. It was great fun to clamber all over them, pretending to be defender of the Tower against marauding vessels in the Pool. They have all been taken away. Some kept behind fences and now untouchable.

Some years before the thirties, a munificent if not far-sighted body of free thinkers, whoever they may have been, decided that what London really needed was a watering place. It was obviously recognised that free choice was all very well when it came down to whether proposed works outings chose to hoof it down to Southend, Ramsgate, or Margate to feast on sun, sand and sea (not forgetting the jellied eels), or, as an attractive alternative to bury themselves in the smoky capital to see the sights. It was instantly recognised that generally speaking the smoky capital lost out. It says a lot for the said body of free thinkers, that even in the days before tourism was the political hot potato that it is now, they had cottoned on to the fact that there might be some money in it. It must have been an inspired and far-sighted individual who first hit on the brilliant idea of a 'beach'. He must have reasoned that it would combine the best of two worlds. For the hordes of anticipated visitors, there would be an occasional glimpse of the sun, and some sand to create the illusion of distant and romantic shores. Provided that they were prepared to forego the jellied eels and ignore the smoky skies, they might be able to enjoy the sights at the same time... what better site for a 'city beach' then, than the foreshore of the Tower Wharf?

Unfortunately, this particular shoreway was just as mucky as anywhere else on the river. This sobering fact did not deter anyone apparently, whereupon soon afterwards thousands of tons of sand were dumped where it was required. On the foreshore of the Tower Wharf. All that was needed to complete the job was to provide the means by which the visitors could reach it, seeing that there was a fifteen foot drop from the wharf. It would have deterred the timid and endangered the lives of the bolder! The problem was overcome by the provision of something very much like a ship's gantry. I expect that it was purpose made to suit the need. On the other hand, it may well have been a redundant item that a local ship breaker had been wondering what to do with for years.

We never had to wait for the gantry to be lowered to get on to the beach. Next to the Irongate entrance out of St Katherine's Way there was a public landing place and stairs to the shoreway under the Tower Bridge proper. This had a very interesting name locally - 'Dead Man's Hole'. It got its attractive name because it was here that drowned corpses were landed. A mortuary was sited beneath the bridge roadway for this macabre purpose. At one time, it wasn't unusual for sixty drownings a week to be brought ashore. Accidental drownings, many of them, but just as many undoubtedly suicides. It was a convenient and well used method for life's weary travellers to launch themselves into the unknown. Unknown as far as their lives and their souls were concerned, for their mortal remains, it was either the mudflats of Purfleet far down stream, or the cold marble slab of 'Dead Man's Hole', or, as it invariably meant, both.

The 'Irongate' had always been a gate on to the Wharf since the building of the Tower, and presumably there had always been a public stairs and access to the river. Because of these ancient public rights of way, the stairs had been retained in the building of Tower Bridge as a dark tunnel under the bridge leading to the stairs down to the shoreway. When the tide was out it was easy for us to reach the beach from here. Even when the Tower Wharf was closed, the beach was still open to us. In any case, most of us would never consider the use of the gantry, that was only for the 'posh' and tender footed visitors. Access from the Irongate stairs was a much more adventurous thing to do. Firstly, we weren't supposed to do it, secondly, it was after all our own private and privileged means of access. I suppose it might have been considered dangerous as it involved negotiating a slippery, muddy, stone strewn stretch of shoreway under the bridge.

Many were the times though when we had reached our objective, that we observed disdainfully groups waiting patiently for some Tower official to lower the gantry. We felt very superior... I hoped that they would think we were special people... After all, we were, we lived there, and princes and princesses lived in the Tower... didn't they?

None of us had any illusions about building sandcastles. We did see a few of the uninitiated trying to but it wasn't that kind of sand. In any case, even we could see that to pile a few grains of sand into the semblance of a castle in the shadow of the greatest castle in the world would be the height of juvenile stupidity. Nor could a few matchsticks imitate the huge bronze and iron cannons whose great muzzles stood just fifteen feet above our heads on the wharf.

It didn't matter whether we were able to get on to the beach because of the state of the tides, or to be driven off because of its rising. We could always go on to the wharf to play on the cannons, chase the pigeons, or make a general nuisance of ourselves. I liked to talk to the 'Beefeaters' who were always willing to explain things to us, show us things and to tell us what they meant. I remember clearly looking over the rail into the dark cavern of the 'Traitors' Gate' whilst it was being explained that the water once came up to the steps and the protective portcullis gateway into the depths of the Tower, explaining how those who entered into it by that dread portal never left the Tower prison by the same means, invariably on a last journey to the gallows on Tower

Hill. I felt the dread and the fear all those condemned prisoners must have felt, to see a massive portcullis rise to let the boat in carrying them into the Tower, and its heavy fall as it closed forever on them. As my Elizabethan dressed informant spoke, I saw the guttering flambeaux flickering a feeble light on to the scene. It was explained that prisoners were always brought to the Tower during the hours of darkness. I shuddered with horror... ghosts of that terror walked as I listened. They walk with me still.

Late evenings in our wanderings, and closing time for the Tower, the big plane trees on the wharf filled with chattering and restless flocks of starlings claiming their roosts in clouds of quarrelling and with the dusk, came the ceremony of the 'Keys' From within the Tower itself, we heard the guard march from gate to gate with the constable to report gates locked and secure... Heard the bugle sound the posts, wonderfully evocative. The deepening dusk and squabbling flocks of starlings, and the sharp call of the bugle as the guard marched from gate to gate and the indistinct shout of a guard telling off the traditional 'Keys'. Once locked and secured, nobody, no matter who, whether King, Queen, Prince or Princess, or the lowest commoner, would leave or enter the Tower until the dawn of another day. In my imagination and memory, I still see it all happening now, and hear it all happening too. Marvellous.

If these things failed to hold our attention, then we could always climb the steps out of St Katherine's Way up on to the bridge. These steps and stairs held a great fascination for me. The granite steps criss-crossed with diamond shapes cut into the stone, the big cast iron balustrade with its moulded shapes. Shields covered with crowns, and heraldic emblems intertwined with vines etc. For some indistinct reason, I was completely captivated by it all. All I wanted to do was to keep going up and down them. When I was down I wanted to go up and when up, to go down again. Lily would become exasperated with my insistence and soon put a stop to it.

It was always good fun to go to the centre of the bridge spans to feel them jump up and down as the heavy traffic crossed over, although I have to admit that I was always very nervous. The brown muddy water racing on the tides under the bridge looked so threatening, I tried not to think of the bridge collapsing into it… the stuff of nightmares really, to go along with 'Tower terrors' and 'Traitors' Gate'. Thinking about it all, the Tower Bridge ought to have been considered a dangerous place for youngsters like us to be in at any time. I don't think parents thought much about the possible dangers and we obviously didn't either, but then we always came home safe, sound, probably hungry and certainly mucky, so what was the point in anyone worrying.

Life in Wapping was hard for everyone. It was no use trying to shield children from the difficulties, dangers, and the hardships. If the kids were going to survive the environmental situation they had to learn early to cope with it, or frankly, not survive at all.

At other times we might explore further afield and Tower Hill, the ancient site of public executions and burnings at the stake, a site good enough for commoners, royal blood was executed away from public eyes within the fortress itself. The block stood on Tower Green. Tradition has it that no grass would grow where it stood.

We had to go to the Tower pier while we were on the Hill, to see the Steam Navigation Company's paddle steamers, those splendid side paddle vessels plying daily trips to Gravesend, Southend and Margate, gleaming white painted and gold brass work sparkling. The Golden Eagle, Royal Daffodil, Maid of Kent etc., berthed at the pier, embarking, or disembarking crowds of those just using the service as a means of easy transport to these destinations or, the milling crowds of 'outings', families out for the day 'on th' river'.

Or into the Tower's moat-side gardens. A narrow strip of railed pathway, thick with trees and bushes overlooking the lawned and waterless moat peeps at the Royal Mint, secure behind high walls, iron spiked railings and huge forbidding gates. I felt the half penny piece in my pocket, and I knew that it had been made here. I thought, 'If only I could get in there to get some more half pennies. How rich we would be'. Sometimes we walked the length of the 'Highway', this marked the boundaries of Wapping to the north, beyond the 'wall' that is. In the thirties it was a lot quieter than its notorious history as the 'Ratcliff Highway', it had been pretty rough then, filled with the worst possible slum housing, doubtful shops, ale houses, gin shops, prostitutes, brothels, and pimps, roving bands of roughnecks and thieves preying on seamen ashore with pockets full of pay. Drunkenness and violence. Vice beyond description. A 'rookery' of total depravation...

By the thirties, there had been a clean-up of the area and the worst aspects of the Highway's reputation had come to an end, but the truth is, that most of its activity had merely been transferred elsewhere. Even in the thirties there was a kind of whispered suspicion that parts of Leman Street and Cable Street in particular, had an unspoken reputation bordering on the notorious. It was certainly cosmopolitan in character with practically every nationality represented. This factor alone was enough to foster the erroneous opinion of the day (and to a large extent to this present day) that cultural and racial differences necessarily meant want of morality. However, it was the truth that the police would not enter into Cable Street alone. Two, three and sometimes four with truncheons drawn ready for any eventuality. Fights and spates of violence were a common feature of Cable Street. There were undoubtedly prostitutes and brothels and everything else that usually keeps company with these activities. There were one or two dirtyish and evil looking cafés that could have been fronts for drug parlours. Idling groups of men that looked as though they were capable of the most desperate actions stood at street corners. A constant babble of abusive language, always simmering at the point of threatened explosive violence and yet, there was also a feeling of a strange kind of overtone. Decent people lived in the street too. I expect that they loved it. It was a street that could be likened to a river with two flows. One sweet and the other foul and poisonous, and the two never mixed. We kids though, were never afraid to walk through it, we thought nothing of the foul, and were never molested.

The Shadwell end of the street though, presented a picture of civilised gentility. Neat houses, the Town Hall, and a treed recreation ground. Cannon Street Road divided the two halves of Cable Street. This was predominantly a Jewish quarter. In fact, it was ALL Jewish and reasonably prosperous. A nice smelling German bakers, kosher butchers, and the Synagogue. A sweet factory, we would stand at its narrow entrance and savour the sweet perfumes of boiled sweets. A mineral water factory. Hairdressers and tailors. Many, many tailors. Every one of them proud to advertise themselves as 'bespoke', 'customers' own materials made up'.

Bearded and long coated Jews with Black Homberg hats on their heads, and strangely mixed in, Anglo-Catholicism. St George-in-the-East church, a huge cathedral-like limestone towered building. Black-cassocked priests and bells on Sundays. Cannon Street Road had a week of two Sabbaths, a Jewish Saturday, and a Christian Sunday. All mixed in together. A marvellous tapestry of contradictions. Saintly piety and devout Judaism, simple folk leading ordinary lives. Poverty and reasonable affluence.

I was never too much at a loss with things to occupy myself when Lily was at school. I have always been an inveterate wanderer, apt to get lost from time to time, most times I was pleased to be on my own. Lily tended to rush me around and I liked the time to just look and watch the things that took my fancy, more often than not lost in a fantasy world of my own making, and there was always plenty to see and watch. The square round the corner from No. 74 during the day when the docks were working, was always filled with lorries and horses and carts.

I was fascinated by a constantly manned police 'box'. Well, 'box' is rather a poor description for what was actually a brick-built office sited in the centre of the square. There was always plenty of work for a continuous presence of the Dock police force. Being visible was part of the idea. Theft and general roguery were rife. It was after all, a well-established tradition of dock labour to supplement poor wages by recycling useful commodities of a consumable nature but woe betide anyone suspected of or caught 'nicking'. The Dock police could be relied upon to do their sovereign duty. Anyway, I liked to sit on the curbed pavement around the 'box' pretending that I was in command and ready for any emergency. When the telephone rang I would pretend to answer it and properly inform the incumbent policeman on duty about my imaginary informant.

Sometimes I would venture further afield into the High Street onto the Wapping Basin Pier Head entrance lock's swing bridge across the road, to watch the ships in the dock being unloaded. At high tides I knew when a ship was due in when the lock gates were opened, and the bridge swung over to close off the traffic flow in the High Street. If I happened to be on the opposite side, and the wrong side for my way back home, I would feel pleased with the idea of being marooned like a ship-wrecked sailor on a far distant shore. The ship in the Pool coming in, turned towards the lock, bow forward, slowly, inch by inch then foot by foot, nosed into the lock. Dock men hauling on thick wet hawsers, looping around bollards loop by loop. Clanging bridge bells and shouting men. There were barely inches to spare in the lock, the ship's sides almost touching the quaysides, rope fenders almost squeezed flat. The shouting and the screaming wet coils of the hawsers, the ship slipped into the lock.

As it slowly passed through and into the dock basin, I looked up to the ship's high sides, portholes, and rust stained streaks, saw the rivets, and steel plates of the hull overlapped. Bored seamen stood at the ship's rails looking down at me. I waved and they smiled. Brown faces, oriental faces. White, sun-burnt brown faces, there was hardly a difference. The ship, a travelling cosmopolitan island of international co-operation towards a common destination. I did not realise that at the time, I only saw what I saw then, and loved what I saw.

Sometimes, up and down the High Street watching the loading and the unloading, most of the men I saw got used to me and took little notice of me, except occasionally to be told: "Keep out of the way sonnie". "Watch out" or some other caution but never really bothered much because I was there.

Frequently I got to be really 'nosey' and found myself in places where I shouldn't have been. I had no hesitations in just walking in uninvited to find out what was going on. I always wondered about what went on 'inside' the wharves. I knew of course that things went in, and things came out. One day my curiosity got the better of me. Spotting an open door, now being quite used to the idea that an open door meant what it implied, I took the opportunity it offered and entered in and climbed a flight of concrete stairway and found myself on the 'floor' of the wharf (as it is locally properly called).

The 'floor' was a low brick, arched and dimly lit area. I could see that it would be vast if it were empty. But now it was half filled with sacks stacked high into the arched roof. A few naked light bulbs cast a dull yellowy light, a few windows overlooking the river shed their small share of dim light onto the scene through panes covered with the dust, dirt, and smoky grime of decades past. The air loaded with dust. Ranks of maroon-red painted iron columns set in rows supported the floors above. Men were working. A ship was being unloaded at the wharf jetty. Shafts of strong sunlight flooding bright semi-circles around the open loop-holes… I took it all in. So far, I had not been noticed and was undecided whether to stay or remain where I was and watch or beat a hasty retreat while the going was good, when suddenly,

I heard a man coming up the stairs and he had seen me. I could not go forward, nor retreat... I decided to brave it out.

He stood, hands on his hips looking down at me. A strong looking man, ruddy-faced, dressed as all of his companions were dressed working on the 'floor'. A collarless rough cotton shirt open at the neck and bare almost to his waist, his chest covered with dusty brown hair, braces and a wide leather belt fastened with an enormous brass buckle. Trousers, heavy brown cords well-worn and stained, spattered with the marks of many different cargoes. Brown stains, white and dusty stains, and oil. The legs tied at the calves with bits of string, a flat cap on his head. Two vicious sack hooks looped into his belt and heavy studded clogs. He must have been surprised to see me turn up in a place where I ought not to be. "Hoi... wot cher doin 'ere den sonny"? "Yer ain't s'posed to be 'ere". He looked so fierce and threateningly angry that I thought that I had better quickly explain who I was and that I had a right to be there. "I'm Johnnie Insole, an' I live up Hermitage Wall, an' I jest wantid to see what you are doin'. I haven't never seen in here before". "Well, I'll be blowed" said he, with a broad grin spreading across his face. Now he was grinning and chuckling. "Yer ain't seed in 'ere before nor neither. Yer will 'ave plenty o' time ter see all yer'll ever want ter see when your time comes I reckon". I thought I had better remind him. "I lives in Hermitage, an' me mum don't mind". Whether she did or not, I was where I wanted to be and I was going to make the most of it. "Yer lives in 'ermitige does yer, an' y' mum don't mind. Well, I'll be buggered she don't. If she don't mind, no more'n I do neither."

With a roar of laughter he lifted me up with huge hands up on to a stack of piled sacks and they crunched as I stood on them. "Yew kip nice an' still fer a momint, I've got ter tak yer darn to th' street in a minit. Yer kin 'av a little look".

68

The sacks of peanuts were warm, and the tropical smell of the hot dusty jute sacks filled my nostrils, mixed in with the smells of other cargoes, nuts, spices, coffee, tea, leather, sugar, and molasses and a hundred other things flowing into and out of the wharves. A vessel discharged today, its cargo stacked, shifted, and dispatched tomorrow, and then another cargo, another ship. Week in and week out, month in and year out.

From my lofty perch I was able to look down into the hold of the ship that was being unloaded, a fat hollow looking ship like the ones that I had watched passing through the locks. They always looked to me to be so solid, but I had never realised how hollow and empty they were!

Surrounded by a flock of lighters, I saw the stevedores crawling over the sacks in the now half empty hold, piling them into rope slings to be hoisted to the loop-holes. Every minute or so the crane on the jetty dipped and up came another load, men at the loops unhitched, others 'on the barrow' moved the sacks quickly to the growing stacks on the 'floor', men grabbing them with their sack hooks, throwing them up onto the stacks, all at a fast and furious pace based on 'yardage or tonnage', governed by the pace that the stevedores worked, a time allocated piece rate in order to turn a ship around as swiftly as possible.

I wondered 'Where do all these nuts go?' I could not believe that there were enough people in the whole world to eat all these. Having been refused some trifling item from time to time, I thought, 'If there is so much why can't we have some more'?

There was a short pause in the work, and my wharf man remembered me, lifting me down. "Good boy sonny, git on 'ome nar". Not before I had filled my pockets with raw peanuts though. I hoped he would not notice my bulging pockets.

In the process of loading in the High Street sometimes the sacks would be split, and their contents spilled. Showers of nuts, figs, dried fruits, or liquorice sticks scattered the cobbled street as a delicious carpet, only to be trodden under the heavy booted feet of the labourers and the horses' hooves. Mostly though, it would be carefully swept up and recorded against 'tally', no one would dare to touch a morsel of it. The local kids though, would often dart in unseen and grab what they could, to be seen later with their pockets filled with the stolen goods. Fists full of and the pavements littered with the half chewed remains. There were plenty more where they came from. No Wapping child ever suffered with constipation when the liquorice ship was in.

I had to get rid of my peanuts before I got home, there was more than the possibility that I would 'catch it' for wandering. I didn't want to explain... not for having the nuts mind you. Not only this, but there were always plenty of 'cabbige' about (Dock police) and I didn't want to take the risks of being caught 'nicking'. I tried to feed my stolen nuts to the pigeons, but their crops were filled with stolen nuts already. They could steal them, and I couldn't. Mine were left to be crushed in the gutter.

Chapter 7

Cinema and Other Entertainments of a Social Kind

The very idea of most Wapping kids ever going to the cinema on a regular basis was about as likely as Christmas coming twice a year.

Dad did take Lily and me occasionally as a rare treat, but the nearest really decent cinema was about two miles from home as the regular Wapping pigeon flies. There were one or two others described locally as fleapits a little bit closer, and probably a reasonable alternative providing one accepted the risks of infestation. Anyway, understandably, if one were disposed to make a treat, naturally only the best option would be good enough. There was, however, no public transport, so it was either 'Shanks's pony' or not to go at all.

Distance was never a problem for me if we were going anywhere with Dad because he usually carried me on his shoulders, 'flying angel' wherever we went. He was of course in my mind, the perfect substitute for a horse and I constantly reminded him of it. "Giddy up… giddy up", I would say, with the appropriate movements to encourage him. "Keep still" he would say, "Or you will have to walk". I kept still for a while.

We were going to the 'Troxy', the newly built and magnificent edifice of cinema Art Deco. All stucco covered without, and brass, chrome, and thick carpets within, all red and gold decor, crimson plush seats. It was equipped with a Wurlitzer theatre organ that rose majestically during the intervals, rising slowly in the glare of spotlights and dimmed auditorium lights, playing a stirring rendition of the latest 'pop' to wild applause. Just to set the pace for the performance to follow the resident organist dressed from head to toe in gleaming white, turned to address the audience, "Good evening ladies and gentlemen. Tonight, I am going to play by popular request a selection from…", whatever current hit numbers were the rage. Down would go the lights, spotlights focused onto the organ… more wild applause, and then ten minutes of stirring music at full volume. Tear-jerking love songs taken up by the audience as the Wurlitzer slowly descended still playing as it went.

My friends sometimes went too. The day after the event would be fully related to those less fortunate, in order to score a moment of triumph. "Las' night we's wint ter Th' Troxy". The great news received with an inflection that intimated disbelief. "Oh yeah"? "We did an' all, wiv me dad an' me mum… An' we seed Amy Johnson on der news". Amy Johnson was that courageous lady solo pilot who flew undreamt of flights from continent to continent. Very much the heroine of those times.

The fortunate cinema goer ignored the disbelief and carried on with the story, in spite of the comments of his listeners and disbelief. "E sez 'e wint t'der Troxy an' seed Amy Johnson… Nar, course 'e couldn't cos Amy Johnson ain't at 'ome at th' momint…sh' is gorn ter America". Now, every Wapping child knew that Amy Johnson was a full blown Wapping girl… She couldn't be doing the things she was doing if she weren't. I was even shown where she lived once. There was no point in me disputing it, even though the house looked unoccupied and there was no response to our determined knock at the door. My informant's explanation was simple "Tolt yer. Sh' is gorn ter America, be back 'ome soon dough."

Another cinema in the Commercial Road was the 'Palaseum'. It was better known as the 'fleapit' but it did put on Saturday morning matinees for the kids - 'the tuppenny flicks' that provided an hour or two of real live imaginary cowboys and Indians and Disney cartoons together with Charlie Chaplin silent ten minute features and children's news reels. I went a couple of times.

The projector was constantly breaking down, leaving the spotty mould-damaged screen illuminated by flickering brightness and dark splodges of faint images. When this happened, pandemonium broke out... the kids jumping up and down and screaming, "Gis our money back... money back... money back!" Only to be stilled finally by a distorted sound like a slow running record and a fuzzy picture slowly forming on the screen as the projectionist recovered his composure to the accompaniment of cheers, stamping feet and clapping. The fact that about twenty minutes of the film was missing made little difference to what was always the plot anyway, finishing off at an exciting bit with the caption 'To be continued next week...'. Most of the films were serial features, hopefully, I suppose to encourage a few more tuppences in the till the following Saturday.

It was still a long walk to get there. Not many of the local Wapping kids managed to get there on time before the matinee began, or the doors closed, 'full house' which usually meant fifty payers and five hundred 'bunking in'.

Chapter 8

Sunday Visiting

Sunday was the day for visiting. Everybody did it, it was the done thing, and the general custom for adults and children alike.

Now, seeing that everyone was on the sabbath move, it ought to have been a very chaotic and complicated affair, but it wasn't. It seemed in some peculiar and mysterious way to work out very well. It was never a case of somebody's visit to somebody else's coinciding with the person being visited and found to be out visiting somebody else. That they ever succeeded in meeting at all would be easy to understand if it were a case of prior arrangements being made. As I saw it, nobody seemed to consider, "Ah, so and so is likely to call round, I had better wait to be sure that I am here". Oh no. For instance, Auntie Rose would never delay her Sunday visit to Uncle Bill just on the 'off' chance that he might decide to pop round to see her. If it came to mind to visit Uncle Bob, 'off', she would go only to find that Uncle Bill and Auntie Maggie had done the same thing. Thereby, killing the proverbial 'two birds with one stone', or as I prefer to believe, Uncle Bill decided to stay put, guided by pure instinct, or some other strange influences, thus avoiding the chaotic situation of lost visitors wandering around looking for each other.

This must sound a very complicated explanation to the uninitiated. How was it really done in practice? There is unfortunately no simple explanation that I can think of. I have already spent years trying to work it out for myself. If I knew the answer and how the system could be made to work in situations other than Sunday visiting there might be some money in it. Rail operators could dispense with the necessity to provide expensively produced timetables and at the same time remove every trace of confusion over connections. Wherever one wanted to go, at any time, there miraculously would be the very train one wanted, at the time one wanted. Also, to arrive at ones destination when wanted. I would be tempted to ask for an appropriate commission, after all, passenger traffic would increase a thousand fold. The only logical solution I can come up with is that grandparents seemed to have suspended Sunday motion and stayed put at home, thus creating the roles of mini solar systems for themselves, within which their progeny revolved around them according to the dictates of familiar gravity so that everybody would be in their appointed place at the appointed time. Which, of course, was the whole purpose of Sunday visiting. I can only finally put it all down to pure instinct and I don't propose to delve into the complicated realms of instinct, or the other intricacies of genetics.

However, Lily, who was an accomplished Sunday visitor would inform me on the right day at the right time, who we would be visiting. Last minute preparations to be made involving as it did, the bothersome ritual of being 'togged' up in Sunday best, coupled with umpteen inspections behind the ears and anywhere else nobody was ever likely to see.. All this tiresome performance punctuated by the repeated warnings, "Keep your socks pulled". "Mind the time". "You be home in time for dinner". Hand in hand we would finally be 'off'. We were going to 'Big Gran' Insole. I didn't have to give any assurances about timekeeping. Lily was in charge. She said that she could tell the time. I had no doubts that she could. I 'fibbed' that I could too but I was always careful to take my cue from her. If she said it was half past Tuesday, I was careful to agree. Mind you, I was always inwardly aware of my limitations even if I was typically prepared to deny them.

If it meant that I had to invent a story… I became quite skilled in inventing them.

The short journey to 'Big Gran' was often spent in trying to convince Lily that those statues we had just passed in Scandrett Street were my friends and they were really alive. I concocted the tale that they had come down to the nursery school room for some hot cocoa and if she looked very closely she would see for herself that they were alive but keeping very quiet and still, whispering to each other the things that only they and I could hear. "Look", I said. "I jest seed them move", only to compound my knowing guilt of 'fibs'. Lily was too wise to accept my desperate 'lies', pointing out the penalties for this obvious 'fibbing' and at the same time, it was because I was little and silly. "They're stone an' stone isn't alive. Nor does it move", but I noticed with some satisfaction that she paid them particular attention as we passed by. I consoled myself with the realisation that she was none too sure herself and behind all of her 'self-assurance' she didn't know all the answers either.

Sunday mornings were always quiet. The docks were not working, and the streets empty of lorries, men, carts and stamping horses or steaming piles of horse droppings, no chaff blowing on the breeze. It was the day of the week that I heard the pigeons. I saw them every day, but it was only on a Sunday that I discovered that they spoke. It was very quiet. The silence was of that kind that one experiences in country lanes, complete with the sound of far off church bells. Even the wharves that we passed didn't look the same as a weekday wharf. A busy working wharf was the easy thing for me to understand. A silent one, in some way was totally different in a strange inexplicable way. Bathed as they were in a Sunday sunshine (the sun always seemed to shine on a Sunday), it cast a strong hilltop kind of sunlight contrasting with the sombre valley like shadows in the streets. A sabbath wharf, a holy day wharf, was quite different to a weekday wharf. Perhaps it was because the usual dust had a chance to settle and the smoke to clear? Maybe it was nothing more than the silence or was it because the only motion that we saw was the many flocks of London sparrows and pigeons? Their normal activities were governed by the constant movement of traffic. On Sundays, their normal perches on the wharf loophole platforms were undisturbed by hoists and sacks, bales and barrels, and their movements were leisurely and unruffled.

Sunday was the day that everything came to rest. The only reminder of work was the ever present wharves and the omnipresent dock wall and an all pervading aroma. A strong but never unpleasant perfume laced with spices. This rich indefinable perfume was peculiar to Wapping, and it was none the worse for that. Sunday people too, moved as if they hadn't a care in the world. Everything they did was in a kind of slow motion. Lily and I were on our way to 'Big Gran' Insole and even we could not hurry.

'Big Gran' was not called 'Big Gran' because she was 'Big' per-se. In fact, she was not very tall. However, what she lacked in height she made up for in width. The kindest description would be 'pear shaped'. I'm sure that lots of similar grandmas are not called 'big' solely on that basis. It might seem inconsiderate and rude. A personal reference to being 'fat'. In our case, our other Grandma Wrighton, who lived in Bermondsey 'over-the-water' was very little. She stood remarkably just a little taller than my four year old head in the region of four feet nothing (and that is not in her stockinged feet). Everything else about her was little as well. Her little flat in Guinness Buildings. Her brother, little Uncle Albert. Little Auntie Maud and Auntie Cis (and all the other aunts and uncles). I never knew Grandad Wrighton, so I suppose he happened to have been little as well. So, for us the descriptions were justified, and it did simplify identification. 'Little Gran' and 'Big Gran'.

'Big Gran' always wore plain black dresses covered with the obligatory flowery cotton print crossover overall. This item of dress seemed to be the uniform of every married lady. One, to do one's daily chores in, and a clean newish one to go out in. One never saw a 'lady' without unless it happened to be the washing and scrubbing time of the day sack apron. Both her black dress and her wrap over overall, because of her lack of height, reached almost to her feet giving her the appearance of an ample William pear. Her progress was slow, and she rolled along with a gently controlled motion from side to side. Fine, wispy hair, she gathered at the back of her neck in a little pretend bun. She hadn't enough to make an ample one! She was always bare necked, her low cut dress and a gold chain resting on her ample bosom. Contrary to what one would expect in Wapping, her complexion was as 'rosy' as any country beauty. Locally, she was known by everyone as 'Aunt Beet', not, I hasten to add, because she bore any resemblance to a beetroot, but because her name was Beatrice. She was actually a sort of Wapping aunt to everybody. The kids and their mums and dads too. She was often a source of auntish advice and often a few pennies to go with it in a crisis. If anything were needed, Aunt Beet would know where to get it, where such an item could be found, begged, or borrowed. Who to ask and how to ask it, and she was our 'Big Gran'!

Grandad, 'Uncle Jack' to the locals, was of typically Saxon proportions. Short and stocky, solid, and also ruddy faced. His dress never varied whatever the seasons, summer, or winter, come wind, wet or shine. He would always be wearing a flat cloth cap, little whisps of white hair curling from under it. A narrow white silk scarf knotted at his neck. Black seaman's jersey and a jacket. He never wore an overcoat. Sometimes, and only for best, he would wear a waistcoat, black boots well-worn and wrinkled but brightly polished. He would only shave two or three times a week and most of the time his chin was covered with a white bristle stubble. Once, it had been reported that he had been seen wearing a tie. He did wear a shirt, one of those with a detachable collar. As far as I recollect, I never personally saw them ever come together, so I have to deny the rumour of a tie. In his wanderings about town, he always walked with his hands firmly clasped behind his back, bent forward with a fag end in his mouth, poised as it were, steadily and determinedly onward as though he battled against strong winds and foul weather. He was a truly solid and dependable man. Always quietly spoken and never given to wasted words. His usual comment on any subject under discussion that met with his approval was an emphatic, "Yus", and that was enough. His disapproval was usually expressed by silence and with that the matter was closed.

Long conversations were never Grandad's thing, although at certain moments he had stories to tell, like all grandads have a tale to tell. I found that the best time to draw him out was early in the mornings alone in the kitchen with the door shut tight so as not to wake gran. Gas burners flaring on the gas stove to warm things up a bit, washing drying on lines moving in the warm air of the gas flare. Cups of thick brown tea, seated at the bath-top table while he rolled his daily quota of 'rollups'. Thick, almost black 'Three Castles' tobacco. He never smoked more than ten a day. I would count them as he rolled. He talked about the times that he worked in the docks as a young man. 'Surrey Commercials' 'over-the-water' (the south side of the river), mostly 'humping' deals of timber from ship to quayside on his shoulder. He told me about 'coal heaving' colliers unloaded by the basket load a hundred weight at a time. About his father and 'his' grandfather, and about fish.

There was a strong influence of fish in the Insole family history. His, and of course, my forebears were fishermen who came to, or perhaps with the Barking, Essex, fishing fleet, some of whom found themselves marooned ashore in Wapping, but fish must have still been in the genetic makeup because by tradition my great grandparent, or is it great, great grandparent, bought fish at Wapping old stairs from brethren fishermen still with the fleet, and sold it to the locals as a means of livelihood. Eventually, he opened a wet fish shop but as Grandad said, "Couldn't make much of a living out of cod's heads and penny a dozen herrings". He also told me that to make a little more out of his shop, he and great grandma started to fry fish in coal fired pans somewhere around the mid to late 1800s. Quite an enterprising thing to do. It was certainly the first fish and chip shop in Wapping. It is debatable whether there were any, or many, in the whole of London itself. Grandad took over the business and carried on the trade. In fact, the business grew. If there was nothing else to say or talk about, he would hum a formless sort of hum matching his actions as he washed the cups.

In company, 'Gran', more often than not, spoke for both of them, interspersed with nods and "Yus", from Grandad to confirm that he approved of what she said. 'Big Gran' was in many ways a perfect 'cockney genteel'. Her bearing was that of a lady of higher birth. It wasn't put on or false, but wholly natural. She had taste in the manner of her dress but not ostentatious with it. Her conversation spoken with a lilt of the 'posh' coupled with her broad cockney accents.

I spoke to an elderly lady of Wapping (Rosie Coombs). We were reminiscing over the times past. "Yer Gran, yer know…", she said, "… was a real lidy. Them 'ats wot she wore an' them black dressis an' 'er gluv's up ter 'erelbers". "Yer Grandad wiv a top 'at on, orf ter de races, in a carriage an' pair". "Us kids…", she continued, "Chased 'em all up the Gravel Lane as if dems were Royals".

In many ways, 'Big Gran' and Grandad were a reflection of better circumstances than most Wapping people enjoyed. They did run a very successful business, but they were also Wapping people through and through. They had shared the same conditions through better times and the rough (there were never 'good times') as any other Wapping resident shared, the same pleasures too I dare say, and the sorrows. Life and the living in Wapping was hard. Very hard, most of the time.

Gran and Grandad lived in what was probably the true heart of what had been the site of the original Saxon settlement. Its main thoroughfare was 'Old Gravel Lane', which suggests its rural beginnings. It is said that St Johns Church, the parish church, had been built on the site of an old Saxon church, sadly demolished to euphemistically 'improve' the area. Old Gravel Lane ran from the Highway of notorious repute on Wapping's northern boundary, to the High Street on the riverside. It has since been renamed 'Wapping Lane' for some unknown reason. I suppose along the same lines of thinking as the demolition of the ancient church. A vandalism on the part of some 'whiz kid' (or likely group of them, in the shape of elected local authoritarians) anxious to wipe out the fascinating history of Wapping's seedy past.

Leading off from the 'Lane', thus preserving the form of an ancient village-cum-hamlet, are Watts Street, Prusom Street, and Greenbank. The 'Lane' had long since taken over the normal role of a High Street and many of the local shops were there. With the development of the docks came the need for rapid building of housing to accommodate a vast workforce needed to work them. Large areas of the typical two-up, two-down industrial houses were built, forming a warren of little courts and alleys on whatever available spaces that were left of Wapping after the needs of the dock development had been satisfied. Dad told me that he remembers that some of the older houses had been left over from Wapping's rural past, "Ancient and somewhat neglected. Some of them wooden framed", he said. Mostly though, the main principle was to pack as many houses as possible into the smallest possible space, along with the greatest number of people to occupy them, and in order to make things a little more comfortable, the close packed streets were graced with attractive rural sounding names. 'Love Lane', 'Bird Street', 'Upper Well Alley', 'Red Lion Street', and countless named and unnamed courts and alleys.

During the twenties, the London County Council, together with the London Boroughs, set in motion the extensive program of slum clearance (probably the main reason why I had the mistake of being born in Dagenham). Vast estates of council houses were built beyond London's boundaries in rural Essex to replace them. Large areas of Wapping's worst slums had been demolished with the original intention of developing the whole area as an industrial complex in line with the docks. Clearing the whole area of residents in the process. However, yielding to vociferous local pressures against the total destruction of the community, Stepney Borough Council, by the sheer weight of local opposition, opposed the L.C.C. plan with the result that extensive blocks of council flats were built to replace them. By the end of the decade and the beginning of the next, during which I arrived on the scene, much of the rebuilding of the council blocks had been completed. A few areas of the old 'not so desperately slum-like housing' still survived, notably Prusom Street in particular, remained to be dealt with at a later date.

In the clearances, 'Big Gran' and Grandad's ancient fish and chip business had been swept away before I was born. I wish that I could have seen it all. All I have is Dad's wonderfully evocative descriptions. "It was...", he said, "... an early old Georgian building that stood on the corner of Choppins Court in the Lane. The shop was open fronted with wooden shutters to close it up at nights. There was a marble slab for wet fish, mostly cod's heads and a few herrings though. Nobody could afford much else in those days". He said, "Along the shop front over the pavement were some iron rods grandad used to thread his kippers and smoked haddocks on. He cured them himself in his own 'smoke hole' in the back yard. There was always a lovely smell of curing fish and the smouldering oak sawdust. The shop always opened till late at night, eleven and twelve o'clock usually on most nights, they had to make a living. Fish and chips were fried in coal fired pans in the back o' the shop". He laughed at the recollection. "A ha'penny bit, an' a ha' p'orth. Just think of that", he said. "You could get two hundred and forty portions of fish and chips for a pound". (There were 240 pennies to the pound in old money in those days) "Just think about that", he continued. "A pound hardly buys a portion of chips now, never mind the fish". He laughed at the ridiculous comparison. "At night times...", he continued, "... there were gas lamps over the shop front, the flaring gas light an' dad's kippers an' haddocks glistening golden brown. Grandad had a good connection too with other local fishmongers, he supplied them with smoked fish, and I think that he supplied one or two West End hotels as well. He was famous for his curing. Gran fried and dealt with that side of the business". Her local reputation was good too. "Fresh, crispy and 'ot", she would say. "Them needed a good dinner, not a load o' rubbish". Only the best was good enough for her patrons. "Fish and chips were a good staple and standby. Sometimes they couldn't even afford that".

Dad had another story to tell that demonstrated the truth of this. Work and pay were never guaranteed in the docks. He told me his story. "Dad and me, were walking up the High Street once. We met a Hermitage fella, there was a half penny piece in his hand and' said to dad, "Jack, put anover wiv dat un fer a pint till I gits paid, and I pays yer back". "Grandad knew the loan wasn't anything to do with buying a pint but that he was desperate to find a little to feed the kids. Dad gave him a tanner (sixpence piece). The very same evening he came into the shop and bought six portions of fish and chips with the same sixpence piece. He had been too proud to ask for charity and I expect he paid Dad back too".

Whatever the benefits were generally in the slum clearances, for 'Big Gran' and Grandad it was a tragedy. The shop was swept away along with their livelihood. They got not a penny piece compensation. The shop was held on a lease. Their freeholder landlord was amply compensated for the loss of his freehold. Grandad got nothing. Aunt Beet and Uncle Jack could beg for their living or apply for parish relief if they qualified. They were however, offered a lockup shop in the 'Lane', a part of the new council block and a two bedroomed flat over it, but he was told that he could not fry or cure fish. Just wet fish. Cod's heads and herrings presumably. He tried because there was nothing else he could do. It failed and he had to give up.

The flat they had been offered and moved into would be considered these days as 'substandard' and inadequate for today's standards. There wasn't a bathroom, but it was provided with a bath in the kitchen. A cast iron bath with clawed feet supplied with a match-boarded lid that did duty as a table worktop. Beside it in a corner, a zinc galvanised gas copper to heat the water. This had a rubber hose and a hand pump to transfer the hot water into the bath. However, it turned out to be a lot more laborious than bailing out water with a saucepan, so the hand pump was relegated to the useless. At any rate, it was a bath and something that had been in very short supply. The story went about, and I see no reason to disbelieve it, when the new council flats were being considered by the planning committee, a particularly (but probably typical) block-headed councillor exclaimed, "Why give these people baths. They will only keep their coals in them"! Fortunately, the 'coal hoarder primitive people' got their baths and somewhere to keep their surplus coals as well. A brick and plastered coal bin were built in the passage from the 'front door'. Not that most people had too many surplus coals that required prolonged storage. Even so, the flats must have been a great improvement on what many of the new tenants had been used to.

'Front door', this seems to me to be a bit misleading too but then I suppose it has always been a problem how to designate a flat's entrance. What is it other than a simple 'entrance'. It certainly isn't a 'front' of anything resembling a street. However, the 'entrance' to No. 8 Jackman House was always referred to as the 'front door' in spite of the obvious difficulties of description because it led off directly from the 'belkney' (balcony), which was reached by a dark plain brick walled and concrete stairway that led off an asphalted courtyard at the rear of the buildings.

Apart from a few fenced off patches of grass and a few small trees planted when the buildings had been completed, not a garden in sight. This particular lack didn't seem to bother most people. The new tenants had never been used to such luxuries. A tiny claustrophobic enclosed backyard perhaps. In any case, nobody had any illusions about what to do with a garden even if they had one. There certainly weren't any illusions about an innate green fingered instinct, many had tried to grow the odd tender, and the not so tender pot plant from time to time but with very little success generally. A beneficial light might have helped but if the sun ever shone at all on any open space, it was likely to be as brief as two minutes flat before it disappeared in its heavenly orbit behind a dock wall or a high building. I just know, as every aspiring Wapping gardener also knew, that their best efforts were bound to end in failure. There were exceptions, and Grandad was one of them.

Grandad had always wanted a garden; any little spot would do where he could grow some privets and a few flowers would be very nice. Just a little space that would get some sunlight in reasonable doses would do the trick. The best he could do in Jackman House were boxes on the 'belkney'. Also, over the shopfronts there was a narrow asphalted roof fronted by a low parapet wall. The only access to it was from the living room windows. He had his privets, some asters, petunias, and geraniums, neatly set out in boxes along the roof and the parapet. I often saw him standing at the living room window looking for all the world like a full blown country gent watching his crops grow. An illusion that was accentuated by the fact that he stood in his usual fashion, hands clasped behind his back, cap, and scarf on, roll-up fag end in his lips. He was very proud of his garden, something that the council hadn't allowed for when the tenancy agreements had been drawn up. Grandad was therefore told to remove the offence. He refused with his usual grunted, "Yus", which gained more meaning by the addition of, "Oh", in front of it, said in such a way that must have struck terror into the breast of the unfortunate council official who had been given the unenviable task of telling Grandad to remove his flowers. Especially as Grandad emphasised the meaning of his, "Oh yus", by removing his jacket with the full intention of rolling his sleeves up as well.

Officialdom in County Hall had always had a healthy respect for a certain nastiness displayed by Wapping gents when they were really upset. Stories had spread to the furthest reaches of the whole of London that would be tyrants had been known to finish up tipped over a bridge rail into the nearest lock, whether they could swim or not. Stories that circulated freely in the corridors of the County Hall and far beyond. The official beat a hasty retreat to puzzle over this extraordinary business of a Wapping man who had the temerity to want to grow flowers. Heads shook in disbelief in County Hall. Not about Grandad's offer to sort it out in the time honoured fashion of Wapping men, that was a foregone conclusion, but Wapping and flowers didn't seem to belong together. For the moment, the 'official telescope' was offered to the sightless eye in the best Nelsonian custom, more in fear that both the official eyes could end up sightless if it weren't than for any reason of human understanding. Grandad was left for the foreseeable future in complete possession of the battleground, for there was no way that he was going to surrender his 'garden'.

The flowers did look nice, but for me the question was where did he get all that earth to fill the boxes with? Nobody knew the answer. All that was known was that the grumpy old parkkeeper had reported to the parks department that he had noticed some holes appearing in the flowerbeds in the recreation grounds and he suggested that the problem might be caused by moles, but the parks department official who came to follow up the report had to tell the parkkeeper that moles had not been seen in Wapping for at least five hundred years, and with that the mystery remained unsolved. I suspect though, that if they had asked the right question in the right quarter, the mystery could have been resolved with a confirming, "Yus".

I recently read a thirties report by some lady social academic conducting a survey in Wapping following the 'transformation' after the council flats had been built. She reported, "The new council tenements are a great improvement on the old derelict slums. Especially...", she said, "... the window boxes and the flowers overlooking the shops in the 'Lane'". She hadn't obviously been told that they were an illegal privilege. Grandad would have been so proud. As he said, "They took me shop and me livin' an' left me with nothing. They ain't havin' me flowers an all"!

Maybe there was some justification on the council's part. The way would have been opened to all sorts of strange additions to the new buildings that could have become unsightly. As it happened, the neighbours didn't follow Grandad's example and the situation did not lead to an escalation of hanging baskets like the fabulous gardens of Babylon, but what they would have looked like after a hundred year drought. Perhaps it was merely that they knew their efforts would look shabby by comparison with 'Uncle Jack's' display, or they just could not be bothered.

Our arrival at No. 8 was always expected in a sort of unexpected way. The flat usually buzzed with aunts and uncles, neither was it only relatives that came visiting. The 'front street' door was never locked. Nobody ever had to knock. It was straight in and into the purpose of the visit if there was a real purpose. Sometimes it was just a quick, "Hallo" and into the subject matter straight away. "Ah, Beat, I havn't asked 'arry yet bu' E sez 'e'll get them things fer yer termorrer", and just as quickly into the 'goodbyes'. "Tarrar, see yer termorrer", and away.

Gran's, "Thanks", (to whoever it happened to be) was often too late. The visitor was probably visiting somebody else by then. Mostly it was a constant stream of 'through traffic', if for nothing else, other than maintaining the tradition of Sunday visiting, or as I have already suggested, 'just resting momentarily in their solar orbits'.

Dad's bachelor brother, Uncle Bob, was always 'at home'. Dad and he were so much alike that they could almost have been taken as twins. I was very fond of him. He worked at Gibbs Soap Works in Greenbank, and always smelt pleasantly of soap. His main mission in life though, was to teach me the noble art of self-defence. A very necessary skill to be acquired in Wapping. He never gave me any indication who these enemies were likely to be but just in case there was an enemy, I had to know how to take care of myself. Most of the rules hovered around the Queensbury rules of engagement but I also received some very useful tips on how to effectively discourage a 'would be' assailant in the event that I found him to be bigger than myself, a bully or just a bit too handier with his fists. "Kick him in th' balls, Johnnie, an' if yer can't reach 'em, kick him in the shin". He knew though, that it was always better in the end for fair and square combat. "Never mind the bumps an' bruises", he said. "Take it all, never turn yer back, nor run away. If yer put up a good show he'll respect yer, an' you'll make a friend of him". Brutal as this philosophy might sound, the truth happened to be just as brutal. It was always a case of survival in Wapping, and it was often the only way of defending the little they had.

Like all Wapping kids, or for that matter children anywhere, I didn't lack in the imagination stakes. For us, it was all we did have in anything like abundance and moreover, we made full use of our latent capabilities. Uncle Bob never ridiculed any of my most fantastic notions about the dock wall and dungeons, secret passageways and hidden gardens, especially live statues. He would always be ready to match anything I said with tales of his own. We would disappear into one of 'Big Gran's' rexine covered armchairs and once out of hearing, we would swap stories. He even assured me that he had seen those statues come down from their niches himself. "They moved all right. Mind you, it was a windy day and I expect they were feeling a bit cold". I caught his meaning really but chose to ignore it as just being an inconsequential comment on the weather at the time. It didn't matter, he believed me and was willing to enter into my fantasies when nobody else did. I am convinced that he was a prime mover in my blossoming career as a bit of a romancer, not as a means of deception but arising out of pure childish imagination. So much so, that I acquired the Wapping nickname of 'Pickles'. Whether it was because I had 'nicked' 'Big Gran's' jar of pickled beetroot, or as I suspect, I _was_ pickled in my brain box. I don't know.

Very soon, the requirements of Sunday visiting having been met, 'Big Gran' and Grandad would disappear too. We all knew where they were going. Grandad, 'orf' to the Red Lion up the 'Lane' for his midday pint (or two) before his Sunday dinner. Gran to our bachelor Uncle Jack's little greengrocers shop, also in the Lane. Great Uncle Jack liked to go to church on Sunday mornings and Gran looked after the shop for him for an hour or so.

It was a little cubicle of a shop, no more than twenty feet deep and eight feet wide, wooden racked and smelling of musty earth. Full of 'taters', whites, an' tater Ed'ards. cabbiges, carrits, unyins, an' cowcumbers. I liked to sit on top of a stack of jute sacked potatoes to watch 'Big Gran' serve the customers. "Five o' dem whites, Beat, please" (Five pounds for sixpence). "Wots them brussels like den"? Gran would answer, "Have th' savoy cabbige luv". As she weighed out the potatoes she explained the sprouts. "They ain't too good. They've gone a bit yeller. Reckon they might be alright underneath but th' savoy is better". Gran knew that Sunday dinner deserved a nice fresh cabbage. The brussel sprout could wait to be sold off cheaply during the week. The customer satisfied. "Alright, Beat. I'll have half den, don't want a 'ole one". "Right", said Gran. "Give Mrs Sullivans 3 half pence change". A 'tanner' chinked into the OXO tin till. I knew that three half pence was a lot of money, so was a 'tanner' and it was probably Mrs Sullivans' last until 'hubby' maybe got some work in the week.

There were not many luxury items sold in the shop. A box of Cox's apples, a few oranges, and bananas. Soft fruits in season. Another customer to be served. "A nice Cox's please, Beat". Gran also knew that she could not afford them and tried to extol the virtues of cooking apples as an alternative that were much cheaper. "These Bramleys luv, yer can eat 'em, they're not sharp at all. Just you have a smell". I was suddenly surprised that you could tell whether something was sweet just by smelling it. I went around sniffing all sorts of things to test the theory to the utter consternation of Lily who thought that I had really flipped this time. As she pointed it out to me, "Yes, but that's apples and things, not chairs and things!" I knew what Gran meant though, and it was something else to impress my friends at nursery school with.

Our bachelor Great Uncle Jack of greengrocery fame was something of a 'dandy'! If one could describe a paunchy middle aged gentleman as a 'dandy'. He was wont to dress in rather colourful clothes and wore an expression of distinctly effeminate gentility, both unusual features of Wapping of the time. We would see him coming down the 'Lane', his light hued violet-lavender overcoat, neat and dapper. My friends would see him too. "Ere cums yer Uncle Jack, Johnnie. Arst 'im 'as he got 'is stays on"? The reference to 'stays' was of course to emphasise that Uncle Jack was somewhat 'the other way', which he undoubtedly was. He was though, just as undoubtedly untroubled by the general view of his inclinations and smiled his way through the implications. He was certainly also an extrovert and always in the forefront of any situation that called for acting a part. He might have been effeminate and of doubtful gender inclinations, often the butt of local fun and derision, but he was a Wapping character. Let anyone from 'outside' Wapping tease him... then feathers would fly.

There was always a Sunday dinner at No. 8. 'A bit of beef', or 'an hand and spring of pork and greens. 'Big Gran' always left the dinner 'doin' while she looked after the shop. We had to go home in time for ours but there was always a spare potato for Lily and me. "Crisp roast potato", Gran would say as she gave them to us. "Them whites roast better than those Edwards. Balls of flour them are". … and they were.

Frequently we would be sent on an errand but only on a Sunday. Gran would give us a large white china jug and send us over the 'Lane' to the 'Three Swedish Crowns' to the Jug and Bottle for a frothing quart of Guinness's stout. "Just for a sip with me dinner" Gran would tell us. "And don't you spill any either". It was rarely a full quart when we arrived back at the flat. On the way back, carrying a full jug was as attractive to local kids as honey is to bees. We would be surrounded by a crowd of hopefuls. "Give us a sip den". "Go on, jest a littul sip". We knew that a little sip would have been a long gulp, so we never gave in to their wheedling ways, but we always sampled it ourselves on the dark stairs up to the 'belkney'. I'm sure that Gran knew that we did but she never said anything. A knowing look into the jug was enough to tell us that we had rather over done the 'perks'. The jug set at the Sunday table and a tumbler set beside a knife and fork. "Dinner's nearly ready", she would say. "Go up and tell Grandad for me". We knew where 'up' was. The Red Lion 'up' the 'Lane', and we went to tell him but there was never any need. We always met him on the way home down the Lane, dressed as he always dressed, arms clasped behind his back, cap on, white silk scarf and a roll-up in his lips. I think I saw him stagger once. Well, not so much a stagger, more a hesitation of foot as if that sudden gust of wind needed that little extra push. He wasn't tipsy of course, but the roll-up had gone out and he hadn't noticed. We greeted him. "Going home now Grandad"? Just his usual grunted, "Yus", and we were gone.

On our way, Sunday people were seen sitting at their front doors, their children playing in the street. At every pub we passed groups of kids with bottles of lemonade and huge arrowroot biscuits in their hands, squeezing as far into the pub as they dared, complaining to their dad's within. "Dad, le's 'ave one o' them biscuits. Le's 'av one. Please". "Oi… Dad, Tommie's jest gorn orf…. 'e sez 'e ain stayin' 'ere".

The threat added just to remind the dad in question that the reward for looking after restless Tommie was slow in coming.

For Lily and me, it was home to Sunday dinner and a long afternoon of other pleasures, or some games in the streets with our mates.

Chapter 9

A Bit of a Party

Wapping probably had more pubs to people than anywhere else in London. Come to that, anywhere else in the UK…unless somebody can tell me otherwise?

Every street corner and every stairs to the river had its pub. Quite apart from those to be found halfway up a street and to cap it all, those on the other side all the way back again. Bearing this in mind it would be understandable if the occasional visitor got the erroneous idea that thirty six pubs in a tiny village sized area like Wapping, could only prove that the population must have spent three parts of their lives in a sodden state of blissful unawareness, and the rest of it in a drunken stupor.

It wasn't like this at all, given that a few individuals might have overdone the 'sauce' a bit too much from time to time… Let's face it, there was always the surprise addition to the family numbers to celebrate, or the loss of a much loved grandma to commiserate. If these things didn't actually involve yourself or your immediate in-laws or family, there were so many friends and neighbours who needed con-gratulations or consolations now and again on a fairly regular basis. On the other hand, there was always the perennial problem of too many odd half pence burning holes in pockets.

It cannot be denied that the pubs were well used… 'Used' incidentally, is the correct Wapping terminology. A Wapping man would never be asked "Where de yer drink?" but "Wot plice de yer use?" Now, anyone not familiar with the local manner of such a question might think that the enquirer was being a little too personal, after all, one 'uses' a lavatory. It could have sounded as though the curious were referring to matters of great interest. In general, we are all interested in the private doings of everybody else, whether we are prepared to admit it or not but there it was, thirty six pubs and every one of them apparently a thriving outlet for the brewers. They couldn't have gone wrong. If there had been forty six, all of them would have made a comfortable living even if their patrons could not.

It is a curious paradox really. On the one hand, observers would be justified in thinking that alcohol had been the curse of Wapping... and so it was, but on the other hand, there was another side to it. The 'plices' used were not generally used as a means for a weekly 'booze up', or even a daily one, but happily frequented because they were warm, bright and friendly. For hundreds of Wapping men, they were a natural meeting place. The first stirrings of labour organisations and union combinations took root in the smoky fogs of a Wapping taproom. Not only for this commendable off-shoot of a public bar, but the pubs also functioned very much like the private members clubs of the well-heeled and better-off. Indeed, it went even further than this. They were regarded by their patrons as the natural extensions to their generally cramped homes. The claustrophobic conditions of most of these, and the children abed in what was often the bathroom, kitchen, living room, and to top it all, often the bedroom as well. The pub's role in their lives is perhaps not surprising.

That is not to say that bitters, brown ales, and Guinness were not consumed in copious quantities. Neither was it unusual to see a stagger or two in the legs of the homeward bound, or perhaps the unfortunate individual being carted off on the 'police ambulance' to sleep off in the 'cooler'. The police ambulance was just like a costermonger's barrow, with a hood like a child's perambulator. The patient requiring assistance wrapped in a blanket and strapped in to prevent his sudden urgent desire 'Ter git orf an' walk'.

This sort of thing happened at all times of the day, not just hidden away in the dark of a late night. I think that the late revellers were not always seen and left to their own devices to find their own way home as best they could. Limp bundles in dark alleys were more likely either to stay where they were until daylight and cold consciousness returned, or his mates found him and took him home.

In my cot at nights, I did sometimes wake to the sound of some homeward bound carousing, singing at the top of his lungs a barely recognisable popular hit. Lily would reassure me, "No, he is only singing". "No…he isn't crying". "No…he isn't lost". He may well have been lost and crying. The noises that he was making couldn't be described as singing either. Generally, these things were rarer than they might have been. Hermitage nights were as quiet as country lanes are reputed to be. The only sounds I heard were the constant blasts of ships' sirens nearby, leaving the dock on a high night tide, others far down river coming on the night air as doleful sighs, sounding like the regretful sobs of the departing, slowly disappearing into the distance. I knew what they were, and I found them comforting. Apart from these familiar sounds, almost an eerie silence. Empty streets dotted with little pools of gaslight from the streetlamps. Silent houses, the deep grey shadows of the walls and hulking wharves, slashed with black voids of deep-set darkened windows, gates and loop-holes. The moon hanging low over the roof tops.

I would creep out of my cot to look out of the window, to see the dock lights here and there lighting the late working quays. Dad's wireless (radio) playing music in the living room. I would watch and wonder at the depth of the sky and the barely seen stars. Dad found me one night kneeling on the foot of Lily's bed, head on the windowsill and fast asleep. He lifted me, still barely asleep back into my cot… I remember it still. The quiet music and the night's wonders had lulled me into deep dreams better than any bedtime story. I feel it now, the warm pleasure of slowly falling back into oblivion. That is if there wasn't a party going on. There never seemed to be a shortage of this sort of celebration going on.

Parties always happened on a Saturday night for the very good reason that a good sleep over the following Sunday went a long way towards curing the after-effects of an over-indulgent 'bellyful' and the inevitable hangovers 'slept orf'. What parties they would be too. Nothing was ever allowed to spoil the events (not at the time that is). The grumpy bad tempers and consequent rows always created at parties generally surfaced later.

Big Gran always held the Insole parties at Jackman House. The neighbours didn't seem to mind, they were probably too busy thinking about their own noisy parties to be arranged and organised in the very near future. They would tell Gran, "Our Kaffy's gittin marrid next munfe, that'al be a 'knees up' an all… mind, it ain't before time if I ain't mistook… by the look on 'er it's a tossup wever it's one or a piggin pair". Not that anyone had to explain or apologise for noisy parties, it was not the done thing to complain, quite apart from the possibility that one might be invited in just to 'wet the baby's head'.

Weeks ahead of our do, which for some reason didn't always appear to have any particular noteworthy cause for celebration, apart from maybe the season for parties had arrived and it was therefore all down to the influences of instinct alone. I can't remember if I was ever told personally that a party was in the 'offing', but I noticed that Gran was laying in stocks of jars, bottles etc. The coal bin lid in the passage pressed into service as an extra storage space. Slowly the pile would rise, and with its increase my own assurance that the time was getting closer rose too. I knew it was even closer on the day that the living room mats suddenly disappeared from off the living room floor and the 'lino' washed, a peep under Big Gran's bed would reveal the whereabouts of the missing mats. I knew then that something was imminent. Next her much prized vases with the handles like entwined vines and the painted pictures of rural scenes and gentle folk would disappear from off of the mantelpiece for safe keeping.

The living room table had wandered into the passage and stood in shameful scrubbed pine nakedness beside the coal bin. Cardboard boxes got out from under the beds, the contents got out and washed. The table's shame covered with a once or twice a year used tablecloth. Crates of quart bottles of light, pale and brown ales, milk stout for the ladies, bitters and Guinness stacked beside the coal bin, boxes of glasses marked 'breakages to be paid for' and a barrel came from the pub, iron-hooped and a wooden tap. 'Watney's bitter' deep cut into the barrel's top and painted red lay on its side propped on stools, a white china basin on the floor to catch the drips.

Sundry smells floated from the kitchen. Rich savoury smells of boiling joints of bacon and roasting pork. Piles of thick-cut Wonderloaf sliced bread, wrapped in blue waxed paper appeared on the bath-top kitchen table. The jars from the coal bin top ambled into the kitchen, to be replaced by bottles with strange shapes and colourful labels, and equally colourful contents: port, rum, whiskey and sherry. The jars opened in the kitchen to add their sharp smells of pickled onions, beetroot, red cabbage, and cucumbers to those of the boiling bacon and roasting pork.

The last of the unwanted furniture threaded out of the living room and stitched into whatever space remained in the bedrooms. Pushing and pulling, Gran red-faced and offering advice. "Nar… not tha' way Bob… Turn i' round a bit… Get out on th' way Johnnie". I was only trying to help. "Put th' mats on th' bed Bobbie… Nobody 'ill get t' kip on 'em anyway".

That done to Gran's satisfaction and the fire stoked up with coke for the last time (it will get warm enough later), it was time for a nice cup of tea, and soon the first arrivals. Except for Grandad, who had wisely removed himself from the scene of operations a couple of hours earlier, "Just fer a breath o' fresh air". I expect he had a 'half' or two while he was about it.

Everybody would be coming, aunts, uncles, sundry cousins, and a few friends who were not involved at that moment in organising their own parties. No one would be missing. No one would want to be.

Big Gran had a piano. It was rarely played at any other time except party times. Mum played it, she said 'By ear'. I had no idea what ears could have to do with it, but I assumed that she knew, and as it sounded alright, and even though I carefully watched her ears and they didn't seem to do anything to assist, I left it at that. The 'peeyana' was an ancient instrument with sconces to hold candles and fretwork panels with faded green silk backing. It was normally loaded with dusty ornaments and things to be put out of the way, stored under its lid, but now it stood grinning with yellowed keys in anticipation, ready to receive the attentions of mums' ears or anyone else's who could produce a tune out of it with any part of their anatomy they chose. It hadn't been tuned for at least forty years and sounded like it, though I was told "That it did a tune". I had no idea what it was supposed to do to a tune, so I suppose it did do 'a tune'.

Mum was always keen on our cultural development, and we had been taught our songs. Lily was forever disappearing into the distance, something to do with 'Red Sails in the Sunset'. She happened to have a very good singing voice. I could never manage anything more taxing on the vocal chords than one song: 'I'm the Little Boy that Santa Claus Forgot'. I remember the first verse. It went something like this:

'I'm the little boy that Santa Claus forgot.

98

And goodness knows I didn't want a lot.

I wrote to Santa, for some soldiers and a drum.

It broke my little heart when I found he hadn't come."

The rest of it I have forgotten… Not that I ever got beyond the first verse. I was prevented from continuing in full flight and about to enter into the spirit of the thing, by a round of very earnest   clapping. I realise now that it was nothing to do with approbation but rather the only way to shut me up. Anyway, it did bring in the pennies and half pence. Lily collected too. We didn't exactly pool our income, she just looked after mine for me.

We always did our bit early in the evening and from then on busied ourselves with cousins, dashing around and getting in everyone's way; hiding on the dark stairs, and up to the upper balconies of the buildings, creeping along them in a game of hide and 'shriek' when discovered. Something we would not have dared to do at any time other than party time. The fascination and wonder of it all for me was the unaccustomed lateness of the hour. Taking surreptitious sips from unattended glasses, gorging ourselves sick with pickles and roast pork, thick slices of boiled bacon wrapped in Wonderloaf thick-cut sliced bread, hours of feast and fun, fading into desperate attempts to stay awake.

Apart from the pubs, Wapping wasn't exactly the mecca of the entertainment world so folk were left to providing entertainments for themselves by any means available to them. Parties were the ideal vehicle for extroverts to exercise their natural high spirits… and they did just that. The party night was filled with a constant stream of things going on, from beginning to the end a lively procession of sweaty and certainly bawdy activity.

The 'establishment' came in for an irreverent bashing, especially the Church. It has to be said though, that nevertheless the 'church' as a physical and sometimes spiritual entity was very important in everyone's lives but sometimes it was of a vaguely indefinable nature, hovering between necessity and practicality. One needed to be pragmatic to survive in Wapping and Wapping people were never short on satire to express their inequalities.

Uncle Bill, Dad's younger brother, was *the* great games organiser. I especially liked his shadow silhouette pantomime acted behind a lighted bed sheet set up as a screen. For example, 'the operation' when ridiculous objects were drawn out of a shadow patient (a volunteer) on an operating table, hammers, saws, strings of sausages etc. Sometimes (actually, most of the time), items of a very personal nature and the dialogue to go with it... "Sorry mate bu' I cut this orf by mistake". Always very funny. Always very bawdy.

That we kids witnessed all this rude humour never seemed to bother anyone, least of all, us. Nobody had any illusions on that score about life in general and none at all about sex. Even for us there were very few undisclosed mysteries about it. If anyone had any ideas or the intention to deceive us with silly stories about storks and gooseberry bushes, they would soon come in for a cultural shock.

A song or two accompanied by Mum's ears on the old 'peeyana', our bachelor Great Uncle Jack of greengrocery fame, dressed in outrageous drag, probably one of Gran's old black dresses, equally outrageously powdered and rouged, energetically and mostly rudely trying to be into everything and everywhere at the same time. As the evening wore on the drag wore off, his face streaming in rivulets of rouge-streaked perspiration.

It wasn't a question of how long we were allowed to stay up. This was governed solely by our own ability to stay awake. I thought I was succeeding very well, but aided by the surreptitious sips of illicit and frankly unnoticed alcohol and the natural process of exhaustion, I always awoke the next day curled up with sundry cousins who like me, had not been able to keep the pace, under a pile of coats on the bed, wondering where on earth I was? I don't think I was alone in that either!!

Chapter 10

A Fiery Interlude - 1935

We were playing in the street. Lily as usual was supervising the construction of the local females' idea of a house. An old piece of mat dragged from under some unsuspecting mum's living room table. A couple of tatty blankets draped over the airy railings made the walls, an old chair and a few bits of rubbish gathered from here, there and everywhere completed the furnishing arrangements.

The 'airys' used to be the basement quarters of the cook and the parlour maid but had long since been quitted as such and turned into basement quarters for a paying tenant rather than the quarters of paid servants. A few Hermitage people lived in these semi-underground rooms in almost permanent semi-darkness. A couple of old chairs had been found somewhere, one minus a leg, bits of string, chipped plates, cups, and well-worn shreds of curtains had been gathered from all over Hermitage. Everything was ready. All that was needed was the application of considerable collective feminine knowhow in setting up a home.

It might have been a simpler matter if it had been left to the whims of a single individual, but seeing that this was a joint effort, and owing to the multitude of personal ideas of what a house should look like to make it a semblance of a 'home', this wasn't going to be easy.

Lily had offered to sort it out... well, not so much offered, or volunteered, it was more a case that she had somewhat forced the issue and taken over proceedings. She was terribly good at that, but she did get things done and organised. She was bringing a trace of order into the developing chaotic situation. One has to bear in mind the sheer numbers of females that had to be housed and the complexity of the individual tastes and requirements for suitable accommodation. Nothing less than a mansion the size of Buckingham Palace would have sufficed to cope with the wishes of every prospective tenant. There was also the knotty problem of possession of the various collected chattels. This factor alone frequently upset the plans. A frustrated plaintiff would complain, although she realised she had provided the dolls cot. The doll belonged to somebody else. She knew she was in imminent danger of being left out of the nursery arrangements. However, she was also a member of a very just society which was more likely to be prompted by the notion that the doll's owner was just about to withdraw, taking the doll with her. A rapid compromise had to be found. Lily suggested "Alright then, you can be th' nursery maid". This isn't what the complainant really had in mind. She reasoned with some justification that the cot being hers then the baby put into it must be hers too. After all, 'nursery maids' didn't go around putting their babies into other mums' cots. It hadn't altogether dawned on her that the doll wasn't hers anyway. Lily of course reminded her of it. "Anyway" muttered the plaintiff, "babies is allus der ladies, not der nursery maids". In the end the planners realising the limitations imposed upon them by the lack of materials available to them, compromised in the only possible way. "Alright den, We'sle tak' it in turns".

Honour, for the time being, was satisfied, the genius wisdom of the kids had won the day. for the moment that is, until… Lily, who was very mature in her approach to the orderly world of adults, suddenly threw a very loaded spanner into the works, by pointing out the obvious. "You can't 'ave babies without a dad". The game came to an abrupt and confused halt. This was something that obviously needed some serious thought. Every blue, brown, grey and green female eye roved around the assembled group. Not a male in sight, apart from me.

The boys knew from long experience where these games usually led and at the commencement of this one had taken the wise precaution and disappeared. I obviously didn't know otherwise I might have disappeared with them but there I stood in innocent isolation; two dozen virgin eyes turned in my direction. I personally didn't have any doubts about my masculine gender, I knew that I had all the bits and pieces generally associated with dads. Apparently, the girls it seems rejected my claims to these necessary appendages. The possibility of me ever performing the role of a father was put out of their minds the moment it crossed them. In their collective eyes I was probably more suited to be the 'product' rather than the 'producer'. Whatever were they going to do now? The whole enterprise was about to collapse for the want of boys. It hadn't occurred to them yet that they couldn't be mums either. Never mind, they didn't know it then, but the day would come when the boys would fall over themselves to play the game in earnest and join in.

It had been a good game. There was nothing else for it but to endure their innocent existence until that fateful day should arrive. I saw that my usefulness had come to an end and resorted to my favourite pastime of lying on the pavement gazing into the narrow slot of sky to be seen on a clear day between the rooftop and the dock wall, speeding away with the clouds from all this worldly triviality. I was just getting into a deep contemplation about the how and why babies came about. Well, I had a rough idea about the 'how', it was the 'why' that bothered me the most. But the sky didn't look at all right. The clouds were quite peculiar and not like any clouds that I had seen before. The cloud I was seeing was long and thin, black, and flecked with red. It came to me all at once... It was smoke, and lots of it. Smoke.

I leapt up from the pavement, "Smoke" I cried out. "Look, look" pointing upwards. Every girlie eye turned upwards. In a flash the game of house came to an abrupt end. Shouting kids scattered in all direction, in their excitement diving into street doors and banging on downstairs windows, yelling to their parents within. "Look mum. Look dad. Tha's smoke that is", "Le's go an' 'ave a see where it is". By now every child and their parents were in the street, watching the growing cloud of black and brown smoke turning rapidly to pitch black and flecked with flaming debris. Streams of people making their way to the High Street… People at their street doors. Very quickly the report came back. "Th' Colonial is alight", "The Colonial Wharf is goin' up in flames", "It's all a-goin' up in smoke".

The house that we had been building was completely forgotten and stood forlornly abandoned. Mums were trying to retrieve their 'borrowed chattels', their warnings: "Jest yew fetch 'em back agin when you's finished wiv 'em", forgotten in the excitement of the moment. There was a fire and what a fire it turned out to be. The Colonial Wharf in the High Street was ablaze. In a matter of a few minutes the smoke had filled the whole sky (there was plenty of fuel for the flames) and was now filling the streets with a thick brown tarry smoke that rolled along the High Street like an angry brown muddy whirlpool, climbing up the walls of the wharves then crashing over the roofs like breaking waves. Wave after wave with a roaring like a storm-whipped sea. Smoke and flaming ash shot out into the street, turning, and tumbling like a huge cartwheel before seeming to flatten, then climbing the walls afresh to burst into the sky.

Pigeons began falling out of the sky too, they staggered into the gutters as crumpled blue bundles of feathers gasping for breath, beaks wide open, pink-mouthed and panting. I could pick them up. I had always wanted to pick them up, but they had always flown out of my reach. Not now though. I was sorry for them, I picked them up and put them where I thought they would be safe and recover, on windowsills, ledges, and doorways within my reach. Lily insisted that I leave them alone. She could see that I was probably doing more damage to them than was necessary in my heavy-handed mission of mercy. Many of them were already dead.

Everything was in total chaos. From the top of Globe Street, a turning off the High Street, we could see the flames leaping high above the wharf roof.

Fire engines were beginning to arrive. In the distance the clanging bells racing closer and closer to the scene. Men and a few constables were trying to push back the gathering crowds who were being pressed from behind closer to the burning wharf by the sheer weight of the crowd's pressure. Things began exploding in the wharf, windows burst out sending showers of shattering glass and cast iron window frames. Showers of burning debris fell even to the margins of the crowds. They moved back very quickly. Lily and I had been squeezed onto the top steps of the spice mill's office doorsteps. We were safe where we were and left alone.

From our grandstand position our view of the conflagration could not have been better. I felt the heat of the flames as a hot breeze on my face. A barrier had been thrown across the High Street where we stood. Fire engines came one after another, some went through to get closer to the blaze, but many were helpless and could get no further. The High Street was so narrow that no more than two engines could be engaged at a time, presumably from both sides of the fire? Water too was a big problem. The few hydrants were insufficient, so they had to pump water from a distance. The tide was out. The nearest source of water was at the Pier Head bridge over the entrance lock some hundred and fifty yards away. Dozens of hoses were run out along the street, hanging over the bridge handrail. They filled fat with water. I could see the throbbing pulses of the pumps sucking the Thames water through them.

Everywhere was becoming so thick with dense smoke that everything was covered and hidden under a gloomy pall. Just like a typical 'pea-souper' fog that we knew so well when one couldn't see a yard in front of one's nose. This colonial fire though was different.

The same smoke that belched daily from thousands of chimneys. The same choking smell but a good London fog was somehow 'natural', the colonial fire was not.

Firemen strode by our vantage point. Long black leather thigh boots, navy blue coated, shiny brass-buttoned and black-belted, axes at their hips, the handles slapping against the shiny thigh boots. The swish of leather on leather as they strode their long-legged strides. Helmets like Britannia's I had seen on my pennies, emerged out of the fog, and disappeared back into it again. Grim faced and anxious like soldiers advancing toward the fierce hot glow and explosive furnace. How I wished that I had been a fireman then. I thought, 'If I had been, the girls would not have rejected me so quickly.' I knew that much about sexual matters!

The fire burned for days on end, it seemed like years to me. The streets and pavements became sticky with soot and tar dropped from the sky as a black rain. It occurred to me that this could go on forever and the fire would burn from one end of the High Street to the other end without stopping. I didn't want to miss a moment of it.

I remember being dragged home from my personal vantage point on the mill steps or from the top end of Hermitage Wall, sat on the granite curb stones late at night and being put protesting to bed... after being scrubbed red-raw. Practically every part of me was spotted with sooty tar. Lily being one of those finicky little Hermitage ladies, rather declined the risk of spots of tar on her crisp clean dresses, it had to be avoided. Me, on the other hand, could not see what all the fuss was about, a few spots of tar didn't bother me and didn't seem to be worth worrying about. In any case, I knew that I would collect a few more tomorrow. I lay for hours listening to the steady throb of the pumps, the crump of falling walls, shouting firemen. I could see the flickering glow in the sky, smelt the acrid smell of smoke and the pungent sweetness of hot burning tar. I woke in the mornings to find that it was all still going on. I wondered whether the firemen had been home and gone to bed just like me?

The cause of it all had been a moored Thames barge at the wharf jetty loaded with barrels of pitch and tar which had caught fire. Stacked as it was with dry and highly combustible materials, there was no way to control it. It could not be towed away from the jetty because the tide was out, and it sat on the shoreway. Neither could the Port of London fire floats get in close enough for the same reason. By the time that the tide had turned there was no barge left to tow away. Only its charred remains floated away on the rising tide. By then of course, the fire had spread to the wharf itself and was well ablaze. Nothing the fire fighters did made any impression on the flames. It flared up and died, then burst out anew, each time fiercer than before. For days on end, it raged out of control until it met the thick brick walls of the neighbouring wharves. This alone checked the fire's progress.

For a week or so, the heart of Wapping's dockland had missed a beat or two. Along hundreds of yards of river front docking ships hurriedly left their berths, half unloaded or loaded. No ships replaced them. There weren't any lorries and carts along the length of the High Street. Instead, dozens of fire engines parked and waiting to relieve the fighting crews. Fresh engines coming bright and shiny... spent engines creeping away covered with filth and soot carrying red-eyed and wearied firemen, heads hung with exhaustion.

At last, the fire had been subdued and the talk for weeks afterwards was of nothing else. The Colonial Wharf had been gutted. There was a hole in the canyon wall that had not been there before, like a missing tooth in an otherwise perfect set. 'Outsiders' came to 'risky Wapping' to look at this unaccustomed openness and marvelled at the thickness of the broken wharf walls, wondering at twisted and quickly rusting steel girders and the still steaming piles of wet and blackened wares.

Visitors came from far afield, listening to the kids' tales of fantastic sights and brave deeds. Pennies were paid out and the stories polished and garnished for the next willing listener, told in the hope of two pence instead. I actually did quite well, I recollect the princely sum of four and a half pence for an evening's series of 'Big Whoppers', some of it the truth liberally sprinkled with fantasy. My particular concoction was to relate the firemen's particular liking for cocoa, who came and shared mine before I went to bed.

Too soon for the kids the outside interest waned. Fewer and fewer of the curious bothered to come. Men came to clear the site, quickly followed by builders and the bricklayers. In a short space of time new walls sprang out of the old like new green shoots of spring. The riverside dock revived; ships returned to their accustomed berths. The High Street throbbed with the familiar traffic but this empty space in the canyon walls could not be left empty, the gap had to be filled quickly. Things must not be allowed to change.

No one who had stood with us and witnessed the Colonial fire could have known at the time the horrific future that was in store for them within a few short years - a trial by fires and blasts that were going to change lives for ever... including mine.

Chapter 11

Hopping Season and a Bit of a Break

As if by some magic signal, the whole female population had come to the conclusion that the very thing everyone needed was a bit of a break.

It was all very well (considering the general facts of the matter) having a party or two, perhaps a walk out now and again, even on rare occasions 'making a day of it' down the river or maybe a trip up 'west'. On the whole though, these rare treats came far too rarely to break the monotony of the daily necessities of life. The outward signs of this apparently spontaneous phenomenon, was the sudden annual urge to pack everything in sight into tea chests. They would be seen going into the front doors empty and coming out filled with pots, pans, buckets, and brushes. The tin baths normally hung out to dry until Friday nights were taken down from their hooks in the backyards and balcony railings and filled with plates, saucers, cups, teapots and the umpteen and various items of household implements. Rolls of bedding, mats and bits an' pieces of curtains would be seen piled up in passageways and spreading up the stairs.

How all this peculiar activity was viewed by the menfolk it is impossible to say. The pub landlords will tell you of a sudden increase in their takings mid-week. Others will say that the gents had been seen at street corners with puzzled looks on their faces, hands deep in their trouser pockets jingling their last few pence and wondering whether to relieve themselves of them in a 'quick' one, or to stay where they were hopelessly watching their wives' antics with some resignation.

Over the years they had come to expect it. It was an annual event rather like a monsoon period or snows in Alaska, March winds or April showers… it was coming up to Autumn in Wapping. In the end they could be seen to jingle their last pennies in their trouser pockets, shrug their shoulders and toddle off down the street, to toddle back a little later to their favourite corner, minus their pence, but looking a little happier and a lot warmer in spirits. The kids must have been in on the secret though. Dashing around getting in everybody's way and collecting little red marks on various parts of their anatomy for their trouble.

The reason for all this extraordinary activity of course was that the hopping season was in.

Toffs might have their 'flat' season or their grouse season or any one of their multiple seasons they liked. Whilst Epsom Downs or the grouse moors were all right for those with high born tastes… this was the 'oppin' season and very exclusive it was too! For the incarcerated 'islanders' the time had come for the annual exodus of the 'hop picking season'.

For countless generations past and during autumn's harvest times, thousands of East End families had made the trek into the balmy rural countryside of Kent (in the days before recent European 'developments' it was justifiably called 'The Garden of England'). Thousands upon thousands of acres of orchards producing apples and pears. Soft fruits, plums, greengages, and cherries. Redcurrants, blackcurrants, gooseberries, and strawberries. Market gardens. Together with vast acres of 'hop gardens' (a crop in great and constant demand by the brewers). Practically all of the fruit orchards are now grubbed out to euphemistically 'reduce' European 'over production'. Result… English fruit no longer available in any quantity… Not available to British buyers (shame). The hop gardens survived (I suppose one should call Kent the backyard of London now).

Over the years the 'exodus' had been well organised. Mostly it was whole streets, courts, alleys, or buildings, or at any rate as many of the near neighbours who would be 'goin' 'oppin' arranged it so they would be going to the same farms. Now this might seem to suggest that neighbours couldn't bear to be parted from each other. The truth of the matter is it was a very sensible arrangement. It solved the problems of transport and overcame the islander's natural distrust and shyness of 'outsiders and foreigners' at the same time.

Transport was of a fairly extensive nature. Absolutely nothing was provided by the Kent farmers to accommodate the hordes of itinerant 'pickers' so it was critical that every possible domestic need was provided for and taken with them, hence the extensive packing. A group of neighbours would be able to hire a lorry, and everything put onto it would be going to the same farm. Imagine the confusion if it was any other way? Chaos in fact. The owners of the loaded chattels finding that the teapot had gone to Wadhurst and the hopping pot to Lamberhurst, when they were both needed at Crowhurst. A lorry's tour of different farms would have inevitably resulted in just that.

In due course the packing done, the departure Saturday arrived. Last minute frantic packing to be done. Last night's bedding had to go too. Rolled up and still warm, put onto the lorry together with the boxes, tea chests, bundles, and the tin baths… Nothing forgotten, and it was 'off' on its journey towards the balmy climes of rural Kent. Last toots on its cranky rubber-bulbed horn as it turned out of the street.. .and it was gone.

Windows to close and street doors to lock. Missing kids to be rounded up and sorted out. Flustered cleanings of sick-stained shirts and pee-soaked knickers. Mums admonishing the guilty. "Yer littel sods…yer clean uns is on th' lorry" "Ne'er min' you'sl 'ave t' do".

As groups left one by one, an unaccustomed silence descended over the 'manor'. Soon afterwards the booking clerks at Wapping underground station would be called upon to issue countless tickets to Waterloo, Charing Cross, London Bridge and Victoria. The exodus was 'on'.

Within the space of a couple of hours, early in the mornings the streets would be empty of children. Local shopkeepers would despair of ever disposing of their perishable goods. Great Uncle Jack (of greengrocery fame) would look at his cabbig's an' greens, knowing that he would watch them as they turned from fresh green to yellow and finally to black. In the end, "Sod it, I'll 'ave t' chuck 'em art", but not until there was no hope left of finding another customer though.

The homes of the departed, starkly deserted for the next four, five and in some cases six weeks, were now bare semblances of their former selves since everything but the proverbial 'kitchen sink' was now on the back of a rickety old lorry wending its rattly way towards the autumnal hop gardens of Kent. Dads, husbands, and the working menfolk would be left at home to guard the home fire and free to 'toddle off' to their hearts' contents.

In the days before it was the accepted right of working men to paid holidays… quite apart from the 'casual' nature of Wapping work in the docks, they had to get work when they could. Even a couple of weeks off generally meant a whole month with no or very little pay.

It was rare indeed for a man to take a holiday "Fer a bit o' a break" unless he had more than a few pounds to spare tucked away. Even then 'hopping' was out, hopping then was by and large a female province and apart from a few unemployed young men (or for reasons of sickness) the only males going would be children. Anyway, because the family were all away, was a 'bit o' a break' for the menfolk I daresay.

Mum wouldn't go hop picking. She thought it was all too low and primitive. She did her best to discourage any attempt to persuade her to go but Lily and I weren't to be so easily put off. We didn't want to be left out. Even Mum's warnings of, "All that damp, damp air" and everything else she could think of wouldn't deter us… we desperately wanted to go 'oppin'. Big Gran, Auntie Rose, Aunt Maggie, or anyone else who would take us offered. "Do 'em good" they would say.

Under pressure like this and our sulkiness, she would at the very last minute relent but she always left it to the last gasp, using our doubts as a tool to extract the maximum good behaviour out of us. For weeks before we were the essence of sweetness and compliance… not an easy thing for us to maintain. Finally at the last minute, if she was satisfied that we had tried hard enough she would tell us, "All right… when things are settled there, you can go for a week. Dad will take you down next weekend". 'Blow it', I thought. Another tiresome week to wait and some more bother of good behaviour to endure, not least the threat that she could still change her mind! She let us go eventually… I'm sure she suffered agonies of apprehension until we returned.

Not gasping out our last gasps as she thought we would be, but actually as brown as nuts and more alive and naughtier than we normally were. Yes. Hopping certainly was primitive and more often than not, damp, but how we loved every minute of it.

Families would often arrive at the 'gardens' before the lorry did with all the bits and pieces on, the drivers explaining the obvious reason for their lateness, the lorries being old and 'clapped out' and carrying such a heavy load they had to stop quite a few times, "Ter let 'er cool orf a bit". It was fortunate that they were able to find a vacant space or two on various pub forecourts on the way down. Ours arrived eventually. They saw it coming. Bumping down the muddy farm track, through field gates and down muddier field tracks, tipping this way and that way, threatening to tip its load into the ditch or to give up the struggle at every yard but finally, to the cheers of the early arrivals, it waddled onto the field accompanied by honks on its croaky rubber-bulbed horn, as if to say, "We made it… bu' we ne'er fought us 'ould".

On the field, set against an overgrown hedge stood a row of 'huts'. These were a row of black tarred corrugated iron sheds divided into cabin-like cubicles, each one no more than eight feet wide and ten deep, each one designated as a hut. The huts were each intended to house a family. There were perhaps a dozen huts in the row. One of the peculiarities of the 'accommodation' was that the dividing partitions didn't quite reach to the roof, leaving a gap of about six inches to a foot. In the Insole hut there was an old iron bedstead with a rusty meshed stretcher, sunk in the middle. It belonged to 'Big Gran'. She had left it there for umpteen years past. In the majority of the huts there were no beds. The pickers had to improvise one with bundles of firewood that the farmer provided for the campfires (faggots). Dirt floors. No lights. A small dusty window beside a badly fitting boarded door, which was secured by a rusty Suffolk latch. Here and there along the row the fanner had placed bales of straw.

The very first job to be done was to see to the bed. From the now unloaded lorry, the right bundle identified, out came the striped bed ticks. Everybody had the same thing in mind and the general rush was on. Break open the nearest straw bale. Stuff great handfuls of the straw into the bed ticks. Hey presto. A palliasse stuffed and bloated like a stranded balloon. It had to be manoeuvred into the hut and onto the improvised bed. Much hilarity and sweaty comment accompanied this frenzied chore. First things were always first at hopping. This was always the bed. Those who thought to change the proper sequence couldn't complain if they finished up with a skimpy bed. Nobody wanted more than their fair share, mind you, but it was useless for a rebel to complain if they finished up with a skimpy palliasse. Once the bed was sorted then and only then could any thought be given to the campfire, the "kittell an' a nice cuppa".

Standing separately away from the huts there was a three-sided iron shed open at the front. Close by a standpipe. This was the wet weather cooking area. The shed provided with a brick hearth to build a fire on, but no chimney. The smoke had to escape as best it could from the open front. The main disadvantage was always that the wind persisted, even on a calm day, on blowing into the open front thereby causing the smoke that was trying to get out to change its mind and try to get back in again. In the end most pickers gave up and cooked in the open, wet, or not, some distance from the huts. Usually, umpteen yards away in the far distant corner of the field there was a faggot pile, bundles of twigs and tree pruning's that the farmer had gathered and garnered through the year. This was the cooking fire's supply of fuel. The kids would be sent for them, pushing an old pram, unsuccessfully as it happened, through the lank wet grass. They would bring as many as they could back to the huts... well as many as an old pram or a dozen noisy kids could carry.

In front of each couple of huts a fire would be set to be shared by both. A few bricks made a hearth, some iron rods carefully put away from the years before became hanging rods for the 'oppin' pot... a blackened kettle set to boil and soon the 'nice cuppa' for everybody. Thick brown tea, plenty of 'Nestlé' sweetened condensed milk... "Luvly".

Next, the hut had to be dealt with. Around the walls the bits of curtains thoughtfully brought from home. The tea chests emptied of the pots and pans, kettle, plates, and cups, stood on their sides became cupboards or an improvised washstand. A piece of material to cover it, onto which would be stood an oil lamp, or candlesticks, perhaps even a clock... the last wisps of straw scattered onto the dirt floor and the domestic arrangements were complete. Time now to relax and think of supper. "Jest sumfink quick'll do... git an' early night an' 'ave an early start termorrer". So, for the kids a quick grab at a hasty meal. A last look around to see whether everything was as it was last year. They will go further afield tomorrow.

Stifled yawns and the desire to drag the day out to its limits and yet, anxious for the 'first night', this would be a wonderful climax to a day already filled with excitement… slightly tearful with exhaustion, tiresome and giggling, awkward to the end, finally giving way to the need for rest and sleep. The lamps and candles lit. The fire's embers glowing, as if it too were desperately trying to keep awake. Little spurts of flame flickered and died in a sparkling defiance of extinction. A wonderful smell of wood smoke hung on the crisp evening air.

Treated to a quick 'sloosh' at the standpipe and sent complaining off to bed… all in together, some at the top and some at the bottom. The first night taken up by establishing rights to a particular place in the bed, accompanied by screams, flomps an' giggles. "Ooo, that there bit o' straw ant arf stickin' in m' bum" or, "git ower…yer in my bit", but finally the palliasse beaten into a hard board, and the contests over. The warmth, the fun and the excitements of the day, the same sounds from all along the row gradually subsided. Lulled by the soft murmur of the ladies gossiping around the dying fire… sleep and the silence of a country night. One by one the ladies blew out the lamps and candles and climbed into what little space was left in the bed, thinking, "Termorrer. We'll 'ave a good breakfust an' a good dinner!"

The first lady up in the morning got the fire going and water boiled for tea. Frying pans were got out. The bacon and the dripping. The early kids far afield looking for mushrooms. Slabs of bread, thick lumpy porridge, crispy rashers of smoky soot speckled bacon floating in pools of black mushroom juice… cups of thick brown tea.

Stiff morning staggers to the portable lavatory. A boarded hut with a board seat over a hole dug in the ground, moved when necessary to another spot and another freshly dug hole… if for just a pee, into the hedge would do. The long wet grass, the briar thorn, and wet nettles.

117

The hedgerow dripping with the early morning dew. The nettles stung my legs as I peed.

The first day was a Sunday and a whole day in front of us for exploration and getting used to things. Stores to be laid in. It was the children's job to get the shopping. Down to the village shop for milk and bread, sliced or nutty uncut. We always got uncut if we could, breaking off little bits of the crust as we came back, arriving at the huts with a denuded loaf. The faggot pile gradually disappearing towards the huts. Long walks into the countryside. Heaps of things to do and see. Hide and seek in dark spinneys.

Tomorrow, on Monday, the 'picking' would begin but today was for relaxing and settling in.

The hop gardens were set out in long rows or drives. Lines of stout poles, at least ten or twelve feet high, strung together with ropes and twine. The hop bins grew on them to the full height and above the poles. Now, at the harvest season loaded with ripened hops, hanging in cascades of green and golden bunches, the air filled with the pungent perfume of ripe hops. The drives looking like long green tunnels dripping with dew. Each family was allotted a 'drive' and several more set aside for them. Provided with a 'bin' looking rather like a folding trestle table, with a deep canvas bag hanging between its legs.

Mums, aunts, grandparents, and the older children grouped around the bins stripping the hops from the vines into it. The younger kids doing everything to avoid it. Soon the pickers' fingers would become stained dark brown by the juice of the ripe hops.

A 'pole man' pulled down the vines and brought them to the bin. He was often one of the unemployed young men, but mostly one of the farmer's regular full time labourers.

As the vines were pulled and stripped the bins were moved down the 'drive' leaving the spent vines behind them. Every few hours or

*Great grandads Fish and Chip Shop – J.W. Insole (Wet, Smoked and Fried)
Est. mid to late 1880s. Demolished 1927/8*

*Dad and me at 4 months,
August 1931.*

Hermitage Wall.

74, Hermitage Wall.

74, Hermitage Wall. Our kitchen on upstairs landing.

74, Hermitage Wall. Ground floor scullery.

“Hoi, Wotcher Doin’ ‘Ere?”

*The back yard and shared lavatory
at 74, Hermitage Wall.*

*Me at 5 or 6 years – poss.
school photograph.*

IV

Tea time on the quay, at the 'Pier Head P.L.A Clinic'.

*Hermitage Wall Loop-hole...
He flied up jest like a sparrer.*

Policeman looking the other way when the sack fell 'off the back of the cart'.

Great Hermitage Street. Goose that chased anyone it did not like.

VI

My friends the statues, Scandrett St.

From my lofty perch, watching a ship being unloaded at the wharf jetty.

Mrs. Thompson's all night coffee stall at the Irongate Tower Wharf entrance, St. Katherines Way.

so, as the bins filled with the hops, the 'measure man' came round, scooping out the hops with his bushel basket. At the sound of his call "Hops, hops" the bin's contents would be 'fluffed' up by the pickers to loosen them. They knew a short measure would result if they didn't. The measure man counted out his tally, "One, two, three…" usually interrupted by protests that his measure was mean. "'Ere yer ant treatin' us'ns right. Them over dere 'as got better hops 'an us. We knows cos we 'as seen 'em".

It wouldn't be right if the pickers didn't complain. He continued his count…

"Right 'en. Five bushel". He marked the picker's book and his own copy. Transferred the hops into long hop sacks and loaded it onto his cart. He passed to the next drive calling "Hops, hops" as he went.

Payment was so much a bushel. If it was a poor harvest then the farmer was forced to pay more unless he wanted his pickers to pack up and go home. A good and heavy crop he would pay less per bushel. It sounds as if it ought to have been the other way round.

Good or bad, the pickers needed to know that their labour was worthwhile. Whichever way it went, the pickers would be lucky to earn as a family something in the region of two pounds a week for six days picking. Good and persistent pickers maybe a bit more.

The growers booked the amount due, officially to be paid out at the end of the season. Most pickers 'subbed' the amount of the 'sub' against the amount due. Almost everybody 'subbed' copiously and had little or nothing to come at the final pay out. It was not easy work. Long hours at the bin, early mornings till late in the evenings the work went on. In the wet and dew dripping mornings, the determined pickers draped old hop sacks over their heads and shoulders and carried on. Whatever the weather they sang, the gardens constantly filled with loud laughter and song. When one group exhausted themselves or paused to take their breath, another would take over and a continuous chorus sped the day.

While the picking went on, one of the ladies of the family group would do duty as a provisioner, throughout the day providing thick sandwiches and billy cans of tea if the garden was too far from the hut fire, bottles of stout and lemonade for the kids. She would also prepare the evening meal. Potatoes and carrots. Onions and meat set to simmer at the fire in the hopping pot. Dumplings made and put into the stew at the right time. More shopping trips for the kids. At hopping times, a maid was kept at home to do the household chores... Wasn't that grand. Tomorrow it would be someone else's turn!

At weekends, dads and the working men would come down, arriving after their own day's work had finished, to spend most of the following Sunday with their families. Excluding the time, of course, for their small constitutional amble down to the village and a smaller sample of a country brew before their dinner, merely to compare brews, naturally.

The kids were glad to see them come and sad to see them go back home. I expect a lot of the mums were sad too.

Lily and I were not so lucky, but for so many of our peers for four, five and sometimes six weeks, it was fresh air and frolics in the open fields, sorties into spinneys late evening under a dark hedge to tell ghost stories and chase the girls. Orchards to be scrumped. Shopping to be fetched. If we were very lucky a trip or two to Tonbridge on the bus for essential shopping. Baths taken under the open skies in the tin baths and dripping nakedness in the cool air. Early mornings in the mist-covered fields looking for mushrooms. Late evenings gathered around the fire listening to the adults gossiping, singing, or just gazing into the darkness beyond the fire's light.

The silence of the nights penetrated by the strange and constant sounds of a rural night. The sound of rain on the hut's iron roof. The hiss of drops on the fire's dying embers. The sound of leaves tinkling like muffled bells in the tall uncut hedge. The cries of a waking child somewhere along the row being soothed in soft tones. The gentle rhythms of sleep's deep sighs. The warmth and the wet-lipped mouths against your neck. Arms and legs belonging to goodness knows who entwined in yours. The exhaustion of strenuous games. The long silent study of the strange and wonderful things of nature. The grind of stiff-legged hours at the bin... and the incomparable taste of stews doled out of the iron hopping pot. The getting up in the mornings, the going to bed at nights. Lungs filled with the glorious autumnal air. Faces all aglow, burned by the late summer sun. We were free. Free of dismal thoughts and the claustrophobia's of the things at home. Far away and temporarily forgotten. Blessed were we and glad to be alive.

The season had to end. The hops were done, and the packing started. A last night's party in one of the farmer's barns had come and gone. All too soon the old lorry would return. The tea chests repacked. Most were sorry that it was all over yet glad to be going home.

Palliasses emptied of their now broken and chaff-like straw and the bed ticks put away. Rubbish tipped upon the last fire burned fiercely as if in protest at the coming departure. Everything must be left in order. The rods for the fire carefully put away in one of the huts, they will be needed again next year. Finally, the too short journey home by train, loaded with bags of 'Oppin' apples for the luckless ones who had stayed at home.

Great uncle Jack wouldn't sell an apple for months to come. Wapping was awash with them.

We knew it had to end and accepted the fact with the best possible grace. For weeks after our return to the dark familiar things we tried desperately to forget, consoled by the thought that next year and the next and the next, there would be another hopping season.

In the meantime, there will be a party or two to help us along!

Chapter 12

Shopping trips, Street Cries, an' a Ride on the 'Rattler'

Lily was always curious about the happenings in other parts of Wapping, for no other reason that I was aware of except to exercise her right of free passage, anywhere. She carted me around with her as a sort of traveling mascot. I think though now, on serious reflection, that she was only getting my legs used to the more strenuous journeys she had in mind for me!

Wherever we went we were accepted as some sort of visiting tourists, accepted that is with the same sort of resignation that residents of popular resorts manage to make obvious behind the smiles as they relieve them of their money, wishing them further at the same time. Personally, I couldn't see the point of all this to-ing and fro-ing. I could on the other hand, understand mum's insistence on certain errands being 'gone for'. Every youngster has these onerous tasks to perform from time to time, in spite of the nuisance these onerous duties and demands make on one's time when one is in the middle of an interesting game. Not much of a nuisance though when one is on the losing side. It occurred to me on more than one occasion, having been pressurised or otherwise coerced into "Go and fetch this" or "Run and get that", that we had gone rather a long way to the Lane to 'get it' when we could have got the same item just round the corner in Hermitage at the local shop. It might just have been Lily's rights of free passage. On the other hand, I'm more than disposed to conclude that it was all to do with her insatiable nosiness about the doings and goings-on of others and she didn't want to miss out. Coming home from one of these unnecessary marathons was always sensibly explained by Lily's insistence that, "Well. They hadn't got it at Mrs Hawkins, so we went up the Lane for it".

Mum had long since given up on a speedy acquisition of the required Oxo cubes and had finally gone for them herself, an inconvenience that took her no more than ninety seconds of her time. Frankly, I wouldn't have minded if we had stayed in Hermitage. As already mentioned Hermitage was reasonably served with shops for the everyday needs. Even so it has also been a source of wonder to me how the local shop keepers managed to make a living. If their shops were anything to go by, not a very good living by normal standards, even for Wapping of the times. Thinking about it, I don't suppose the combined wages of the whole wage earning population of Hermitage amounted to very much more than four to five hundred pounds per week. I expect that rent and the brewer had prior claim to most of that. None of the local shop keepers looked as though they were about to retire on their fortunes.

In Hermitage, during the working days there were of course quite a few 'itinerant' workers. Lorry drivers, carters and any number of dock allied tradesmen serving various industries sprinkled liberally throughout Hermitage. There was always a regular and constant volume of traffic in and out of the docks at any time. Except on Sundays.

There was a coffee shop tucked away in a back street which I vaguely remember was called The Greengate Cafe to cater for these hungry souls waiting for a load. It advertised itself as a 'Good pull-up for carmen'. The fact that there was nowhere to actually pull up anywhere in sight was apparently neither here nor there, any carman taking the advert at its face value pulling up at its door would have brought the whole of the docks traffic to a standstill. As for the 'greengate' connection, nobody had ever seen a greengate in Hermitage, still it had to be recognised as something I suppose.

This wasn't the only eating place on offer. There were a couple of coffee shops in the High Street. One eating shop certainly fascinated me... a faggot and peas pudding emporium in Great Hermitage Street. I think that it must have had a very brief existence. Nobody I have spoken to seems to remember it at all. I expect it was one of those overnight wonders that blossom hopefully, like mushrooms overnight, only to be scorched out of existence in the fierce glare of reality. The shop itself didn't give the impression that the proprietor had overdone it on the investment. In fact, I should think that about five pounds would have covered the whole risk... They probably lost it in the end! Faggots, saveloys and peas pudding were about the full extent of their wares. It wasn't a very bright shop, seeing that it had probably just been taken over after a rag and bone man had been forced by unforeseen circumstances to quit it. Its bare wooden floor still bore the marks and stains that had proved to be unscrubable of various previous trades.

It had a hastily constructed scrubbed wooden counter by the shop door, under which were some flat blackened heating pans from which the delicacies were served. Scattered about the shop, some worn and battered pine tables and a few odd kitchen chairs for the customers to eat on the premises, but it was mainly 'takeaway'. Dishes and basins brought by the patrons to be paid for and eaten at home (there really is nothing new under the sun is there?). I never had faggots and peas pudding at home. Mum said they were made with 'bad meat'. I liked the smell of them though and I would have liked to taste them.

Apart from the shops, we were visited daily by hopeful street traders. On Sundays, the 'cockle man' would come round. Pushing a costermonger's barrow (it probably did duty during the week at Billingsgate fish market) loaded with shrimps, whelks and cockles, the shrimps tied up in string bags or heaped on white enamel trays, calling out his impossible to describe street call.

Every trader had his own personal yodel, whether those sounds bore any resemblance to the wares to be sold was more a matter for the imagination than it was for public information. The cockle man had his own brand of warble to advertise his presence and his regular stopping places. At the first sound of his street call (which sounded very much like a very sloshed newt's mating call) people would emerge from every direction, dishes, and basins at the ready. The first customer held out her dish, "Pint o' shrimps luv"? He would measure out the pink delicacy in a pint pewter pot serenading his purchaser with his mating call but like all wary Hermitage mums she wasn't going to be seduced by fine words alone and delivered her rejection. "Oi. Shake it darn a bit, or it ain't a pint". His measure had to be generous or at the least, fair, otherwise, there would be no point in his coming next week. He could try if he dared and shout his lungs out until his shrimps went rotten. A short measure would have 'done him'. At three or four pence a pint, shrimps were a luxury that people might afford for their Sunday tea but not on any other day of the week.

During the weekday evenings the muffin man might chance his arm and have a go. Presumably though, during the summer months when his wares were definitely out of season, he was robbed of the opportunity to perfect a reasonably recognisable call. It would never do if potential customers expecting one thing were completely deceived into thinking it was something else. Everybody's time would have been wasted for the muffin man to have to explain that the tray that he carried on his head did not contain cats' meat or fish, so he used a bell, sometimes with a practise call thrown in, but uttered with no great conviction that it would drum up that little extra bit of trade. A vigorous clanging of the bell and an almost inaudible, "Muffin" usually did the trick. Although, I think in all honesty, I ought to put one little matter of possible conflict right. Although he was called the 'muffin' man he really sold 'crumpits', but still, they were very nice toasted at the fire on a cold night oozing with a dab of the best.

At fairly regular intervals the 'rag and bone' man came on his rounds. He had a little cart pulled by a pony. He too used a bell, but he also had a call that everybody knew. It went something like this: "Heniholhion", ignoring the phonetics for the moment, it could roughly be translated as "Any old iron". He collected rags and bones too, and never known to refuse jam jars, lemonade, and beer bottles, for the value of their returns at a penny or two pence a time. Rags though, were usually worn through several generations until there was nothing left to collect apart from the holes. As for the bones, I don't suppose there were enough redundant bones in Wapping to make a teaspoon full of glue or a decent rub of soap. He also collected any item of trash that might fetch a penny or two. One could hear him coming from miles away. Strangely, his call from a distance sounded clearer than standing up close. "Heniholhion" became good plain Oxfordian English, coming over the smoke-soaked ether as clear as any BBC announcer. "Heniholion" and a clang on his bell. Off he would go again… long pauses to deal with an old shovel or a broken fender. He rarely gave money in exchange for scrap, but cups and saucers and all sorts of cheap white china, he could however be persuaded to part with a copper or two if something were offered that wasn't too old, too badly broken and which had a resale value as it stood.

I remember once 'Big Gran' had a big hopping pot, one of those oval black iron pots with a handle to hang at a fire. It had done good service for years, but age had caught up with it in the end and rust had finally eaten a small hole in its bottom. Gran had waited for the 'rag an' bone' man and now was her chance to get rid of it. "Tak' this down to the man Johnnie, an' ask him fer a tanner for it. Tell him I don't want any ol' china. He kin either give a tanner or we keep it us selves. If he won't, fetch it back 'ere". Useless as it was, Gran wasn't going to part with it for another useless piece of cheap china. It was going to be a cash deal or not at all. The 'old iron'man came into the square at the rear of Jackman House, "Heniholhion", a clang on his bell... "Henihol...", "Woa dere" to the pony... "Wa's dis den sonny"? He could see what it was I had got, but I thought that he might not know what it was, so I had better tell him. "It's a 'oppin pot an' me Gran wants a tanner for it". "Well nar" says he, "Yu tell yer Gran I 'as some nice cups an' sausus, wot I knows she wants". Gran, who had been watching proceedings from the balcony, called out, "Yew just bring it back 'ere Johnnie. Is 'e deaf, is 'e? We don't want any of his cups an' saucers... or his plates".

As the old iron man had not yet seen that there was a hole in the bottom, because I still kept a tight hold on it, and it had its lid on and Gran had also given it a shine with Zebo black-lead polish, and it looked in good condition... well on its outside, it did! Having visions of at least six or seven shillings on a resale and seeing that I was more disposed to do as Gran said than to stand there and argue the 'toss' with him and that I had started back to the stairs taking the pot with me, he suddenly changed his mind. "Righto son, 'ere's a tanner... put it on the cart son". Then he searched in his deep trouser pocket for the unwilling six penny piece... muttering "Taint worf it dough". It wasn't, but Gran hadn't said that it was, and if he was prepared to give her sixpence for it, as she said, "That was his look out wasn't it"? She also said later with a chuckle, "I didn't tell him it was a goodun, did I"? I'll bet a fiver that the old iron man looked very closely at old hopping pots ever after, especially in Wapping.

Apart from these itinerant hopefuls, Wapping was also served by the usual daily things: a travelling fruit and veg, bread and milk and a weekly coal man. He had to come on a weekly basis as pretty well everybody either couldn't afford big loads or had nowhere to store it, especially in the 'buildings'. The coal bin provided in No. 8 might have taken a hundred kilos if completely empty, or in those days weight measures: two hundredweight, fifty kilos being roughly equivalent to one hundredweight. The coal man had a horse and cart. There wasn't any need for big loads. At three shillings and sixpence (17½ pence) a hundredweight he didn't sell much. Most people bought a hundred from time to time and eked it out with coke. This could be purchased from the coal man, but it was a little cheaper to get it from the gas works in the High Street. It was mostly the kid's job to go and fetch it.

You took your own bags, an old pram, or a homemade go-kart to carry the bags home on. A bit of a nuisance if you lived in the 'buildings' on the top balcony and ten flights of stairs to reach it. There were no lifts. The coke was weighed out in a scuttle like scale pan in fourteen pound lots (a stone or sixish kilos). The coke man used a big shovel that could scoop practically a stone in one go. The required amount was asked for, "Two ston' mister". 'Woof', would go the shovel, and as quick as a flash the coke would disappear into the proffered bag, to the utter astonishment of the purchaser whose obligatory response had to be that he questioned whether the coke had been weighed at all since its tenure in the scale was no more than a split second, but then no Wapping purchaser, young or old, stood meekly by while a vendor gave them what he thought he would give them for their money. They always let them know, "We's not aving none o' that there. We's knows wot's right, so let's be 'aving yer".

The coke man knew from long experience how to play this game, he had heard it all before. "Oi mister tha' there pan dinant go darn or it ain't a ston'", but Mr Coke Man was an old hand at it and countered, "Don' yew be sa cheeky yer littal sod", to which the required answer had to be to complete the deal to everyone's satisfaction, "But I's tellin' of yer the pan dinant go darn an' I's s'posed ter ain't I"? There was never any need for the coke man to add a little more to be on the safe side, he was always generous anyway, but the kids were duty bound to try for it. If you hadn't got a bag it was straight into the old pram or go-kart, much more of a problem if you live the ten flights up, but then there was never a need for big loads to cart or perambulate up the stairs. Another stone tomorrow would do if there was the money for it that is!

The local dairy man had his rounds and some people preferred fresh milk, but in the main it was either tinned Nestlé sweetened condensed, or bottles of sterilised bought from the grocers in the Lane. The milkman would be happy to sell you his sterilised on the basis of cash now, having discovered that a regular delivery of the same did not always mean a regular delivery of the debt at the end of the week.

I remember too, a hand cart with milk churns (even this was becoming a rarity in the thirties). A pewter milk measure dipped into the churn and then into a jug you took to fetch it in. I didn't see this milkman very often. 'Big Gran' was convinced that they sold watered down milk... and probably right about that.

Very infrequently we were visited by the India Toffee man. His particular strange wares were carried in a box with a lid suspended from his waist with leather straps. He sold a chocolatey kind of confection that bore no resemblance to 'toffee', but who could dispute its description? It was declared to be 'Indian', and I supposed that was good enough reason to be different. I think it was made with desiccated coconut, it looked like tobacco. It might have been better smoked! He didn't come very often. The most likely explanation is that Wapping did have a rough reputation, quite apart from being a difficult place transport-wise to get to. I personally thought it was because of his frequent visits to India for fresh supplies!

The trader that I liked the best though was yet another enterprising rag and bone man. He didn't collect much in the way of rags or bones, his method of bringing in the pennies was largely dependent on a gaily painted roundabout roughly the size of a couple of beer barrels on the back of his cart. The fee was a half penny for a few dizzy turns to view the local scenery composed of solid walls about ten feet away in any direction. If you hadn't got a half penny a clean jam jar would do.

Many a half-filled jam jar was offered in payment. He used a bugle to summon his trade, but the locals were never treated to a spine tingling cadence of stirring military taps. By the look of the bugle, it had been battered and bent on the Somme before being pensioned off to do the duty calls of the rag and bone man. A few shrill blasts were all his repertoire could muster. The bugle and he had never been on the Somme to learn a respectable tap or two. At the first blast of the said bugle, kids would come running, jam jars at the ready, some evidently filched from mum's cupboard whilst she wasn't looking. He wouldn't accept the half-filled one, with the remark, "That un ain't no good. I ain't 'aving ev'ry bleedin' worsp a follerin us darn de strit. I wants th' clean uns".

The honest reason for the rejection was more to do with the recollections of irate ladies chasing him up the street, and sometimes down again, for the return of tonight's tea, than it was for any fear of wasps. After all, these interesting insects had not been seen in Wapping for at least a millennium. Flies? Yes. Fleas? Possibly. Bed bugs? Well, no doubt. Wasps, bees, and butterflies... no chance. They wouldn't have survived an hour, let alone follow the rag and bone man. The jam jars did get recycled though, so I suppose he was doing his bit for the environment.

Other things like clothing, boots and shoes, bedlinens, etc, had to be got out of town as it were. One could get these things, however, from Nora Leech. There wasn't much in the way of personal and household things that she could not get for you - blankets, shirts, coats and gloves, trousers, suits, and skirts. Boots and shoes were a constant worry for parents, but Nora would let you have them for as little as sixpence a week, sometimes less if she knew you well. She always got her money in the end, because to let her down meant that there would be no more credit.

Nora Leech was a tally lady, friendly enough so long as her clients kept to their side of the bargain. Apart from Nora and ready cash considerations, the out of town source might be Whitechapel Road, or for us it was generally Watney Street daily market in Shadwell. To reach it one could have a penny's worth on the underground from Wapping to Shadwell, one station down the line, or it was Shank's pony. For most people it was Shank's pony. It was a twenty minute walk for normal legs, but for me without the towing hand of Lily, about four times as long.

Watney Street was then a quarter of a mile-long street out of Cable Street to the Commercial Road, almost entirely composed of shops. It was also a daily market, stalls along both sides of the street. Every kind of goods on sale from groceries to… well, you name it. The stalls frequently duplicated the goods on sale in the shops. So, what was not got inside because customers would not accept the invitation to 'step in', they got outside instead.

Whenever it was announced that we were 'going up Watney' I was overjoyed. Not that the excitement was prompted by any illusions of becoming the possessor of a much desired object. Even though I might come home with a new pair of boots, which was all right as far as boots can be the objects of juvenile desire, there was so much else that I would rather they had bought me instead. I liked the dark evening trips the best. The stalls lit by flaring and spluttering incandescent lamps, rows of hissing beacons of yellowing light along the street that dimmed and flared in tune with the breeze. The bright light shed by them made everything displayed look ten times more attractive. The cabbages greener, the apples rosier, the best of them banked in slopes at the fronts of the coster's stall. Items hung for display twisting and turning in the breeze… and the sounds, a constant babble of the crowded street. Groups just gossiping. Shouting stall holders calling out their wares. "Luvly apples luv" … "Ripe an' sweet" … "'Ere yer are luv, two punds for a tanner" … "Sweet oringis" … "If yer kin find sweeter you's lucky".

A few selected oranges invitingly cut in half to show how ripe and juicy they were. "Fresh an' sweet gals, yer can't find fresher". A pause for breath and into his 'patter' again. "Get yer taters 'ere gals, five punds fer five an' arf". That was a half penny cheaper than his nearest rival selling the same apples and oranges. Everything was to be got in Watney Street. Jewish tailors by the dozen, every one of them proud to claim, "Bespoke and quality assured", the named tailor standing by his shop door making irresistible offers to an incredulous public as they passed by. "Got a nice coat 'ere madam, ordered an' not called for" … "Going cheap to clear" … "Von't her step dis way?" … "Try it, there's a luv…" … "Very cheap" … "Luverly quality". He probably had a stock of readymade to suit every size under the sun… Cheap it was… cheap and nasty!

Furniture stores. Mats and lino, linen drapers, windows a riot of haberdashery. Hats at one and nine pence, stockings at sixpence.

Their competitors up the street, windows filled with the same items with the same hats at one and eight pence, stockings five pence, three farthings. Farthings meant a lot in the thirties. The draper might even give a packet of pins with your purchase, just for the sake of his 'good will'.

Fishmongers. One of them I noted with interest was also an Insole. Most definitely related. Maybe one or two generations back, but how and by what mystery of familiar connection, nobody could tell me! Butchers and bakers.

Sainsbury's had a small but typical store too. Marble slabbed counters, bulk cubes of fresh butter, Wiltshire Special and Devon cream or some such varieties. Groceries, tinned fruits, and vegetables. Eggs and bacon sliced on a hand operated slicing machine, glistening in red enamel and gleaming chrome... swish, swish, back and forth. The bacon and butter weighed out on tall brass scales... eggs sold at the front stall, thirteen for a shilling (a baker's dozen - why thirteen I have no idea).

Tucked away in a side street, the second-hand stall, screened off from the main street and dimly lit. It was only shadowy people who bought at the second-hand stalls, nobody that anyone would ever know. If folks did by mere chance meet there, it was an apologetic greeting: "Jest thought I'd 'ave a look" ... "Yer might find something fer patching".

Nobody would ever admit to buying anything to wear. There must have been a lot of patching in the East End of London. There were always a lot of shadows around the second-hand stalls.

Watney Street was always crowded. A few vehicles moved up and down the street, but only those who had business there, their drivers honking and shouting "Yer backs there, galls", inching forward in fits and starts. The street was virtually pedestrianised in a sort of unofficial way. It was possible to wander back and forth to your heart's content. That is if an equally wandering crowd permitted it. I was never permitted to dally though. There was always the more important item to be got elsewhere except where I wanted to be. Constantly I was told, "You can come back later an' 'ave a look" but the promises were never kept, always forgotten. I forgot too and the original fascination dimmed by some new wonder.

If the shopping trip was long and loaded, two other Watney Street treats were in store: one, the possibility of a ride home on the 'rattler' and two, some pie and mash. These treats always came together. If the shopping was light then we usually walked, heavy and loaded... my cup of delights was full and brimming over... It was all I needed to hear. "I think we'll 'ave some pie an' mash an' ride 'ome".

The Watney Street pie and mash shop was situated under the archway that carried the Fenchurch Street Southend line across the Street. The shop was brightly lit and warmly welcoming, a delicious smell of baking meat pies wafting into the street. Filled with marble-topped tables, the seating either low backed benches or some bentwood chairs. Sawdust scattered onto a scrubbed wooden floor. On the tables stood pint sized bottles of vinegar, in which floated masses of peppers and chillies. At a marble-topped counter were steaming heated brightly polished copper pans and piles of gleaming white soup plates and basin-like bowls. In one pan the mashed potatoes. In another a thin green parsley sauce. It wasn't called parsley sauce, but 'liquor'. A strange mystery perplexed me for years until ultimately, I suddenly realised the meanings.

I often heard the servers call out in some strange language, "Liquorloluv" and "Piesloluv". I wasn't much into foreign languages, I knew something about 'back slang' but didn't want to ask, because I didn't want to reveal my ignorance. Back slang was often used in markets or in situations where 'private' conversations were conducted in crowded places and the speakers preferred not to be understood. Certain people used back slang that was only known amongst themselves. Market traders for instance, and racetrack bookies especially.

Those strange words taxed my muddled brain for ages then suddenly it 'clicked', and I felt rather stupid for not understanding it from the beginning. It dawned on me that the servers were merely calling out for replenishment of the liquor and the pies!

The pies. Black baking trays on a worktop behind the counter, filled with individual meat pies in little earthenware dishes, covered with a crispy flaky pastry, sizzling from first to last on the trays smoking straight from the oven. Fast and constant baking was essential. Trade was always brisk. It was 'self-service', ordering your meal at the counter and paying for it: "Pie an' mash please". The pie whisked out of its little dish onto one of the soup plates. A wooden spoon plunged into the mashed potato and a generous helping scraped onto the side of the plate, next a ladle full of the liquor poured over.

At the table lashings of vinegar from the pint sized bottles, spoon and fork raised (knives and forks were not pie and mash etiquette) and then sheer heaven. Simple and perhaps strange as the meal may sound to the uninitiated, one might travel the world over sampling strange and wonderful cuisines and never come across anything so individually flavoured. Genuine London pie and mash will never be imitated and certainly never matched. The meal cost about three to four pence (two pence in today's currency) and extremely good value too.

If, on the other hand, you were really 'flush' you could go in for stewed or jellied eels. Pie and mash shops always sold stewed or jellied eels, or it wasn't a pie and mash shop. With eels you got a thick chunk of bread as well as the potato. Stewed eels that is, jellied were always eaten cold, but you still got a chunk of bread with it. I worked it out that they got the bread because the proprietors recognised that the 'toffs' had a fuller pocket. A very necessary qualification if you went in for eels... and as I have already said, a tanner was a lot of money.

The ride home on the 'rattler' didn't take very long. Just one station down the line from Shadwell to Wapping. Our fares paid, a penny each for 'Big Gran' and Aunt Rose, Lily a half penny and I went for nothing. Tickets to be clipped by the porter, down a couple of flights of wooden stairs that smelled strongly of decay and carbolic, which the station porters sprayed around constantly out of garden type watering cans, and then onto the platforms.

Shadwell underground station was a dimly lit affair. The few scanty lights didn't quite reach into the girdered and arched roof. There was a constant drip, drip of water droplets forming little puddles everywhere. The station was distinctly 'run down' and slowly decaying. This didn't bother me too much; all I was interested in was the arrival of the rattler.

The trains had been deservedly given this name, since they had all done service on other more lucrative lines for at least a hundred years and were never relegated to the old East London line until they were a little too serviceable to scrap, and a little too old and dilapidated for anywhere else, but good enough to get us from Shadwell to Wapping. They were so noisy that you could hear them coming ten minutes before they arrived. But arrive they did. Stopping at the platform with a screech of brakes and groaning coachwork, air gushing from the braking system like some leviathan 'fart', air pumps thumping to make up the loss of air pressure.

One selected a door that was already open, or had been left open by an alighting passenger, since choosing one that was shut and if you insisted on trying desperately to open it and the guard was unaware of the problem (the doors frequently stuck tight closed) could result in having to make a last second dash to find an unopposed entry, or just be left standing on the platform watching the train 'rattle' off on its way. Having successfully boarded the train it was always a wise policy to leave the door open otherwise the door problem could well prevent one alighting on arrival at one's destination, which in turn did nothing to reduce the noise as the train lumbered through the tunnels.

Wapping station is deeper underground than Shadwell, as it is situated on the river with its front at the Thames Tunnel entrance. The Thames Tunnel was built by Brunel in the early years of 1800, but not completed and finally opened in 1827. Being the first tunnel ever to be driven underwater, Brunel encountered mounting problems, including several floodings, loss of lives and not least the continuous lack of funding. In its construction Brunel devised a method of preventing collapse. A shield worked at the tunnel face being dug was moved forward foot by foot whilst the tunnel brick lining was put in place behind it. A method used extensively to construct the tube tunnels for the whole of the London underground system, and it remains the method of tunnel construction the world over. Brunel was quite an innovator but not until the Thames Tunnel got the undeserved name 'The Great Bore'. It was a long time in the building and in fact, abandoned for a year or two before it was finally completed.

I suppose that in its original design it had been conceived as a general traffic crossing to complement the growing docking activity, but in the end it finished up as merely a foot passenger tunnel and it was never a great success. For one thing there were never many Wapping folk who had the least desire to cross over the water, and nobody over the water wanted to come to Wapping anyway. For another, there was the major consideration of the tolls charged. Apparently, having paid to go one way did not entitle you to come back again. There was always the suggestion that it should ultimately be extended for vehicular traffic, but nothing came of it. For a long time, it was virtually abandoned. Its ultimate fate was to be included into the growing network of the underground system of the East London railway.

It wasn't an unusual occurrence in the thirties (in fact well into the forties) for steam hauled goods trains to come through. Black sulphurous smoke filled the tunnels and the stations for hours afterwards. A thick acrid fog of fumes slowly leaked its way out of the ventilation shafts. At one time it was all steam hauled. The high brick arched roof of the station still bore the smoke and soot stains of those times (and probably still does). The platforms were no more than four feet wide (still are!) and permanently wet. The station was dark, if not darker than Shadwell. The Thames water cascaded down everywhere and was only prevented from soaking the passengers by a corrugated lining over the platforms.

To reach the street one could climb the stairs circling the shaft. These 'were' the original Brunel stairs to serve the tunnel. There are two separate stairways, originally one for the up direction and the other presumably for the down, making their separate ways by a series of circling flights to match-boarded stall-like landings, each with a sit-up-and-beg type bench for the weary ascending or descending passengers to rest at.

I am sorry to say that although they seemed to be in a fairly good state of preservation, in a mad rush for modernisation some mindless bureaucrat (or a collection of similar mindless) decided to destroy them and replace them with the excuse that the cost of refurbishment was prohibitive. However, they missed the flights directly down to the platforms and they still survive.

We could climb the old stairs, or we could take the lift. It had nothing to do with Brunel, it had been installed long after he could have envisaged such a thing, but on the other hand, one should never be surprised at anything he may have conceived. I'm sure he would have approved of it from an engineering point of view. It ought to have impressed a youngster like me too, but I had a quarrel with a lift in which I had come off the worst. I was always inclined to give lifts as wide a berth as possible. I preferred the stairs.

Chapter 13

Summer Days an' a Pub Crawl

In the gaps between hopping times and parties, it was realised that something had to be done to fill in the spare time.

During the hot summer months especially, no one felt too much like exerting themselves, so the organisational abilities of the entertainments experts were suspended for the time being, and a lackadaisical attitude descended over the whole business. Parties were definitely 'out' for the duration of the long summer evenings. The pubs however were the best resorts, affording cool refreshments when they were most needed.

Big Gran and Grandad might, for a change of scenery, decide on the spur of the moment on a 'walk-about' around the island parish to meet old friends not seen since yesterday, and as an annual treat sample the rare delights of further afield establishments providing the essential cool refreshments. Spurning their usual that they normally 'used', they would toddle off. Grandad with his usual disregard for the season, dressed as he was always dressed... cloth flat cap, white silk scarf and jacket and with the obvious token of courtesy due to visitation to friends at any season... the obligatory waistcoat, clean collar, and a tie. 'Big Gran' with a clean flowery wrap-over overall, sedately swaying from side to side or beam to beam like a vessel under sail in a gentle swell, setting course in the direction of the 'Ramsgit'. This was of course the famous old pub situated on the even more famous Wapping Old Stairs - The Town of Ramsgate.

The pub hadn't always been known by this name, it had originally been called The Red Cow or The Black Bull or something like it, a rural sort of name that might have been more appropriate in the far off marshland farming days before the dock building. Whether the islanders realised this subtle point or not there is no way of knowing, all that can be said with anything like certainty is that according to the time-honoured Wapping tendency to rename anything and everybody with a more suitable appellation that fitted in with local sensitivities, the pub came by degrees to be renamed... The Town of Ramsgate.

It was here at the stairs that many of the Ramsgate fishermen came to sell their fish. Grandad said that his father, my Great Grandad (who it transpires had himself been in his youth a fisherman or closely involved with the Essex fleet) had bought fish from his brethren fishermen at the stairs. However, some local wit in the distant past, on seeing the crowd of itinerant Kentish salts, remarked, "Th' 'ole of der tarn o' Ramsgit as come an' all", and since the misnamed pub on the stairs hadn't really appealed to the local taste in these matters, the more obvious name for the pub stuck - The Town of Ramsgate. Anyway, it must have made the visitors feel more at home and welcome.

It was same Wapping Old Stairs that Gustav Doré had sketched so vividly, and where it is also recorded that it was the practice of enterprising magistrates of the not so distant past, in order to save the expense of transportation (never mind to Botany Bay, but also to the much shorter and ultimately final destination of Tyburn!) caused to be erected a gallows on the shoreway and ordered incorrigible local villains to be, "Hanged in chains till they be dead". Hanging the said villains in chains was not apparently the actual cause of death or, at any rate, just in case it wasn't, they were left hanging in chains and let the tide do the rest.

Tradition has it that the minimum period the luckless victims had to remain on these unique gallows was for three full tides. Not only were they to look quite dead, but thoroughly beyond redemption and presumably beyond resurrection. It is also recorded that the spirit of the law which demanded 'three full tides' was always carried out to the letter. However, it was not unknown (so it is said) for corpses to remain on the gallows until they simply rotted away, since according to the same just laws, it was the responsibility of relatives or friends to remove the body for burial. Not infrequently, there was not a soul who cared enough to perform this last duty, so the mortal remains of the lonely and the unwanted rotted away tide after tide. This barbarous form of hanging was used (if not actually instituted) by the infamous 'Hanging Judge Jeffreys'. Eventually, he got his comeuppance at the hands of those who had suffered under his murderous tyranny. After the abdication of James II, he was captured at Wapping Old Stairs, dressed as an ordinary seaman, trying to escape to France. He was taken to the Tower where it is said he died (probably assisted by those anxious to cover their own tracks and misdeeds). It would have been a nice touch of ultimate justice if he had been 'hanged in chains' on Wapping Old Stairs shoreway, but then in a way I suppose he was, by his own rash decision to come ashore for a last drink... presumably at the Stairs pub or whatever its name was then.

There was another site in Wapping for such macabre hangings, at 'Execution Dock', but it was reserved for the punishment of sea pirates, shipboard mutineers and minor misdemeanours committed at sea. Execution Dock was a merchant seaman's province and beyond the interference of the civil authorities. Ship owners and merchant companies had their own Parliamentary approved law on the high seas and carried out the punishments at the home port as a salutary example to any who might be tempted to break them. Lashings, scourging's, and a hanging at the yardarm at sea were not publically seen. A ship berthed at a riverside jetty in its home port had plenty of witnesses.

For civic matters and Wapping Old Stairs, another considerate punishment for those who wisely decided to commit their crimes at a season of low tides, sentenced to umpteen years at that famous Australian holiday resort, Botany Bay. A reward incidentally, that did nothing for local entertainment and amusement.

The 'gramps' having satisfied themselves that all was well at the 'Ramsgit' and feeling sufficiently 'refreshed' by a sip or two with old friends, decided to continue their periodic 'pub crawl', accordingly 'set sail' in a fair wind to the next port of call - 'The Prospic'.

Further translation reveals that they were heading for the famous old riverside hostelry known as 'Prospect of Whitby'. A place of refreshment and entertainment established in 1509.

Many famous individuals, apart from Big Gran and Grandad have swilled its popular brews over the centuries, including Samuel Pepys and Charles Dickens, who when he was not rescuing his dad from the broker's man or away on far flung Pickwickian travel, liked to order his favourite tipple of 'porter' at the 'Prospic' and gaze contentedly at the chaotic river scene from a veranda on the waterfront (since demolished), confronted before his very eyes by the evocative scenes that found their way into his eternal novels. Characters like Mrs Gamp, Quilp, The Chuzzlewits and Sam Weller to name but a few. I believe he drew them for eternity out of London's docklands and East London, I believe much of his inspiration grew out of the fertile earth of Wapping itself.

Interestingly, another aspect of the pub was that besides the rich and the famous, the place was well thought of by the poor and the unknown. It had been the natural haunt of river pirates, thieves, smugglers, and the just idle ne'er-do-wells lost for an hour or two to entertain themselves. Seamen ashore with money to spend and 'interesting' company ready by any means to relieve them of it. These thirsty souls were too often tempted to barter curios they had brought from overseas for just one more pull at a quart pot before they sailed away. An enterprising landlord of yore was apparently willing on the best possible terms, to himself to take the dubious articles as a little bit of security on a trifling loan, like a quart of porter.

As frequently happened to sea faring folk of the day, things like 'missing with all hands' or simply just getting too friendly with the natives of those faraway places often interfered with the otherwise good intention to come home to redeem the debt. The result was that the pledge could not be kept, and the landlord kept the pledged. In time this became something of a problem for the said landlord, whose living quarters were becoming like a chandler's shop. He evidently hit upon the brilliant idea that his clients might just be forgetful rather than dead and if he put them on display it could just jog the befuddled memories and jolly up a few of the outstanding pence.

In the thirties I think that his heirs were still waiting for most of them (if not all of them?!). It's just a wild suggestion I suppose... Charles Dickens may well have got his inspiration for the 'Old Curiosity Shop' from the 'Prospic'? Anyway, Sam Weller was every bit a Wapping character if ever there was one!

Once again, the pub had been called The Red Cow or Black Bull or some other rural appellation. However, in the ancient tradition of Wapping sensitivities, it was close to the permanent berth of a vessel called the 'Prospect of Whitby'. In the perversity of the local tendency to rename anything and everyone rather than as nature had intended, changed the name of the pub to suit seafaring tastes. I suppose the logics are that seamen are better acquainted with vessels than with landlubber matters like bricks and mortar, pubs, and houses. The same thing had happened to the 'Ramsgit' and incidentally, for a good many other Wapping pubs as well. By the thirties though, the 'Prospic' had fallen out of favour with the majority of the locals, even then it had become something of a tourist attraction. The pub, along with Wapping as a whole, had a 'reputation', the locals regarded it with some suspicion, the generally unwelcome 'outsiders' gradually forced the locals out. It was all right for a 'walk out' on a warm summer evening though.

On a recent reminiscent visit, I was somewhat disappointed to discover the 'old' character of the pub had been dramatically changed - probably with the object of 'improvements' in mind. The old veranda had been demolished; I expect that it simply rotted away. Not only had its outward appearance 'gone modern' but the interior had been destroyed and a pseudo 'old' had replaced it... What a pity. Too late... too final.

Since the evening was still light and long, there was no rush for the gramps to get home, still plenty of time for a wander around to visit a few more pubs. 'The China Ship' in Hermitage, named after a record breaking voyage by a tea clipper of the 'Cutty Sark' vintage and practically next door the 'Scott's Arms' - how it got and kept this name is a mystery.

Wherever the gramps went it was never very far to the next. If only to meet old friends and renew promises to come again soon.

Having found that there was a little time to spare for a very quick one on the way homeward (discovering too that the weather had somewhat worsened as there were now deepening swells and slanting decks), a visit to the ancient Hermitage 'Turk's Head' was advisable. Yet another of the ancient riverside pubs of the 'Prospic' period of establishment, squeezed between the encroaching wharves at a dark narrow tunnel-like passage leading to stairs to the shoreways. Its claim to fame was that it served as the last stopping place for the condemned to be hanged at Wapping Old Stairs, who were given a last drink before being taken to the gallows. The pub no longer exists, having been closed as a pub late 30s, to become a dining rooms and finally destroyed in the 1940s Blitz. What a pity it did not survive for just a few more years. Maybe, just maybe, it might have still been amongst the dwindling features of the old and ancient Wapping.

As they had spent their evening stroll so far from home, popping in for so many quick ones, they thought that they had better pop into their usual retreat 'The Cuckoo' in the Lane... merely for social reasons! Just in case the regulars had noticed that they were missing and had taken up a collection, "Fer jest a few flars".

If Big Gran was too busy for a walk out with Grandad his favourite recreation on Sunday afternoons after dinner, was a walk down to Tunnel pier. Every Wappingite knew it as Wapping pier... so that was that.

The pier is situated on King Henry's Stairs out of the High Street, a girdered walkway led from the stair street landing to a floating pier landing stage. Its original purpose was a 'stop-off' and landing place for river passengers. At one time it was anticipated as a means of getting into and out of Wapping, at those times it was either river borne transport or Shank's pony, there was no other alternative.

It didn't take very long for the river traffic operators to discover that the service was not an economic success. Hardly a soul wanted to come to Wapping, and nobody seemed to want to leave it. However, it started life as a public landing place and that's how it remained whether anyone landed, embarked or not.

On summer evenings and Sunday afternoons it was the quietest place in Wapping. Grandad made full use of it. He would stand for hours on end, elbows planted firmly on the handrail, gazing downstream. I never saw him look the other way toward the city, always downriver toward the open sea. Lily and I, on one of our outings saw him once. Standing there. The evening light was fading, the setting sun threw a fiery stream of flashing sparklets on the river, borne by the ebbing tide toward the sea. I wanted to go to him, but Lily knew that this was Grandad's private time and wanted to stop me. She relented and let me go on to the pier, warning me, "Just for a minute then". Grandad knew that we were there and said nothing. I was going to be full of chatter, but the silence of the moment reached me. I suddenly saw what Grandad was seeing. The sun setting in the west, its long shadows softening the harshness of the dirty riverbanks. The tall cranes on the jetties now at rest, stood motionless. Black silhouettes, their latticed masts reared against a darkening sky.

A departing vessel going downstream on the falling tide, almost in darkness but carrying with it little points of brightness, lights twinkling at portholes and swaying mast head. A shouted command and a bell's clang came to us softened across the water. The ship churned onward, turned toward the southern banks, and slipped silently into Limehouse Reach and was gone.

The ever restless pigeons flew up, fluttering at their roosts on the lumbering wharves. Gulls called to each other from out of a darkening sky. The sound of the lighters bumping against each other, moved by the swift flowing ebb tide racing toward the sea, the splash of the racing wavelets against their gaunt black steel hulls.

The lowering shadows of the high riverside wharves stood stark against the shimmering ribbon of a silvered river; its filth hidden beneath the glancing evening light. The south bank and distant shore of Bermondsey, darkening and mysteriously pierced here and there with flickering lights. Ships at their berths slumbered at the jetties. Bored seamen on watch at the ships' rails wondering at the unaccustomed stillness of the ship and the unnatural quietness of the docks.

We stood for long minutes not daring to speak. I was enthralled, caught in the magic transformation of a scene I knew so well. Turning from dull, dirty, noisy, and ever-busy into a scene of inspiring beauty. I shall never forget it.

Grandad stirred. From around the bend out of Limehouse Reach downstream a ship lighted all over. A bright mass caught in the dimming afterglow of the setting sun. He spoke for the first time,

"'Ere comes th' Golden Eagle, Johnnie. Back from Ramsgate". It came abreast of us, side paddles thud, thud, thudding the greying muddy water, throwing up a sparkling white path of foam at its wake, caught for fleeting moments in the dying light. As it passed us it was all light and noise. Its passengers almost at the end of a day 'darn der water' returning from Ramsgate, Southend, or Gravesend, were soon to arrive at the Tower Pier.

Journey's end for the ship, but, for the happy revellers a tired and merry trip to their homes. As if reluctant to end it all 'too soon', their last boisterous efforts to enjoy themselves seemed to increase the nearer they got to the journey's end. Last pints of stout were drunk, the last bawdy songs were sung. The noise of it all echoed around the darkening river banks, then silence once more. My excited observation, "Ant it big Grandad" merely drew out his usual grunted "Yus" as he settled back into his private dreams. What marvellous dreams they must have been. All around us a constant reminder of all that was worst and suddenly, on a warm summer Sunday evening, to come upon a scene of the river at its most beautiful best.

Grandad's gaze was always downstream toward the widening riverbanks and the sea. What instinctive siren calls did he hear?

It is fairly certain that the advent of the Insole family tree in Wapping began with the arrival of seamen who are recorded as being connected to the Essex fishing fleet based at Barking, which seems to have moved up the East coast to ports like Grimsby and Yarmouth. It may be fanciful to suggest that some of the fishing fraternity decided to abandon seafaring, perhaps persuaded by the siren songs of the land-based lonely lasses. Or nothing simpler than the alternative opportunities for work offered by the developing London Dock developments. Suffice it to say at this particular moment, that the Insole family are recorded as originating from Worcester as a single sourced family name and had dispersed, presumably some of them down the River Severn to become blue-water fishermen, arriving ultimately all around the UK coast. It is said, but with absolutely no genetic evidence to support it, that once sea salt is in the blood the lure of the sea never leaves.

What instinctive calls did Grandad hear? Did he, on Tunnel pier, discover that the call of the sea was closer to him than anyone would ever know?

We left him there in the darkness to his dreams. Bright trails of sparks from his glowing fag end, a faint smell of the distant sea on the cooling evening breeze. How long he stood there after we had left I don't know. Sometimes I feel that he stands there still. Whether anyone else will ever see him cannot matter. Time will never erase from my memory the few minutes spent with Lily and Grandad on Tunnel pier.

Chapter 14

The Not So Wonderful World of Wapping Men

Now and again, for reasons that are no longer clear to me, I was got up very early in the mornings. On these not too rare occasions, I found myself being taken over Tower Bridge to Bermondsey and Little Gran, presumably because Mum was going to work?

When this happened, it was usually just light enough for me to know that the night was over, and just dark enough for me to be unsure. The strangeness of the unaccustomed hour only clearly defined for one very good reason. I had just as often experienced the late homecoming when Wapping streets were always quiet. There were never very many people about and the wharves shut tight and in darkness. The deeply recessed gateways looking like endless dark tunnels, the gates themselves hidden in blackness. Lightless windows stood out, the only lights that I saw were the dim streetlights dropping little pools of yellow light around themselves, like stepping stones in the darkness, laced along the cobblestoned streets, the cobbles themselves frozen like rippling wavelets of sparkling granite water.

Mornings were very different, now there were hundreds of people about. Mrs Thompson who lived in Hermitage, already doing good business at her all night 'coffee stall' by the Irongate Wharf and the St Katherine's Way Tower entrance. The Tower Gate not yet open to the public but revealing early stirrings in the Beefeaters' guard room behind it, as its light sneaked under the closed gate. The wharves were lit, work of the day already started and from their open gates the light flowed into the street.

Everything was on the move. Lorries and carts were beginning to arrive for the early loads. Drivers stood bunched around the coffee stall supplied with huge wedges of bread and dripping, sizzling hot sausage or bacon sandwiches. Huge mugs of steaming tea. Cranes and hoists, and open loopholes ready to receive or discharge yet another cargo. Carts and horses and men moving in that slow morning listlessness before the chaos of the day, so... I knew this could only be morning!

We were passing a dock gate. A crowd of men were assembled there. Fifty or sixty, maybe even a hundred? All of them silently gathered listening to a man shouting at the gate entrance. It was not an unusual occurrence. This was a regular daily event, not only at St Katherine's Dock gate, but at every gate in the port.

Dad had gone to work. I knew that because I had been got up early enough to see him go. I knew too that he would not come home again until I had been long in bed. He wasn't at all like most of my friends' dads. They mostly worked in the docks, going to work every day too but it was by no means certain that they wouldn't be home again soon afterwards to have to tell their wives, "No luck today gell... dinant get took on". Sometimes they didn't even bother to go home until later. Sometimes regretfully, not until the little money they had left, had been spent on a pint or two with their equally luckless mates. It was easier to forget their troubles than to have to listen to a worried wife asking how she was going to feed the kids or pay the rent man tomorrow or maybe even today. No matter, "Sumfink'll turn up termorrer". All too often it was a matter of hope rather than confidence that something would "turn up".

There were regular full time jobs available in the docks, and together with the various industrial and service activities associated with the dock operation. I do not at this moment know the answer, but it would be a fair estimate on my part that this factor might have employed about twenty five to thirty percent of the available Wapping workforce. There were also regular jobs 'Outside Wapping'. Dad worked for an engineering firm in Dagenham. His brothers 'Bill and Bob' both worked full time in Wapping. The Insole's family on the whole were locally recognised as well provided for, in fact relatively "well orf".

On those mornings of my early visits to Bermondsey and Little Gran I had seen them. The fifty to sixty or maybe even a hundred gathered at the dock gate. Every one of them hoping to be "took on". The shouting man I had seen was a dock Superintendent Officer. He stood behind a chain stretched across the gateway. He wanted his quota of men for the day's work on offer. He knew how many he wanted. Not one more or one less. Glancing at his papers he picked his men, "Rito lads.. .two gangs… no three berth", pointing to his chosen men. "Charlie… Harry".

Charlie and Harry were gang leaders or top men. They had their regular gang members, consisting of usually ten men, eight 'strong uns' and a couple of 'old uns' to grease the barrows and fetch and carry and help the other lads along. It was the only way that the 'old fellers' and the becoming infirm would have got 'took on'. The Superintendent would never have chosen them.

Charlie and Harry were the gang's 'top men', their titles meaning exactly what his work role was. He was literally the man at the top of the hold directing the loading or discharging of the vessel. He knew exactly how to discharge a cargo without upsetting the trim of the ship, and how to load it without endangering its stability at sea. He knew by the shape of the vessel how much it could safely carry and where to stow it.

At rock bottom, whether the dock masters and superintendents knew it, or for that matter cared, the 'top men' were really the real masters in the dock. The one and only thing he could not control was whether there were going to be any vessels in the dock to load or unload. Even so, it was they who chose the men who would be 'took on'. It was either the whole gang in or not at all. In the end it was also a case of whether a cargo got discharged at all, the 'top man' negotiating with the 'super' the price for an awkward or a dirty load, like graphite for instance. He would also receive the payment on behalf of the gang on completion of the job, paying off the members their dues, usually in their chosen 'boozer' over a pint of bitter to the chagrin of their wives waiting at home for some overdue housekeeping, and to the delight of the pub's landlord who would even put a little of their hard earned cash aside in the pub's savings club 'for a rainy day'. There were not too many fair to bright days in Wapping.

These clubs were run very efficiently. Not ostensibly for the direct benefit of the landlords and the brewers. They were used as a kind of bank where a little saved from time to time could always be drawn on when times were really hard.

Every year a secretary and a treasurer would be elected, whose jobs were to maintain an orderly banking system. At the end of the year if they had carried out their duties well there was usually a little interest to add to their savings. If, on the other hand, the saver member had the misfortune to have to draw on his savings, the drawer was faced with the prospect of paying a little interest for the privilege of borrowing his own money if he never had enough of his own in credit. Never mind, he usually got his loan to tide him over. Wapping men had to look after themselves, nobody else was likely to.

The selection at the gate went on. There was always a great surplus of labour available with sometimes as many as fifty percent of those at any gate in the port. 'Out of luck and out of work' and 'on th' stones', literally on the stones of the quayside and not 'took on'.

A top man could argue his and his gang's cause as hard as he could to make the best bargain he could. The awful fact of life in the docks was that ninety five percent of the work on offer was casual, when there was work... maybe? If not, it was back on 'the stones'. Not only this but ultimately, it relied on 'selection' at the gate at the 'super's' discretion and if one was not liked, or rather not wanted or awkward... A slow gang didn't get chosen again. It was also vital for the dock's survival at all. A ship stood at a berth too long was a financial loss to its owners. If there wasn't a quick enough turnaround it didn't come into the dock again next voyage. The 'selection' went on, "Tom... Arthur... George...", until the supers' lists were filled.

A hundred men had stood at the gate. If there were plenty of ships and work most of them would 'cross the chain'. If not, then fifty of them went home. Tried another gate or "Eff it... we're orf ter der boozer... sumfink might turn up termorrer". For the lucky ones there might be work for two, three or four days. The minimum could be as little as four hours. Then for the next four five or six days, nothing. If there was a little credit in the club... if not "Sumfink'll turn up termorrer".

In the mornings in my cot, I often heard the St Katherine's Dock bell ring. It would be rung at twenty minutes to eight and again at ten minutes to. This was the 'call out' bell, if and when ships were in, and men were required, it would ring. No ships in and it stayed silent. It didn't matter if it were two men wanted or two hundred, the bell would ring, and crowds would make their way to the gates and face the selection in front of the 'chain'. Only ten men wanted   , then the rest could go home, or as far as the 'gaffer' was concerned, "Go ter 'ell". The only saving grace for the call out was it did tell them when there was work and when there wasn't. Maybe try another gate? Casual men could be summoned at any time of the day between eight AM and eight PM. It wasn't unusual for work to be started late in the evening and go on all night. At St Katherine's the bell was the key if it rang. No matter what time of day. Get in front of the chain as quickly as possible. No opportunity must ever be lost to work.

At one time (not too many years before the thirties) when men gathered at the gates 'ticketed' men crossed over the chain without selection. The 'ticket' was a brass disc with the dock company's title and a number, it didn't mean that its possessor was permanently employed. He was still a casual worker along with all the rest. But it did mean they were the earlier counterparts of the 'top men' and always got first choice for any work available.

Beyond this privilege the number of men required to make up the gangs were matched with an equal number of brass discs. These were then thrown into the crowd at the gate. It must have been nothing short of a sheer riot. Every fist and foot lashing out. Those who got to a ticket and managed to hold onto it 'crossed the chain', those who didn't went home to beat their frustrations out on the wife and kids, or rather than that, go to the nearest 'boozer' to drown their sorrows and forget the bruises.

By all accounts and living memories it had not been unknown in the past for many a luckless one who just hadn't the strength to fight his fellows for the magic disc, now weakened by age, sickness and hunger and with a wife and kids at home desperate for wages and finally unable to hold his own in a real 'tooth and claw' fight for survival of the fittest, not only went to the nearest pub to drown his sorrows for the moment but stepped to the nearest stairs and drowned himself forever. I do not refer to the early 1800s but the 'ticket fight' persisted into the early 1900s. By then this heathen practice had been stamped out. Not because the employers had realised that it <u>was</u> heathen, but because the 'dockies' decided to do something about it themselves. They came together to agree a course of action. They weren't going to tolerate fighting amongst themselves any longer for the crumbs that were thrown at them daily in front of the chain. They began to fight back.

It wouldn't be difficult to imagine the look of shocked surprise one very auspicious morning on the face of the 'gaffer', having tossed the discs into the crowd at the gate, only to see that every one of them stood their ground, not moving. Nor is it too difficult to imagine how hard it must have been for the really desperate to see lying at his feet dinner for the kids, money for the overdue rent, and not be tempted to pick it up. The stupefied 'super' calling out "Come on then... forty five of yer terday". The men just turned their backs and walked away.

The wonderful thing is that the same thing happened at the same time at every gate in Wapping (and quite a few elsewhere). Not one of them daring to pick up a ticket unless they were really tired of life itself and did not want to work tomorrow. Those poor weaker souls who could not resist the temptation were dealt with in due time. They probably never worked the docks ever again. Not in Wapping anyway.

Wapping men had quite a feared reputation in the 'outside' world. There was not the remotest possibility of outsiders being brought in, or for that matter just coming in as an opportunist hoping to find work that had been refused by local men. A blackleg had never been known to survive for very long. He would have had to work alongside a Wapping man. It was well known amongst the 'aware' that 'strangers' had never been welcome on the 'Island', a fair few would-be trespassers (or a blackleg) found out this truth for himself only when he was gasping for breath floundering in the dirty brown waters of a convenient lock... an accident, of course!

Apart from this inevitable risk things got accidentally dropped. A reputation like this was enough to frighten off anyone prepared to hazard the consequences of stealing Wapping work. No individual or even an organised group determined to break in by sheer force of numbers would dare to confront the combined phalanx of Wapping fists. I don't know where Norman Tebbit's dad went to find work on his bike in the thirties. It certainly wasn't "Darn Wappin' way". He would have soon found himself pitched over a bridge rail into the lock… bike and all.

Many will be thinking 'What a terrible way to behave', maybe… but this is not seeing the situation the same way as Wapping men would have seen it. The labour situation on the 'home ground' had always been difficult enough without outsiders coming in to make matters worse. Darwin didn't need to go to the South Pacific to discover the realities of natural selection and survival of the fittest. Wapping men were only doing just that. Whatever their attitudes were towards strangers and outsiders, justice Wapping style was always extended to everyone accepted as true islanders, every one of them, the weak and the frail, the simple or the strong. The only qualification was that they were Wapping weak and the frail, the simple or the strong.

Nobody went hungry if it could be given. If there was little to give it would be found somehow. Survival meant that to keep the little that they had demanded that they discourage anyone from 'foreign' parts who would take that little and leave them completely destitute.

The mere threat of violence - and sometimes real violence - kept their own country as bad as it was, and for as many reasons, as good as it was for themselves. The only way for Wapping men to protect themselves and to achieve a viable (and social) community was to 'combine' (an unwelcome idea in some circles), but then it would be surprising if the system of selection at the dock gates would have changed much if the 'dockies' had not combined to change it.

Eventually, the dock authorities were forced to accept the demands for minimum conditions, one of those resulted in the setting up of the Dock Labour Board which embraced the traditional principle that no one worked in the dock except those who were approved of by the 'rank and file' (yet another unpopular activity in some circles!).

For most of my contemporaries and incidentally for many generations of their ancestors before them, the only prospect for them was to eventually go "Inter der dock" and at the same time this was a prospect that was only open to them. Virtually nobody got a job, any sort of job, unless he was spoken for, or he was known and prepared to pay a premium to the union. I don't think that many of them did!

It wasn't ever a case of an outsider coming in with the cash. There had to be a very good reason why a Wapping man could not fill a vacancy, because ultimately he had to be approved of by the rank and file. If he wasn't then it didn't matter whether the vacancy was never filled. He wouldn't get it, not even if he offered to treble the premium. No amount of cash would buy them off. The system ensured that nobody picked up a bale or wielded an office pen unless he was 'spoken for'.

My friends and peers, when their time came to be spoken for, it was normally a relative, his father, brother, uncle, cousin, or grandfather. No matter whether the lad was weak or strong, bright, or dim, the only qualification had to be that he was a Wapping lad and 'spoken for'. Neither did this mean that he would automatically get regular work but if there was work on offer he would step over the chain along with his relatives. Casual along with the fortunate... work today... perhaps tomorrow, and then 'back on the stones'. The system of casual labour survived throughout the existence of the London Dock complex. There was never a permanency of labour... with the exception of managerial posts perhaps? The most that the dockies could achieve was the 'knock-on' and even then not until the late forties when the Port of London Authority was reluctantly forced to introduce it.

Each officially recognised and registered dock labourer was issued with an official Dock Labour Board book. So long as he presented himself at the dock gate for the available work that was on offer, not very much different in some respects to the old selection in front of the chain, and if there was no work available he got his book stamped... the 'knock on'. If there had been no work for a whole week, he was entitled to a small payment for his 'stand by', it wasn't much but enough for a minimal 'tide over' and better the little than nothing at all.

In the thirties there was no such thing as holidays with pay if you worked the docks, no sick pay or work related retirement pensions. To supplement the minimal state pension Wapping dock workers had to work as often as they could for as long as they could, quite literally until death or total infirmity ultimately caught up with them and they were at last unable to do the most simple of jobs, greasing barrows or making the tea. Death of course solved everything. Age and its infirmities were predictable, but the spectre of sickness loomed large for the young too. Lack of certain and permanent employment and the constant worry to feed and house a family all took its early toll.

Perhaps things were not quite as bad in the early to mid-1900s as they had been in the previous century. Nevertheless, the same conditions and the lack of work prevailed, frequently with the same disastrous results. The greatest advantage though the islanders achieved over the troubled past was the unique and wonderful social institution of Wapping togetherness and solidarity. Strangely it seemed though, to any outside observer, that it was a 'something' that even Wapping men themselves were not aware of. Also, it may have been a condition that was generated by nothing more complicated than if disaster struck anywhere, to an individual or otherwise, it struck them all. If ships stopped coming to the port it affected no single person individually, but everybody.

There were divisions, as with any other social grouping anywhere, but on the whole though, bread if it was needed, they got it, or a penny for the gas meter. Given today in the sure knowledge that your own needs would be met tomorrow. Wapping may well have been a non-existent geological island, but it was theirs and theirs in more than one sense. Alone.

Mind you, they could squabble and sometimes fight between themselves too. The usual human characteristics of jealousy, anger and so on, raised their ugly heads and even hands-on revenges now and again but in the end if this interfered with the peace of the community as a whole it got sorted out according to the dictates of normal Wapping justice and a 'bust-up' today always finished up over a friendly pint and pleasantness on the morrow. Bloodied noses and broken teeth forgotten... problem 'done with' until the next 'blow-up' that is.

I now live in Suffolk. Recently I had the misfortune to have to call in a plumber. He came out. His strong cockney accent immediately gave away the fact that he was not a local. "Oh" I said, "You're not from around here are you?" As if it wasn't obvious. Without a moment's hesitation he replied, "No I ain't, no more 'an you are neither". He asked the usual difficult to answer question "Where d' yew come from then?" (meaning whereabouts in London). I knew it would cause the usual problem, but I told him anyway. "I come from Wapping". His immediate reply didn't altogether surprise me. "Bloody 'ell, rough lot them weren't they?" He went on to explain. "I come from up Mile End way. One night me an' me mates went up the 'Palaise' to a dance. There was a bit o' bover over the other side o' th' hall. A chap was in a bit o' trouble wiv some lads. Jumped up on t' th' stage. Band stopped playin' an' he shouts out, 'Anybody 'ere from Wapping'? Well, there was a few", he said. "In two minutes flat dems 'ad th' 'all cleared... no trouble after that".

They were no tougher or rougher than the Mile Enders... a Wapping lad was in trouble; it was all they needed to know. Between themselves on the home ground they could scrap like cats and dogs. Outside Wapping it was quite another story. It didn't matter whether the victim of 'outside' abuse, even if he (or she) deserved it, even ones worst enemy at home... trouble with over the borders foreigners, then feathers would fly.

So, you see what I mean. Wapping's reputation still survives even to this present day for those able to remember. It certainly did for the bemused plumber. I wasn't at all surprised or upset by the implication that anyone who owned up to coming from Wapping was of a rough turn of character and reputation. Interestingly, nobody I ever knew from Wapping at the time did or said anything to deny the myth. For that is what it was, they were neither violent nor aggressive... except when Wapping and its social order was threatened.

Chapter 15

And Something for the Ladies

Because of the men's by no means certain income, most Wapping ladies found it necessary to have a little income of their own.

Nobody I knew of took in washing or did domestic work for their neighbours, because their neighbours liked to do these drudging chores for themselves as a sort of penance for not being able to pay anyone else to do it for them but circumstances being what they were, with the general family income on the debit side of bliss and comfort and what with the usual needs to keep house and home together, the rent and other incidental expenses, some way had to be found to supplement the lack of ready funds.

Now. There was a lady who lived in Reardon Street who was very good at driving her neighbours in the houses nearby out of doors. She made pickles at home to sell and the pungency of her trade hung in clouds about six feet above the pavements for at least four hundred yards in any direction, depending on which way any one of the seven miraculous Wapping winds happened to be blowing.

She displayed her wares on the pavement in front of her house on various articles of redundant domestic furnishings like discarded tea chests, boxes, and a broken chair or two, the overflow of her considerable stock balanced on the downstairs windowsills. The displayed jars of her delicacies very reasonably priced with the advantage of a half penny refunded on the returned jar. I was very fond of pickles as everybody knew, collecting along the way somewhere and somehow, the interesting nickname of 'Pickles'.

Everybody in Wapping had a nickname, usually based on some obvious characteristic of the person, physical or otherwise. It applied to places as well as persons. Perhaps it suited the purposes of identification better than a normal and proper name. Not only this, but it helped everyone to see the funny side of things, or maybe it was simply nothing more than an aid to memory.

Then there was a lady who was very good at 'laying in', officiating at those most interesting moments of family developments, not only at the 'laying ins' but she was also very skilled at 'laying out' the dear departed for a small neighbourly consideration of half a crown or thereabouts, whatever she thought it was reasonable to squeeze out of the dutiful mourners, measured, no doubt, on the extent of the wetness around the eyes of the bereaved. She was for me the very real living example of Dickens' 'Sairey Gamp' and I have no doubt the 'small sips' left on the mantelpiece went with the half a crown as well.

I remember particularly a very old lady who lived nearby in Jackman House who had the temerity to unexpectedly die suddenly. She was only, on the best information possible, barely ninety four next birthday. 'Big Gran' recommended to the old lady's not so young daughter that this 'layer in and layer out' be invited to perform her special skills and arts on the corpse. "An' she only charges half a crown", said Gran. "An' she do make 'em look lovely". I think Gran got a small commission for her recommendation from the grateful 'Sairey Gamp'. Anyway, a tanner or two always came in useful and would be worth Gran putting herself out for it.

Tailoring was always an occupation for young Wapping ladies (particularly of the 'unwed' variety!) reflecting the enormous number of 'stitch establishments' and virtual 'sweatshops' in the East End engaged in this useful trade.

Skills learned at an early age could always be turned to good account later on in life. Many a Wapping 'wed-just-in-time' mum 'made up' for her own kids and as a side-line would 'make up' dresses, skirts and trousers for the less agile fingered mums who had an old coat just right to be converted into a pair of long overdue trousers for 'Jack'. Poor 'Jack'. Very often the resultant trousers were well made and fitted perfectly with the wise provision of room to grow but in a yellow kind of tweedy material that had done duty as a coat for Auntie Amy at Auntie Florrie's funeral in 1901… and half a dozen various family marriages since. "Hardly worn" of course, but I think for Jack it was taking economy and prudence just a little too far but then, better than no trousers at all.

Mrs Thompson and her 'coffee stall' had got it right. Nora Leech, the tally lady had it made. There was also a lady who was a dab hand at a cobbler's last who would snob the kids' boots and shoes for a small consideration. A very necessary requirement in Wapping was for soles and heels to be steel shod. Studs and 'Blakey's' came as an optional extra, all much cheaper than going to a regular 'snob' though.

There were regular jobs for the young single girls at 'Meridith & Drew's' in Shadwell. They had started making ships' biscuits for the ever-busy maritime shipping in the port. Gibbs soap factory in Brewhouse Lane, Wapping, The Metal Box Co. in Hermitage, egg packers and the like, and of course the ubiquitous 'sweatshops' of Aldgate and Whitechapel, machining for a few pence a dozen. At the 'Minories' in Middlesex Street, high class tailoring, making officers' uniforms of all sorts, resplendent with gold braid and tassels.

The bottling cellars of the British & Foreign Wharf Company in St Katherine's Way. Some of these jobs also provided 'perks', things that conveniently fell off of the machines into apron pockets… "Just as a sample mind you".

One of the best tales I heard about the borrowing and sampling ways of Wapping ladies came out of the British & Foreign Wharf Company's bottling cellars. The ladies solved the problem of how to get the bottles of spirits and wines out without being detected. The 'gals' overcame the technical problems by wearing loose 'stays' and those copious 'bloomers', long-legged and elasticated at the knees. As the bottles fell off the machines they were expertly prevented from smashing onto the floor and making a mess by a swift automatic manipulation into the bloomer legs. The management knew that things were going missing. A search now and again produced no evidence of how it was done. In those less enlightened days no gentleman would dare to ask a young lady, "Er... humm... will you please take your knickers off", not under those circumstances anyway, perhaps under the more private, maybe? Even so, searches would be carried out now and again... nothing ever found.

These were always conducted at the 'clocking out' at the top of the stairs leading out to the street. It was arranged between them that the first few out would always be 'clean' and to pass back the news "search" to warn the girls following in the queue as a warning. One night the ladies were surprised to learn that the searches were being carried out by females... the queue already snaking up the stairs. The word was passed back down the stairs. They all clocked off innocently and went out clean but left behind them a trail of bottles left on the stairs. They must have walked home a little more comfortable about the crutch, and a little less bandy than on other nights.

The young girls either left full time work when they married or had babies, whichever came first. For the married ladies however, without the benefits of 'perks', work was provided by the fortuitous requirement that the city's offices needed scrubbing, dusting and polishing daily. They were not too far away from home, the most distant not more than half an hour's walk each way. Early in the mornings, very early in most cases, groups of history's first Mrs Mops would wend their way 'up west', sometimes to be home again in time to see the kids off to school. Some preferred the evening shifts and scrubbed the evenings away when the kids were abed. I am sure that half the city's cleaning ladies were recruited from Wapping's worn and well-scrubbed streets. The ladies must have been very skilled at it. As the old cliché says, 'practice made perfect'.

Chapter 16

Something about Churches, Church People, and the 'Sally' Army's Retreat

Dockland Wapping had witnessed in its past many migrations and immigrations. People came and went. Sailors from distant ports stranded on shore. The dispossessed of the city. Vagabonds, villains, and thieves.

The English, the Scots and the Vikings, Danes and the Welsh came to the big city to find enough to feed their families, only to find themselves marooned in a strange place called Wapping, where the living was cheap, and it didn't seem to matter whether you robbed and cheated to survive or tried to find work. The majority of course, were of basically good stable character and managed to get themselves out of the hole they had accidently fallen into and settled in decently. If not, it was easy to join in with the happy bands of rogues.

Those things apart, the advent of the dock building brought the arrival of hundreds, if not thousands of Irish emigrants, who in turn brought with them Roman Catholicism. The coming of the Irish is easy to understand. It was those indefatigable 'Navigators' who came to dig the docks but dug themselves in so deep that they couldn't dig themselves out again, decided in the end to stay where they were to help to work the finished dock. Finally, it was the Irish and Roman Catholicism that stamped its marks on the pages of Wapping's history.

Their masculine numbers were profuse to begin with because it is true to say that there had always been an Irish presence in London's already very cosmopolitan population. It wasn't long before they became aware of their masculine loneliness and promptly added to their numbers an equal number of otherwise abandoned Irish 'Colleens' to keep them company.

In the best tradition of ladies and gentlemen together with nothing better to do, their numbers soon became a flood receiving Catholic Baptism and Catholic Communion. The ultimate result was entirely predictable. By the very laws of social averages, it had to be Irish names and Roman Catholicism in every corner and situation on the island, from the highest to the lowest position in the dock.

Now, I am very aware at this moment that social and temporal matters are one thing and can be discussed openly without too much fear of offence, they may be very contentious and generate a fair bit of heat in the arguments. A contestant putting forward this or that theory may display some justified annoyance at their opponent's lack of understanding and resort to all sorts of name calling and insulting comments about the other's apparent ignorance. Racial and religious matters on the other hand are quite different. Secular things can be discussed as heatedly as the contestants may feel disposed and on the morrow be as friendly as ever. When it comes down to religious differences, fall out with your opponent over a matter of 'dogma' and you have made an enemy forever.

In Wapping's case, mere secular matters paled into insignificance where ecclesiastical matters were concerned. As we know these areas of 'interest' are thick with dangerous statements, a veritable minefield littered with the bones of the unwary, but I shall have to risk it and accept the possible consequences gracefully. Thankfully, most of the locks have been filled in!

From the early 1800s the grip of the Catholic Church on Wapping's social history was tremendous. Wapping became to all intents and purposes an enclave of Irish dominance, almost as strongly as Dublin itself. It was of course a source of terrific bitterness to the indigent Protestant residents. However strong the local claims might have been to a 'native's rights of residency' apparently, it didn't matter. It could be argued that Wapping's history being what it is the Irish had as much right to residency as the native or anyone else did.

It seems that the natives (whoever they were) weren't too bothered about considerations of the new-cum-old dogmas in their midst because there was not a great surplus of religious conviction at all to be found amongst them. If the problems came down to anything at all, it was the perennial problems of unadulterated racism. Catholicism and Protestantism were merely the banners attached to a racist banner and dogma had very little to do with it.

It has always been easier to identify racial differences when it is a matter of colour. In this situation to be either 'Catholic' or 'Protestant' was the only identifiable non-racial difference. What bothered the 'natives' more was that the 'newcomers' were playing their own game of 'combination' and were winning all the advantages in the process. As time went by, in the docking activities it became easier for a Catholic to get a difficult to come by job in the docks. The senior officers and bosses were almost to a man of Irish and Catholic extraction. Usually (it is a fact) the first question asked of any job seeker was, "Are you Catholic"?

Have I any need to go further than this?

But something extraordinary happened in the mid-1800s that began to take the steam out of the situation… well, up to a point it did. The Catholic versus Protestant problem was never really solved. Whether it would have persisted into this present generation of general and tentative moves toward 'reconciliation' is a difficult, if not hypothetical question to ask, never mind to answer it.

Wapping has now become a history of fading memories (my own included). Regretfully some of the 'last' generations of us that remember still display evidence of a lingering bitterness at things that are best left in the past, but there it is. Unfortunately, division of some sort or another does eternally dog the pathways of human relationships with one another and in particular stumbling block ideas of a sectarian nature tend towards uncompromising and unforgiving attitudes.

The 'something' that happened reached into the very hearts and minds of the island's people and began to change things for the better in spite of the fact that the 'something' might be said to have been just as uncompromising as anything experienced by them before or since.

It was the coming to the island of two inestimable gentlemen of 'the cloth'. First with Father Charles Lowder (1869-1880), then followed by his successor Father Lincoln Stanhope Wainright (1873-1929).

Father Lowder's role was exceptional in that he was a product of the 'Oxford Movement' who were otherwise known as the 'Tractarians', a group of Oxfordian ecclesiasts who pioneered the reinstatement of the Catholic ceremonies within the Church of England, better known ultimately as the Anglo-Catholics. Father Lowder's greatest achievement was the creation of the first Anglican National Home Mission - the St George's Mission in London's East End.

His first experience of Wapping was to be chased out by a generally hostile mob of Roman Catholics who evidently objected to his calls for reconciliation in the matter of the ceremonies and the sacraments between the two churches. Tempers were no doubt fanned by the priesthood who would hear of no reconciliation short of a total return to the Roman fold but gradually by perseverance to his cause, he and his faithful missionaries came to be grudgingly accepted. At first stoned and subjected to mob violence, then ridiculed and treated as simple madmen, then ignored and simply accepted as harmless cranks. However, Lowder would not give up. He regarded the whole of Wapping's people as his own parish and told them so, something considering the insularity of Wapping folk, they were none too sure about whether they were Anglican, Roman Catholic, or nothing at all. Finally, during the cholera epidemic of 1869 all their doubts that he meant what he said were swept aside and he gained the honorary title of 'Little Father'.

Wapping people were dying by the hundreds and the disease was raging in the tight overcrowded little streets and alleys. The 'authorities' largely left them to die. Such was the fear of the plague that no one would venture into the crowded courts, alleys, and tumbledown tenements. The 'Little Father' however and his assistant priests, together with the Anglican and Roman Catholic nuns went fearlessly into the worst infected areas in order to care for the plague stricken people, regardless of whether they were Catholic, Protestant or nothing at all.

Father Lowder would carry the dying children wrapped in his cloak to the London Hospital in Whitechapel regardless of the dangers of infection to himself, trundling their parents there in wheelbarrows. It was all the people of Wapping needed to know. He was their champion from then on and his mission completely accepted. Well, almost completely. The Roman Catholics gave him their grudging respect if not their devotion and kept their distance. They no longer opposed his mission by the mob and stones, allowing him to build a little tin chapel in Calvert Street (now renamed Watts Street). His unofficial title of 'Little Father' had been given to him by the children. It meant the parents could resist him no longer and his dreams of Wapping as one large family community came closer to reality... well, almost.

Father Wainright joined Father Lowder as one of his assistant priests in 1873, for by this date the little tin chapel had been replaced by the beautiful church of St Peter's in Old Gravel Lane. Financed by money extracted from the city merchants, principally by far the largest donation came from the Charrington Brewery. Enormous interest had been generated by the mission's work, especially in an area with the worst reputation - Wapping. It had always had a bad reputation, inhospitable and sometimes violent. Anything that showed the least promise to change this had to be encouraged financially, even if that meant finding the money for a grand church, so be it.

Lincoln Stanhope Wainright came from a privileged background. As a young man at Oxford, he was a dapper and fashionable youth, careful that his dress was up to the fashion. A typical Oxford student of the times, surrounded by privilege and opportunity, wealth and power would have been open to him for the taking. As with students of any generation it wouldn't have been untypical for a young man of spirit to decide on an adventurous course of action, like climbing the Matterhorn or joining some dangerous and untried expedition to the ends of the earth. Usually though, the exuberance of inexperienced youth generally gives way to the stolid paths of formality, after a period of useless excitements, to fall back into the enfolding restrictions of a social 'status quo'.

At Oxford, persuaded by the 'Tractarian influence' his ambition was to work with Lowder at St Peter's, London Docks. The Vicar and the strangeness of the place attracted him. Even though Father Lowder had pacified some of the more violent attitudes towards himself and his mission, it still wasn't a safe place to be an assistant priest, even Father Lowder's! If one was not liked or worse, not trusted, one stood the risks of being pitched over the nearest lock bridge rails, or having things accidentally dropped on one's head. However, all things went well for Father Wainright and he entered into the work with total commitment and zeal for the challenges confronting him and perhaps more importantly, with utter devotion.

It would be near impossible to tell adequately in a few words what the whole of his life-long ministry amongst such as the people of Wapping was like, nor can it be properly expressed what in mere physical and secular terms, that ministry meant for them. His 'spiritual' influence and motivation apart, no words can express his total charity. How he gave away his shirt from off of his back, not only because of his benefactor's need of a shirt, but because he also knew that a man would not get work without that essential garment... not once, but many times... his jackets too. Given away to the needy even in spite of his own immediate need for a coat.

How his housekeeper frequently found that his blankets had mysteriously disappeared overnight; of his nightly patrols about the parish... every night... intervening in fights, getting the drunk safely home, sorting out the frequent domestic squabbles. Attending to the sick and the helpless and the lonely, comforting the sorrowful, whose needs always seemed greater in the small dark hours of night. People abed would hear his hob-nailed boots marking his nocturnal progress and took comfort from it, knowing that when their own turn came to need help he would be with them too, no matter what time of day.

He would not sleep while anyone needed either physical succour or spiritual comfort. It will never be known how many times he sat at the bedsides of his own flock or the meanest unknown rogue dying in the hospitals of the London or St George's, nor tell how many times it had been heard said, "Ol' missus so-an'-so died las' night...! S'all right doe, Wainright wus wiv 'er", or old George or Daisy... neither of them would have died alone, he would be there.

One bleak wintry night, a constable found him seated on a cold doorstep near the London Hospital struggling to keep awake. "Are you all right sir"? Asked the bobby. "Yes thank you, but will you please see to it that I do not fall asleep. I must be back to the hospital to be with Rosie. If I am still here in an hour's time, please give me a shake".

The Whitechapel bobbies knew who he was and where he came from. He was a legend even beyond the walled and bridged confines of

Wapping itself. He begged and scrounged for holidays for the children, pleaded for boots and shoes and clothes for their backs. He instituted midday meals for the children - as many as three hundred every day. The meal cost one half penny, and no child was ever turned away for the lack of the necessary coin.

We shall never know of his joy when a group of gutter urchins came to him with a little ragged lad and asked, "Kin yer gives littul Jim 'ere a dinner cos 'e ain't got no mum an' dad an' ain't got no ha'penny". Little Jim got his dinner... and the next day and the next for as long as he needed it.

From the day that he joined the mission he laboured night and day without once taking a break for seven years as Lowder's curate, until finally at his Vicar's death in 1880 he became Vicar of St Peter's, London Docks.

When Wainright came to Wapping, it completely changed his whole way of life. What may have begun as a youthful adventure completely transformed him. Nothing of his former life was retained. Fine airs and fashion disappeared; affectation vanished. He thought nothing for personal possessions and kept nothing for himself in a self-inflicted poverty, saying that nobody had the right to claim that they understood poverty, hunger, and deprivation unless they themselves knew hunger and went without. He could not bear to eat the meanest meal while he knew that any of his flock who had nothing went without.

His room became a mean cell with its bare boards and furnished with little more than a broken chest and a rickety chair, a truckle bed with broken springs and a hard straw mattress. Bed coverings, a few blankets that he frequently gave away so that the sick should be warm.

He became one of the same people that he ministered to, held by them and the dark dismal alleys of this strange island. He would never leave it, or them, for more than a few hours, never days. He never missed a morning Mass although, he too had his own assistant priests. In the fifty six years of his ministry, he never took a holiday. He was once though persuaded after a long illness to take a break to convalesce. It was very much against his will, but to please those who had been concerned for his health, he had agreed.

After a few days he was back in Wapping carrying out his normal duties. On being asked, "Why?" he explained that he could not stand the quietness and openness of the countryside any longer than he had because it made him depressed. The honest answer (as everyone knew) should have been that his devotion to the place and its people were all that he lived for. He could not be parted for too long from either.

Much has been said and written about the Anglo-Catholic Revival within the Church of England. Many will turn up a disapproving nose at the mention of 'revival', re-introducing as it did, so much that had its roots in Roman Catholic tradition, but no one should disparage the results found at St Peter's, Old Gravel Lane, Wapping, nor cast a slur on the memory of the worthy and much loved 'Saint' Father Wainright. "If ever there was a saint...", said one of his people, "... he was one, and it should be made clear to the Church of England that there has been a Saint in her midst". *Menzies, L. (1947). Father Wainright: A Record.*

There were the clubs that he set up. Boys' clubs, men's clubs, a dance club, a rowing club where they became very skilled in Thames rowing matches, taking on 'all comers' and winning; girls' clubs and ladies' sewing and cooking clubs encouraging a better domestic life and ability.

No one who ever went to him in need was ever turned away. A few pennies when it could be spared out of his own purse, half a bucket of coal given out of his own sparse provision. He could also be stern and disapproving of misdemeanours, never hesitating to say so, but never unforgiving. No one took advantage of him either. Whatever one feels about his insistence on the Catholic ritual, his views in the end should take precedence over any dissension. He completely accepted Father Lowder's concept of the situation in Wapping.

"The people..." he said, "... oppressed as they are, the cold and the hungry, they deserve that their church services should have everything that ceremony can provide, to surround their worship with light and wonder".

For Wainright, this meant abandoning the nineteenth century's obsessions of taking away from ceremony anything that smacked of excess, as a sort of spiritual fasting, a sacrifice that might apply to those who were spiritually wealthy and sitting well-fed and warm amidst their physical plenty, but his people had nothing else to surrender or sacrifice but the means of mere survival and life itself. Lowder and Wainright knew as well as anyone what this meant. Answering his critics Wainright replied, "As far as I am concerned I would be satisfied with a plain service", but for his parish and the people of Wapping only the best would be good enough for them.

A well-wishing friend sent him ten shillings (50p) pointing out that it would buy a lot of unsold fish at Billingsgate Fish Market, and it would feed a lot of people. "Oh no", said the Father, "this is going to a man who is recovering from a long illness, what he needs is a good beef steak". If I had been the giver of that ten shillings, I would have taken that as a severe rebuke. How dare his friend suggest that a load of putrefying fish was good enough for his people!

The original parish church of St John's on the corner of Scandrett Street and Greenbank, before the establishment of St Peter's, London Docks, was the centre of Protestant activity. It actually stood on the site of an earlier Saxon church and tradition has it that there was a medieval structure even before that.

Not an unsurprising assumption when one takes into account the continuity of Wapping's history... the misconception that it began with the enclosures and building of the dock is not all together right. Stepney as a whole, which included Wapping, had been well populated in a kind of itinerant and rural fashion.

Records show that the East End diocese of Roman Catholics numbered 16,000, probably made up of Irish or Irish descendants, including the indigenous peoples that had managed to cling on to their tradition at the separation of the churches.

With the building of the dock complex, prior to 1840, the Wapping Roman Catholics hadn't had their own church since the destruction of the Virginia Street chapel (now Pennington Street) during the Lord Gordon Riots in 1780. The numbers of Irish Catholics had been boosted to such numbers, that a church of their own became increasingly necessary. The Roman Catholics, thinking that there might be an opportunity of converting the lackadaisical Anglicans of St John's, built their own chapel right next door to them in Greenbank, dedicating it to the well-known Saint Patrick. However, the St George's Mission had pre-empted the dangers imposed on them by this evidence of an excess of free enterprise on the part of the Roman influence, by the simple expedient of the establishment of St Peter's in the Old Gravel Lane (now Wapping Lane). The Mission's terms for the establishment of St Peter's were dependent on the service and the ritual should be as nearly Roman Catholic as it was possible to be without the dangers of an action for infringed copyrights, terms that were faithfully adhered to, coming, as it happened, to having the ultimate effect of actually drawing the two sides of the congregations closer together and yet still separate at the same time.

At a stroke, as some would have it, 'by Devine intervention', or as others would insist, 'a providential accident' (whether there is a difference in the two propositions), whatever the answer, the endemic threats of an intolerable sectarian situation were reduced. Not all together eliminated but reduced or at the very least pushed further away into the background. This may be an over-simplification. There was still a (too) hefty lump of religious bigotry and racial conflict going the rounds but at last it had become manageable. As yet, others would also have it 'Solomon, in all his reputed wisdom, could not have devised a better method'.

Poor St John was very much in the shadow of these exciting events, quite apart from the fact that the church was 'low-ish' in the ceremonial ratings and ought to have suited the less diligent in these matters. It was sadly, after the coming of St Patrick and St Peter, impossible to consider the 'lowly' St John anywhere in the race.

It did absolutely no good them reminding Wappingites that theirs had been the benevolent society who had served Wapping's people for generations, that had built the very first free schools long before these spiritual 'upstarts' had arrived on the scene. Therefore, they were the elder statesmen (and stateswomen) whose wise counsel was ignored at their peril. It made no difference at all. The populace was deaf to the warnings and were thoroughly absorbed by these new(ish) ideas.

The Irish and indigenous Roman Catholic kids had had the benefits of a church-based education from around the 1770s, arranged outside Wapping. The elders and the priests of the Roman Catholic faction realised that the St John's charity school could not (or perhaps would not) cope with the wandering hordes of Roman Catholic kids, they had to have a school of their own on the home ground of Wapping itself. The main purpose of which was primarily to instruct the wanderers into the mysteries of good Catholic behaviour, together with the useful science of reading, writing and basic arithmetic thrown in. It wasn't until years later that Father Wainright realised that St Peter had been out-manoeuvred, concluding that that if the Roman kids were to have the benefits of an education, then 'He' ought not to be less diligent with 'His' own. St Patrick was perfectly willing to take on this responsibility, because lots of Anglican kids had already found their way to the Catholic school without much help from their parents anyway.

St Peter came to the conclusion that a Roman influenced education was all right when it came down to matters of reading and writing. The arithmetic was also useful in a purely secular situation but when it came to more Holy considerations, that was quite another matter. They had to have their own school to cater for those who would otherwise be left out of the race for literacy.

Father Wainright pulled out all the stops, scrounging and begging the City's merchants again for funds to build, and he got it.

The advent of the St Peter's school opened in 1870 and put the three congregations of St John, Patrick, and Peter at last equal in the field of education... sort of! It remained to be seen who would be the next to take the initiative.

Any successful explorer in the region would have searched in vain for any enterprise on the part of Methodists, Baptists, or any other non-conformist congregations. They just did not exist. There might have been a few exceptions of those whose persuasions might not have been able to accept what was on offer locally but then from what I remember of the condition, they must have been a rare breed, rare enough not to be easily identified.

I did hear rumours of a tin chapel buried somewhere in Hermitage. I spoke recently (well, twenty or thirty years ago) to an elderly lady who claimed to remember something of the sort but could not shed a flicker of recollection on what kind of denomination it represented or whether it boasted a congregation. The fact of the matter is though, that if any local dissident had any inclination to step out of line, they kept very quiet about it. There was no point in rocking an already unsteady boat. Competition was already lively enough as it was. Any aspiring radicals probably realised how much harm could be done to such a finely balanced situation.

If they didn't realise it, they must have been guided by some mysteriously strange motivation into the right paths. Maybe only primeval instincts of self-preservation drove them in spite of their personal inclinations, an instinct incidentally, generated by the ever-present nearness of bridges and murky locks.

In the mysterious ways of the inexplicable, with the advent of Anglo-Catholicism it had become marginally easier to live with the Roman Catholics (and the other way round). It did not remove the inherent conflicts altogether, but it brought those problems into a manageable framework. Without the people themselves realising it, they rejected the multiplicity of ways and ideas. The Anglicans and the Romans were dogmatically so close together that they were almost indistinguishable. Had it been otherwise, at the very least, on religious grounds, the results could have been disastrous, bringing with it more complex sectarian divisions and destroying the whole social structure with it. There was still in spite of this, far too much intolerance around, but I believe that it became largely directed towards real or imaginary threats from 'outside'.

It seems that the kids were just as aware of this inward looking protectionism as their parents or elders were, regarding alien ideas with the greatest suspicion.

Chapter 17

The Sally Army's Retreat

It was reported that the Salvation Army had overcome the bastions of Hebrew Whitechapel and were surging over the breastworks of the highway. They had been seen pausing here and there on street corners to regroup, the scattered battalions came together at the top of Old Gravel Lane.

Having infiltrated the territories of the mystified Jews singly and unnoticed, the purpose of the regrouping was to declare to an astonished public their triumphant capture of the street corners, pausing only long enough to sing their songs of victory and to invite the natives to join them in the battle to come.

Their splendid battle arms displayed to encourage the fainthearted, drums and banners, trumpets, tambourines, and cymbals blaring and crashing, drawn up and drilled. Victory songs rang out, indicating to the puzzled Jews their confidence in the proposed mission - a determined assault on the brazen stronghold of idolatrous Wapping.

This was their big mistake. Like bad news which travels fast. In this case the good news travelled faster. If they hadn't made such a noise about it, they could have opened their attack and complete surprise would have been achieved. Wapping's defenders had been forewarned. The cry went out, "The 'Army' is a-coming". Runners sounded the alarm, shouting their call to arms in alleys and courts as they sped over the cobbled streets. "The 'Army' is a-coming".

From every corner the troops ran to man the defences. The island of Wapping was easily defended, entry was only possible by crossing a bridge. Infiltration was out of the question. The bridge over the lock in Old Gravel Lane was threatened. Within minutes of the first alarm the defenders rushed to man their posts. "The 'Army' is a-coming".

Out of the wintry gloom they came. The Salvationists constricted on a narrow front and squeezed between the dock wall on each side of the lane moved toward the bridge. Not a step further could they go, the far shore on the Wapping side thick with Wapping's troops. A mass of keen young folk come to their country's banner in the 'nick of time' ready to defend to the last of them the sovereign soil of their dear country. Trumpets raised to their lips, the invaders sought to intimidate but this was to be no modern day 'Jericho'. The walls did not crumble at the trumpets' blast, nor did the defenders waver in their determination to deny the island to the Salvation Army.

It wasn't so much a case of hurled missiles or cast insults, it was just the massed ranks confronting them that looked so menacing... it was enough. The Army suffered in infrequent defeat and the confused retreat was on, chased up the lane by the derisive cheers of Wapping's 'light foot' infantry.

It was many years of constantly trying to gain some ground in Wapping, in fact I don't think that they ever did make very many successful forays over the bridges. I have vague recollections of the Army and carols at Christmas times, that were apparently 'tolerated', everybody was well aware of the 'Good Works' of the Salvationers and understood the motivation and commitment of their efforts but even so, I do not have a glimmer of doubt that the most significant factor that deterred organisations like the Salvation Army was the traditional reputation that the islanders were violent and could turn nasty toward anyone that displeased them. It was a complete myth. It was certainly true of perhaps reputation and past history. In the thirties and after, I never came across a single soul who went out of their way to disprove the myth. It served the islanders wonderfully to keep outsiders as outsiders.

There was a very real nervousness bordering on fear amongst 'foreigners' about coming over the bridges, something that I discovered through my own experience. In the mid-forties I invited a Jewish friend to visit me at home in Wapping. He refused point blank. "But why not"? I asked (I should have known the answer before I had asked the question). "Oh, I'm not coming down there". He lived barely a couple of hundred yards from the lane bridge and incidentally, within Wapping's parish boundaries of the St George ward. He didn't actually give me any other reason for refusal. He probably didn't want to upset me by suggesting that he thought Wapping people were rough and violent, and he would get short shrift and a watery burial if he ever dared it.

The idea that these conditions actually existed were too deeply engraved in the folk memory of outsiders to be removed by any assurances of mine. He must have thought that I was one thing when outside and another at home on the home ground. Luring him by pleasant smiles, but as soon as I crossed a border I would revert to my true character and deliver him up to the heathens and a watery grave. Anyway, he never came. I would be very interested to know whether any other Jewish neighbour on Wapping's borders ever crossed a bridge and if they did, I would like to know whether they ever came out again.

We kids were well aware of the fears of foreigners, and never did or said anything to give it the lie. The main objective was to reinforce the myth with factual 'prefabricated' evidence. If not actually 'factual', a good dose of the imagination would do nicely.

Not that the adults were far behind in the game of scaring the pants off would-be visitors. They too had to maintain the notoriety. They enjoyed the joke of it as much as we did and would never dream of spoiling the 'punch lines' that it wasn't like that at all.

In the end though, it did stop anyone with fanciful ideas from giving them a whirl "Darn Wappin' way".

* * * * *

It has been impossible to do full and adequate justice to the memory of Father Lincoln Stanhope Wainright. I have drawn freely on Lucy Menzies' record of his ministry, for which I fully acknowledge my indebtedness to her and St Peter's Church for allowing me the privilege.

Today, mention his name to anyone who knows Wapping as it was before the closures of the docks, and they will know instantly who he was and what he did.

Father Wainright died after fifty six years of continuous and uninterrupted service, on the evening of the 6th of February 1929 and yet his name will remain a legend for generations to come. Strangely, not only the Anglican community respected and mourned his passing, but every inhabitant darkly encompassed within those dismal walls.

It was a fulfilment of Father Lowder's dream of one Wapping family, no matter who they were. No one has ever begrudged him his right to claim it. At his funeral, the salt of RomanCatholic tears mingled with those of the Anglicans.

He is laid to rest at Plaistow Cemetery amongst countless of his flock.

It had been just another of his acts of charity to secure a resting place for his people... there had been nowhere in Wapping to bury the dead. A large plot was found at Plaistow for the exclusive use of his parish. He lies with them now, in his rest, as he lived with them and for them in life.

* * * * *

In spite of an outward calm, a spirit of one-upmanship stalked the highways and byways unabated, not that the kids did not enjoy the ideas of their separated identities. Sometimes things did get steamed up and a shade nasty, but on the whole they associated together, played together… not too infrequently, ultimately married and lived together. If there was any really marked separation of identities, it wasn't so much a case of differing sectarian belief that kept them apart, but something more tangible and physical, like stone, bricks and mortar, church school, etc. Maybe where the parents and adults stood there was, but amongst the kids it did not seem so important, especially where the two church schools were concerned. Each had their own differing calendars. Holy days important to the one faction and not the other, had the effect of producing different half holidays.

It wasn't unusual for the Roman Catholic kids to be enjoying an afternoon off school after having been herded into church in the morning for the celebration of a saint, while the Anglicans slogged on. An air of God-given superiority hung over the Roman Catholics like a silver cloud. They were only too willing to rub salt into the wound, thereby losing whatever Holy virtue they might have gained. No matter, the 'boot would be on the other foot' shortly and an Anglican revenge would be certain.

The Roman Catholics ever keen to put on a good show, many years ago formed a boys' drum and fife band. A number of tried and tested boys who showed a glimmer of musical appreciation were gathered together and provided with instruments suitable to their talents, but not always to their size as the two rarely matched. Kitted out with a minimal uniform consisting of a cap with a tin badge, a tie, and a belt... the rest was optional, so long as it was clean and tidy... not too many muddy shoreway stains that is!

Thus, provided for, and after months of frustrating practice the band was brought out for the ultimate test of competence into the public domain.

The function of the band was to escort the many Feast days, Saints days, Confirmation processions and occasionally, on warm summer evenings (usually on a Sunday and presumably to drum up a few church going laggards into the right paths) and finally the parish boundary processions.

In the end there were so many processional days the band didn't get a lot of time for practice but over the years they gained quite a proficiency in the repertoire of half a dozen or so tunes bequeathed to them by their ancestors... it had to do.

The processions were very colourful affairs with the band marching upfront followed by the church and civic dignitaries. The band members totally convinced that the rest of the procession following them were only included to keep them company. The church regalia and the banners carried high.

Little girls on their first communion dressed in white, pink-faced and smiling (how I fell in love with every one of them), fluttering behind each one of them trails of crimson ribbons tied to every conceivable projection of the happy child. Tightly clutching little bunches of 'flars' got up Watney Street markit' yesterd'y.

Boys too on their first communion, drawn up in tidyish ranks trying not to be seen holding a new prayer book. Grimly self-conscious and smirking, spruced up in their Sunday best and totally disapproving of the whole affair, creeping along or rather dragged along by the compelling thoughts of dire threats to their comforts when they got home if they 'showed orf an' misbehaved'. Yet thinking all the while of

186

homemade scooters and go-karts and other matters of boyhood tastes, demonstrating to all the numerous spectators along the way that they were only going along with all this fuss and bother, not because they wanted to be there, but had really only agreed to come along to please their elders and parents. It was obvious to everyone that they would much rather have been on the shoreways wallowing up to their necks in the black oozy mud.

All this fine musical display did not go unnoticed by St Peter's. It occurred to them that if St Patrick could have a drum and fife band then there was no reason why St Peter shouldn't have one as well, so... they formed one. With this absolute stroke of genius, the Anglicans removed the evils that struck at the heart of every musically inclined Protestant boy. After that it wasn't uncommon to see hopeful lads of either congregation on their various errands around the parish, equipped with a pair of drumsticks drumming on door panels to the desperation of those within. On pavements, walls, fences, and windowpanes, or anywhere that produced a drum-like sound. The sole purpose of this irritating habit was, "Ter git a bit o' pracktis, an' arsts ter jine der band".

As one of the Protestant faction, I suppose I would be considered 'duty bound' by honorary affiliations to claim that the St Peter's band was the better. At the time I would not have dared to suggest otherwise. I done know whether it is safe to now. The truth is though, St Patrick's was the better, even though their repertoire was limited to about three tunes and a selection of parts from about a dozen others, it more than matched very much to the advantage, by comparison with the competition.

Having conceded as much, it behoves me to add that they had no monopoly where processions and ceremony was concerned. St Peter had 'His' too... always careful that the two did not clash. Now, that really did need a lot of diplomacy to sort that one out. They were also just as colourful and impressive and the girls were just as pretty, which did make it a lot easier for me to forget the alluring Colleens… even if the band was not so good.

Chapter 18

Changes on The Way - Dagenham & Bermondsey Blues

As it has been said, and if experience is anything to go by, then my own ought to be enough to prove the point. 'All good things come to an end'.

I suppose, if one has enjoyed a full life filled with excellence and plenty, then it is ultimately guaranteed to 'come to an end' sometime merely as a feature of natural processes, as I once reminded a doctor who I had to visit for some minor problem I thought threatened my continued existence, but nobody else did. He reminded me by pointing out, "Mr Insole, there isn't yet a cure for everything". "Oh, yes there is...", I corrected him, "... but most of us are not willing to take the risk in case we end up in the wrong place".

We learned that No.74 Hermitage Wall was going to be demolished (not before time, surely)? Thomas Allen's who owned all the houses at 'our end' wanted the space to extend their depot, not incidentally, because the houses were long overdue for demolition and unfit for human occupation, in those days this simple fact did not apply, but wholly on the grounds that the houses stood in the way of the proposed expansion so for us, there loomed the prospect of another move. Stepney Borough Council offered to rehouse us, but for the half dozen families affected there was no way the council could, or would, find us accommodation in Wapping so 'when needs must' it was either back to the sylvan fields of Dagenham, or nowhere at all. We had to return to the energising airs and country promises of Essex climes.... I didn't like the idea at all. To me, Wapping was home. As 'grotty' as it might have been, I loved it. Dagenham had no attraction for me.

When the time for removal finally came, it was discovered that Allen's had agreed to make some reparation to the displaced families by offering to accept the cost of removals. On 'the day' it was revealed what was meant by 'accepting' the costs. Everybody affected was informed that the removals would not be done until after their normal Saturday workday, well past midday, and that they would be providing the means of transport, so no move would start before one or two o'clock in the afternoon. Not the best kind of arrangement for a moving day. To add insult to the injury, finally the transport arrived. One large Thomas Allen Tractor lorry and flatbed trailer which was intended to carry the possessions of every family in one single load to every location. Can you imagine something like this? Six families with all their worldly goods dumped onto a flatbed trailer, the unloading of the appropriate items at the appropriate place of arrival would have been a nightmare scenario.

Mum, who was something of a hard nut when disturbed, took a hand in dissuading the driver and his single 'mate' who came to help out with the loading and unloading, by assuring him that neither he, or his mate, would touch a single item of her own or anyone else's possessions until proper and appropriate 'moving' arrangements were met to her own, and everyone else's satisfaction. Not an easy thing to accomplish on a Saturday afternoon with everybody at the depot 'gone home' including the 'management', and there mum stood determined not to give way. Everything packed and ready... it was going to be done properly or not at all! Everybody involved took their cue from mum's stand, including the driver and mate, who no doubt saw the impossibility of getting the move done without the risks to his own wellbeing caused by half a dozen angry mums like 'fire-brand' Mrs Insole. These thoughts far-and-away outweighed the prospect of the ten shillings he had been offered to drive the lorry the short distance to Dagenham. Anyway, he decided that discretion was the best option and he beat a hasty retreat. The outcome, so I am informed, was that somehow the message got back to the 'managers' at the depot and finally, very late into the evening of the Saturday, after proper arrangements had been organised, not flatbed lorries but covered pantechnicon type vans had delivered at the various destination addresses, households and homes separately to everyone's satisfaction.... late. Very late in the evening of the moving day. "Better late than never", mum said. By then of course, I was in no fit state to know what, or whether we had arrived, or where, never mind when. Details of the event are as mysterious to me now as they must have been at the time and as it turned out, best forgotten anyway. Quite apart from the disturbance in our lives and new surroundings to get used to, I hated the whole idea. Dad did his best to reassure me that we would go back to Wapping to see Big Gran, grandad, aunts, uncles, and cousins occasionally. A promise that I was none too sure would be kept. For me, the move might as well have been to the ends of the earth with no earthly chance of a return.

As if getting reconciled to being where I did not want to be, I had somehow reached that time in life when every child thinks that he/she has entered into that bigger adult world and takes on the mantle of superiority which is quick to declare, "I'm five an' I go to school". A condition in life which tends to lord it over those not yet arrived at that magic age. Lily had had this state of 'lordship' over me for the past five years but now, I thought, as I went to school too, I was at last equal to the greater mysteries that she had been party to and had not revealed to me. I could not complain because she had passed onto me over the years, the rewarding skills of reading. I had always shown great interest in her books and her competence in letters and words. In her enthusiasm to show me how clever she was, she explained everything to me as we went along. In a way, this early and pre-school instruction

191

might have been a disadvantage in the long run because this school business came as a great surprise to me. I started school believing that reading was as natural as breathing and found it difficult to understand why so many of my contemporaries hadn't the foggiest idea. As a consequence, I simply ignored the usual introductions to letters and reading as being 'old-hat' and beneath my dignity to pay any attention. I suppose it was one less problem for the teacher to bother herself with. She let me get away with it. A situation that was going to cause me a well-remembered and embarrassing 'comeuppance' shortly afterwards. It wasn't going to be the only problems and disturbances to cope with.

Things were evidently not right on the house front. Lily looked grave and silent. I doubt that even she could have put her finger precisely on the problem either. Neither of us could, but there didn't seem to be very much in the way of conversation between mum and dad. There was a creepy silence that both of them were evidently trying to hide from us but in the process miserably failed to do. Dad, like grandad, was a quiet and 'too' easy going kind of man not easily roused to anger, but we noticed his grim looks and saw the hurting in his eyes. He couldn't hide these things from us.

Mum had always been strict with us. We never went without a full belly or clean clothes. She was excessively house proud, and everything gleamed and glittered with far too much 'Mansion House' wax polish. We never went out of the house with mucky shoes or dared to come into it either, nor did we lack from chastisement. Lily was too often the main recipient of what I thought to be disproportionate punishment for the tiniest indiscretion. For me, it was mostly the 'threat' but sometimes though, I did manage to 'cop it'. (I must have done something mum thought warranted it)? A particularly 'hair-raising' punishment was to be sent out to the local 'Oil-shop' with a penny to buy a bamboo cane, sent on our way with the awful admonition, "And it better be a nice swishy one", and as if this weren't punishment enough, to feel the lash of it round the legs when we got home with it. "Now, that will teach you to behave yourself". (It is quite a debatable proposition for me, to quote, 'Spare the rod and spoil the child'). Sometimes, for my own improvement, having been sent out for a cane, to have it left lying on the table for days and me waiting for the threatened 'swish' to come. Sometimes it didn't. She always broke the cane in half when finished. Once, the cane had been left sitting on the table staring me out when on an impulse I picked it up and broke it myself, only to be sent out for another... but this time I did not have to wait for the swish. I thought that this was very unfair since she always broke them herself. She governed undaunted. Whilst dad grew daily more morose and evidently sadder, Lily and I whispered in bed. We never heard or saw any signs of noisy anger, just an unnerving silence. We whispered in the dark until sleep mercifully took us away from it all.

How long this dreadful time of uncertainty lasted I cannot remember. Too long I suspect. It was not only the silences, but it was also mum's long absences. "At work", she told us. "We need the money". More often than not we were left in the care of neighbours after school and then frequently until dad was due home from work, when mum would come back with just enough time to get us and dad a meal. In silence... then a long evening of silence with dad trying to read his newspaper or listening to his cherished 'wireless' in a sort of unhearing kind of way.

Frankly, not much else can be said about unhappy Dagenham, or is it worth remembrance except for one very clear and distinct recollection. The morning came when we awoke, and mum had gone. "Not just to work", dad tried to explain... "But gone". It was all he could say to us... "Not coming back".

Suffice to say, that her sudden and dramatic going in such a manner... no goodbyes... no explanations... just 'gone', burned as big a hole in our lives as the fire at the Colonial Wharf had done for the high street but for us, there was going to be no reconstruction. From the very moment of our waking on that fateful day, everything was to change for us. For Lily, and for me, and for dad. The little we had had been completely destroyed. In 1936 there was no help to be had. Dad could not take mum's place to look after us supported by 'Social Security', he had to work.

Instant, and I mean instant decisions had to be made. Lily was mature enough to be considered able to look after herself with a little help from neighbours. Me, I was the big problem. She could not be expected to look after me as well. Virtually, within an hour of waking, a bag was packed for me (there wasn't much to pack). Lily went off to school. I can't imagine what sort of day Lily had wondering what she was going to come home to. Before she went we sat in the bedroom and she said, "We had better kiss a hundred times so that they last". She must have known that this was probably 'forever'. Strangely, I took it all stoically, seeing it as merely an adventure that surely would come to an end. Like our adventures around Wapping, they always come to an end eventually.... Back home safe and sound.

The big question of the day was, what was to be done with me?

It was either 'Little Gran', in Bermondsey, or... dread the thought of what might have been my fate... Doctor Barnardo's in Stepney Causeway. Fortunately, no such future was seriously considered for me as an option. I had often seen that 'ever open door' and know why it never closed. Once through it though. Easy enough to pass in, one rarely got out... The solution had to be 'Little Gran'. Within hours I was on my way. Just a small bag with clean clothes, everything else of my few possessions had to be left behind. "You can have them later". My tinplate lorry like the 'Tommy Allen's' that I had always wanted. A few favourite books. A much battered 'teddy bear' that was so big that it always sat on the only bedroom chair... that was about it.... Left behind.... I never saw them again. We were on our way.

I said goodbye to number 26 Verney Gardens and have never entered its doors again. Even then at that very moment, I somehow knew that Dagenham was a closed chapter of my young life. Dad and Lily stayed on there for longer than they should have done. Dad clinging onto the hope that mum would return... 'perhaps'? In the end he had to give up, moving back home to Wapping to live with Big Gran in Jackman House, just as I would later but there were a few years yet to run out their strange windings before then.

In the meantime,... Bermondsey blues.

Chapter 19

'Little Gran' - 1936

As little as she was, and as little as she was equipped in her two bedroomed basement flat in Guinness's Buildings in Snowsfield, Bermondsey, to cater for a little boy of between five and six years old in her little flat, sharing what little space there was with her little bachelor brother great uncle Albert, and her unmarried but nevertheless little daughter, aunt Cis.

Everything about her was 'little' but her heart was as big as the dome of St Paul's. Little great uncle Albert had one of the little bedrooms that lead off from the tiny living room cum-kitchen cum-everything else. Little Gran and Cis shared the other. I had to sleep on a folding bed-chair in the living room beside her one and only large item of valued furniture. The piano.

It was always loaded with flowers, fresh and strongly smelling of perfume in the summer months and paper artificial ones in the winter. Everywhere around the walls were Bible texts, colourfully printed cards hanging on little bits of red or gold twisted cord. She also had an enormous aspidistra which grew vigorously at one of the windows in spite of the four tenths light that managed to penetrate through them (the flat was below ground floor level). What it apparently lacked though in the usual requirements of plants generally, it more than made up for by the lavish care which was showered upon it. It must have been at least a hundred years old. I think it must have been a family heirloom for umpteen generations, coming down to Little Gran from her mother. (My maternal great grandma, unknown and unknowable Smith). The slightest sprinkling of soot laden rain and it was stood out in it. It was washed weekly with milk and watered daily with cold tea from the teapot. It might still be going on strongly somewhere because it had a mighty youth, and a mightier middle age.

Uncle Albert wasn't very much taller than me, which is saying something because I have never been known for my stature, but rather the lack of it. So, he called me 'Robinson the hairless'. I soon got my own back. I found a very battered and coal blacked copy of 'Robinson Crusoe', in the bottom of the living room coal cupboard. It had belonged to aunt Cis, she said I could keep it. I cleaned it and sorted out a few pages that were out of numerical order, wrote my name on it, and read it. I felt like 'Robinson Crusoe'... marooned.... Hence forward, Uncle Albert became 'Crusoe', the other half of 'Robinson'. He thought it was a great joke. From then on we would perform the same ritual. Whenever we met he would enquire, "Hello Robinson, how are you today?" I would reply, "No ships yet today, Crusoe". I really was marooned wasn't I.

Little Gran did everything she could to make me feel wanted and cared for, so did my aunts and uncles plus one or two cousins. Even so, everything felt so incomplete for me.

Dad wasn't there. Big Gran and grandad, greengrocer great uncle Jack, aunts, uncles, and cousins... all missing. Gone in an instant... especially Lily. Nothing left. All gone. Mum. My few books and special toys... all gone. To me, it felt as if they, and it, had all died, never to be seen again this side of Little Gran's promises of the 'great beyond'. She never said these things to me. It was a subject that everybody had decided was best left alone. Nobody could say anyway whether there was to be a reconciliation, nor that there never would be, but I worked it out for myself. After months of 'silence', Sundays came and went by.

Lily didn't visit anymore. Nobody came... not a letter... not a word... nor did mum. For me, they might as well have died, because I had.

It would have been so easy for me to have walked over the Tower Bridge to go back home to Wapping. Lily and I had done it so many times I knew every step of the way... pretty well every paving stone and cobble. It was forbidden. Everything I wanted was so close, and yet so far away.

Aunt Cis (perhaps too unkindly but she couldn't hide the malice in what she felt to be the truth) made it a point in telling me, "They don't want you Johnnie. You're dumped on us". She was none too pleased with her elder sister either. I knew though, that it wasn't really true that I wasn't wanted, it just felt as if it were. The reality of the situation was that this kind of situation was something that most folk of the times, including the Insoles of Wapping, would not believe such a thing could happen. It was virtually unheard of. For a woman, any woman, to abandon her children (never mind the husband) was unthinkable. The Insoles heaped the blame onto the Wrightons of Bermondsey because such a thing was Bermondsey. The Wrightons point of view was the same. Well, what can you expect from Wapping people? I fell between the two warring sides and became 'isolated' as a result. Neither 'wanted', or 'unwanted'. Merely written out of the question. Still, I just had to cope with it, Little Gran had to cope with it too.

I soon discovered that Bermondsey was very different from Dagenham, and certainly Wapping. Whatever it was, as young as I was, I 'felt' rather than understood or could explain it, but there was something indefinably 'different'. It was here that I first witnessed 'street violence' that was neither rooted in racial or religious causes. I had seen the odd 'punch up' or two in Wapping, fought between an aggrieved pair over some apparently insignificant matter, but it usually amounted to a hurried 'scrap' resulting in a bloodied nose or a broken tooth, but nothing worse than a bruised pride and a blackened eye that always seemed to regard its giver the next day with as much friendly feeling as it had in its un-blackened state. The Bermondsey fights were something else. I was really terrified. I mean, it wasn't just a swift angry flying of fists in a moment of anger or annoyance, but weapons of the most terrifying sort were used. Axes, knives, staves. Whatever came to hand. And blood. Red streaming blood and screaming antagonists. What was worse was the crowd were mainly women and the women fought the hardest. Whatever the reputation was with Wapping, some of it (perhaps most of it) deserved, but such a thing had not happened in Wapping for many years... not amongst themselves, but anything, or anyone from 'outside' that presented a threat would never risk a phalanx of combined Wapping fists anyway.

The Bermondsey fights would be broken up by the local 'bobbies'. Whistles blowing and truncheons swinging. The guilty along with the guiltless 'frog-marched' protesting, into the 'Black-Maria's' (the horse drawn 'police meat waggons' of the day) to spend the night 'banged up' in a police cell and a morning 'up' in front of the 'beak' on a charge of ABH – GBH and anything else that could be thrown at them.

Truth to tell though, I was quite comfortable with my situation on the whole. I had no reason to feel that I was unwanted. I was getting an unlooked for whirl of attention from all sorts of people. I'm afraid I have to admit that I was actually becoming too puffed up with my own notoriety and apparent to me, my own importance, especially coming from the local rascals who showed me all manner of condescension's. The news had gone the rounds of the Guinness Buildings internal telegraph system, that I was to be welcomed into the inner circles of the various fraternities. I had plenty of invitations to join up with this faction and that. There seemed to be a determined effort to secure my affiliation as a sort of triumphal mascot. Fortunately, I was wise enough to work it out that it suited my purpose better to remain uncommitted which was driven more by thoughts of the inducements offered... comics, the odd sweet or two, not least the whiles of feminine eyes and charms to lure me (I was wise enough to realise that). The well-remembered girlie identical twins, both as alluring as each other, who competed with each other to 'mother me' with favours. I could not make up my mind which one of the two I should marry.... In the end I made the only compromise possible in such an impossible situation and said I would have to marry them both. They seemed happy with this arrangement, and it got me out of an awkward 'triangle' of interests. I learned fast... because I had no choice.

As if this wasn't enough for me, the members of the 'Arthurs Mission' had been reluctantly acquainted with as much of my 'awful news' as Little Gran felt able to tell. After all, it was her own daughter who had abandoned us. The embarrassment and the shame must have been unbearable. The consequences were that I found myself showered with dozens of comforting text cards, an endless variety of coloured cards printed with the messages 'God is always with you', etc., 'God is the unseen guest in this house'. I took this message all too literally and pointed out to Gran, "It's a good thing that He is invisible. Where would He sleep?" The texts were given to me with the kindly intention to make me feel better in my supposed grief which in truth, I did not feel. It was all bitter anger. I was also the recipient of endless cuddles which I decided were far more comforting than the texts. Sometimes I had to suffer the indignities of many a whiskered matron's chin quite manfully. When it came to girls though, of a much younger sort who felt the ooh's and ahh's of my lonely state, I was really in bliss. I knew without being told that these sympathies were sexually loaded because I never once felt the need to be cuddled by their brothers.

Underneath all this wild excitement I always knew what was missing because I also knew that it was only because it was a case of 'forbidden' and it all still existed, but I could not be part of it. I had been used to being surrounded by those of my own name. In Bermondsey I felt that my name set me apart and somehow because of this, I was alone. There would have been no terror for me to have crossed over the bridge.

No harm would have come to me. Many times, I was able to look across the spans to glimpse sadly mental images of streets and alleys, brooding but safe walls. In my imagination tracking my way home. So close but so far away and unreachable.

I rarely saw much of mum either. I knew as much as anyone what she had done. I didn't want to see her anyway. Well-meaning comforters would insist on trying to tell me, "Your mum had to go to work. Won't it be nice when she comes home", and such like. All of them knowing the truth and trying to avoid the reality. I saw through it all. In the end keeping my own counsel. Preferring in the end to avoid the issue myself. Awkward questions always needed awkward answers and the best way was for me to keep my own opinions to myself.

Little Gran did her best to make it all up to me. She almost took Lily's place where outings were concerned. I was carted around Bermondsey and far beyond, visiting out of the way Mission halls of the City of London Mission. Up the Old Kent Road on shopping trips, she spent precious pennies on day trips to Greenwich Park. She showed me the observatory and the meridian line. I thought it was all wonderful. Sandwiches brought from home and a bottle of fizzy lemonade for a picnic seated on real grass. If I had been reasonably well behaved, and I always was, treated to a 'Snowfruit', triangular strips of fruit flavoured ice, wrapped in wax cardboard (which imparted its flavour to the ice), purchased from a 'Walls' ice cream seller. 'Stop me and buy one', painted in white lettering on to the dark navy blue icebox mounted on a tricycle. The 'Walls' ice cream man resplendent in a white coat and navy blue trousers, blue wristbands an' lapels the same colour as his 'trike'. Breast pocket badge with 'Walls' picked out in red, and a black shiny peaked cap. "Snowfruit please mister", I asked… "Strawberry please". Ice cold whisps of frosted air curled from the opened lid. My proffered fingers stuck frozen momentarily to the wax paper. A penny worth of magic and red stained lips. A red stained melting wetness snaking between my fingers. Grans 'quick lick

201

an' a wipe' relieving me of the soggy pulpy mess of waxed card. "What a state you're in". We would sing choruses all the way to Greenwich Park and all the way home again. As we got nearer to home we would sing…

We've had a good day today,
We don't know where we've been,
We don't know what we've seen,
But we've had a good day today.

There were to be many good days and just as many bad days. Little Gran seemed as though she was managing. I seemed as though I was managing, but it was a situation that could not go on.

Little Gran and her cheerful little brother great uncle Albert, in their earlyish teenish years had performed together 'On the Boards', in variety theatres. I have no idea what their act was. Gran was a real old trouper performer. Song and dance certainly came into it. She wouldn't say much about it but give her a broom, or an old hat, book or walking stick and away she would go. "Never mind", she said… "I got married to your gran'father an' that was that. We called ourselves the 'Smiths'. Now, there was a great stage name to catch the imagination". She couldn't get the acting 'bug' out of her system though. Any opportunity that presented itself to act out a part, Gran was there with it. A natural entertainer. A good mimic and character impersonator. Uncle too, in odd moments played the comic. I laughed at them both and they laughed with me. They might have succeeded in variety. Apparently they got plenty of engagements.

Gran organised a holiday break for us at the seaside. The South London Mission had a holiday retreat at Winchelsea on the Kent coast for the likes of us. For the thirties, it was an adventurous enterprise on the part of the Mission. It was a big house and garden in which were several tiny one roomed chalets ('Billy Butlin' did not have all the best ideas). Little Gran was in her element. From noon until night, and in the mornings too. The broom and the book, all the necessary 'props' to hand, and away she went. A real old trouper entertainer. Impersonations, songs, recitations… some of it quite close to ribaldry. Nobody complained. Great fun!

In spite of all the fun and games, there was still the Bermondsey blues. Underneath it all, I was suffering quietly… something had to be done about it. For once, Grandma's joined forces declaring a truce for the moment and took matters into their own hands by the simple expedient of reminding mum of her own responsibilities. They were successful in so far as without prior arrangement or warning of intent, I was literally dumped onto her doorstep, thereby they reasoned preventing a refusal.

Little Gran liked to help out with (as she said), "The old ladies" at Arthur Mission… making the tea, playing the piano (by ear) for their weekly ladies meetings, sweeping floors, and stoking the turtle stoves with coke, "To keep th' old dears warm and comfortable". Many of those 'old dears' were a decade and more, younger than she was but then nobody minded that. Gran certainly didn't.

Next door to her little two bedroomed ground-floor perma-dark flat at 153 F. Block, Guinness's Trust Buildings, tucked into an odd corner of the ground floor F. Block, was a single room set intended for single person occupation. No. 154 with the benefit of a single shared toilet with all the other tenants of the four ground floor flats, plus the single shared cold water tap, and shallow earthenware sink, and small shared laundry room that nobody used. No bathrooms shared or otherwise. The only personal facility provided in each flat was a very small coal fired kitchen range with hob and oven (still in use in the 30s). Lighting was gas, there was no electricity available! There was also a gas supply connection for a gas cooker and most tenants had a black iron stove for cooking in preference to the coal range, both conveniently in the only living room.

No. 154 was occupied by an elderly 'old dear' who was really a decade or two older than Gran, so it was only to be expected that she would naturally 'look out' for Missus Bangs. She was as far as anyone actually knew, an elderly maiden lady with no known family. Least ways, if there were, she was never visited by anyone other than a few local ladies on social calls.

She was, however, relatively independent of physical help, she washed cleaned and cooked for herself as I have no doubt she had for all of her lonely life. Even so, Gran made it her responsibility to 'do' little errands for her and generally help out when asked. One of her regular (not so much a duty but more an act of neighbourliness) was every morning, just an enquiry to ask if she wanted anything and if everything was O.K. with her. A duty that was mostly tied fairly regularly with Missus Bangs regular visits to the one and only shared toilet.

Little Gran had been up for some time. Uncle Albert had gone to work as usual. I had been got out of my chair bed beside the piano... nothing unusual with this arrangement, getting ready for a normal day. Gran and I sat at breakfast. I noticed that she kept looking at her clock on the mantlepiece and saying, "Missus Bangs, is late this morning". After a little while, Gran thought she had better knock to check whether she was up and O.K. There was no reply. Gran came for Missus Bangs key. She had left it with Gran because 'just in case'. Just in case of what? Nobody could tell.

I followed her without giving it a moment's thought other than as a response to my irresistible nosey curiosity. Little Gran had never had to get the key before, so I realised that something was 'not right'. Gran knocked again to make sure that Missus was awake. It might be that she had only overslept. Again, no answer. Gran finally made up her mind to turn the key and open the door into her room... carefully, so as not to alarm the old lady. Suddenly, Gran threw open the already half open door…

It was too late for me; I saw what she saw at the same time. Missus Bangs gas cooker was just inside her room, close by her front door. Gran rushed into the room and over to the tight closed windows to open them quickly to get some air into it. Missus Bangs lay on the floor in front of her cooker, slumped over onto her side, facing us as the door opened to reveal her face. She had gassed herself. Her blackening lips and her gaping mouthed protruding tongue. I saw her sagging chin stained with her dried spittle. Half-closed misted sightless eyes, staring into empty space. There was nothing that Gran could do, nothing anyone could do now. It was too late.

Gran suddenly realised that I was in the room, and she ushered me out and told me, "Quickly…" (although there was nothing to be done to help Missus Bangs), "… go and get the 'Super'" (the building's superintendent).

Off I went as quickly as my legs would carry me. I found him in the 'square' sweeping around the rubbish chutes. "Gran says will you come quickly; Missus Bangs has gassed herself". "Oh Gawd", said he. He dropped his broom and ran with me back. Gran had closed and locked the door to 154 already. It was now the super's responsibility to make the necessary arrangements. The doctor and presumably the police? The coroner would release the body for disposal eventually after an inquest, whose verdict would merely establish cause of death' and her suicide, and not why.

Missus Bangs could take no more. The story of her lonely life went with her and maybe it will never be told elsewhere. Just a few pence for the gas meter were all it took. Just a few pence worth of gas and it was done. There was probably nothing of what little she had left that was sufficient to pay for a decent burial? There would not have been a living soul who would have regretted it or noticed her passing.

Committed just as she had lived, alone. No mourners. No family tears. No headstone. Just an unmarked paupers grave as the silent witness that she had ever existed.

Bless her. Let this be her epitaph. R.I.P.

Chapter 20

Coffee Shop Days 1937/1938

I do not remember very much about the journey from Bermondsey to Forest Gate except that it was left to Little Gran to deliver me to mum's new address. I had no idea where I was going or what to expect when we arrived except that it was going to be as much of a surprise for mum (and whoever else was concerned), as it was going to be for me. We had got the bus from Aldgate, and I discovered that Little Gran had about as much idea about where we were going as I had. She had to ask the conductor to let her know when we arrived at the 'Princess Alice', Forest Gate. She confided in me that she had never been to Forest Gate before. "Never mind, we'll ask when we get there". All she had was an address which didn't do much to help me sort my mind out and prepare myself for whatever lay in front of me. My frequent questions, "Where are we going? Who? Where? What? How?" could not be answered beyond a reassurance of, "You'll be alright. Everything will be alright, you'll see". I sensed though that she was none too sure of the outcome herself, her reassurances were as much for her own benefit as they were for mine.

Ultimately we found the right address. 92, Upton Lane, and I was surprised to discover that it turned out to be what the sign board declared it to be... Hall's dining rooms. Suddenly, 'the penny dropped' for me, and all the little bits and pieces of information gathered over months and months fell into place. Here was where mum had 'euphe-mistically' been 'going to work' and had ultimately not bothered to come home.

Gran and I stood at the door into the 'shop' and looked at each other. "Well, here goes", she said. "Let's get it over with". She gripped my hand, pushed open the door, and we strode in together. There were a few customers seated about, one or two showed some surprise to see this unlikely pair of potential customers suddenly stop in our progress towards the unknown. There was no time for formalities apparently because I just as suddenly found myself gathered up and hurriedly hustled out of the dining area, through the 'staff only' parts, and up a flight of stairs before I could say 'Jack Robinson' hello, or even 'Robinson Crusoe', and deposited in an upstairs sitting room... and there I was left sitting for what seemed an eternity waiting to see what happened next. It wasn't until much later that I realised that I never saw the going of Little Gran. There had been no goodbyes and it was years before I saw her again, or Uncle Albert, or anybody else from Bermondsey either.

From the very first moment that I had been told that I was going to be taken to mum at 'Forest Gate', I had naturally begun to wonder and speculate about the 'where's, the what's, the how's and the why's? A picture of the strange, as yet unknown destination had formed in my mind of an actual 'gate' entrance to a real forest of the Robin Hood variety. All the way on the journey I kept asking Gran, "When are we going to get to the 'forest'? Does the bus go into it through the 'gate'?" Gran said that she didn't know so, "We had better keep a look out for them as we go along". There was a tree or two here and there but nothing that came anywhere near to what I would expect a forest to look like. Other than these promising indications of 'forests', or probably gates into them, I saw nothing but houses, shops, people, buses and carts. When we arrived, the conductor's assurances that this was indeed the 'Princess Alice' and 'Forest Gate', turned out to be a bit of a disappointment because there was neither a forest nor a gate to be seen. I had even wondered and worried about what sort of reception I should expect. I often listened to the guarded and whispered conversations about the 'situation', not just about the 'situation' but the 'dreadful situation' and mum's role in it. I already knew, nobody had to explain to me (or to Lily) what she had done and what she was still doing. I didn't have to be told how hurt Little Gran was either. Although it was something that was never voiced, I was aware of the shame this 'situation' brought upon her, and the family of the Wrightons, because I knew that I was a member of both the Insoles and the Wrightons... and felt the shame of it too.

As Little Gran and I had stood hesitatingly at the door of 'Hall's dining rooms' (or 'coffee shop' as these establishments were generally better known), I sensed her own anxieties in the grip of my hand. The deep breath and the barely audible, "Oh well, let's get it over with". I knew then that she didn't know what sort of reception to expect ether. And there I sat, waiting for whatever was going to happen next in this extraordinary situation. I was doing what mum had asked of me. Patiently waiting. "Wait a little while", she said. "I am very busy at the moment. I'll get you something to eat shortly. You will be able to come down later, but we are just about to get busy for lunch and you will get in the way for the moment. You will meet Uncle Arthur soon when he comes in from work, so be a good boy for me and wait. I'll send you up some dinner. Are you hungry?" I hadn't given it any thought whether I was hungry or not. I wasn't, but said, "Yes please".

In the meantime, I thought I had better take stock of my immediate surroundings because the way things seemed to be developing, it looked as if I was going to be permanently billeted. If I had any doubts on that score there was my little suitcase and the odd bag or two of my worldly possessions to prove it, so I had better get used to the idea pretty quickly. Once I had got over the other surprise presented to me. Who on earth was this new and unknown Uncle Arthur? Who would be home from work soon? I didn't know or had ever heard of an Uncle Arthur. This, I thought as I sat patiently waiting, is turning out to be quite different to what I had expected. The truth is I had no idea really what I did expect. The transition from 'expectancy', albeit to curiosity and uncertainty, had been so sudden. There had been a few quickly gathered glimpses of the 'coffee shop' dining room, surprised customers, the kitchens, pots and pans, plates, and cups, the warmth of the kitchen area and sundry smells of cooking both strong, savoury, and sweet. Mum's shock and surprise at mine and Little Gran's sudden and unexpected arrival, her obvious confusion and reaction revealed to me that she had been caught unprepared and that we were none too welcome at that moment.

I could not understand at the time why it was that Little Gran and I had so obviously been separated and I had been whisked upstairs temporarily 'out of sight' as it were, and 'harm's way' (I understand a little better now).

As I sat trying to think it through I felt nervous and frankly 'unwelcome'. It was difficult for me at the time to comprehend the reasons for mum's confusion and what felt very much like rejection, and the worst of the situation, I was very much alone too. There was no Little Gran to stand by me. No one. I knew though, that for better or for worse, this was something that I was going to have to cope with on my own because there was nobody else to rely on. So far, mum was an unknown quantity, so was the prospect of the promised meeting with the unknown 'Uncle' Arthur, and what he was all about? What was his role? What would his reactions be? Did he know anything about me? Who I was? I knew by this time that Little Gran had left without me. What if he said that I could not stay? I wondered if I could find my way back to Bermondsey and decided that the only problem to prevent me doing this if necessary, was whether the few pence I had in my pocket would be enough to pay the fare, and if it wasn't, it would be a long walk.

As promised, the dinner came in due course. The young 'lady' who brought it to me said, "Hello. What's your name? Mine is Flo. I hope

210

you are hungry?" She had a nice smiley face and I thought, well things can't be too bad if I am being smiled at so nicely. I told her my name, "Johnnie Insole", but she said, "I'm not able to stop long because we are very busy. The 'misses' said that you will be able to come down when it's quieter an' she wants to know if you want anything?" I wanted to know everything but soon realised I was going to have to wait before I got the answers. Who was this 'misses'?... But she had gone before I was able to ask.

Time was beginning to hang very heavily on me. I heard the noises of whatever was going on 'downstairs'. Voices, sometimes loud voices, and laughter. The clatter of plates and sounds of people coming and going, coming in and going out. Street sounds, people, lorries and 'trolley busses', cars and carts. I went to the windows overlooking Upton Lane, watching, and waiting for some answers. I took stock of everything in the room I was sitting in. It didn't look a bit like Dagenham, Wapping, or Bermondsey. Everything looked so new and sparkling. Green and gold upholstered armchairs and sofa. Matching draped curtains and crisp white nets. I marvelled at the carpet that was not just a mat in the middle surrounded by oilcloth or stained bare boards but fitted right up to the skirting. Porcelain ornaments on a well-polished sideboard; vases and 'art deco' models of scantily dressed dancing girls. I liked them but the central 'pride of place' ornament that really took my fancy was of a bold looking knight in bright steel armour, seated on a huge charger with lance held high and ready to do battle. I understood perfectly that what I was seeing was pretty well-to-do and rich by any usual standards I had ever experienced. I was duly quite impressed and wondering. The dinner was very nice too!

Somebody was coming up the stairs. I knew it was mum because she called out to let me know who it was, and there she stood. Nothing was said. I stood almost frozen to the spot and for what seemed an endless time of indecisions. What should I do? How should I deal with those feelings of excited anticipations and fears that had been

building up in me for those last few hours? What were those feelings
sweeping through me? Should I stand aloof and unresponsive? Hurt or
angry?... I had felt these feelings, and the abandonment. I had known
of the angers, hurts and bitterness of Big Gran and grandad. Lily and
dad. I had seen and understood the shame of Little Gran and the
Bermondsey family. Felt the atmosphere that had been created in both
Wapping and Bermondsey. In that instant of meeting and the forced
confrontation of all these influences, I didn't know what to do, or what
to be. Where did my loyalties belong? No matter what, she was mum
after all. The solution was instinctive anyway. She held out her arms to
me, I could not resist. Everything will be alright now. The 'ice' began
to slow thaw.

She began by making an apology. "I couldn't stop when you came
in, I was very busy. Gran said that she would see you soon, hopes
everything will be alright and comfortable for you. You'll soon meet
Uncle Arthur, but before you do I want to speak to you, and I want
you to understand and remember what I am saying. One day you will
understand why, but for now I want you to do something for me... for
us both. You are going to have to live here with me". So far, I thought,
so good. There was a long pause. "Now, this is going to be very difficult
for me, and for you"... and then there was the threat. My blood ran
cold, and the big freeze began again. "If you can't do what I want,
you won't be able to stay here and you will have to go into a 'home'.
We would both have to go into a 'home' because I could not stay here
either". So, it was to be no choice. She looked at me closely and saw
that I was willing to do what she was about to ask. It finally came.
Bluntly and forbiddingly threatening, "You are never to call me mum".
Fair enough I thought, no real big deal. I nodded my agreement...
she had more to say. "You must never call me mum. I am your aunt,
and it is to be aunt and uncle Arthur, and my name is Mrs Hall... not
Insole".

I was to become part of her own 'lie' and her conspiracy. I said I would do as she asked but I wondered if I could. What would happen I thought if I made a mistake and the truth slipped out? I would be in big trouble and that threat of a 'home' loomed very large indeed. This was going to be a big, big problem.

I solved the problem. 'Uncle Arthur' was not the same. For one thing, I had not yet met him, "When he comes home from work", had not yet arrived. I decided that I would call her nothing at all, neither would I use 'aunt' to address her, or mum, then I reasoned I could not slip up. If I was ever asked an awkward question that might have been quite a different matter. As time went by, I became quite skilled at evading any questions by the simple expedient of keeping myself to myself.

This whole business of Forest Gate was going to be one big problem for me but there was nothing to be done about it. I realised that I just had to get used to the idea. The alternatives were too terrifying to even think about. From that moment the ice never really completely thawed – ever.

While we sat, mum tried to explain but couldn't. I think I understood better than she thought I did, so for me and the necessities of the moment, I didn't want to even listen to mum's point of view and useless explanations; a fact that I was trying my best to hide and cover up. We spoke about other things too. She assured me that I was going to like 'Uncle', there was going to be a life of plenty. "You will want for nothing. I am doing this all for you (and Lily). Life was going to be full of promise and the future a world of blissful plenty". Suddenly, the downstairs door to the stairs opened and a voice called out. "Hello, are you there? I'm home". Mum quickly recovered herself, "Oh good", she said, "Here he is now". She took my hand, and we went to the top of the stairwell. I looked over the banister and surprise surprise!... So, this is 'Uncle Arthur'. I discovered that I had known him all along. Uncle Arthur and I had come across each other way back in my Hermitage days. Uncle Arthur had been the regular gas inspector who came to empty the gas meter at No.74 Hermitage, who had given me two pence for sweets and had been entertained, (I have no doubt) he enjoyed a welcome cup of tea while I went out to buy them. I wasn't in any hurry to return home with them. He said goodbye to me once as I sat on the step of the corner shop in the high street enjoying my own entertainments. As I looked over the stair banister and saw his upturned face saying "Hello. Hello" again, I think mum must have been able to get in touch with him to tell him of my unexpected arrival. He didn't seem very surprised, but it was alright. He wasn't at all frightening and intimidating. I had a recollection of tuppences and mums assurances of the good things to come. He wasn't going to be a problem. We had a sort of masculine 'understanding'.

Not a word of what mum had been saying to me about the 'situation' didn't then, or ever, pass her lips. Frankly, I even began to wonder if the reality was that he did not know what my relationship really was but the necessities of those moments (and whatever the future was likely to reveal) was that I should be very careful in what I said to him, to mum, or to anyone. I constantly worried about what the consequences would be if I accidently slipped up, so the best policy was 'silence'. It was a subject that for both of us became almost a conspiracy of the 'unsaid and undiscussed', and for as long as it remained like that, I could feel relatively safe in what was after all, an insecure situation of my belief that only mum and myself knew the truth. I was never sure whether Arthur did or not? In any case, there was nothing I could do or say to change the situation. It was really a case of 'get on with it' because the threatened consequences of not 'getting on with it' were far too horrendous for me to even think about. I didn't even feel comfortable with the 'request' that Arthur should be called 'uncle' because that still implied a connection, in my mind, with the lie of 'aunt', and neither could I call him 'Arthur'.

I quickly adopted the 'coffee shop' staff designations. Mum was the 'misses' and as good a reference point for me as any. I didn't like 'guv' for Arthur but as I had seen a comic character somewhere and at some time or other who was called 'Pop', I reasoned that would be good enough to mask whatever he was supposed to be to me, so 'misses' and 'Pop' resolved my problem. That was neither 'aunt, or 'uncle', 'mum', or 'dad', achieved by the simple means of unrelated identification. Even so, the same policy seemed to fit the requirements, whatever name I used to refer to them both. The truth is I _never_ felt comfortable with the deceit and the underlying feeling of insecurity this produced. Silence and a virtual withdrawal from reality _was_ the only safe option. It was a case of 'getting on with it'.

To give 'Pop' his due, I know now that he did his best to make me feel comfortable and wanted. I believe that he genuinely, as far as he was able to under the difficult circumstances, 'adopted' what was after all a somewhat unwilling 'adoptee'. However much he tried, he was never going to replace dad, and what's more, whatever mum had been, or not been to us, 'misses', or 'aunt' was never going to replace that. In retrospect, it had been far too heavy a burden to put onto the shoulders of a not many months beyond his seventh birthday diminutive boy like me. The wonder of it has to be that nature itself provides the means of adaptation to whatever circumstances confront us all from time to time. It is finally what makes us what we are. 'Getting on with it' and making the best of adverse situations either breaks us or makes us and the choice is always our own.

Mum left us together on our own to get acquainted better saying that she had lots of things to do. The coffee shop generally closed early to match the end of most working men's days. She added, "When things had been sorted out downstairs I would be able to come down and meet the 'ladies' and see what 'Hall's Dining rooms' were all about". The 'downstairs' moment finally arrived. I expect mum had prepared the way for me to meet the 'ladies' who worked at the 'coffee shop'. It was evident to me at the time that mum had created the cover story for my sudden arrival by telling them that I was actually the son of a mythical deserted sister, and I was to be staying with her until matters had been 'sorted'.

Not one of the 'ladies' ever referred to such things, presumably on the basis that 'such things' were the untouchable subject and not to be spoken about. Whether they did so between themselves is quite a different matter (I am certain that they did). In any case, such were the moral considerations of the times and mum's relationship with Arthur... To put it into context of the times, she was a married woman with two abandoned children living in 'sin', unmarried with another man. Had this become known by everyone... as she reminded me, not only could I not stay at 'Halls Dining Rooms' (Coffee Shop, or Forest Gate), neither could she, or Arthur. Their customers would have deserted Hall's Dining Rooms in droves. Nobody would have had the courage to be seen as offering 'support' and implied approval by accepting the hospitality of a meal and a cup of tea. No matter how good and welcoming that meal happened to be, as far as the 'ladies' were concerned, their very jobs depended on their silence too.

I actually know this to be the case because 'Flo' (of the pleasant smiley face) later (on another occasion), intimated, hesitatingly... but barely implied without actually saying it directly... looking very closely at me for my reaction... "We know you know", without telling me what it was that 'we know'. She just left it at that. I have no doubt, because she had seen my reactions of real fear, that the secret was out and I could not 'tell', as I said. She too knew, as I did, the consequences of telling what *she* knew. Her job (which was relatively good for the times) as a virtual 'manageress' depended on her silence.

But for ever after, *I knew* what it was she knew. She knew that I knew she knew too, and again, it was always best 'unsaid', but we did share a conspiratorial 'look' at each other from time to time. I suppose it was this alone which indicated to her that she was right in what she had always suspected. It must have been her way of confirmation. Unwittingly, I was the one who provided the confirmation. For the rest of the 'ladies', it was a case of 'best unknown and unsaid'... everything depended on everybody's silence.

On coming downstairs, there they stood waiting to see this unfortunate victim of circumstance who had turned up out of the 'blue yonder' in a mysterious way. I did not quite know how I should behave. Should I look sad, or happy? Or should I look nothing at all?... It just happened to be quite an easy decision because I didn't really know what I felt. It was neither happy nor unhappy. I think it was more a case of stunned uncertainty and the same feeling was communicated generally. Fortunately, duty done by the waiting ladies in their welcoming 'hello's', they could now depart and leave me to my own thoughts. Fortunately, there was plenty to take my interest. At long last, after a very long day for me filled with the unknown and unknowable, I felt that I could begin to relax and take stock of my new surroundings. When I had set out in the morning I had no idea what to expect. I knew of course that I was going to see mum again, but not whether I should be staying with her at Forest Gate or coming back with Little Gran to Bermondsey. For me, the future was full of uncertainties and insecurities. I didn't know then whether I wanted to see her at all?

There had been that event at Bermondsey... I had suffered a bout of 'sunstroke' and the doctor had been called out. Mum had naturally been informed and she duly came to see me. I had nothing to say to her. I felt the real anger of her abandonment. I had not seen or heard from her since that fateful morning she left Dagenham... and she must have felt as unwanted as I had felt. She was desperately trying to sooth me, believing that my distress was the result of my indisposition, but it had nothing to do with it and I could not tell her why... I dare not. She sat on the bed, both of us in silence. Finally, she spoke... almost angrily. "What are you kicking me for"? She must have known why? Soon after this she left, and I had not seen her in the many months since and now those readjustments had to be made in order for me to sort myself out. Arthur…'Pop', stepped into the situation and rescued a developing difficulty of 'what now', by suggesting that I needed a tour of 'Hall's Dining Rooms' to get me used to where things were and what things were for, starting where it seemed appropriate to start.

We had come down the narrow enclosed stairwell from the upstairs regions at the bottom of which was the door into the 'dining rooms' kitchen area. I had so suddenly been whisked through with just a short glimpse of all the activity going on and the first thing that took my attention now was the biggest (obviously industrial type) coal fired kitchen range I had ever seen. Little Gran had a virtually unused small domestic coal range in Guinness's Trust buildings which she used primarily for heating purposes, but this was a great beast of a range, still glowing hot with various large pots simmering on its hob. It must have been something in the order of seven or eight feet in length equipped with two massive ovens, the whole fronted by as huge a fender as the range itself, and one or two other gas stoves and ovens, and a catering steamer. The centre of the kitchen occupied by (again in my eyes), a massive well-scrubbed pine table. Along one wall was an equally large pine dresser that was fitted and shelved up to a lofty ceiling loaded with white plates, boxes of cutlery, cups, and saucers, also trays of the more regularly used mugs, all brightly gleaming and scrubbed in mum's usual houseproud manner. The 'shop', or dining area, fitted with typical and traditional coffee shop style with a range of stalls of fitted sit-up-and-beg seating sufficient for at least six diners in each. The whole seating altogether forty eight diners, and as I soon learned, regularly filled to capacity four or five times at a mealtime sitting.

I was taken on a lengthy tour of a range of sculleries and preparation rooms. A normal domestic bath filled with peeled potatoes immersed in water to keep them fresh. Sacks stacked of unpeeled potatoes. Nets of cabbages, onions, and carrots. I was shown a storeroom filled with sacks of flour, salt and soda and boxes of dried fruits, dates, and raisins. Racks of shelving stacked with catering sized cans of fruits and vegetables, boxes of other smaller boxes of goodness knows what... large brown paper bags of tea. Bottles of this and that... for me the wonder of it all, a veritable grocers shop of goodies. A big fridge cooled by an enormous melting block of ice filled with bacon and butter, margarine, and lard and eggs by the boxload. The coal store in the backyard holding enough to provide at least a hundred weight (50 kilos) a day to keep the coal range going and the constant heat of its daily work always present. Racks of pots and pans, dishes and basins, bowls and rolling pins, knives, and ladles. Big sinks and plate racks, buckets, and mops... and the smells, sweet smells and sudsy. Savoury perfumes of bacon and sizzling sausages, stewing diced steak for tomorrows speciality, steak and kidney pie or steamed steak puddings. Apple pies and steamed syrup pudding. Spotted dick and baked jam roll, and for those with more delicate tastes, the lighter touch of steamed or baked sponge puddings, creamy rice puddings baked and nutmegged. Altogether a real working man's coffee shop-cum-dining room. Traditional fare designed to satisfy the hungry and the palate. Whatever mum was, she was a good plain cook. Clean, and certainly efficient at the job.

Next, I was to be given the spare bedroom on the top floor when the required bed and bedroom furniture could be provided which rather impressed me, with the assurance that it would be my own bedroom all to myself, which to say the least, was quite a big change from the bed chair made up beside Little Gran's piano in her little living room or for that matter, the bedroom shared with Lily way back in the days of Hermitage and Dagenham. Also, I have to admit that this sudden elevation to possession, somewhat went a long way to accepting that this remove to Forest Gate and Halls Dining Rooms was going to offer me a few welcome advantages. I began suddenly to believe mum's assurance, "It's all for my own and Lily's benefit" (how easily we are coerced into justification??) especially as Pop had promised that on the morrow he would take me to his 'gents clothiers' in Upton Lane to kit me out appropriately. Not that I was badly dressed in the first place, mum had always been keen on our appearance and had always sent various articles of the needed when needed, but I was going to have to go to school too and that was going to be arranged soon. In the meantime, for the first night I would have to make do with a temporary sleep arrangement. I was so tired anyway that the recollection of a first night has disappeared or for that matter, the first and the second, if not a good few others as well, blanked out in a confusion of new events, new experiences, and new places to get to know.

The new school was fairly close by in Upton Lane and known simply as Upton Lane School. There again, my first days, or maybe it was months, have disappeared into the mists of forgetfulness. There was not very much about the school in any case that aided memory. The school was as much the same as any other school within the London County Council influence. The very buildings themselves never, or rarely differed. Just as the pupils have equally disappeared into that misty time induced void of no recollection, the influence of them and the school in any case, was so brief that the mind really hadn't time to establish rememberable persons, even the images of them no longer exist. All that remain are merely those indefinable vague images of my contemporaries. I made no friends. I could not afford the risk of the awkward question of my past and of my present that friends would be bound to ask. Beyond the obvious moments of being with others in general normal activity, my instinct was to keep myself and my secrets to myself which was altogether unnecessary because nobody was ever likely to ask the awkward question. Nevertheless, they could speak freely about their brothers and sisters, cousins, and their mums and dads, uncles, and aunts... I never could, and the dangers of doing so were always constantly in mind. Except for one boy of nearabout my own age.

Next door to Halls Dining Rooms was an unremarkable kind of shop on the corner of Gower Road, which had no displays in its blanked out shop windows because it was not an ordinary kind of shop. It was in fact the store of a firm of travelling tallymen run by the family Moss. It was a quiet and un-rushing kind of operation that carried on there. Nobody seemed to come or go and yet there was also an air of economic success about the premises and the family. The unusual thing about them, I soon learned, was that they were Jewish. Not that this made them especially unusual but the discovered fact that they were practicing Messianic Jewish Christian did.

The Moss' were five in family. Mum and dad, two teenage girls and Derek, of my own age. Somehow we seemed to fit together. He too went to Upton Lane School, and we chummed together for some unexplainable reason. I was ok with Derek. We played together and usually managed to get into the same kind of scrapes and mischief. At first I was worried about the usual worrying things, but Derek's parents never asked any awkward questions. I must have been seen by them as a suitable and safe friend for Derek. In some ways there was also a similarity about our situations, me with my own problems, and Derek's family's problems of being ostracised and dismissed from the normal Jewish community because of their conversion into the Christian faith. Not that I have any right to suggest such a thing, or any reason beyond what I have said, Derek said nothing to me about such things, neither did his family and neither did I speak of mine. It is just that somehow these things come about for no reason other than an instinctive motivation. Maybe this was the only reason that we gelled together so well? We were no threat to each other for reasons we could not have understood or explained, except that we allowed ourselves to be the boys we needed to be.

Chapter 21

The Gathering Storm – No "Peace in our time" The first evacuation 1939 Tunstead, Norfolk, and a 'Punch up'

In spite of myself and the original worries that had given me so many problems to begin with, I had to admit that mum's promise that I should have everything I needed (within the bounds of necessity), and Little Gran's assurances, "Everything will be alright, you'll see", things had turned out 'alright' and I had been more than compensated in a pecuniary sort of way, as far as the possession of those really wanted items were concerned. (Sometimes though, it even transpired that it was not only my own ideas that came into consideration). Pop had suggested that I would really like a train set that could be set up on a full sized sheet of plywood that had been knocking about and surplus to some repair or construction work at some ancient date around a century or so ago. I agreed that this would be a suitable use for what had been a bit of a nuisance taking up space in a dilapidated shed in the back yard that desperately needed to be got rid of. From that moment of my agreement about the idea of a train set is where my own input into the construction ceased and I merely became the justification for Pop, and his younger bachelor brother 'Ern' (who was lodging temporarily at Halls Dining Rooms) for them both to enter into the spirit of the enterprise. The board was duly brought in and dusted, and space found on the floor of his bedroom which was simple enough because 'Uncle' Ern's bedroom was empty apart from a small single bed and a collection of boxes used as temporary storage for his possessions. Mum grumbled a bit about the whole project but as I was offered as the legitimate reason for the whole exercise she reluctantly agreed, but only on the strict terms that everything having been got out and set up, it was to be just as willingly 'put away' again afterwards. A condition that was accomplished by fixing everything that could be fixed to the board and everything else easily packed away. The board itself stood up against the wall. A condition that somehow gradually got overlooked on the grounds of the train set being for the moment 'only being planned', and the wasted playtime setting it up and putting it away again got in the way of development. I didn't even get to choose the set. It simply duly arrived delivered... and wonder of wonders for the times, a real working, gloriously realistic Hornby electric train set. Well, that was alright, I supposed I could claim to own such a wonder, but I did also wonder when was I going to be allowed to get my turn to operate it on my own? "When we have done this" or "Done that". "When the electrics are sorted out". "When the track has been readjusted"... It all seemed to be running well enough to me, but then I was really only a spectator of the whole operation and in the end I realised that I was merely the excuse for the undertaking anyway.

Derek and I got it all out once when everybody was at work and out of our way, and we had a great time with it. The strange thing is that it worked perfectly apart from a too enthusiastic derailment or two, but we had made our point and after that we were allowed a little more freedom with it, but it might have been only down to some kind of adult embarrassment which had entered into the situation and their enthusiasms had somewhat diminished, and we could at last let our own imaginations take the place of frustration. Sometimes the electrics did fail. Sometimes the tracks did get out of alignment but now we could move things around, build bridges. We had reclaimed our right of childhood... it was great! Somehow, for Derek and me, it had become a real partnership of joint possession. Finally, it was neither my train set, nor his. He showed no trace of envy and for me, it was simply a case of mine, but not mine. Frankly, the reality is that I couldn't grasp the idea of Forest Gate and possessions as a single entity. In some inexplicable way the whole Forest Gate, Halls Dining Rooms, Upton Lane situation... It all had that atmosphere of unreality about it.

Young as I was, I was aware of a feeling of 'not belonging', not actually being wanted. These feelings in turn engendered a stronger awareness of me being a nuisance, even a risk that in a flicker of an eye I could destroy everything including myself. At barely eight years old, yet inexperienced, I was already a million years old and with an awareness of this very potent fact that something that was never explained, or ever mentioned... I knew it. My very few precious books with my name and my addresses laboriously printed on their flyleaves heavily scored out by mum so as not to identify me with anywhere, or with anyone, especially herself. I felt that I no longer existed.

Mr Waller of the City of London Mission and Arthurs' Mission in Bermondsey, had given me a red cloth bound Bible... I still have it. The flyleaf with my name and address heavily scored out remains to me as a potent memory of those difficult times, including the good times and the good memories, enough of them to cancel out the bad (sometimes)! In hindsight, and perhaps better understanding, whatever happened was just as much the fault of the times as anything else. The need for the deceit and the lies to protect themselves from stiff inflexible moral attitudes. Perhaps it is right and proper to have those standards? Perhaps not? Nevertheless, it could never be right to subject me, and I include sister Lily, dad, and both families in this area of condemnation, to subject me in particular, so directly to become party to their deceit. At the time it might have looked as though I had everything I needed. Maybe in a physical sense, I had. Inexplicably, I knew that I had nothing. A state of mind that was no less compounded by the fact that Pop had four brothers of whom 'Ernie' was the only bachelor (for that matter, incidentally, so was Arthur), but that is by-the-by… (to all intents he might just as well have been married, if only in common law of cohabitation). Three of the five brothers at least had legally married partners which somewhat also compounded my problem…. Apart from Pop who (even he) was suspect from my point of view, of whether he actually knew that the 'misses' was actually my mother and not my aunt. It further increased my constant worry. Did any of them know the truth? I know now, of course, that the reality was that they ALL knew it. If I had any questions to ask myself (even now), I constantly wondered what they ALL thought about the whole situation? I shall never know, not that it matters now anyway.

Not only his brothers and their respective partners, and in amongst them only one that had children, and only one of those who survived into adulthood. There was also the mother who lived quite close by in a flat opposite Halls Dining Rooms over a fish and chip shop. She was quite an imperious kind of dark faced lady… constantly seemed to me to be a threatening presence and likely to be the only most likely to ask the awkward and unanswerable question. She always gave me the impression of hurt disappointment in life. The kind of person that shows it and demonstrated her belief that she had deserved better. There was always an air of upright disapproval of about everything in general, and everybody but herself. She had an 'if only the world could take notice of me and my behaviour', kind of attitude. I wonder what SHE thought of the situation in her quiet reflections. The answer might explain her disappointments. She positively radiated a resigned, 'just look at what I have to bear'. A kind of, 'please take notice of me and learn by it', sort of way. I did not like her at all. For me, she represented the ultimate timebomb kind of danger ready to 'blow up' at any moment soon. I think it was more like fear than dislike. I have no idea what her first name was, I can only imagine that it must have had something a bit Germanic and Teutonic about it. She always seemed to appear on the scene accompanied by Wagnerian rides of the Valkyries symphonics. Not exactly true, but it is the best way that I can describe her now. Her reactions to me in some ways were similar to all her sons and her related. Whenever I was in 'the presence', so to speak, I sensed the obvious discomfort that they all must have felt… they were after all, family, and as always, families stood or fell together. The 'blood thicker than water' syndrome. The idea of brother, or son, or family, living in an adulterous situation was never something to easily admit but there I was, not family, and a constant reminder of their own guilt of compromise. Every one of them preferring that I was not there at all as a searching reminder.

I got the same messages by means of the same messenger. I was mostly ignored, pushed into the background out of sight and hardly worthy of notice, frequently barely spoken to, and even then out of sheer necessity. I was to all intents just there, and I wished I weren't just as much as they did, so it was a mutual feeling of rejection… a kind of revenge on my part.

Pop of course, was alright out of sheer necessity of acceptance. Uncle Ern was alright too. He was prepared to engage with me in what I believe now was a kind of repressed release of boyishness on his part. He had been the principal mover in the train set project. There were also walks on Wanstead Flats and Wanstead Park and the jam jars and nets dredging for pond life. The evening spent in a darkened room screwing one eye into a microscope eyepiece desperately trying to get a view of cyclops and spirogyra, and other unnamed and strange pond life, all very amateurish and uninformed. The very posh and upmarket microscope had been purchased simply because my being there was the excuse for purchasing it in the first place and perhaps, if only to regain some missed opportunities of his own to discover things.

In one way or another, considering the otherwise difficult situation, I seemed to be doing relatively well enough to feel comfortable with myself. There has to have been more than a trace of 'The Lord Fauntleroyishness' about me as I wallowed in this unlooked for, and in some ways unexpected 'state of plenty' that was being lavished onto me. Halls Dining Rooms were evidently a very successful venture and recognised locally as THE place to get a good and satisfying meal. As far as it affected me, there were the benefits of 1930s luxury, and there were Pop's brand new Austin saloon car and the telephone to prove it. I watched and marvelled at its installation 82 years ago, on the landing at the top of the narrow stairs and still remember its number. Grangewood 3550.

There had been no calls after a few days. I thought, 'Whenever is this thing going to ring'? And one evening suddenly and alarmingly it burst into life with its strident and clarion demand to be answered... "Oh"! Said mum in answering it. "This is Grangewood 35... er... wait a minute, I don't remember". "Well, this is Halls Dining Rooms", only to discover that it was only Ernie phoning from a public telephone just for a lark and the pleasure of activating this new miraculous means of communication. Apart from this, it didn't seem to get used much. In those days, the telephone was not really found too often in domestic situations. Shops, and even then not too many of them, larger businesses maybe. Local authorities and offices certainly, but not Halls Dining Rooms. It was really quite unnecessary from a business point of view and in some respects merely a mark of its success. Almost the same kind of boast I personally perpetrated at Upton Lane School to further impress my contemporaries... "We have a telephone". What a little snob I was becoming! But, like everything else in my so far short existence of eight years and a trifle more, measured in weeks, things had never seemed to last very long for me... there never had been anything likely to become permanent. Things had been going along quite nicely for a while at Forest Gate and Halls Dining Rooms. I might even have got into the way of thinking that this was going to be forever, and yet at the same time there was something in the air that threatened some kind of 'yet another' indefinable change. I was beginning to hear anxious 'talk' and noticed that the 'talk' was of war.

Dad had a set of volumes about the Great War (the first world war). I had been fascinated and at the same time found the pictures illustrating the horrors of death and destruction frightening... and now this 'talk'. The newspapers and the 'wireless', and more 'talk, talk, talk'. Then there was a short trip to somewhere unremembered, to be fitted and issued with a smelly horrible 'Mickey Mouse' (without the ears) kind of black menacing rubbery gas mask, and the awful feeling of hands holding my head still... I could see nothing because the cellophane kind of eye piece had already steamed up. A voice said, "Breathe now Johnnie". I had to, or I thought I would perish by suffocation, hands tightening the straps to keep it on securely, I was afraid to breathe and lose that last gasped gulp of air... I could hold it no longer; I was forced to exhale the last desperate breath and suddenly, feeling the rubber sides of the mask vibrating against my cheeks as the air escaped like a wet rude raspberry. At last, whoever was fitting it was satisfied it was a good fit, and a few unsuccessful attempts on my part to quickly get it on as directed... or, as I was warned, "You must learn how to get it on quickly or the gas might kill you", I wasn't sure whether I would be able to do it.... just another thing to worry about. I did manage it in the end, and to realise that I wasn't really going to be smothered wearing it. I hoped I wasn't going to have to use it in earnest, but then I didn't want to die either. I thought that if it meant not being able to breathe, how terrible that would be... like drowning I suppose? Then, I was taken to somewhere else to be registered and get issued with an identity card and ration book. I still have mine. Posters were being put up everywhere telling everyone what to do in an air raid. Leaflets being delivered in the morning post explaining how to prepare for making a room gasproof. Windows everywhere being reinforced with gummed brown paper strips in crisscrossed patterns as a guard against flying blast shattered glass. Appeals for able bodied elderly and those yet too young to be called up for the armed forces, to join the volunteer public defence organisations like the A.R.P. (Air Raid Precaution), or the Auxiliary Fire Services. How to make a safe place to shelter in the expected heavy air raids. How to provide adequate 'blackout' provisions and the penalties to be expected for showing the merest chink of light at night, at any time, whether a raid was in progress or not. The newspapers and the wireless broadcasts put out in heavy headlines on a daily basis the news from the continent. All of it geared onto the 'threats' and the constant political attempts to avert the risks of the threatened catastrophe that could plunge Europe and the world into another desperate struggle. In those short few years, and finally months leading up to the 'the last word', it was impossible for anyone (including the young like myself), to remain unaware of the 'moods' and the grim-faced worries of everyone and everything going on around us... everyone knew that the conflict and the consequences were bound to happen. There was an inevitability about the whole situation. The belligerent demands of 'Herr Hitler', and the frankly pitiful attempts of the compromisers to defuse the growing explosive nature of the times, were nothing more than diplomatic ruses to gain a little more time for the far-too-long delayed decision to make effective defensive preparations to be put into effect. Everyone knew that 'peace in our time' had failed even for us children at school, we were not permitted to be unaware. Daily, we were given instructions about what to do when the 'warning' sirens sounded. Everybody must be kept calm and do exactly what the teacher tells you. Most schools were provided with either shelter trenches dug in the playgrounds, or reinforced ground floor classrooms with bricked up windows and strong wooden beams to protect against structural collapse. There were daily gas mask practices. One was instructed to carry it wherever we went, to know where it was at all times... in fact, never let it out of sight. Not only these significant matters of the worsening situation were brought to our attention. Having returned to school after a weekend, we found that the school playground had been taken over by several R.A.F. blue lorries. Huts had suddenly appeared, and mysterious enclosures formed by stacked sandbagged walls. The ground littered with boxes and bales, and all the other paraphernalia of a military nature. Blue uniformed

R.A.F. men unpacking a huge canvas covered roll of whatever it was. Teachers seemed surprised by this unaccustomed intrusion into the normal daily routines, just as we were. The very idea that any semblance of order and routine was going to be regained, was for the moment suspended until the excitements of these strange activities had diminished and some sort of lesson routine established. I clearly remember the desperate attempt to get some mental arithmetic going and the teacher asking the class, "How much does a tuppeny bar of chocolate cost"? And putting my hand up to answer it when suddenly pandemonium broke out with a teacher shouting, "Everybody under the desks. Quickly". The classroom suddenly darkened and loud shouting's of panic came from the playground, and a moment of chaos and screaming children, and shouting teacher... bouncing against the windows was a huge, bloated silver barrage balloon. The panic of course, was that the balloon was filled with highly inflammable hydrogen gas and likely to burst into a ball of flames engulfing the school and in particular, the classroom we were in. The balloon operators had inflated the balloon for a trial run and had not taken a slight breeze into consideration and consequently had lost control of it. The consequences of what could and what might have happened is unthinkable. We might have been the first casualties of the war, as yet undeclared. They managed to get it under control eventually and also, better organised whenever the permanently inflated balloon was allowed to rise during 'practices', against the day when they would have to let it rise in earnest in defence against low flying enemy aircraft. Usually, the officer in command let the school know when these practices were to take place, in which event, we had to evacuate the classrooms overlooking the playgrounds. As I recollect, it turned out to be a regular daily event, not only when it was going up, but also when it was being hauled in.

The balloon was always kept in a state of inflated readiness. Inflated and tethered, constantly bouncing around on its restraining tethers like some huge, bloated silver whale. I liked to watch it from the classroom windows when I should have been concentrating on all that boring stuff, like lessons. Fascinated by its rhythmic swaying, bobbing, and bowing in the lightest movement of air, its air deflated tail fins hanging limp at its stern like a whipped spaniels tail tucked between its legs. More and more frequently we had air raid drills. We had not yet been subjected to those stomach churning wavering howls of the air raid warning sirens. In the meantime, the head used his loud hand bell, and to make sure that everybody understood its meaning, he also used a shrill police whistle. At the first clarion clang and the screech of the whistle, everything stopped. We had been daily instructed in what to do and how we should form calm and tidy ranks but quickly in the gaps between the rows of desks, the nearest rank to the classroom door, left first, followed by the second and the third, passing through the door in single file. It worked perfectly in practice. Fortunately, we never had to do it in an emergency. It might have been a different story. We would be marched down to a ground floor classroom that had been reinforced as a shelter. Thus installed, we stood in tidy ranks and counted off against the register to ensure there were no missing stragglers. On the command… "Gas masks on"… woe betide anyone who had left it in the classroom, or worse, forgotten to bring it to school, or just lost it. We had to carry that ubiquitous cardboard box and its contents everywhere we went.   EVERYWHERE!

The news was getting worse by the day. There were too many who remembered the carnage of the first great war and were in no mood for another blood-letting. The frightening images on news reels and in the daily newspapers of the Spanish conflict, and the horrific prospects of an aerial warfare and the alarming predictions… 'The bomber will always get through', bolstered as it was by the German propaganda of the might and the technical superiority of the Luftwaffe bomber and the sheer numbers of them ranged against us. The stark warning 'The bomber will always get through', could not be ignored.

Pop and brother 'Ern' decided they ought to provide us with a secure cellar shelter. The main problem was that Halls Dining Rooms at 92 Upton Lane did not have a cellar, but the fish and chip shop over the road where the Empress Teutonic mum lived in state, did. Permission was duly sought and granted. The Empress would have none of it because there wasn't going to be a war. "Hitler", she declared, "Would not risk such a thing". She insisted that, "There were such wonderful things happening in Germany". "There would be too much at stake to lose everything that had been gained". "It's a great pity that the warmongers don't follow their example", etc., etc., etc. Without being too picky about it, there was a little too much Nazi sympathy sloshing about in that quarter. The Teutonic Empress lost no opportunity to preach the Nazi gospel, even to such a soft target such as little innocent me. "Well mum", Pop dutifully said. "Perhaps there won't be a war, but it makes sense to be prepared in case there is". "Well, alright then", said she, with an air of patient resignation. "If only people would take notice of me, but don't expect me to sleep in a damp and dirty cellar for no good reason", and that was the final word from her except for a mumbled and very audible protest now and again.

Once this reluctant permission had been granted, the first problem was to decide the best way to construct a secure and safe cellar shelter. The real business of the how's, and with what materials, were gone into with a degree of professionalism that had no idea of how to build a safe and secure cellar shelter. Anyway, the decision was made to use sandbags and stout timber shorings. Measurements and rough drawings were made, and calculations entered into. How many bags and how much sand? Next, the problem of getting either the sand, or the filled sandbags down into the cellar. Finally, the sand was ordered and the timber joists. Umpteen dozen or so cubic yards of soft sand delivered and tipped half onto the narrow pavement and the other half onto the busy roadway to the extreme annoyance of the pedestrians, and a traffic jam stretching back half a mile to the utter disgust of trolly bus drivers and their passengers. In other words, an extreme annoyance to everybody. As well as the sand there was what looked like a brown mountain of jute sandbags to be filled. Conveniently, there was a coal chute on the pavement (which had been part of the plan anyway) and a couple of willing hands who had been offered a few 'bob' for a couple of hours shovelling and filling the jute sandbags to be transferred into the cellar down the coal chute. In the end, the project took a few weeks to complete which included a couple of benches that could double as beds. Emergency stores, a paraffin stove, and a kettle for same, paraffin lamps and candles. Bottles of water, tins of evaporated milk, sugar, and biscuits to allow for the necessary cup of tea.

Nobody had dared to envisage the possibility of being entombed under a collapsed fish and chip shop... if they had not, I certainly did, and shivered at the prospect. Nobody expressed the risk verbally. It couldn't really happen... could it? I was none too sure that it felt as safe as it was thought. The shelter was eventually finished and ready for any emergency. A splendid example. Luxury set up for relative comfort and every contingency.

As far as I know, the shelter was never used by any of us. Soon after it was finished the Empress fell and broke her hip, shaken and screaming in pain she was taken to hospital and thereafter, never returned to her flat. I was told years later that the shelter had been used by the new tenants during the blitz, so perhaps all the planning and the hard work might not have been wasted.

What I do know for certain, is that the fish and chip shop was totally destroyed during the blitz and at the time of writing there is still an open and empty space in Upton Lane where it stood (see drawing), so perhaps for the sake of future archaeological information, this must stand as the explanation for all that sand. In any case, the situation that had existed warranted the precaution. At the time, there had been a grim sense of foreboding and fear of the future. Austria had been annexed. Czechoslovakia had succumbed and fallen under the Nazi jackboot and now Poland was threatened over the question of the Danzig corridor. The news coming out of Germany itself told of terrifying events and Nazi brutalities.

There was talk at school about the possibilities and that arrangement for the evacuation of the children could be imminent. Parents had been warned. The newspapers were advising them to consider the good sense of sending the children to places of safety. Pop and the 'misses' had been informed that the school was organising and planning for the mass evacuation of the whole school in advance of such an eventuality taking place and wanted to know how many children would be involved. All this kind of preparation was going on at every school in the affected areas of danger for months before war was actually declared. I was consequently asked whether I would like to go? I said that I didn't mind. I was reminded that I would be with all my school friends and if I didn't like it I could come home... and maybe it wouldn't be as bad as people feared it might be.

Suddenly, it all came about in such a way that to this very day, I have very unclear recollections of how it did come about. Vaguely remembering that I went to school on what must have been the appointed day with a small suitcase and the ubiquitous gas mask in its cardboard box, and a short trip to Stratford station on a London Transport red bus, a fairly clear memory of a steam train compartment filled to capacity with my Upton Lane School contemporaries, who to this very day remain as shadowy figures of a dreamlike unreality. I cannot recall one single name or fix one single face in my memory. It's as if they never existed. It is probably a case of neither do I to them.

I had absolutely no idea where we were heading and neither did any one of my temporary companions in our compartment. To all intents it might be said that we were all alone with our own thoughts and our own futures. In fact, the whole episode of the journey has somehow vanished from my memory with the exception of those shadowy recollections already described. Consequently, I have absolutely no idea where that particular part of the journey terminated or for that matter, how I came to finish up where I did. I know now, as I suppose I knew then, that I had somehow arrived at a little backwater cum village or community called Tunstead, Norfolk, nor for that matter, how it was that I had been mysteriously allocated to a billet with another boy of about my own age who might have been a member of the Upton Lane School party, and he might not have been, with a small family of a couple and a small child of about three years old (gender unknown), who lived in a group of 4/5 red brick cottages that seem now to have been a thousand miles from anywhere, and about as close to nowhere as I could ever possibly describe, apart from a terrace of 4/5 two-up and two-down Victorian industrial/farm workers cottages set at a right angle to a narrow road, to which I am unaware whether it led anywhere other than straight into the Norfolk Broads.

A recent search via old maps and Google, as well as an extensive visit to the area, have finally revealed the whereabouts of these cottages. The best way for me to illustrate my impressions is to offer a description dictated more by recollection than by fact and hope for the best result.

I do remember clearly that the cottages shared a joint access to their rear formed by a kind of wide yard/pathway. Each cottage had its own 'outside privy' and dilapidated 'wash house' reached across the communal access. There were gardens-cum-allotments set on a field on the other side of the road, hedged and gated, on a slight incline formed in long traditional East Anglian farming 'pightle' strips. At the top of the incline there was a well (the only source of water to the cottages). I remember it particularly because it became a daily chore for myself and my fellow companion evacuee in grief, to draw the daily two full buckets of ice cold water. It also reminded me of the old nursery rhyme 'Jack and Jill went up the hill to fetch a pail of water'. I could never manage a full bucket and usually lost half of it on the way back only to be sent back again for another to make up for the deficiency. It was a daily routine for everyone to draw the days needs for water. A routine that always occurred at the same time, arranged this way presumably as the house ladies means of distributing local gossip and the current scandal and other equally important matters of public concern. Most times, we... that is myself and my un-nameable companion evacuee in grief, had to wait our turn at the well handle and roped bucket, and usually not until everyone else had hauled, gossiped, and filled and departed the scene, filled also with the pleasing satisfaction of disgust, or contempt of the alleged doings of Mr X, or Mrs Y. This was something that I remember very well because I had a very distinct feeling of 'us' being the object of sidelong glances and the whispered conversations. Lots of ex-evacuees I have spoken to over the years have expressed the very same feelings of their experiences, who had been regarded as the unwelcome, the unwanted, unwashed, flea ridden city kids of predictably doubtful character.... Incidentally, there is no doubt at all, that there were the unwashed and the flea ridden of doubtful character, and I dare to say, the great unwanted too. Sometimes, the local children were no different from their parents in this respect.

I was once sent to a local farm close by with a can for milk. On the way there I passed a group of local rascals playing in a roadside coppice. I was followed on my way by the threatening shouts of, "Go home you dirty pigs. You're eatin' all our grub", and such like. One or two stones followed their frightening words. Fortunately, they were not there on my way back. I suppose it was something to do with a country isolation and a distrust of city ways and 'townies like me'. As for 'eatin' all their grub', it certainly didn't feel like it to me. We were never allowed into the house during the days (the schools incidentally were closed for the summer holidays), so there were a lot of days out of doors for us including the weekends, but provision was made for the probable event of rain and thunderstorm. We could shelter in the old, dilapidated washhouse. I think the husband did a bit of nightwork as the local poacher... Around the whitewashed walls (or rather the one time whitewashed walls) mostly dripping with fresh blood, were any number of pheasants, hares, rabbits, and pigeons. There must have been a fairly constant movement of game because they were never the same ones from day to day. It couldn't have all been down to household consumption either. If it was, we never saw any of it, or tasted a morsel. I think the little family must have fared quite well though, although I shall never know for certain because there was never an occasion when we sat at table with them to find out. We had to fit in with an arrangement that functioned very well and very economically for the household budget. At mealtimes we would be called into the house to finish off what was left on the table after they had had their fill... and there was never very much left for us. It was also obvious that even the scrapings off their plates had been collected together with a few cooling items of whatever the meal had been. From my point of view, it was only sheer hunger that drove us to eat what was on offer. The same system applied to every meal. At breakfast, when the husband had left for work and the little innocent had been fed and was satisfied, there was the cold toast and a spoonful of marmalade on a saucer. Small portions of cornflakes and barely enough milk to moisten them left in the jug. The last dregs of tea left in the tea pot warmed up by a dash too many infusions from the kettle on the hob, spoiled any illusion of tea in the cup.

At the end of the day... the wonder of wonders. I don't know how the allocation of evacuee billeting had been organised, or what checks, or inspections of foster homes had been carried out? The simple fact has to be that no such checks or inspections could have been undertaken at that very special billet that I and my fellow evacuee in grief had had the good fortune to end up with. Probably, the principal was that Mr and Mrs so-and-so, had a spare room. The only drawback was that it was all there was because there was not a stick of furniture in it.

Not a trace of floor covering, but bare knobbly boards and a window naked of decency by any kind of curtains. We had been provided with a couple of skimpy blankets and the bare boards to sleep on... added to which insult, we were constantly hungry and reduced to stealing raw carrots and anything that seemed edible from the cottage allotments.

I wrote home asking the 'misses' to send us some food because we were hungry. I got a reply very quickly in the shape of mum herself on a surprise visit. The house lady was VERY surprised (and very confused). "Oh, hello Mrs Insole. How nice to meet you, I'll make some tea, and will you have something to eat with it"?... "No, thank you", said mum. "John and I are just going to go for a little walk". "Now", she asked me when we were alone, "What's this all about? I want to know why you are hungry. I want you to tell me about everything". I explained about how we only got to eat what was left on their table. How we pinched apples and carrots because we were hungry. I explained about the sleeping arrangements. "Well," she said, "You will soon be getting something to eat but we have something to do first". It wasn't a very long walk. "Right", said mum, "We will go back now".

When we returned, Mrs house lady had carefully prepared a tray of tea things and laid out some cakes and bread and butter. "I could boil an egg for you if you would like it", she asked. "No, thank you", said mum. "I would like to see where John sleeps first".

There was a definite flurry of confusion on the face of Mrs house lady and her uttered apologies for what she knew of, "Where John sleeps", and what mum was bound to discover. "Ar, well we are waiting, and it will be coming soon when we can arrange...". Mum cut her short. "I want to see where he sleeps please". Mrs house lady had no choice but to comply with the request. I sat and waited downstairs, eyes glued on the provisions waiting to be consumed and dared not to touch any of it.

They came down, mum grim faced. House lady uttering her red-faced apologies. Mum wasted no time on ceremony. "Pack his bag this minute". "Here, Johnnie, eat those cakes and bread and butter". The house lady, still confused, tried to explain again. "Some of his clothes are in the wash". "Then put them in wet" retorted mum. "We will wait". The suitcase packed, and we were ready to leave. Mum was not done with it yet. There was still something to do… and she waited for the right moment to do it.

"John has told me all about the treatment he has had to put up with here. I see you have a little (girl?). I wonder how you would feel if some cruel stranger had treated her as you have treated him. What would you think? What would you do? I expect you would do what I am just about to do to you. The lady stood open mouthed and un-protesting, shakily excusing herself… "My husband…", but she didn't finish what she was intending to say. My mother's hand flashed across her face and met her open mouth. I remember the hollow 'plop' as it struck her. Mum withdrew her hand, clenched her fist, and flew at her. Her enraged fist landed, and the lady dropped to the floor… "Now", said mum, "I expect you will report me to the police. If you do, I will see to it that your name in these parts is mud. Never mind you reporting me. I shall see to it that you will never have another evacuee. I shall make it my business to report you and your husband to the billeting office and every other authority I can think of". With that, we strode out into the road and shook the dust of Tunstead off of our feet.

I often wondered what happened to my 'partner in grief'. I expect he was removed soon after. He might even have come home like so many others like me. In hindsight, it is perhaps appropriate to mention the one constant memory of bad memories associated with what had been an altogether bad experience… the declaration of war.

I heard it the very first time it was announced. The Prime Minister was due to speak to the nation on the 'wireless'. Everybody waited to hear what he had to say. I think everybody knew what it was going to be. His words when he spoke, confirmed their worst fears. "I have to tell you; a state of war exists between the United Kingdom and Germany". The 'Empress' had been wrong. Building the cellar shelter had been right. Suddenly, barely minutes after the radio announcement, as I stood outside in the rear yards, I heard for the very first time that stomach churning air raid warning's mournful waves of high and low wavering howl, coming from somewhere in the middle distance.

At the end of the common right-of-way at the rear of the cottages, there was a hedge, and in a gap overlooking the fields beyond there was a compost heap or a general rubbish dump... a kind of 'midden' in lieu of dustbins. I ran to the gap and climbed up onto the heap as the siren's warning was fading away in a low moan (and yet still barely heard). I thought I might see the expected advancing ranks of attacking German squadrons coming to blow us all to smithereens... there was nothing to be seen. Maybe it had only been the reckless foolishness of childhood to be so fearless of unknown dangers. A curiosity driven on by the fascination of indefinable horror??

Somebody saw me standing on the top of the heap and shouted to me. "Come in... quickly. The war... the war has started", and he feared that the anticipated destruction, death and the danger was about to begin. "Come in. Come in quickly and be safe". Apparently the air raid warnings were sounded everywhere. Nobody knows why. Somebody at the War Ministry had probably pressed the wrong button in his panic, or just excitement.

Once again I have to reluctantly admit that I have absolutely no recollection of the journey back to Forest Gate beyond a vague image of a coach trip from somewhere or other, equally lost in that 'black-hole' of forgetfulness. It seems that the whole experience of the pre-war evacuation from Upton Lane School has been somehow compressed into a narrow band of memory concentrated around those four or five terraced farm workers cottages and extending no more than a few hundred yards around them, almost like a stage on which was enacted a play of the life and the images of a past age, a glimpse of which I was merely a brief spectator.

Even in the 1930s and in the terms of social progress generally of those times, and the virtual 'dead-end' isolation of Tunstead and its people, were apparently still linked inseparably to the umbilical cord of its rural past. Therefore, it is no surprise to me to understand how it was that the event must have seemed to them like an alien invasion and a virtual occupation by enemy foreigners, the evacuation was impossible for them to cope with. Like the children themselves who were convinced that I was robbing them of their food. For their parents, it was a disturbance that was threatening to destroy what was (and always had been), a too finely balanced social order governed by the oppressive dictates of the rhythms of the land, the rising sun, and its setting. The church and the gentry. They rose in the morning at daybreak and went to bed at sunset. They ate off the land and drew their water from out of its depths. Rarely left it or travelled any great distance away from it. London was a world apart and impossible to imagine.

Many years later I was asked by an elderly very rural Suffolk lady (long since gone to be with her ancestors) of about the same generation, or maybe before my Tunstead period, "You come from London don't you", she asked. "Yes", I said. "I have a cousin who lives there", she explained, and went on to tell me, "They have a shop in the High Street. You must know them"... And this, in a nutshell, is exactly what I mean about Tunstead. My conversation with the lady took place fifty-five years after I had left it behind me.

I had returned to Forest Gate no more than half a dozen weeks after I had left it, and yet somehow the whole world had changed in that short period. Forest Gate of course, was still Forest Gate but in those early days of the war and during the still great uncertain pause of its realisation when it had dawned on everybody that what had been expected to happen didn't, and what might happen now, nobody knew?

Whatever that turned out to be, the urgency was that everybody and everything should be ready and prepared for the worst. The general 'blackout' had come into effect. Streetlights switched off. Bands of white paint appearing everywhere wrapped around lamp posts and telegraph poles. Edges of curbs and steps whitened. Windows everywhere crisscrossed with brown gummed paper strips. Car and bus lights and lighting (even the traffic lights) dimmed to meet the blackout regulations. Sandbags everywhere stacked against important buildings. Wardens' posts established. Shelters being built in the streets. Police, steel helmeted and gas mask packs. The bus and train windows covered with a heavy white mesh leaving a tiny diamond square or circle of clear glass in their centres to see out of to check where one was, or whether one had missed the stop several stations ago.

The mobilisation and call up. First to go were the young men, 18-29. Sons and brothers mainly. Friends and sweethearts maybe. The marriages will have to wait (if they ever happened at all). Wartime regulations issued and devised, and the news... none of it good... all of it conducted in a sort of grim-faced sweaty excitement. A kind of atmosphere of anticipation and of the unknown that even I managed to feel. The apparent urgencies together with what is now known as the 'phoney war', produced an atmosphere of total unreality over everything.

Something that was exaggerated to a large extent for me by the unusual fact that Upton Lane School was closed. Every school was closed throughout the whole of the London area, presumably because so many children (and their teachers) had been evacuated in the first pre-war 1939 evacuation which meant the schools would not be worth opening for the few children left. It was actually very much like the day after the 'Pied Piper' had visited. However, arrangements were put in place by the relevant and the apparently still functioning L.C.C, or Essex County Council educational authorities to provide some sort of makeshift semblance of schooling by setting up classrooms (for the few) in private houses.

In my case, I was pleased to find out that the Moss' next door had agreed to offer their sitting room on the first floor 'over the shop' for this purpose. Not only was it to happen next door, but I should have Derek with me too. It made it a little easier to cope with. In some ways it was also a disadvantage in the sense that it was too personalised to be useful. It merely represented an extension of a playground for us. In any case, I think he stood too firmly on his right of possession, and nobody was going to tell him what he should or should not do in his own home... I naturally followed his lead. Not that it made any difference in the quality and educational value of the facility, or that any one of the half dozen or so other fortunates gained anything from it (I think it was most likely very much on the loss side for us all). For one thing, it was never established on a regular basis of school time normality. At best it might have been an hour or two in the morning. Maybe starting at nine o'clock... and maybe not. Maybe Monday or Tuesday... or perhaps three mornings, or four, a week. Never five. We might start at nine or ten, or not at all. Never afternoons. Even if we did start 'something', there were never anything like text or exercise books, just a few bits of scrappy paper and broken point pencils and nothing to sharpen them with. The teacher (for want of a better description) was not really qualified beyond the basic requirement of being able to read and write. Anyone who might have gained a school leaving certificate of the three R's sometime in the eighteen hundreds; and it seemed to me those generally no younger than ninety were deemed qualified enough to teach (if they could remain awake long enough). I should not seem to be too unkind though because as I understand it now, it was all a voluntary and public spirited effort on their part even though we did not exactly see it in that worthy light at the time.

There might even have been a distinct feeling abroad that whatever benefit there might have been in this effort, it would all be a waste of time anyway...The news was getting worse by the day... The waiting and the 'phoney' war had ended.

Europe fell under the Nazi jackboot... The Battle of Britain was about to begin.

Chapter 22

The Mass Evacuation – "Where's a to 'en" – 1940 – Camborne, Cornwall.

Mum said to me, "Your dad has suggested that you should be evacuated with Lily. Do you want to go with her"? As if she needed to ask. Lily and I had not seen each other since that fateful day in Dagenham… How I had missed her and Big Gran Insole and Grandad, and especially Wapping. Dark and mysterious Wapping, nestling close up to the Tower and Tower Bridge… How I had missed the teeming river Thames and the humming docks, cranes, and the lorries, some of them steam driven, solid tyred, leaving a trail of steam and acrid smoke behind them as they went. The big canvas covered waggons drawn by the huge 'shires', steel tyred wheels. Sparkling horseshoes struck from the granite cobbled streets. Dark narrow streets winding between the massive riverside wharves. The noise and the men… Ships sirens as they departed downstream on the swift ebb tides… Tugboats and red sailed Thames barges… My aunts, uncles, and cousins too. As if I wouldn't have wanted to be evacuated with sister Lily. I would have risked the gates of Hades itself to go with her. "When"? I asked. "When are we going? Who are we going with"? Of course, she couldn't answer any of my anxious questions. "I don't know", she said. "We shall just have to wait until your dad lets us know. Maybe it will be tomorrow. Maybe it will be next week. We shall just have to be ready".

Correctly, dad had decided that if it was thought to be urgently necessary to undertake such an extensive and complete evacuation of the children, then it must be that the dangers were extreme. In any case, the news was getting worse by the day. A German invasion was thought to be imminent… Therefore, it was only right that Lily and I should be together.

Nobody at those times could know what those dangers could mean. Perhaps there might be an invasion? Certainly, heavy air raids. Everybody had been issued with a gas mask. Maybe mass gas attacks? Anything was possible. A ban had been imposed on the ringing of church bells. In the event of an invasion, the bells would ring out the general alarm. Local defence forces were being mobilised. A.R.P. wardens manned the 'wardens' posts'. The local defence forces organised 'Home Guard' (which later became Dad's Army). The nation was gearing itself up for a long hard struggle.

Winston Churchill's stirring words rang out loudly. No one could mistake their meaning… He only promised, "Blood, sweat, toil and tears". "We will fight on the beaches, in the streets", etc., etc. "We will never surrender". No one could begin to imagine what this might mean. Perhaps thousands of deaths. Perhaps hundreds of thousands. Thousands of homeless. Thousands of orphans? Such things happened in Poland and Czechoslovakia. To France and Belgium, the Nazi juggernaut had swept over Norway, Holland, and Denmark. All under the Nazi heel. The big question on everyone's lips… What if? Could we suffer the same fate?

Daily we had listened to the news reports. Battles had been lost. There had been the retreats, the defeats. People openly spoke of 'compromise', 'give up', 'make terms'. 'Let them have Europe then leave us alone', but the general will, was to fight on. Never surrender. 'The Hun' was getting too big for his jackboots again, he has to be cut down to size. As Churchill reminded us, and the free world, "If the British Empire were to last a thousand years…" (it was not to last another twenty) "…this will be their finest hour".

Hopping in the 1930s. The huts at Paddock Wood.

Big Gran and great aunt Daisy, picking hops at the bin,
Paddock Wood, Kent in the 1930s.

"Hoi, Wotcher Doin' 'Ere?"

Aunt Rose, uncle Harry 'French' and Big Gran having a Sunday tea break at the huts, 1940s.

On Sundays, the cockle man came round.

Watney St. Market. 1968 (c.Tower Hamlets).

Original Turks Head pub Hermitage – destroyed in the Blitz 1940.

Big Gran and Grandad on a pub crawl.

Winchelsea, July 1938.

Winchelsea, Little Gran acting as Mrs Mop, ITMA.

Winchelsea, Little Gran – acting as itinerant preacher.

Hall's Dining Rooms showing the Blitz boarded up shop front, 1940.

Marler's Farm, Tunstead, Norfolk.

Marler's Farm,
Tunstead.

Brewhouse Lane School destroyed in the Blitz 1940.

Evacuation 1940. Elmhurst at Treswithian Downs, Cornwall.

Back yard and privvy at Elmhurst, 1940.

The Battle of Britain would be fought over the channel and the fields of Kent and Essex... Biggin Hill attacked. Hornchurch, Debden, and all the other front line fighter airfields... 15 German aircraft reported destroyed, eight damaged and six possible. Our own losses said to be seven... We would all want to believe it... but...??

Better that Lily and I should be together. Against all events, whatever they turned out to be, we should have each other.

Mr and Mrs Moss next door had also suggested that as they were planning to evacuate to a family cottage in Brentwood, it might be better that I should go with them. Derek and I would be good company for each other. I was asked and would not decide right away. My answer was left until the very last minute on the eve of their next day's departure. I wanted to go with Lily.

How long I waited for dad to call. I can't remember any more than I wondered whether he had forgotten me, and that she had left without me. They were anxious days. Waiting... just waiting. I was in a whirl of nervous anticipation. 'When is he going to call'? Meanwhile, mum had bought a fancy new backpack and had put together all the listed items. A new comb. A new hairbrush. New, this and new that. She, "Wasn't...", she said, "... going to send me away looking like a tramp". What she did not know or understand was that I hated the whole idea of overindulgence obviously to create an image of what I thought to be too much on the side of 'posh', especially centred around her choice of those childlike blouse like shirts with elasticated waistbands. The pair of carpet slippers with button over straps and stupid bobbles on the toes. All very childish when I thought that the times and the troubles meant that we had to be 'strong, adult, masculine and brave'. How I despised the fancy new sponge bag with its blue ribbon drawstring and new bar of 'pongy' soap wrapped in a new 'fluffy' face flannel. Thinking about it, it couldn't have been easy for her knowing how things had gone with the Tunstead situation but at least I suppose she must have decided… this time wherever we finished up, Lily would be with me. I would not be alone.

A few minutes ago, dad phoned. "Tomorrow morning…", he said, "… if Johnnie can be ready by 7:30am at the latest, his 'Gran' will come to collect him". There was no time to chat. It was arranged that I should meet 'Big Gran' Insole at the bus stop at the top of Upton Lane at The Princess Alice. "He has to be at Brewhouse Lane School (in Wapping) no later than 8:30am". There was not much sleep for me on that night. I was up at four… or was it three? "Not yet" mum said. "Go back to bed".

I sat on my bed and waited impatiently for the right time to get up. Trying the weight of the new backpack, newly packed. Getting dressed and undressed again. I slipped that awful spongebag under the mattress… I wonder what she said when she found it. She never said. I thought the night would never end.

I went to the top of Upton Lane just before 7am on my own. I wouldn't have anyone else go with me. I knew that this was going to be a tearful reunion. She was waiting at the bus stop. "How you've grown", she said as she wiped her eyes. I didn't think I had grown at all so it was obvious that she could not see me very well. She didn't say very much either just then. She explained, "I have got a frog in me throat. Anyway, we 'ave to hurry else we'll get there too late". It seemed to me as if the bus would never come.

We were only just in time. Arriving at Brewhouse Lane School with just enough time for quick hello's and a hasty hug and a hasty kiss. My name included onto a register. A label written out and tied onto my lapel. Children were milling around everywhere, it all seemed to be in an excited and utter confusion. Teachers trying to muster their charges into tidy ranks and a registration called, then lined up in the street. At last, all seems to be in order, and everyone accounted for. "Off we go now. Heads up everyone. Let's have no tears… not yet anyway".

Wapping children did not cry... and we were off to fight the war all on our own.

Parents had been advised, in fact, it had been forbidden to see their children off either at the schools of departure, or at the stations because it was recognised that tearful farewells would be too upsetting for both the parents and the children. (Probably more so for the parents than their mystified children).

A tidy march from Brewhouse Lane School to Wapping underground station, no more than a hundred meters distance, and then a confused and chaotic tumble down the station stairs to the platforms and the special underground train waiting there to take us to Paddington Station. Nobody could tell us where we would be going from there. Nobody knew. For most of us, Paddington station would have been quite far enough and a good deal further than a good many had been in our whole lives before. It was the last time that many of us saw Brewhouse Lane School again other than as a pile of rubble. Soon after our departure the school was destroyed in the blitz. Coincidentally, also, Upton Lane School was severely damaged but then so were dozens and dozens of other London schools, either damaged, or totally destroyed.

I lost Lily somewhere on the trip to Paddington. She was on the train with her friends. Somehow, I suddenly felt as if I didn't really belong to the group... I didn't know anybody. It had been such a long time ago. Wapping ought to have been no more than a distant unforgettable memory for me. Lily had grown up. I hardly recognised her and anyway, it had all been a long time ago. A little girl took my hand, looked up at me and said, "I'm five an' I've lost me sister". She had taken my hand for safety and protection. Goodness only knew, I felt as if I needed protecting myself, but I was nine years old and had to be very brave and manly. My little lost and trusting companion held my hand very tightly. We comforted each other. "Don' tell me sister", she whispered. "I couldn't 'elp it. I has wet me knickers"! I blushed for her and kept her secret. She was eventually reunited with her sister (as I was too) and gathered into her family fold. Her busy worried mother for the duration... big sister... all of eight or nine years old on strict instructions, "Jest yew look after little sis, don' yew let 'er out of your sight. Hold on ter her very tight"... and probably brother too, and everyone else who wanted looking after... and I expect that she did.

The underground train rattled on its way through the underground tunnels on its lumbering way to Paddington station.

Paddington station was packed solid with children and their teachers arranged in school groups on the concourse. There was no public passenger for several hours in the mornings in order to get as many evacuation trains away as quickly as possible... thousands of children (amazingly quieter than one would expect a thousand excited children to be). Just a low murmur and the clear voices of the accompanying teachers issuing instruction or chastising the recalcitrant and the reluctant to comply. I think that we were all mostly too far subdued to chatter or step out of line. The sounds of shuffling feet. Normal big station sounds. Hissing steam and the smell of smoke. Trains arriving empty, squealing wheels echoing loud, gushing steam as a train departed loaded. No panic. No hurry. Everything moving quietly and orderly just like carrying out the normal school routines and disciplines.

Trains standing at the platforms. All sorts of carriages made up into endless trains of twelve and fourteen coaches. Brown ones, cream liveried, green ones and red. All kinds of shapes and colours drawn from every region of the national network. Some so evidently dilapidated that they were little better than scrap but pressed into service in order to get the kids away and out of danger quickly.

The nearest group to ours as we stood in line on the concourse waiting for instructions was a distraught and screaming boy hanging onto his equally distraught mother who had evidently ignored the instruction to stay away from the station. A furious evacuation official telling her loudly and angrily, "Get that stupid child home mother, and get yourself home as well. You stupid woman. You're upsetting everybody"… and that was the end of his evacuation experience. You would not catch a Wapping boy grizzling like that. We were tough and brave. After that we felt very confident and superior! Suddenly a station official signalled to us, and we were on the move. "Right", said 'Miss', "Here we go children. Pick up everything". "Now everybody, keep together… keep together. Follow me… follow me". "Quickly now", to the stragglers.

Our instructions were to go to the first two coaches of the train on platform one. Just what we expected, Wapping kids were always up in front! The march from the concourse and along platform one seemed endless. I counted as I went along… one, two, three, four… eleven, twelve. Thirteen and fourteen were the first two coaches. Number fourteen was the first coach behind the steaming engine. It sounded to me as if it were vibrating in its pent up restraint ready to haul us to goodness knows where. All aboard in an excited rush to sort ourselves out. Friends separated and desperate to be with each other. A chaotic few minutes in and out of compartments up and down the corridor accompanied by disputes over who should sit where. 'Miss' shouting to be heard above the chaos of noise and movement. "Quiet now. Settle down now". Slowly but ultimately, we did settle (for the moment anyway).

We were aboard and into a compartment. The notice over the seat said 'Four Seats'. Four seats each side of the compartment would mean eight persons, but I counted thirteen of us, and then myself, which made fourteen crammed in, but it was alright. I was squeezed into a corner by the corridor door. I didn't mind… Lily sat opposite me. 'Miss' was calling out the names in her register. "Jack"?… "Here". "Harry"?… "Here 'Miss'". I waited for mine to be called and it didn't come. I thought, 'I've been forgotten', perhaps I shouldn't have been here at all. I asked Lily. "What about me then"? "Don't worry", Lily said, but went to ask anyway. "What about my brother Johnnie"? "Oh, dear me", she said. "He isn't on my list" and wrote it in herself. "There", she said. "Now you are here aren't you", and then with evident relief... "We are all here".

There was a little more time to wait before the train was filled. Not a spare space, or a spare seat anywhere. Fourteen coaches and probably a thousand children from a dozen schools. Slowly the train began to move away from the platform. Urgent grunts, straining gushes of high pressure steam, spinning and screaming wheels and little sharp jerks as the tightening couplings took the strain. Coachwork was groaning and creaking. The woof, woof... woof, woof of the engine. We slowly gathered speed. Suddenly, there was a general chorus of questions. "Where are we going 'Miss'"? "I don't know", she answered. "Truly". Some said, "We is goin' ter Scotland". "Nar, we aint", said another. "We is a going ter Wiles", but of course, nobody knew. We suspected that 'Miss' did know but wouldn't tell us. All she would say was, "We shall all have to wait and see". No doubt she was as interested and as curious as we were, and then confused us even more by suggesting that we noted the stations as we passed them by, but all the station name boards had been removed or blacked out so that an invading enemy wouldn't know where he was. We certainly didn't.

The train's progress couldn't be described as fast by any normal stretch of the imagination. After a while, the train made a jerky stop at a station somewhere. It might have been Surrey, or Hampshire, or anywhere. We had no idea where. There were lots of aproned and overalled ladies on the platform handing out drinks of watery squash in enamel mugs and some buns and thick cheese sandwiches. You had to be quick about it or you got nothing. We were told to leave the mugs on the platform to be washed and ready for the next evacuation train and the next, and the next I expect. What a day this was turning out to be and not yet arrived at our mystery destination, and the station clock had said half past one o'clock. I wonder how much further we had to go before arriving wherever we were supposed to be going. On and on we went. More stops and more watery squash. Every time the train stopped at a station it got shorter and shorter as coaches were slipped off the end of the train. At least the coach's passengers knew where they were going even if we didn't.

A shout of excitement went along the train… "The sea". "The sea", and the red cliffs of Devon, but on we went. Plymouth and the 'Sound'… yet another excited shout. "Cor, look at dem ships". Big ships and little ships were scattered over the 'Sound'. Grey ships and black dazzled camouflaged destroyers, cruisers, and frigates. Dozens of war ships bristling with action ready trained guns.

"Brunel's Saltash Bridge", 'Miss' said. "Children, we are now crossing over into Cornwall", but added, "Where in Cornwall we are going, I do not know". One or two stops later there were just two coaches left and the station clock said half past six. 'Miss' said, "We have just passed Redruth", but we did not stop and then the train slowly drew into Camborne station. Suddenly it was "Everybody off the train now, this is as far as it is going. CAMBORNE".

The train had come to rest. The engine seemed to me to be panting to catch its breath. Standing in the cab with enamel mugs in their hands stood the driver and his fireman. Oil stained and Great Western Railway coal and smoke stained, grinning at our bemused and silent group as we were divided into smaller groups. Busses were waiting in the station forecourt to take smaller groups to different schools in the Camborne area. Suddenly, I realised that Lily had been put into a different bus to mine, this wasn't going to do at all. I wasn't going to put up with that… after all those years of separation and having come all this way to be separated yet again on Camborne forecourt. Absolutely not! 'Miss' agreed. "Oh, alright then", and altered her lists.

Lily had boarded the bus that was going to Kehelland. In that case, I was determined to go to Kehelland with her or they could put me back on the next train to Paddington... I went to Kehelland.

There might have been no more than a dozen or so of us out of the Brewhouse Lane School group who finally arrived at Kehelland School. 'Miss' and the other teachers had gone with the larger groups elsewhere and with that, walked out of my life and mind, and I saw them no more.

Waiting for us at the school were the 'reception ladies' who had arranged sandwiches and buns and warm drinks of milk for us. They had also 'rounded up' local people who were willing to take in and 'foster' an evacuee. In the course of a long and weary darkening evening, foster carers came in, in ones and two's, and met and selected those who they would foster. It was all conducted rather like a human form of cattle market. If someone liked the look of 'Tom', or 'Dick', or 'Harriet', then 'Tom', 'Dick' and 'Harriet' were settled in no time at all. All that was needed was to sign the billeting officer's forms. The government will pay ten shillings and sixpence per week (in old money), fifty two and a half pence current values, or nineteen shillings for two (95 pence). "Here is a prepaid postcard to send", to 'Tom's', or 'Dick's', or 'Harriet's' parents, to let them know where they were and that they arrived safely. The address is... etc., etc.

Nobody in any reception area knew who, or how many evacuees would arrive at any particular reception point. It says something about the kind people generally, who took into their homes those little lost urchin souls mostly on complete trust. Even the most angelic looking evacuee could turn out to be awkward at best, or just downright villainous at worst. A few angels amongst them surely sweetened an otherwise reputation for some difficulties. Much has been said about the uncontrollable and unruly side of things and yet there was also the unconsidered side too... the evacuee. Torn as they were, almost in all but name, in a sudden and strange and often frightening way from familiar surroundings. Home, and everything this meant to them, and their security, was lost to them. The child had no way of knowing whether this was to be temporary, or if it might be permanent. Young as most of us were, we knew perfectly well why we had been sent away. We had come to understand the violent nature of war. Not one of us ever lost the unspoken fear that our parents might be killed, and our home destroyed. What would become of us then? Then, there were the strange new ways of the new situations to be coped with and learnt. The whole foreign differences between the rural and the city ways.

In some ways, it could be said that the evacuees had been thrust into 'nearly' orphanage situations. It also says a great deal for the general run of evacuees, that they coped as well as they did!

Slowly as the long evening wore on, fewer and fewer evacuees were left to be fostered until finally there were only two left. Late in the evening and nobody likely to come in, and less likelihood of finding at this late hour a willing fosterer willing to take them in… Lily and me. Nobody could be persuaded to take two evacuees, a brother, and a sister. I was the problem. I would not agree to be separated. I was resolutely determined that I had not come all this way to lose my sister again. It was no use appealing to me by assurances, "Lily will be staying just across the way; you will be seeing her every day". Neither threats nor promises would make me give way in my determination to stay together. Lily might well have been as exasperated as everyone else, and probably wished me anywhere else other than at Kehelland School. "What are we going to do with them"? Was the whispered conversation. "They will have to stay at the school overnight". Camp beds were to be 'gone for', blankets were to be fetched. The discussions were muted, and the questions asked, "Who will stay with them"? "What about breakfast"? And "We will have to sort it out tomorrow. There is nothing to be done for tonight". Names and places were suggested. "I wonder if Mr 'So-and-so' has a spare room"? Or "Mrs

'Thing-a-me'"? Or, "Perhaps Mrs 'Do-dah' might... just for the night"? Johnnie Insole, the cause of all the problems because he would not be separated from his sister, had meanwhile found the empty milk churn stood against the wall in the boys cloakroom. He had wearily sat on its cold shiny lid, leant against the cool cream painted wall, and had fallen fast asleep in spite of the imminent risk of tumbling off of his precarious perch.

Goodness knows where he might have been wandering in his confused and troubled dreams? He probably had some vague idea that he was anywhere else other than sitting on a cold metal lid of a milk churn in the boys cloakroom of the little school in a little Cornish village called Kehelland... a long way away, and a long, long time ago from where and when he had started out hours and hours ago... or was it yesterday? Or, last week? Or last year? Perhaps it was really all a dream, and he would wake up later in his own bed. If only he could think where his own bed might be? A voice was coming through my dreams and a warm hand was shaking my shoulder. "Hello 'en. An' what are we got 'ere"? The voice continued. "What are we got 'ere 'en"? Mr Mitchell, who worked for the Milk Marketing Board at the Treswithian depot, had come to collect the empty milk churn. He had delivered milk earlier in the day for our warm drinks. The problem was explained to him. "Well, Johnnie won't be separated from his sister and we can't find anybody willing to take them both. They will have to stay at the school overnight"... "Nothing we can do about it tonight". "Well," said he. "Then I reckon that they had better come along wi' me then for tonight", and he collected more than an empty churn... and a surprise for Mrs Mitchell when he arrived home with us. Two very tired 'waifs and strays'. So it was, that we found our foster parents, or I suppose it would be more correct to say that _we_ had been found.

Mr & Mrs Mitchell lived at 'Elmhurst', Treswithian Downs, who became Uncle Charlie and Auntie Hilda to us both. (I had no problems with that arrangement)! They had two children of their own,

Rodney and June, both a little younger than me. It turned out to be a tight, happy squeeze, but wonderfully I never noticed it other than the kindness and the understanding shown to us.

"Where's a to 'en"?

The first memorable introduction to the Mitchell family and 'Elmhurst', was late... very late in the evening of the eventful journey from Forest Gate, filled as it was by excitements, curiosities, fears of the unknown, and anxieties for whatever the future would be. It seemed to me at this unaccustomed late hour, to have been so long since I walked to the top of Upton Lane alone to meet 'Big Gran' in complete ignorance of where I should be before the day was through. The excited trip on the bus and then the 'rattler' from Whitechapel to Wapping and Brewhouse Lane School. The noisy chaos of the 'rattler' to Paddington and the long, long haul of the creeping train to Camborne and Kehelland. All this felt like the proverbial 'Month of Sundays', ago to me.

Wearily, Lily and I climbed into the driver's cab of the Milk Marketing Board lorry. There wasn't very much in the way of luggage to transport. It was to be 'Uncle' Charlie's last call to return the empty churn to the depot. How long it had been before I was finally able to descend into forgetful sleep, I don't really know. All these years on, and my recollections only allow me to assume an indefinable period of making those final adjustments to a relaxed state of mind in which sleep would be at all possible. I was probably still in that state of semi-sleep. For all I knew, I might still have been dreaming, draped uncomfortably on the cold shiny lid of the milk churn? Our arrival at 'Elmhurst', certainly caused some disturbance in the usual family routine. (If anything was calculated to thrust me into sudden wakefulness), our unheralded appearance threw everything into a burst of confusion. Neither we, nor the gathered Mitchells, knew quite what to do first. Names to be sorted out... Who was who? What was what? "This is Rodney. This is June". "You had better call us Auntie Hilda and Uncle Charlie. Will that be alright"?... We assented to this sensible arrangement... "Oh yes, that would be nice".

Uncle Charlie was trying to explain why he had brought us home with him. "Just for the night Hilda. I couldn't leave them to spend a night at the old school". "Of course not", Auntie Hilda agreed. There was relief all round. What would have happened if she had not agreed? Be sent back to the old school I supposed?

Rodney was sitting at the living room table, his supper unheeded and mouth agape in bewildered astonishment at this sudden invasion of strangers. June, also eyeing Lily with some trepidation... Is she an enemy, or a friend? Somehow amid the confusion... warm drinks. "Are you hungry dears"? All I really wanted to do was to sleep and just be able to shut my eyes and sink into merciful rest, but they seemed to have a will of their own and refused to stay closed. There was far too much to take in.

The little living room was almost filled by the big kitchen table. The coal range dimly nestling in its chimney recess. The soft warm light of an oil lamp in the centre of the table casting a bright flickering circle of light on the ceiling. Shadows lingering in the corners of the room. The dim red glow of the range fire. A kettle gently steaming on the bright shiny black hob. Glinting sparks of reflected light dancing on the polished points of gleaming brass. Dark looming furniture casting deep shadows around themselves. The walls where the light of the lamp glowed, soft yellow papered. Cotton primrose tinted curtains drawn against the little deep recessed window and the night. The ceiling, low and thinly beamed.

Beds and bedding to be organised. Who was going to sleep where? Sheets to be got out, pillow slips and bed covers piled on a clear space on the kitchen table. Rodney's supper was still untasted, he was never going to eat it now! Auntie Hilda taking a quick look into my backpack.

Lily sorting herself out. "Do you have pyjamas m' dear"? "Ah, yes". The 'jama's nicely new, folded and packed. Then, the new slippers, new and embarrassingly 'bobble toed'. "Ah", said Auntie Hilda. "Take your shoes off and put these on". Those bobble toed abominations were a source of embarrassing shame. I hated them but mum would insist. At the very first opportunity that came my way I was determined that I was either somehow going to lose them or cut the stupid bobbles off. Suddenly, I had a guilty vision of the missing spongebag left under the mattress at home and I worried that there was going to be sent an irate letter on the morrow, complaining that I had been sent away without soap, face-flannel, toothbrush, and toothpaste. Though, being a relatively normal nine year old boy, these deficiencies didn't bother me too much, only a sense of foreboding at the menace of possible punishment for my misdemeanour but for now, all I wanted to do was to sleep.

Candles in white enamelled saucer-like candlesticks were lit to light us up the dark narrow staircase toward bed… Oh, blessed bed! I wouldn't have cared much if it had only been blankets and a bare floor like at Tunstead. I could barely climb the steep stairs. I was to sleep with Rodney in the big high double bed which was squeezed into the tiny middle bedroom (it was more like a big cupboard than a bedroom). (Much later, Auntie Hilda told us that she had no hesitation in making this sleeping arrangement. Her preliminary examination of our possessions had assured her that we were from good homes, and clean).

I climbed wearily up onto the bed barely able to make it unassisted. Cool, soft bed… crisp and sweet-smelling sheets. Rodney wanted to talk, and I desperately struggled to stay awake. "Where's a to 'en"? He asked (meaning where do you live), but I was unable to answer him because I didn't know then what he was asking me. His strange Cornish accent was totally beyond my comprehension. I was blessed with a broad cockney accent, so between us both I did not understand him, neither did he understand me. We giggled over our misunderstanding. I tried hard to fix his question in my mind and work it out what it was he was asking me? "Where's a to 'en'?... "Where's a to..."?... "Too, 'en to...'n'"? Then, happy oblivion, I heard his voice no more, and I fell fast asleep.

When I woke the next morning, I lay for a few moments to gather my senses together, trying to raise sufficient courage to get myself out of bed, collecting my thoughts together in some semblance of order to be able to make firm decisions about what to do next. Should I get up? Should I present myself downstairs? Do I stay where I am and wait until somebody came by and relieved me of having to make the decision for myself? Everything was so quiet. Not a movement. Not a sound that I could identify as an indication that the house was not deserted. For one chilling moment, I imagined that everybody had deliberately left me alone to sort myself out. Silence, except for the songs of birds singing beyond the curtained window and the raucous chatter of flocks of squabbling rooks.

The sun shone through the thin curtain casting a narrow beam across the wall, chasing dancing motes of dust floating up and down the tiny floral pattern of the faded wallpaper as the curtain moved in response to a light waft of air from the open sash. I just had to see what was beyond the window. Slipping carefully off the high bed, backwards, my foot settled onto the brim of the 'gazunder', the ubiquitous night chamber pot, and over it went! Fortunately, it had not been used in the night, so no embarrassing explanations were necessary.

I had no idea what I expected to see beyond the window. I gently pulled aside the curtain. The bedroom faced the front of the house (all the rooms faced the front). At the front of the house there was a long cultivated garden filled with rows of growing vegetables. The garden on the lane side was flanked by a long low wall topped by upstanding granite stones reminding me of the battlements that I had seen atop of my own familiar Tower of London. Low, untidy elm trees barely more than the height of the house lining the field side of the garden, dotted black in constant movement by the arguing rooks.

Beyond the house and the garden there were fields, and beyond those, more fields all around. The very house stood detached and alone amid field beyond fields, bounded by gates and hedges of low grass topped stone walls. Cattle grazing the lush green meadows.

I hadn't known what to expect to see out of the window. Lily and I had come here when it was dark and had seen almost nothing beyond the dim headlights of the lorry. Perhaps there would be darkened blacked-out houses which I was used to, but there were none. Just one barely distinguishable grey slated roof peeping above the height of a distant hedge bearing witness to a habitation, a chimney trailing a thin spiral of smoke barely visible in a morning summer mist. Further off, a smoky smudge and almost imperceptible... I guessed it must be the town of Camborne, the scene of our arrival from Paddington the late evening before, so long ago now (in my mind)... so far away from home!

Somebody was coming up the narrow stairs. The room door slowly opened. "Oh, hello. You are awake then"?... "My, you have slept haven't you". It was Auntie Hilda. I began to stammer out some sort of appropriate reply in apology for my probable failure to wake at the right time. Confusion together with a coordinated 'sorry' for the upset pot and the equally unnecessary explanation for it. "I only wanted to see out of the window", as if I had somehow overstepped the bounds of decency by not asking if I may. She merely smiled at my confusion. "Of course, my dear". I gave up trying and left it all to her reassurance and let her sort me out. "I expect you would like some breakfast"? She asked. "Do you have tea, or milk"? "How about cornflakes"? Taking no notice of my confusion, she simply accepted the obvious fact that I was dumb with shyness. It wasn't shyness, I was practically speechless with the sheer anxiety to do and say the right things. She obligingly sensed how things were for me. "Never mind", she said. "We'll soon get things sorted out for you". "Get dressed now and come down to breakfast. Rodney and June have had theirs. Your sister Lily has gone out for a little while". As she turned to go downstairs she remembered a very important item of concern. "Oh. I expect you will want to go to the lavatory. I'll show you where when you come down". I hadn't really thought about it but now that it had been mentioned I realised that such a visit was long overdue. I wondered where this strange mysterious 'where' should be? In what wonderful secret spot would the usual WC be hidden away? "Yes please", I answered her.

The 'bucket privy' turned out to be 'outside' in the backyard. A little brick built shed-like lean-to set against the house wall, tucked into a corner out of sight behind a little tumbledown extension that served as a scullery type of kitchen, or rather a complement to what would be a kitchen if cooking went on in it. There was no kitchen sink. No piped water or drainage. The annex doubled as domestic storage. Shelves for pots and pans. A cupboard. Whitewashed walls and windowless, but in order to qualify the extensions pretention as a kitchen, stood a narrow table, a 'Champion' oil burning oven and a methylated 'Primus' stove meant to supplement the coal range if needed. On a rickety handmade trestle table outside the match-boarded back door, a small enamel basin. This was the sole household washing facility. It was usually cold water, and a quick dash indoors was always enough for me. Some warm water when it was really cold. I was always asked, "That was quick. Have you washed properly"? Naturally, I always answered that I had!

Auntie Hilda showed me where the 'privy' was and left me to attend to myself and to survey at my own leisure, my new toilet experience. The black painted boarded door which didn't quite fit its intended frame, well and liberally bored with ventilation holes. Quite unnecessary as there was a wide gap at both the bottom and the top of the door. The smooth board seat polished bright by countless generations of constant usage. A hole in it to sit over the 'bucket', far too large for my miniature dimensions. The whitewashed walls, brown, damp stained and flaking. A piece of 'lino' for the feet. The only apology for luxury and comfort was a small square of worn carpet. (It was never intended that one should overextend any unavoidable visit. The privy was not that kind of place. One did what one had to do and left). A bundle of cut squares of newspaper hung on a bit of string nailed to the wall… an essential item of toilet equipage! One could sit and read last year's news at the same time as contemplation. I always came out better informed than when I went in. I especially liked the comic strips from the Daily Mirror.

On this first morning call, long overdue, having finished my normal morning exercises, I felt embarrassed at the usual problem of what I had to do next. Somehow, I felt quite guilty about having to leave undone a usual performance. A habit that had been formed by a year or two of constant practice… I looked for the usual 'chain' and could not find it. Eventually, I gave up the search, but I did come out smelling sweetly of carbolic disinfectant.

School

I was very disappointed to discover eventually, that this evacuation adventure was to be no holiday from the onerous duties of normal school days. The chances are that somewhere down the line, what with the Tunstead and 'no school' then, back to Forest Gate and a part time hour or two of educational opportunities wasted away, I had (and I have no doubt a good many more like me) reached a temporary erroneous conclusion that this 'war evacuation business' was going to turn out to be one long holiday from school. Some lucky children I knew usually went on holidays off to the seaside perhaps. Others might have gone to aunts or grandmas in the countryside. It's true that Auntie Hilda and Uncle Charlie were not 'real' aunt and uncle, but they had said that they were for as long as we stayed at Elmhurst, and by that interesting twist of convoluted reasoning, I considered that we were therefore on holiday!

One morning, just as we had finished breakfast and just as I was thinking that I would like to go out and do a bit more exploring around the local neighbourhood, Auntie Hilda dropped her bombshell which blew all my holiday illusions and expectations to smithereens. Lily, who had been up and about long before me, had already been wandering about around the immediate neighbourhood. As it was explained, "Waiting for me to get up and ready". "You both have to go to the school today to sort things out and get you settled into school". Lily already knew this and was only waiting for me. Uncle Charlie had arranged to take us in his lorry, he would be passing shortly on his collecting rounds picking up milk from the local farms.

The relatively short journey in Uncle C's lorry seemed even shorter than our exhausted trip to 'Elmhurst' on the eve of our arrival at Kehelland. Really, there was no need for a ride in the lorry as Kehelland village and the school were little more than three quarters of a mile distance from Treswithian Downs. In spite of the short distance, it was made to feel further by a delay caused by a herd of cows being driven, as Unc' C' explained, "Bein' drove" from the farm's milking parlour back to their grazing meadow. Nobody seemed to be hurrying. The herdsman did not appear to be at all aware of the looming presence of a large lorry behind him. Whether he was or not, he never bothered to acknowledge the fact. This was so different to the sort of 'hurry up' honk and hooter blare of London streets. "Get out of my way. I'm coming and I want to be gone" syndrome. From my vantage point, I watched in amazement those multiple hindquarters waddling erratically from one side of the narrow lane to the other, sampling the vegetation at one verge and then at the other. Great pendulous udders that I thought were grotesquely out of proportion to the animal, and hind quarters smeared with caked excrement.

From that moment on, if ever I was likely to have an idealised view of cows, it was totally destroyed. If in the future, they were to be viewed by me as objects of natural beauty (the like of natural born tigers for instance), I decided then that the best way to view cows at all was from a distance. Close up, one must agree (albeit a breeder of cows might claim that certain features of the beast could be said to be attractive) however, cows are not generally accepted as the most attractive of nature's natural creatures. Perhaps it is because they are not natural that they are so… well, just ugly! This might be just a matter of my own personal opinions. Beauty will ever be 'within the eye of the beholder', I suppose?

As far as I was concerned, any delay in getting to the school was O.K. with me. I was never too certain about 'school' under any circumstance. The thought of yet another 'new' school to be got used to and to be coped with. New teachers. New people. New children. The whole prospect of new problems thrown up by the inevitable unanswerable questioning. The lies and subterfuges that had been created around my very existence. I had just about learnt to cope with it at Upton Lane School and now yet another 'move on'. So far, my relatively short school career had managed to encompass as many schools as my years in age. I really ought to have been used to a nomadic wandering through the realms of academia by now!

We arrived at last. The teeming playground alive with noisy children at play as only children released from unwilling studies can be. The evacuees of yesterday's arrival stood in a silent group waiting, I discovered, to be registered. We were not going to be given too much time to think about it. As soon as we had been properly and formally documented, we were disposed about the school according to our various age groups. Not, alas, according to size or merit. Mine fell somewhere around the middling to the positively diminutive age, and an academic ability set against my years didn't seem to be in coordination. It didn't matter whether there was a seniority of years on my part, or my juniors. Everybody was bigger than me.

For some inexplicable reason I always found myself positioned in a back row. The advantages this peculiarity gave me was that I could just disappear into its obscurity and still see what I needed to see in a crowd betwixt legs in comfort and security or, I could just melt away into the background. In hindsight, it was never a case of being overly introverted, in essence the opposite is more likely. It is just that I preferred to be left alone. It was my way of dealing with the awkward questions and being trapped into revealing 'the truth'. It was generally better if I managed to keep my own counsel.

During my whole time at Kehelland, this preference to keep myself to myself and at a safe distance from avoidable association was ultimately accepted. My favourite place in the scheme of things was the doorstep of the boys entrance. On it, I felt comfortable so long as I was left alone watching at my self-imposed lonely post. I would frequently join in games and get myself into the usual mischief of a normal boy, it was just that I preferred my 'think post'.

I need not to have worried about getting used to Kehelland School because I soon discovered that there was a certain 'slowness' about a Cornish village school in direct contrast to my usual London experience. For one thing, there were not the vast hordes of energetic children arranged in tiers and disposed throughout a vast number of classrooms on umpteen floors of a monstrous Victorian 'prison-like' structure surrounded by high walls and spiked fences. Everything institutionally hard and virtually sterile of any growing or blossoming thing, including childhood. Overseen by equally over energetic and harassed teachers whose principle objective in school life seemed to be merely to get through the day. Good teachers there certainly were... many good teachers I dare to say, but inevitably all of them must have felt the same overbearing sterility of the schools no less than their pupils would.

The head teacher of Kehelland school taught two classes that were separated by no more than an artificial line drawn from the 'Tortoise' coke stove at the front wall to the back wall. Each class could have been no more than a dozen to fifteen children ranging from five years to tenish, or eleven. More often than not, my own interest was more fully occupied by what was going on, on the other side of the invisible line than it should have been with our own. The headmistress was the soul and meaning of patience with my lack of concentration… sadly her name for the moment escapes me. A tall slim lady of indefinable vintage, certainly adult as I saw her then, but now her image returns to me in the pinkness of youngness. The obligatory teacher type glasses set on a slim pink nose, pink of cheek and lip. Her smile was as pink as it was both comforting and encouraging. She sang well in a slim pink voice as she played the piano. She made an announcement suddenly and startlingly. "We must have a choir, and we will sing carols at Christmas". Considering that we had not yet got further into the year than June or possibly July, it might have been a little premature but a choir she would have. We were accordingly set up in lines like a military parade and whilst we tried to sing some prearranged ditty, the pink lady listened to each of us in turn rejecting the frankly outrageous voices, or otherwise, as the case may be. However, as nobody was rejected but merely reshuffled into something approaching 'far enough away not to be heard', the selection process turned out to be something of a marketing ploy to create a 'must have' desire for an otherwise unwanted intrusion into our private lives.

Sometimes we went home for dinner. Sometimes Uncle Charlie would bring some sandwiches on the day when we stayed at school. Sometimes, and on the special days for me, he would bring hot 'pasties'. Before we left for school in the mornings, I always knew when that special day had arrived because Auntie 'H' had got out her mixing bowl. The vegetables and the meat neatly diced. The range fire stoked and burning brightly to heat the oven. The living room table cleared and ready for the great day. Flour and the dripping for the pastry. Rolling pin and her clean white apron. Potatoes, leeks, and onions fresh from the garden. The turnips or swede and the salt and pepper. Even before the promising ingredients had been put together, I could taste in anticipation the final perfect result. Dinner time would not come quick enough for me. Uncle Charlie would bring them to us smoking hot and straight from the oven... delicious!

* * * * *

If for no other reason other than to create as many problems as possible in the shortest possible time, nature herself began to wreak her own very special brand of havoc amongst the young population. 'Diphtheria'. An ancient scourge of mankind (so rarely spoken of, or encountered these days), raised its 'gorgonian' eyes in our direction and began to select her victims. One by one, and then two by two, rapidly spreading into epidemic proportions. Diphtheria was a remorseless killer infection. Once taken ill, it frequently ended in the death of the sufferer. Isolation in every case, and hope for the best. There were no antibiotics. Just care, poultices, and a prayer, was as much as anyone could do, the only defence was precautionary inoculation.

An urgent program of mass inoculation was put into effect under the wartime emergency powers legislation. Every child who had not previously been inoculated was given the injection whether parents or guardians wanted the child vaccinated, or not. Under wartime measures refusal could mean imprisonment at best, and/or a death sentence at worst (depending on the nature of the offence of course). There was no choice in the matter, every one of us on the appointed day at Kehelland lined up to be 'done'. Painless of course, but for some of us frightening. Nevertheless, as we were told, "This is much better than that terrible ol' dippy". "Smile and be grateful"... There were some screams and fights... "There. It didn't hurt did it"?

As if Diphtheria were not enough to contend with under the most chaotic of circumstances, next on the list of Medusa came 'impetigo', an irritating pustular infection of the skin together with a companion scourge, 'scabies', to keep it company. Both irritating, disfiguring, and highly contagious. Children burst out all over in weeping sores and scabs. The rumour went the rounds that the Germans were responsible. Dropping infected sweets (surely probably the first suggestion of biological warfare in history)? Absolutely untrue of course, but nobody would put it past them though! Kids dare not scratch without risking a thorough examination, sometimes with disastrous results.

* * * * *

I don't ever remember Lily being at school. I knew that she had been registered along with all of our evacuation group but for some reason, I had simply assumed that she had been in an older age group and therefore, in a separate classroom. She tells me now that she was hardly ever there at all. "The reason...", she says, "... is because there were too many of us in the older group of evacuees and were only able to attend school in two's and three's at a time. The school could not cope with the extra numbers". "Usually...", she said, "...I was only able to go to school for two or three 'periods' during the week. One on a Monday, or a Tuesday. Perhaps in the mornings, perhaps not. On a Wednesday, or on Fridays, maybe in the morning, maybe the afternoon. We never knew when it would be until we had finished for the day's session and were told then when to come back next". She says... (and it was not uncommon during the war years) "My education from about the age of twelve was almost non-existent".

Education suffered for all children of school age during the war years (there might have been a few exceptions of the privileged minority who came off better). Teaching was not a 'reserved occupation'. By this, I mean that the profession was not exempt from military, or war-work. The most able and young teachers were called up to become the Officers' Corps, fighter and bomber pilots, navigators and wireless operators, naval artificers, and khakied officers. Some of the more 'gifted' university professorial lecturers and from the 'private' professions, enrolled as 'code breakers' or makers, drafted into intelligence and secret services.

Education authorities everywhere were hard pressed to find the best available candidates to fill the ever widening gaps. The result was that schools generally had to make do with whoever came by. In the end, anyone who seemed to have little more than just keenness was engaged more in hope than confidence, I dare say. Everyone was expected, in a true 'Nelsonian spirit', 'to do their best'. 'England expects' syndrome. In the end it was this alone that got us all through the worst. The common threat drew the best out of everybody. The wonder is, that we got an education at all!

Most 'all' female staffed schools like Kehelland, were fortunate to be able to carry on with an already established staffing more or less as usual, in spite of the shortages of material. Books, paper, pens, and pencils were unobtainable. It was make do and mend, skimp and scrounge. If a ruler broke... it broke, and there was no replacement. Exercise books, every inch carefully garnered, not one scrap must be wasted. As far as Kehelland was affected, these problems apart, the big problem was the sheer numbers that had descended upon them. This factor alone caused as much disruption in the school's program as anything else. It was almost impossible to cope... They did their best.

What Lily did with her spare time; she has declined to say!

Chapter 23

Town, Cinema, Shops and Recreation and One or Two Essays of a Rural Sort

Camborne was no more than a mile walk from Treswithian Downs and 'Elmhurst'. Shopping days were usually once a week but in the main, Auntie Hilda got regular deliveries of bread, milk, and groceries too. Umpteen other grovelling salesmen came on an irregular basis. Oil being an essential item for lighting and some cooking, especially during summer months when it was often really too warm to light the range. Coal and coke deliveries were also one of the regular necessities. The perishables, like eggs and most vegetables, were produced in the garden in better pre-rationing times. The butter, more frequently than not, came from the farm, but for the rest, the 'big' shops of Camborne and Redruth were necessary to visit from time to time. If for nothing else, Auntie 'H' did a weekly just to break the monotony, and when we weren't at school we would go with her. I liked the 'Penny Bazaar' that was situated under the clock tower of what was a cinema (on my last nostalgic visit it had become a night club)! Piled onto rickety trestles were heaps of tatty goods on display, not that there was much one could buy during the war years that was not 'in short supply', or definitely unobtainable. The Bazaar presumably managed to make some sort of a display mostly, I suspect, of pre-war unsold and frankly unsellable, rubbish. Good writing or drawing paper were things of distant memory. There was of course, wartime substitutes which were not unlike newsprint and frankly better suited to wrap cats and dogs meat in, or fish and chips. Horrible brownish and sometimes greyish, flecked with lumpy blemishes, or better still, simply just 'not available'. When one did manage to get some, it was generally useless for either writing or drawing on. The pen or the pencil had to negotiate its way around lumps and bumps of undigested rubbish not removed in the manufacturing process. Unpainted pencils whose leads were so soft that three short straight lines or half a dozen words sufficed to wear the point down to zero... crayons... ditto!

There wasn't much to be 'got' in the Camborne shops no less, and I don't suppose any more than anywhere else. Rationing and the scarcity of unrationed items, produced queues for every 'wanted' item, sometimes even for an unwanted item. The truth is, that wherever queues formed, folk would join it. Whatever the queue had formed for, it had to be worth getting whether wanted or not... frequently to be told just as one had reached the point of purchase, "Sorry, sold out. Might be getting more next week". "Might", more often than not, said in hope rather than certainty. A few toys could still be purchased, generally though, they were wartime influenced. I was very keen on diecast models of army lorries, howitzers, and army equipment. Balsawood self-build models of 'Spitfires', 'Hurricanes', bombers, and barrage balloons to hang from the ceiling. There was one particular model that I coveted, an army lorry with its trailer howitzer field gun but the set cost half a crown (12 ½ pence). For me, at that moment, unobtainable riches.

We did get irregular 'pocket money' sent to Auntie Hilda. She was the official keeper of the purse on my behalf and regulated its disposal. To this day, I don't know who sent it. Whether it came from dad, or from mum? I have no idea. I pleaded for an advance, but the request fell on deaf ears. I wrote home to mum who I thought most likely to respond favourably. I got a letter in reply complaining that I never bothered to write to say how we were getting along and that everything was alright, and now it was only because I wanted something that I had bothered. That said, with it came a postal order for the two shillings and sixpence (twelve and a half pence).

Days later and the postal order cashed... only to discover that the coveted lorry and trailer field gun had been sold. "Sorry, we might be getting some more later". I never did get the trailer and lorry. I have no idea what I did get with the money? Sweets? Well, although sweet rationing did not come into effect until much later in 1940, that did not mean that sweets were plentiful and freely available. Scarcity was really more rationing than otherwise. It is a cruel fact of life though, that those with 'power' and 'money' rarely found any difficulties in 'resourcing scarce supplies'. Shopkeepers usually sold more from under the counter than ever went on display. In some ways, this was not used unfairly. Most shopkeepers knew the value of their customer goodwill and his regular customers who consequently were looked after. Strangers would clear out limited stocks on display in two shakes of a warden's whistle. Rationing at least ensured that everybody got a fair share of what was available. I always bought the few sweets I could afford at a little 'house-cum-shop' in Kehelland village. A tiny front-room-general sort of shop that sold everything from A to Z and back again. A, for 'Aspirin' and 'apples', to Z for 'Zebo' black lead, to 'go, suck a Zube'... My favourite when I could get it. "Only one, young man"... a sticky tuppeny Mars Bar...

I didn't always sit on my granite doorstep and think of nothing in particular. Certain individuals sometimes took my attention rather more than others. Strangely, the recollection of quite who, has become rather vague with the passage of time, with one notable exception. Dare I mention a name after all these years? Oh well, why not... Heather!

Now, I would never have considered sharing my rare Mars Bar with anyone... absolutely no one! I couldn't even bear the thought of breaking into it... yet. There was far too much at stake. I would offer some to Heather if I could summon up enough courage to do it. Playtime came and went. Dinnertime came and went, and again, playtime... The Mars bar remained complete, unbroken, un-smelt, untasted... Ah well, I should jolly well have to eat it all myself!

Later that evening and with a borrowed table knife, I sat upon an upturned rusted clothes boiler in the coal shed with the door closed tight. I cut slices as thin as I could into the melting confection with the blunt knife... One for me... Yum!... A slice for Heather (who might have benefitted if it had not been for fate and greediness)... much better. Yum! The bar by now reduced to a soggy mess, sacrificed at the altars of Aphrodite.

School apart, and town excursions, there were a good many other things to discover which entailed a thorough exploration of the neighbourhood. I have always been an inveterate wanderer (mostly preferred on my own). 'Elmhurst' surrounded on all sides by fields, just green meadows wholly given over to grazing. Field gates to climb over, footpaths and dry stone walls capped by soft mounds of grass and yellow eyed daisies. The fields covered with daisy white and speckled with cowpats. I liked to sit atop one of these walls at the crossroads leading down Strawberry Hill into the valley of Reskadinnik (the fact that Heather lived in Reskadinnik had nothing whatever to do with my chosen post of watch)! Up on my lofty perch, I pretended that I was defending my castle mount, reliving those dreams when I lived close up to the Tower of London. Imagining ranks of steel helmeted and armoured guardians, patrolling along the battlemented walls and towers. Glinting pikes and bows and arrows ready to fly at any attacker or, just to sit and view the 'downs' and speculate on more distant places beyond the hilltops and the blue misted horizons. The busy smudge of Camborne and distant Redruth... the misty mount of Carn Brea pointing its mysterious finger towards the sky... wondering what lay beyond the ridge of the Downs?

Sometimes, at weekends or school holidays, Uncle Charlie would take us one at a time on his farm rounds collecting milk churns (cows were milked seven days a week, 365 days a year including Christmas days or holidays, and the milk had to be collected daily. Uncle 'C' very often had to work seven days a week). When my turn came... up early. He would collect me as he passed the house later. I had to be ready because we never knew when he might come by. I sat on the field gate opposite the house and waited, chewing a frond of grass like a full blown countryman. It had seemed to me that every farm worker needed to chew a blade of grass!

He came eventually. Up onto the high step, and a struggle into the driver's cab. I could just about see out of the dusty windscreen; my nose came at about the same level with the dashboard but if I sat up straight, I could manage to see the road surface at four hundred yards distant. It didn't matter too much because this was going to be a journey of discovery. I was confident that I was about to see those distant places only dimly imagined from my vantage point atop the dry stone wall.

Uncle Charlie drove a big flatbed lorry of uncertain vintage, never at a pace that was likely to break the current speed limits (if there were any current speed limits), not that anyone would have known if it did. Vehicle and pedestrian traffic were virtually non-existent on the local roads and byways. We generally had them to ourselves. The lorry lumbering along. The clank and metallic clash of the empty milk churns as we meandered down this lane and up the hill. Crunching over the narrow verges, just about able to turn into farmyards between granite gateposts that leant this way and that way, every way but upright. Gates hanging from them that would never be opened and never closed. Bottom rungs dug deep embedded into uncut and knotted grass. The farmyard littered with decaying farm machines, an elderly tractor lopsided on flattened tyres and battered by years of hard labour and left finally to bury itself. Muddy stone paved yards and the obligatory farmyard chickens scratching hopefully for loose grains. Cowsheds and milking parlours, granite built, and sagging slate roofed.

Half a dozen full milk churns on a raised platform, Uncle Charlie unloaded the empty sterilised returned churns first. 'Clash'... 'clash'... 'clash'..., as the battered rims rang on the cobbled stone yard and then the hump and the bounce of the lorry as the full churns were loaded. He was a big strong man. Ruddy faced, he lifted full milk churns as though they were filled with air or feathers. I found it was impossible for me to move, let alone lift, an empty churn. Full ones with as much as ten to fifteen gallons in each. A dozen of me would still have found them immovable.

At most farms visited, the full churns were collected and the empty churns for tomorrows milk delivered, usually went unnoticed or acknowledged. Farmyards empty of a man or beast (excepting the untidy flocks of farmyard free range chickens). Sometimes, there might be a loose kind of wave from an ever open farmhouse door. A feeble toot on the lorry's cronky horn and we were away to the next call... and the next.

Once, Uncle Charlie disappeared into the farmhouse emerging minutes later with a cheery... "Bye now. Bye", and a broad smile. Back in the cab he winked at me, putting a packet and a cardboard tub under his seat. "Fresh farm butter on 'yer bread for tea tonight m'dear"... "An' are y'oom ever ha' splits an' clotted cream"?... mmm... nice!

Under normal peace time circumstances, this would be a no 'big deal' kind of transaction. Fresh farmhouse butter and clotted cream, but now with rationing beginning to 'bite', butter at two ounces per person per week, and cream totally and completely unobtainable, rationed, or unrationed, these illicit items promised a rare treat. It was criminally illegal for both the farmer to supply them and for Uncle Charlie to receive them. It could have been a prison sentence for both.

"Mum's the word. Don't tell on it m'dear". I didn't even mention it to Auntie Hilda. I wondered how she knew when to buy the splits from the bakers delivery man this morning. The raspberry jam appeared from somewhere as well...mmm, they were nice!

* * * * *

On my very first trip on the milk round, Uncle Charlie said he was going by the North Cliff road over Reskajeage Downs on his calls between Gwithian and Portreath. Most of the local farms were generally (in today's terms) little more than smallholdings of under a hundred acres or so. Dozens and dozens of them boasting an acre of two of arable fields but mostly it was milk and dairy production as the mainstay. A dozen or two of 'milkers' and a modest cultivation of vegetables, cabbage, hay and mangolds for winter feed. I was told they were 'mangelwurzels'. "I will stop and let you see 'Hells Mouth'", he said, "An' th' cliffs". This trip was turning out to be a real adventure of discovery!

As we drove over the brow of the downs, my first sight of the crystal blues and greens of the Atlantic Ocean. White capped waves as the long Atlantic rollers dashed inshore to break foaming on the granite bastion of the North Cliffs of Reskajeage Downs.

The road passed so close to the 'lip' of 'Hells Mouth' no more than ten to fifteen yards distant. Uncle Charlie parked off road but kept a tight hold on me as we approached the brink. "Not too close now m'dear", he warned, but didn't let me get any closer. I was too fearful anyway as it was. I thought I felt far too close to eternity for comfort but there was a terrifying fascination in the great yawning chasm which fell straight down from where we stood to the waves crashing into the base of the cliffs. Awe inspired fear gripped me in a tightly held breath. I knew then, why it was called 'Hells Mouth'!

Off to my left, the white finger, misted by sea spray of Godrevy Lighthouse on its granite island and beyond the deep blue, white wave speckled Carbis and St Ives bays. To my right, wave battered high cliffs, greys, and browns, topped by tangled scrub of heather here and there dotted with purple splashes, and the short nodding clumps of pink sea thrift. Reskajeage Downs and the North Cliffs were little more than a mile as the proverbial crow flew from Treswithian and 'Elmhurst'. "Y'oom must never come here without an adult", Uncle Charlie warned. I promised that I wouldn't but wanted to come again and somehow, I knew that I would.

On our way back, Uncle 'C' stopped at the bottom of the valley separating Reskajeage and Treswithian Downs to show me the 'Red River'. A narrow, rapidly flowing stream on its tumbling way down to the sea at Gwithian, stained muddy red like blood. He explained that the red hue was because of the flow of water continuously pumped out of the deep shafts and galleries of the local tin mines still working at Redruth and Carn Brea. Another fascination for me to wonder at!

Ever after perched on my dry stone wall mount, I knew what was beyond the ridge of the Downs. In my mind, I could wander down the lane cut between its high banks, down the valley bottom, and dream of blood red water pumped from the bowels of the rocks beneath my feet and the green meadows, and the cows lazily cropping and chewing over the cud unaware of what lay beneath their green carpet of liquid milk.

Some tin mines were still working. Hundreds more had shut down as uneconomic years ago. Rotting and derelict, pumping and winding engine buildings stood like gaunt and grey monumental gravestones. Stripped bare of machinery, ancient and rusting heaps of amputated beam engines littered the landscape and were sinking into it. Wartime measures were put into action belatedly to step up production. Tin and seams of copper ore both precious and unobtainable imports. It would have taken years to reopen and re-equip deep mines. Far too long to have any real effect in the wartime effort. It is said there is more tin still in the ground than was ever taken out.

This morning a letter had arrived for Auntie Hilda from home. She had read it and waited for me to come home from school to tell me what mum had to say. "Johnnie. I have something to tell you. Your mum has asked me to tell you what it is when I thought it was the right time. I have decided to tell you now". In her hand she held the letter. Putting it down on the table, she looked at me carefully and saw the puzzled and frightened look in my eyes. Somehow, I knew that the news was going to be something bad. All sorts of terrible things flashed through my mind, and I stammered an anxious, "What"? That's all… a nervous, "What", that I didn't really want to know the answer. She hesitatingly continued evidently trying to find the right words. "Your mum has asked me to tell you that your friend Derek, who I believe lived next door to you, has been killed in an air raid with all of his family"… I could not take it in. There was nothing more that she needed to say. It had been Derek, my really only best friend. It was the fulfilment of that constant unspoken fear of 'what if parents were killed'? 'What would become of us'? Grandparents, aunts, uncles, cousins, friends, or neighbours. Anybody or everybody. I wouldn't believe it, but there it was laying on the table. The memorial card. Three days after leaving Forest Gate and evacuating to Brentwood in rural Essex… October 20th, 1940… in rural Essex… It did not occur to me at that moment, and I can't exactly say when it did, but one night I could not sleep…. Was I dreaming? Could I hear it? Yes, I could hear it. A repeated, 'boom', 'boom', a constant booming. Would I hear the bombs exploding all this far away from the blitz? I wasn't sure. Suddenly, I thought of Derek and was afraid. In the morning I asked Auntie Hilda… "Last night I could hear the bombs dropping. Could I hear them all this far away? It kept me awake". "Oh no, my dear", she explained. "What you can hear are the waves breaking on the cliffs. Uncle Charlie will tell you". "Oh yes", I said. "I had seen them and heard them too". Suddenly I realised if I had not been here at Elmhurst, if I had chosen to go with Derek to Brentwood instead, I would have been killed too!

It is almost unbelievable that the Moss' had delayed going away until the night blitz had started. There had been the massive daylight attacks on the docks and the East End on the 7th of September, a mere week after we had left London, and the 15th of September, but it had not yet affected places like Forest Gate until the Nazi's realised that daylight raids were far too expensive in aircraft and crews to sustain the attack and so resorted to attack by night instead. The result was that they lost the benefit of seeing where they dropped their bombs on marked and strategic targets and went in for carpet and terror indiscriminate raids in order to destroy morale as an alternative. One of those indiscriminate bombs probably jettisoned from a lost bomber desperately trying to get back to its base, fell onto a rural cottage in the fields of rural Essex and killed a whole family, and that awful fact is what the mass evacuation was all about. The blitz continued for fifty six consecutive nights of terror. There were to be many more Derek's and his family brutally killed before it petered out and finally came to an end, leaving behind it thousands upon thousands of houses destroyed and hundreds of churches and historic buildings reduced to blackened piles of rubble. 20,000 people killed (some reports suggest twice as many), and many thousands more injured, many thousands of them severely. Thousands of children might have been killed or severely injured and permanently maimed if evacuation had not taken place. We, who are still here to tell the tale, should feel ourselves fortunate to be able to tell it. My own story is only one of a million similar stories that could be told... as it happens, both the good, and the bad!

Even in the quiet corner of Camborne and Treswithian, very occasionally an air raid warning sounded. The nearest siren was positioned in Camborne - we barely heard it. Mostly at night, and for us, it frequently went unnoticed except one particular night when there was a bit more activity than usual. There was gunfire, and flares were dropped over Camborne and Redruth, clearly illuminating Carn Brea in a bright white light. No bombs were dropped but flares, one after the other, slowly descended until they spluttered out. It was quite exciting really, like a firework display.

In spite of the assurances given to me, an instinctive fear gripped me. The news about Derek was still raw like an open wound which I tried manfully to hide, and no one knew of it. A fear that warned me because it could be me next time... neither could anyone offer me a soothing word because there was nothing to be said.

It was suggested that the German pilots over-flying Cornwall after raids on either Cardiff or Bristol, had got lost and released flares to light up any identifiable positions like Carn Brea with its prominent finger pointing the way. Falmouth too, was sometimes attacked at night. I saw the twinkling flashes of shell bursts in the sky, infrequent reminders that there was a war going on and there was still a threat of German invasion.

Chapter 24

Milk Marketing – Whitegate Farm, Kehelland

As if the excitement and adventure of Uncle 'C's milk round had not been enough for one day, as we passed 'Elmhurst' on the way back to the depot at Treswithian, he asked me if I would like to see what happened to the milk that had been collected. By now, the flatbed lorry was loaded to the tailboard with full churns labelled and marked to identify which farms they had come from. "Yes please". We didn't stop at the house but went straight by to the Milk Marketing Board depot situated no more than a few hundred yards along the lane at Treswithian village, a few dozen or so houses to the corner shop at the crossroad (still in business), and the 'Cornish Choughs' public house. The Milk Marketing Board depot was a large oblong red brick building of two storeys in height. The depot was reached by a semi-circular driveway off the Treswithian downs lane just before the main road junction. The frontage planted with well-tended shrubs and flowers. Everything immaculate and tidy.

Uncle 'C' turned heavily into the driveway crunching over the well raked gravel onto concreted loading and unloading bays and backed up slowly to a raised glass covered platform. Everything scrupulously washed and scrubbed. White coated operatives were on the ramp wearing white trousers and white plimsole like soft shoes. Breast pockets picked out in blue embroidery with 'Milk Marketing Board'. The full churns rolled from the lorry on their rims to waiting white coated 'examiners', each churn tested for quality, cream and fats content. This value and that content determined, milk that proved to be under standard was rejected to be either returned to the farm of origin (for animal feed probably, not for human consumption), or if contaminated, set aside to be disposed of. The good milk emptied into a stainless steel hopper which fed stainless steel tanks inside the main building, to be processed. Whilst the lorry and its load were being unloaded and tested, he asked me if I would like to see inside the depot. "Oh, yes please". This was too good an opportunity to miss.

We entered through a swing door at the side of the building and climbed a brightly lit short flight of stairs, painted a brilliant white, and through a swing door out onto the first floor receiving area. Spotlessly white tiled with white coated and capped operators, stainless steel tanks fed by gleaming stainless pipes and red rimmed stopcocks everywhere reflected onto the white tiled walls. The red quarry tiled floor gleamingly clean. It smelt of warm pasteurising milk.

Steam pipes hissing, here and there little spurts of escaping steam. Up another flight of stairs and a swing door to the upper story, gleaming tiles just like the first floor. Pipes and tanks, stopcocks, dials, and gauges. In the centre of the floor (as far as I remember), two or four maybe, large butter vats, slowly turning, first one way, then reversing the opposite way. Hour after hour, separating the butter from the whey. At the far end of the 'floor' from where I stood, a large cold room refrigerator door was open and issuing cold vapours into the warm moist air. Stacked with brown waxed cardboard boxes filled with two pound blocks of butter, wrapped in waxed paper and stamped with a crown and W/D (war department)… none of it for domestic consumption but requisitioned by the War Ministry to supply the navy, air force and the army. When I was told this, I was pleased, and felt proud that the airmen who were chasing these bombers away would have butter for their tea too, because we had collected the milk to make it!

Fat short 'tankers' stood at the loading ramps waiting while pasteurised homogenised and skimmed milk were pumped into them. Shiny like the depot and carrying the legend on their tails ends, 'Milk Marketing Board'. Later, they would deliver Cornish milk to bottling depots all over the UK.

There was not a real shortage of milk during the war years, production had increased so much that there was actually a surplus. However, sometimes supplies were interrupted or limited for all sorts of reasons. A local milkman might have to tell his customers, "Sorry luv, can only let you have two pints today. Deliveries are up the spout again"! Not an unusual feature of wartime Britain. "Might get some more next week... might not"!

* * * * *

During my time at Treswithian, the 'Board' began a program of experiments to produce dried milk in a separate unit at the depot. A new machine was installed looking like a huge stainless steel mangle. Two steel rollers, one above the other, super-heated by high pressure steam, they revolved against each other. Milk was introduced onto the top roller drying rapidly into a dry flaky sheet. When it reached the bottom roller every last drop of moisture had been removed. The final product scraped off by close set blades and collected into a hopper.

It was all experimental really, the dried milk looked like flaked rice paper and didn't reconstitute very well. They also tried by the same method to dry vegetables. Finely shredded cabbage, carrots, onions, and turnip. I think it was never intended for the domestic market. It was packed into large, tinned containers, painted khaki and marked W/D and the crown. Some probably turned up in the deserts of North Africa, naval vessels, and submarines... so, Treswithian was 'doin' its bit'!

Whitegates Farm Kehelland

Uncle Charlie and Auntie Hilda were on close friendly terms with Mr & Mrs Bennet of Whitegates Farm, Kehelland. Whitegates was a typical Cornish farm of the times. A large rambling granite farmhouse fronted by a square farmyard just like hundreds of similar farms we visited on Uncle C's rounds.

The yard surrounded on four sides with stone built cowsheds with grey slated roofs. On one side of the square, cowsheds with half a dozen pens, on another, various stables complete with two huge 'shire horses'. Open fronted sheds under which were farm carts, horse drawn ploughs, reapers and binders, carts, wooden iron shod wheels. A high sided 'hay wain', horse collars and tackle, rakes, and pitchforks, leather belts, and a veritable galaxy of old rotting implements, dating I suspect, from at least a century past.

Close by, the farmhouse in a separate part of the farm buildings (as ancient as the rest), was used as a diary. Freshly whitewashed and quarry tiled floor, all scrupulously clean. A deep butler's sink (and taps), a big stainless steel cooling tank, stainless buckets, china bowls and jugs, scrubbed wooden racks, and the churns to be filled at the next milking. Of course, the obligatory farmyard chickens who no more regarded the ever open farm gate as the limit of their territorial range than the average Cornish crow, or the farmyard sparrow! Scattering occasionally at the approach of an infrequent vehicle daring to pass the farm gate over their part of the road.

When we visited the farm (quite frequently as it happened), there was always something going on to grab our natural curiosity. We were always greeted long before we arrived at the farm gate, by loud growling barks of warning, letting us know that our unwarranted presence had been noted and sterner means of deterrence would be resorted to if we dared to come any closer. However, suddenly the barking would cease and 'Shep', the black and white collie dog, would bound towards us;

tail wagging in a kind of circular orbit at his rear, greeting each one of us in turn in order of preference or seniority.

Shep was an old and retired dog and a trifle unsteady on his legs (hence his revolving tail). He was also totally blind. Misshapen eye sockets declared his canine darkness and yet I wondered, how did he know that it was us long before we had reached the farm gate? Surely... I wondered... surely our combined footsteps would make it impossible to identify individuals, but he knew who was who! He knew his way around the farmyard, sniffing his way from point to point with a certainty that gave no indication that he was unsighted. I even saw him chase a determined chicken who refused to move out of his way. He turned at the precise moment in the precise direction that the bird turned, snapping, and turning, following every move the startled chicken made to avoid his bared fangs, until it flew off in a squawking protest and drifting cloud of loosened feathers.

Whitegates was a mixed farm. A herd of a dozen or two of 'milkers', a heifer or two, some calves together with a ring nosed bad tempered bull who had his permanent indoor quarters in a separate pen, gazing out and chewing the cud over a seemingly too flimsy boarded half stable door, frequently scaring me with a loud bored bellow and a stamp of his forelegs. I always gave it a very wide berth. The two shires were stabled next door to the grumpy old bull.

A few grubbing and squealing sows surrounded by a cloud of uncountable piglets penned into a muddy paddock adjacent to the farmhouse. Naturally, the flocks of obligatory free ranging chickens and a field or two of arable crops. An acre or two of cabbages, broccoli, carrots, and turnip. A few hay fields and mangolds (mangle-wurzels) for winter feed, and half a dozen acres of cereals.

Mrs Bennet had heard the commotion and stood at the ever open farmhouse door to greet us. She was an unexcitable lady, short of stature but of comfortable proportions, face glowing with the retained farmhouse bloom of a young girl, although to me, anyone past the age of twelve was regarded as ancient grownups and well on the way to the declines of old age. Mr & Mrs Bennet could not have been much past the age of thirty. Uncle Charlie and Auntie Hilda much about the same ages. All four adults probably grew up amongst the same age group of local children. I like to think that perhaps they even went to the same school together in Kehelland… all pure speculation on my part more than a certainty. Mr & Mrs Bennet were childless, yet over tolerant of us mischievous kids rampaging around the farm and getting ourselves into bother and extremely muddy at the same time. Mrs Bennet especially. Her responses to our flood of excited questions were always patiently awaited whilst she considered her careful way, her replies were then delivered in a calm and comfortingly measured manner. I always felt safe.

The big rambling farmhouse of the ever open door to all comers, including the farmyard chickens which ran the gauntlet of Shep's guardianship over what was rightly his own territory, wandered in and out of the house just as they pleased. The front door led into a wide passage boasting a wide staircase to the upper floors. The hallway passage floor laid with worn quarry tiles, red and white with black bordering. Off to the immediate right, a large high ceilinged farmhouse kitchen, tiled like the passage. A large pine kitchen table and a usual black coal fired kitchen range darkly tucked into a deep chimney recess. The floor seemed alive with wandering hens, under the big table and even fluttering up onto it to scavenge for stray crumbs. Mrs Bennet's ineffectual wave of her hand and her slow unconvincing, "Shoo", merely removed them for a few seconds. At which fowl determination, she only smiled the smile of resignation to their frequent depravations of the family board. She saw my total amazement and wide-eyed wonder at this strange farm spectacle. "Oh", she said. "We get used to it". I wondered whether they wandered upstairs to bed along with Mr

& Mrs Bennet at night-time. Did they sleep on, or under the bed? I didn't think it was wise to ask the question, but it lingered on my lips.

* * * * *

Since our arrival at Treswithian in early September 1940, we had been 'established' for a couple of busy months already. I was comfortable and well used to the family routine and reasonably happy at school. It had proved to be never too laborious and threatening and also, accepted in the sense that I had more or less been left alone and no awkward questions asked. I was used to the neighbourhood and yet constantly still surprised and fascinated by the different ways of country life, but at the same time liking very much the openness of the somewhat bucolic grandeur of my surroundings. From the very first day, I had wondered about the disposal of the privy bucket contents and had never found the courage to ask.

Just over the way from Elmhurst, was the house of Mother. That is, Auntie Hilda's mother, the image of whom was Auntie Hilda herself. The existence of the house came as something of a surprise to me as it was virtually hidden away out of sight from the road, buried deep in a tall standing of trees and dense hedges. With Mother, lived two elderly bachelor brothers. Baynard and Telfer, who might have been uncles to Auntie H. I was never sure what the relationship was. Telfer, who might have been the elder of the two, spoke mostly in Celtic Cornish with a mixture of barely recognisable English and I never understood a word he said. Both weather beaten faced farm workers wont to wear at all times, their regular work clothes. Trousers frequently tied at the calf with bits of binder string. As Baynard explained to me, "Them al rats do sumtime run up th' legs an' tickle them knees". Mud stained hobnailed boots, wrinkled with wet and preserved with greasy yellow saddle soap. Their hands were as large as their normal sized 'pasties' and gnarled with thick calluses. Weather beaten strength, yet as gentle as lambs. Soft spoken and permanent smiles of Cornish wellbeing. Often short sleeved and big leather belted, as if this were not enough to maintain natural decorum, twisted ancient braces (the elastic a thing of its distant past).

Baynard cultivated and produced the vegetables on Elmhurst's garden plot and looked after the chickens… early mornings I would see him coming. A fork of ancient design and a long straight handled heart shaped spade carried over his shoulder. His first task between the rows of cabbages, carrots, and potatoes, was to spit on his hands, grasp the long handled spade and dig a narrow trench. Having completed this to a measured depth, he downed the spade and visited the 'privy'… not long enough to negotiate his way conveniently out of belt and braces, but to emerge carrying the 'bucket'. Back at the trench, he tipped the contents in an even line along it… the solution to the puzzling mystery of disposal! Now, I had the answer. I wasn't too sure about the vegetables though? Baynard guessed my surprise. "Tha'ill do them taters a worl' o' good. Be as big as pumpkins an' sweet as 'oney. You'll see"! Hmm, I thought, I'd take his country word for it, but it never put me off pasties! A sensible arrangement perhaps. Certainly, such a practice had never hurt a country soul for perhaps thousands of years.

Water too was a scarce resource depending entirely on rainfall and ground water levels. Daily needs were drawn by hand pump from a shallow cistern in the corner of the backyard, cut into the underlying rock, no more than a few feet deep. Uncle C would regularly open a wooden cover to see how much water was in the cistern. If it was low, urgent economy of water 'use' was adopted. In any case, low water levels, or high, every drop of 'used' was thrown close to the cistern and the hand pump so that it would permeate back into the cistern through the soil – 'cleaned'?? Now, I also knew why we had infrequent baths. I worked it out that a few days later I could be drinking somebody's bath water in my tea. Whenever I had a bath in the old tin bath in front of the kitchen range, I was always careful to avoid an occasional accident that I had experienced from time to time. Sometimes, I couldn't help myself, in which case, I just had to bear the thought manfully, and hope that nobody had noticed.

Chapter 25

Christmas 1940

In spite of the fact that 1940 had proved to be as difficult and different to me as any of my previous years, as far as it was possible for me to make any means of comparison, one year with another, it could be said to be 'business as usual'.

I had been assured in the normal process of understanding, that seasons were guaranteed to follow each other in a regular pattern, year in and year out. As far as I know, certain of these conditions had followed the natural pattern, albeit somehow disturbed by events of human making. Things like the war. The evacuation. Tunstead. Bermondsey and Forest Gate. Not least an event of almost unthinkable and unmentionable awfulness, the death of Derek and his family, tempered to some degree by the peace of Treswithian and the feeling of security. I felt as if I had been evacuated away from the greater disturbances faced at home.

The springtime had followed the winter, summer, and Whitegates Farm. The harvest gathered home, threshed, and stored... Christmas would soon be upon us. A wartime Christmas... there really wasn't much in the way of goods or good news to cheer the season. We would have to make do and accept the best available (not that peacetime Christmas's had been comparable with today's bonanza of luxurious waste).

It was a well provided for family even then, who could afford more than the general rule of scarcity, especially that scarcest commodity...

money. Most of us children of those times were content (if not a little envious of the obviously 'better off'), to receive the gift of a much wanted toy together with few items of welcome pencils, crayons, a colouring book, or a book to read and the traditional 'surprise' pillow slip mysteriously stuffed and deposited at the foot of the bed on Christmas morning. Every one of us, of the so thought to be innocent of the truth of 'Santa', knew how the pillowcase full of promise got there but were glad to pretend we didn't know. One or two packaged surprises, apples and oranges, nuts, and a few minted chocolate pennies, helping to fill out an otherwise empty package of promise. We were well satisfied with the scant contents.

By Christmas 1940, oranges and bananas had disappeared and were practically unknown or unremembered by the very young. Toys were almost unobtainable. Everything was of poor quality but even so, 'lucky acquisitions' if one managed to get something. Parents did the best they could. Wooden substitutes 'knocked up' by handy dads (who were not away, lost and running for their lives in some North African desert, or swimming for their lives in the Atlantic, or scrambling to the next, and perhaps their last sortie). Dolls clothes stitched together by needle skilled, and the not so skilled mums producing the 'better in the end', expensively purchased bauble soon to be discarded.

Turkey and its trimmings were only a tradition to be read about. Perhaps the local butcher might… but only might, be able to get a few scraggy capons for a Christmas dinner. Perhaps a small joint of cheap cut pork that would absorb a full months (or two) of meat ration for a whole family. He might on the other hand, just might, be able to supply a few sausages to go with the non-existent turkey. No tinned fruits more than one had ration points to purchase, and even then, generally home produced fruits. There again, maybe a (lucky acquisition), a rare tin of pineapple and even rarer, peaches.

A fruitless and tasteless imitation of the Christmas cake iced with sugarless icing… two ounces of butter each, and bread. The iniquitous apology for white bread, heavy with all the substance of wholegrain but not exactly wholegrain brown, but a grey homogenous mass of grey solid for the lack of baker's yeast (yeast was too scarce a commodity). Bakers found ingenious means of making their bread a little more like the real thing!

Mum had sent a parcel with a few goodies. Some of it euphemistically saved from her own ration but frankly, like Uncle C's butter and clotted cream, most of it illicit. Something for each of us marooned country folk. Packets of tea and sugar, sweets, and a selection of chocolate bars (including Mars bars), jam and a tin or two of fruit. A model barrage balloon for me, and a football for Rodney. Also, a note in the parcel to say that she would try to visit us for Christmas.

Time was not the problem, but travel was. One could not simply decide to go anywhere at a whim. Travel permits had to be applied for and if the issuing authority decided that the journey was not justified they refused the request (restrictions that applied to long journeys principally). The risks of travelling without a permit could land one into a lot of unnecessary bother. If a passenger were asked (which they rarely were) for their permit, they could be taken off the train to face an interrogation if they couldn't provide it. All was in order for mum, and she did come for a once only visit. (It also happened to be the last time I saw her for the next three/four years).

Christmas had come and gone. School, and the winter was upon us. There was horse drawn ploughing at Whitegates, the raking and the drilling. We 'helped', but Mr Bennet's farm hands might have described it another way. The one acre field had been planted with winter cabbage. Bundles of tender two leaved plants and a 'dibber' setting them out in neat rows at regular intervals. Milking time, on rare early visits. The cowhand dairyman milking in the cowshed by hand. "Would 'e like t' milk 'er'"? He asked me. The pendulous udder washed, and my hands washed and a three legged milking stool and a stainless steel bucket somehow tucked between my legs. "No... no... not like tha'". The patient cow kicking against my rough treatment. "Here, like this. Squeeze an' pull... 'n squeeze an' pull... Not t' 'ardly now. Tha's right, gently now". Two fat warm teats between my fingers, a squeeze on one and the pull on the other in a slow gentle rhythm. Thin jets of warm frothy milk splashed into the bucket, first one teat and then the other. I laughed at my newfound skill. "Tha's right me dear. G'ye on 'en". I had to go on until there was no more milk. The cow contentedly munching her ration of cattle cake. I was offered a cup of the fresh warm milk and it tasted rich and creamy on my lips. My cup of contentment (and pleasure) ran over.

* * * * *

Apart from our frequent weekend visits to the farm (welcome as they were), a time of the year had arrived when farmers were thinking of bringing the harvest home. The farm suddenly awoke from out of a lazy dream of high summer. Machines were wheeled out from their sheds, dusty and chaff soiled. Washed, and cleaned oil and tested, sharpened, and repaired. Harnesses and traces gathered from here, there, and everywhere. We were sent off on this errand and that. "In such and such shed y'll find such and such". "Will y'get he for we m'dear", and equally as often asked to keep out of the way. We were told, "We are t'cut five acre in th'morning. You will come if y'like... early mind". It wouldn't matter how early... "This I must see"!

One of the shires had been harnessed, up and early, long before we had arrived. Even 'Shep' was quiet, as if he knew what was afoot, and also knew when to keep out of the way. He had probably had a few kicks in the days of his wild youth and dared not to risk one now. He wandered aimlessly and shakily, his tail revolving furiously in its accustomed circular motion. Everything was ready. The shire (for want of a remembered name), its iron shod hooves impatiently stamping the flagstone yard. His driver of the reaper and the baler took up the reigns. "Right... cum on, hup now boy". Hup, hup, hup", then... "Steady... steady... too fast now", and a sudden cry... "Woah... woah there... hold it. Hol' it now". The reaper and baler, its flimsy flail in serious danger of being tangled up with the farm gatepost... but finally out on the lane. "Lead on 'en. Cum hup now... steady... steady", and off at a steady plot towards the five acre field, through a five bar gate and over a meadow with cows grazing in a far corner. Shep creeping and hobbling along to keep up with the procession. Half a dozen casual helpers, and Rodney and me. Mr Bennet had a two bore gun split and hanging over his shoulder with the barrels pointing down to the ground. "Rabbits m'dear. See 'en run fr' under the reaper. Dinner for some of us'ns". Somebody else interrupted him. "Only if 'e's a better shot than las' year". A rabbit bolted for the stone wall hedge. Close by me the first barrels discharged and tumbled the rabbit. "Not always though", somebody said. "That was a fluke boy but keep y'head down H'ill 'ave Y scalp. He don't always aim true". Five acre field... ripe wheat standing tall and straight with golden stems and full ears bending coy-like nodding to the earth. The early sun warming the cool autumn morning. The field of gently moving wheat exuding a malty perfume of ripe wheat and shedding light clouds of misty dust.

The reaper lined up and the shire being pulled into position, "Cum on, hup now... steady boy", and the flail turned and the first cut, all of three feet wide. A slow plodding speed... a shower of cut wheat spilled out at the back. "Whoa... whoa. Stop". "What now"? "Th' binder twine wis not feeding through". A few minutes of adjustments... "Right. Away we go". The flail began to turn. Swish... swish... swish... clickety clack... clickety clack. The cut wheat moving on a belt into the mysterious 'gut' of this strange horse drawn heap of bits and pieces. Suddenly, out of the back of the reaper and binder shot a bound sheaf, and then another, and another... leaving a long line of bound sheaves behind the reaper. The horse nodding with every sure step. Head down, pushing into its heavy collar, plod... plod... nod... nod... as the sheaves tumbled out at the back of the slowly retreating machine, like a big animal leaving a trail of droppings behind itself.

Our jobs were to stack the sheaves into 'stooks'. "No, not tha' way. Like this'n". Showing us how to stack the 'stooks' the right way to allow air to circulate upwards through them to dry the wheat. Explaining that if the wheat did not dry, it would ferment in the 'rick' and be ruined. As the day wore on, the field of wheat slowly got smaller and smaller as the reaper creaked along one side of a diminishing square and then a turn along another side. The shire bucking and turning to turn the reaper in the right direction, repeated at every turn onto every side to complete the 'round' of the field.

Three or four limp bloodied rabbits laid in the shade of a dry stone wall; dozens more had bolted unharmed. 'Bang'!... "Drat. Missed". 'Bang'... 'bang'... both barrels this time... both missed. The same performance repeated throughout the day. He was not a very good shot. The expenditure of the cartridges used so far for the paltry 'bag' of half a dozen rabbits could not be regarded as an economic proposition. Some of the helpers were having more success catching them with heavy club-like sticks... even Shep managed to corner one.

The field was cut. At the end of it I was tired. My hands were red raw with handling rough straw and the file like full ears of wheat. Aching and sweaty but thoroughly content and happy to have been there. I had no difficulty getting to sleep that night. The reaper and binder had not yet finished its annual duties. There were one or two more fields yet to cut and stook. One or two days more for us.

The close cropped fields sprouting sorry looking stubble, lined with regularly spaced rows of drying stooks. A few more days of fine weather and the harvest could really be brought home. I was determined that I would be there too.

* * * * *

The patient old Shire now harnessed into the shafts of the high sided 'Hay Wain' loaded with pitch forks (newly sharpened), two long curving prongs mounted on long birch handles worn smooth and golden by generations of harvest times. The hay season and the wheat harvest. Half a dozen pitch forks and half a dozen casual helpers... Not for us... dire warnings. "Keep well clear of the fast swinging pronged tines".

Bottles of cold tea and battered tin mugs. We also brought a few solid blocks of thick cheese sandwiches with us and a 'Tizer' bottle (tuppence for the returned bottle) and a bottle of water. A ride down to the five acre field on the 'Wain' with solid un-sprung wooden wheels and steel tyred rims, crunching the uneven lane surface and leaving in its wake two thin white lines of crushed chippings. On the field, the wain was positioned between two rows of stooks. Two pitchers, one each side of the wain. Two shirt sleeved stackers on the cart each with a pitchfork... the spit on the hands, belts tightened, and caps pulled, "Right. Hup now". The horse, seeming to know from years of harvest experiences before, just what was expected of him and drew the wain forward and stopped.

Pitchforks whirled each side of the wain in a kind of circular motion, spike a sheaf on the ground with the long curving prongs and quick as a flash, the fork swung in its arc over the pitcher's head, the flying pitched sheaf landing precisely at the feet of the stackers... every time, six to eight sheaves to a stook. The wain moved slowly down the row of stooks at just the right pace for the stooks to be broken and pitched and stacked properly to form a level and balanced load. Twenty... forty... sixty sheaves pitched in a matter of minutes. The stackers had to be quick to keep pace with the pitchers. The further the wain moved along the rows, the higher the load and the higher the sheaves to be pitched, until the pitchers could no longer reach high enough. "This load will do". I thought so too. The golden load hung over the sides of the high sided wain and seemed to me to be ready to tip over. It stood as high as a red double decker London bus.

Rodney and I got to ride back to the farm on the top of the load. The stackers were to stay where they were so it would be fun, even if for me, a little scary. "Climb up on th' ol' wheel me dear". A large red hand swung a foot or two too high over my reach. A rickety old wooden ladder that had been brought from the farm for this very reason I suspect, was brought from the side of the field for me. Up I went somewhat nervously and flopped thankfully into a rough trough of sheaves as far from the edge of the load as I could. I felt very insecure as the wain swayed one way and then the next, as it turned towards the field gate and bumped over deep rutted tracks. Finally, when onto the road, I felt relieved and less nervous and forgot my initial fears. This was really fun. High above the walled field hedges. Close to my ears the singing telephone wires looped in the descending curves from tarry post to tarry post, sometimes above my head and sometimes below the level of the high load. I risked a peep over the front edge. The huge Shire looked so small now. Ears erect, head nodding in time with every steady paced stride. 'Clip', 'clop'… 'clip', 'clop', in a steady unhurried rhythm. His back muscles rippling and draped with leather straps. The reigns thrown carelessly over it. He knew his way back to the farm, there was no need for him to be led, but someone walked at his head and talked to him anyway. Brass buckles, belts and rattling chains attached to the nodding shafts; shoulders pressed into the thick collar.

* * * * *

A little paddock like field just off the lane adjacent to the farmyard had been from time immemorial, set aside and always spoken of as the 'Rickyard'. The remains of last year's hay crop scattered over the site of last winters 'Rick' (haystack). This year's crop of golden hay still streaked with traces of the summers meadow green, baled, and stacked, solid looking, and a house high, was thatched and roped against the wet and the wind. Precious winter feed for horses and the cattle. I thought it needed windows, a door, and a smoking chimney, to complete the picture of a farm cottage. This year's wheat crop, the first of which was on this very 'wain' as we turned into the rickyard, and the rest of it still stooked in rows yet to be brought home, was 'stacked in Rick' (as it was obligingly explained to me), in the yard until it could be threshed. "Perhaps in a few weeks' time". "T' thresher do come in a week or two T' flail the wheat out o' them ears". Seeing that I was somewhat mystified, the explanation was left at that, and no further enlightenment offered beyond, "You'll see m' dear".

* * * * *

At the rickyard, the first load spread carefully on the prepared ground in a neat square layer. Sheaves laid in different directions like house bricks. The next layer in the opposite direction. "Th' rick 'ould blew down at th' fust good blew m'dear"…. I should have known the answer even before I had asked the question. That done, it was back to five acre. Load after load, the stooks were fewer and fewer. The rick grew higher and higher until finally all were safely 'gathered in'. The final tarpaulin weighted down with suspended stones that served the same purpose for generations of past harvests and would do service again next year… Start a smaller rick for the last few loads… The day's work was done. As the early night crept over five acre and the darkening rickyard, we walked home along the darkened lanes.

* * * * *

The school summer holidays were upon us. It behoves us 'tearaways' to find things to amuse ourselves and keep us out of real mischief. I had a wild idea to bring the city to the countryside. I suggested we would build a stage and organise public (and paying) variety shows.

299

A stage with curtains tucked into an out of the way corner beside a garden shed. A labour of hours to collect together the bits and pieces finally resulted in a stage somewhat reduced in scale to the original conception. The idea rather petered out when it was realised that the first essential variety performance was the performers, and there was a lack of them in the immediate vicinity of rural Treswithian... never mind. The stage stood forlorn for some few days until some new idea took root and the bits and pieces required to perform elsewhere.

Holidays were never short of things to do. There were the Whitegate days and milk round days. Frequently, I was able to slope off on my own tours of discovery. When I was really bold and determined to risk the consequences, I managed to find the path up to the North Cliff. Not too far mind you, and not too close to the cliff edge. I had a healthy fear of the ultimate risks. As I stood at the cliff edge of Hell's Mouth with Uncle Charlie, I didn't like the sensation of my imagination of falling into the threatening gulf, but I wondered at the grandeurs around me, and the Atlantic rollers crashing and leaping up the granite cliffs. It was marvellous.

I explored the whole length of the Red River valley path almost to its outflow at Godrevy. In those days, the banks of the bloody stream were littered with rusting iron wheels, decaying and broken troughs, and sheds fast sinking into oblivion. Iron and bolts, wood, and iron frames, rusting and returning into the natural elements of disintegration. Reminders, I was later told, of the recovery of tin out of the red silt washed out of the tin mines of Carn Brea and Redruth. An operation abandoned at last because it became uneconomic, and the remaining tin was swept out to sea.

A little further down from the crossroads close to 'Elmhurst', I had noticed a five bar gate into a field, well padlocked and further restricted with barbed wire and a notice printed in red declaring 'Danger! No admittance'. It was a small course meadow, grassed, and overgrown with bramble and scattered with broken stones. I never saw cows grazing or crops growing. I asked, "Why can't we go into that field"? Auntie Hilda explained with all the emphasis that the heavily chained and padlocked gate implied. "Never climb over that gate, or ever go into it. There are mine shafts that are extremely dangerous. If anyone ever fell into one it would be the end". "There is deep water at the bottom of them. So, now you know. Don't ever go near the place". After that I always gave the gate and the field as 'wide-a-berth' as possible. I had a terrible fear of suddenly being swallowed up and lost forever in the black depths of the abandoned mines.

One evening, Uncle Charlie came home with the news that the 'thresher' had finished at, "So, and so's farm". "He tells me that he is 'threshing' at Whitegates tomorrow". To me, he asked, "Ar' you ever seen threshing m'dear"? Well, of course I hadn't, so I answered, "No". "Then I'll take 'e both, up to Whitegates in the morning". Rodney and I were up at the crack of dawn, full of excited anticipation. Finally, Uncle 'C', on his way to pick up the milk at the farm, collected us at the back gate of 'Elmhurst' as usual. Off we went, aided by a thin pencil of light of the lorry's dimmed blackout headlights and a brightening dawn beginning to glow low in the east. As we passed the school at Kehelland and made our careful way up the lane to the farm, I saw a thin trail of black smoke rising like a thin pencil into the lightening sky. We stopped at the rickyard gate and almost fell out of the lorry's cab with hasty and excited speed. "Behave yourselves, and don't get into the way", Uncle 'C' warned. "Be good... Bye" ... and left us to our own enjoyments.

* * * * *

The 'Rickyard', usually so quiet in its isolated guardianship of its silent ricks, was now a scene of activity that reminded me of visiting fairgrounds. On one side of the yard, a collection of iron shod wheeled caravan trailers. A black tarred water tank on iron wheels. A flat trailer stacked with bags of coal, and best of all a steam tractor. It's long chimney standing erect and glinting, brass capped, mounted on a slim grubbyish green painted boiler bound with polished brass straps. Front wheels that looked too flimsy to carry the heavy weight of the tractor. Huge iron spiked rear wheels carrying the 'footplate' and boiler fire. Fly wheels lazily turning, the spinning 'governor'... brass dials and steam leaking valves. A horizontal knobbed steering wheel and its long threaded column dropping chains that turned the direction of the front wheels into the direction of travel. Topped all over by a canvas covered roof awning.

Quietly 'chug'... 'chug'... 'chugging' fly wheel and governor slowly turning. A sudden glow on the face of the driver as he opened the fire box door to feed more coal into it. A belch of black smoke rose out of the chimney. The long black pencil I had seen in the sky as we passed the school.

Standing by the recently built tarpaulined rick, the big wooden red painted threshing machine was waiting to be connected to the tractor. A long four inch wide belt lying on the ground between the 'machine' and the tractor fly wheel. There was not enough pressure yet to begin the Threshing. Helpers pulled off the roped tarpaulin and helpers were up on the 'rick', and others up on the threshing machine waiting to begin. At last, all was ready. The steady chug of the tractor... more coal and the tractor increased its tempo. Hissing steam and a soft 'whoof... whoof' of smoke issuing from the chimney, it was time to connect the belt to the thresher and the tractor. The heavy leather belt held over half a dozen shoulders and slipped over the stationery fly wheel. Next, the thresher's... a few sweaty under breath uttered curses and a few shouted instructions, the belt was threaded and looped and crossed over the thresher drive wheel. A big heavy hammer drove home the belt connector. "Right 'en. Let 'er going 'en". A last minute check that all was as it should be and safe, the fly wheels slowly took up the slack. The regulator opened another notch. 'Chuff'... 'whoof'...

'chug'... 'whoof', in increasing tempo. Belt slapping wheels turning slowly at first then gaining speed. Riddler boxes, oscillating wheels, and protruding spindle here and there, took up the refrain.

Everything working on top of the thresher, the helpers introduced the first sheaf. Nothing happened, then the next sheaf and the next... nothing... and the first trickle of loosened grain fell sparingly into the sack hooked at the rear of the machine to receive it. More and more sheaves swallowed into the hungry machine. Dust and more dust. Hankies tied around the lower face. Dust, and now a steady flow of husked wheat fell into the rapidly filling sack. Chaff building up under the machine. It will be used as feed. Spent straw cast out saved for litter, I think the bran too was somehow gathered, but I have no idea how.

Soon the sack would be filled and replaced quickly with another. Swiftly and deftly stich-sealed with binder twine... a hundred kilos perhaps, hoisted onto a waiting cart to be taken back to the farmyard and stored in one of the farmyard buildings used as a temporary granary until sold. The old Shire horse had his part to play in this 'mechanised' monstrosity of modernisation too. He had to haul the carts back and forth from the farmyard and fetch and carry. The steam tractor glowing hot and hissing steam, the flying regulator valve spinning captive steel balls in a misty circle of bright steel... coal and water. The water tank hauled by the shire to be refilled. A black faced driver watching over his firebox, dials, and gauges. The whole tractor was shaking and straining against the captive belt and the vibrating thresher and there was black acrid smoke. It was sweaty, heavy, and dusty work. The ricks grew smaller and smaller, and the stacks of grains grew higher and higher in the temporary granary.

Threshing time was a busy time for the travelling harvest time itinerant tractor team, contracted to go from farm to farm to thresh the cereals. The team that had arrived at Whitegates had arrived as a long caravan of half a dozen trailers pulled like a train by the steam tractor, in the early hours of the morning. A short rest and early breakfast, the men cleaned out the fire box and set up the thresher and got organised. A new fire was set to raise steam for another days work. Whitegates did not have much grain to thresh but there was enough work for a long day. Eight hours later they cleared and tidied up and hitched up the living caravans. They would sleep overnight in the rickyard and move onto the next job early next morning.

A mountainous farmhouse supper of massive pasties and brown earthenware flagons of Devon/Somerset, or West Country cider, or chipped white enamel tin mugs of brown tea (which was Rodney's and my repast). I would have liked to try the cider! Mrs Bennet even discovered a spare pastie each for us both (and for one or two other hopefuls hanging around the open farmhouse door). I don't remember Uncle 'C' calling to take us home. A wonderful climax to a wonderful, tiring, and evocative memory. A wonderful end to the day at the sun's setting… Unforgettable.

However, a threatening shadow of disaster began to overtake events. June had suffered the indignity of impetigo, her luxuriant crop of dark curls had had to be shorn, she wore a bonnet to cover her embarrassment. Rodney and I were not affected.

As for me, an annoying itch which I tried valiantly to hide troubled me. My arms showing the disastrous blotches and purple scab… scabies. That awful scourge sweeping relentlessly through the ranks of our school fellows. I was infested. Parents and guardians were required to report these infections and there were penalties for not doing so. The local doctor was informed, and I was duly diagnosed. "Yes, I am afraid it is scabies". There was nothing else for it but for me to suffer the ever present threat 'hostelisation'. We all knew about this threat.

Auntie Hilda was sympathetically concerned for me as well as her concern for the family. She had no choice anyway. Isolation of the infected was compulsory. It was a case of submitting to the inevitable! "I'm sorry m'dear. We have to do what we are told".

Chapter 26

Tabb's Hotel... Concentration camp number 1 - 1941

Later... the very same day.

There was to be no time to think about it. The doctor, there and then, made out the admission order. Admit one, male. Insole, John. Age nine. Home address... London, etc., etc. Guardian... etc., etc.

"You will need ration book, identity card, gas mask. Change of clothing. No toys or books can be taken. All tagged with name". Instructions completed; a faint smile of condolence flickered for a split second. "Everything will be alright Johnnie. Tabb's Hotel is very nice. You will have a nice time. Don't worry". He might well have known something about its real reputation if his rather 'over the top' reassurances had anything to do with it. He knew more than he was telling. I was not reassured. Amongst those who had already experienced this 'Tabb's treatment' and returned to civilisation... cured... still bore the psychological scars to prove how 'nice' it had been.

Bag packed, bus times checked, there was a trip to Redruth from the top of the lane at Treswithian. I had never been to Redruth, so this took my mind off the purpose of the journey for a while. Auntie 'H' produced a small bag of boiled sweets. "Put those in your pocket m'dear, for later". A tiny sparkle of a tear shimmered in the corner of her eye. Mine threatened to erupt into a flood but a pretence of manliness forbade it.

A short climb up the sloping Redruth high street, passing the clock tower… "Tabb's Hotel, m'dear"? Auntie enquired. "Over there m'dear". The lady pointing with a quizzical look at me. The lady knew why we wanted Tabb's Hotel. Its reputation had gone before it.

It had been closed as a hotel for many a year. The local authority had requisitioned the empty building to carry out its liability to provide centres to accommodate the 'blighted'. I was about to join the ranks of the inflicted and felt decidedly 'dirty'. At that moment in Redruth high street, I felt like the lepers of the Bible stories I had heard about in my infrequent exposures to Sunday schools. I felt as though all I needed was the bell to announce my coming!

Some belated attempts had been made to brighten up the otherwise near derelict premises. A double fronted three or four storied building, the woodwork in serious need of paint. Between an imposing pair of ground floor windows was an equally imposing entrance with doors shut tight. A notice said, 'Please knock and wait'. Somebody came eventually in answer to auntie's loud knocking. "This is John Insole. I have been told to bring…". Her explanations of introduction suddenly cut short. "Oh yes, come in please. This way please", she said, holding her hand out for the admission documents. We followed as instructed through a short entrance lobby and swing doors to the main hallway entrance, with a cold tiled floor devoid of covering and not a vestige of furnishing. "Please wait here, matron will see him in a moment". (There were no chairs or seats to ease what proved to be a long wait).

Passages to the left and to the right disappeared into the dark uninviting interior. Above us, a high stairwell and staircase rising the full three storeys to a glass roof window that bore the grime of generations, permitting very little natural light to percolate the dusty stairwell and the ornately carved staircase to the three upper floors. The whole had seen much better days of décor. Wallpaper that had been applied many years since, torn, stained, and in many places quitting its crumbling plaster anchorage... not a reassuring prospect for me. There was also a pervading aroma of rot and decay mixed in with that hospital smell of disinfectant. Attempts had been made to cheer things up a bit. One or two pictures on the walls. Lace curtains over the street facing windows stretched skimpily and drooping. The pictures may well have been uncleared items left when the hotel closed for business. Everywhere was chipped and worn. Stained and darkening varnish to doors, stairs, wainscoting. Everywhere there was darkening black woodwork adding to the overall dismal aspect of the place.

Most astonishing were the inmates. They were everywhere. Climbing the stairs, disappearing into this passage and that passage, passing into and out of the downstairs rooms. Instructions shouted from within. "Shut the door", repeated impatiently. "Shut the door will you"? (How one passed through a doorway and closed it at the same time I failed to understand). What completely threw me were the children. Some were wandering apparently aimlessly. Some fully dressed, others in white gowns and little else. Some too long and others too short. Some hair shorn, but the most amazing thing was the blue. Blue arms, blue legs, necks, and faces painted with a bright blue gentian dye. Some of them even sported elaborate designs of a blue ship, or a car, or a lorry (the boys of course). Tabb's hotel was a mixed sex hostel. The girls kept themselves well wrapped and accommodated separately. (Rumour had it though that they also sported their own preferred designs but kept them well covered).

"Ah, Mrs Mitchell, come this way please". We obediently shut the door on request. No ceremony. This was going to be a brief interview. Matron sat behind her desk. "Right, this is John is it? Have you brought his ration book? Identity card?... Good, good. Change of clothes? Good, good". Interview over. "Right, Mrs Mitchell, there is no need for you to wait. The doctor will see him later and we will let you know when he may return home". She coughed. "I mean, back to your foster care. You will let his parents know of course". With that, Auntie 'H' was sent on her way, and I was left alone with destiny. "Right John, now let me see. Ah yes, scabies. I'll take you up to see the doctor now, then we must get you settled in. You will soon meet some nice friends". She stood up and I went to pick up my bag of clothes. "No, no", she said. "Leave those with me", and she took the bag away from my tight grip. I wasn't going to surrender it without a struggle. The little bag of boiled sweets was in it. It was the last I ever saw of the bag, and I didn't get the sweets back either.

I climbed the long staircase in her wake, not being fast enough for her wonted pace. "Come along now, we haven't got all day". The stair suddenly depopulated of children aware of her threatening presence. I learned later that 'matron' was best kept at a distance. 'Where are you going, and what are you doing', needed some very fast thinking if one were to avoid some irritating occupational task imposed upon the luckless slow thinker.

At the top floor I was deposited into a sort of anti-room adjoining the doctors surgery. There was nowhere to sit and wait. The room was furnished with a W/D trestle type table and a folding chair set upon a dusty scrap of frayed carpet. There were cardboard files piled haphazardly in corners of the room. The 'office' (for such it was designated) overlooked the front of the hotel. A lace curtain suspended on nails hung limp against the window. A naked lightbulb hanging by a dusty perished length of wire threatening to part company with a lopsided rose. I had time enough on my hands while I waited to see the doctor to absorb every detail of the hastily set up provision of an 'office'. A very essential provision of any and every organisation efficient or otherwise, not that very much ever seemed to take place in this emporium of officialdom. The door into the doctor's room opened. "Come in". It was the brightest room in the whole building. Clean and freshly painted with the usual array of clinical furnishings. New 'lino' on the floor and the usual oversized leather topped desk. Tidy papers, a stethoscope, pens, and pencils lined up in neat rows. "Come in". The matron standing in the doorway in servile deference to the mighty doctor. He was a stout fresh faced gentleman that spoke of a natural joviality. His spectacles balanced precariously on the very tip of his nose, he looked at me over the top of them with a big bedside smile on his face. Involuntarily, I could do no more than return the courtesy with a big smile of my own. The first genuine smile that I had seen so far. "This...", I thought, "... was not going to be so bad after all". "That's right. That's right", he said. "Now, let's see what this nasty business is all about. Arms up... Humpf... Yes, yes. Up with your shirt... Good, good. Ah, yes, well... well... oh yes, dear me. We will soon get you put right".

To the matron, who stood with her notebook and pencil poised, the treatment was described, and prescription made out. "Twice daily". I'll see him... now let's see... yes, yes, this day next week at... 10:30". The examination was complete, and I was released into the tender care of the matron and her staff. Matron, suitably subdued for the moment by her confrontation with her revered superior, smiled at me. It was the first and the last time that I (and I have no doubt, many like me) ever saw her smile at all!

* * * * *

Once out of the doctors presence, the matron seemed to unfold out of her subdued opinion of her own smallness and grew suddenly in the sunshine of her inestimable greatness and authority. The smile had remarkably vanished and was replaced by a thin line of concentrated efficiency. "Now, let me see. Where are we going to put you?.. Ah, yes, there is a vacant bed space in the 'ballroom'". Off we went, children scattering in all directions at her dreaded approach, but she was too busy to deal with this particular personal irritation at that moment. Down the stairs to the first floor and a sharp turn to the left into a long corridor of unfurnished ex-hotel days. There were guest rooms on one side of the corridor and on the other, a row of windows overlooking the rear of the hotel. The floors were bare of any covering and the windows naked of a curtain to grace any one of them. The corridor ended at an open door. In the ancient days prior to 1940, Tabb's Hotel had boasted a largish reception room. Hopefully designated 'ballroom' as described in old lettering on the open door, but now it echoed to a very different kind of music. Children shouting, laughing, and creating all kinds of juvenile mayhem. "Quiet... quiet", bellowed matron. A sudden hush fell over all. One or two of them, not yet made aware of her sudden and unheralded appearance, still babbling for all their worth. "Quiet now... Qui...et... That's better. Now, Tom, what are you up to again"? Tom, too nervous to say, was letting go of Harry's last remaining tuft of hair. For the want of another ear to bend, or just to comfort herself, she muttered audibly for everybody's information. "The sooner that child goes home the better", a sentiment that Tom would no doubt subscribe to gladly. This very moment would not have been too soon for him... or Harry... or any one of them, including me. To me personally, she said, "You WILL behave, won't you? I don't want any more bother than I can help". In other words, woe betide me if I was a bother to her. Tom smirked and put up two fingers at her turned back merely to indicate that he at least, was determined to be as much bother to her as possible, threats or no threats.

The 'ballroom' presented a picture of perhaps three or four dozen children pretending (for matrons benefit only), to be busy at something, and an equal number of ex-army camp beds set out in four or so rows. The ballroom was just as dingy and as derelict as the rest of the building. On one side a large open fireplace, empty but for a pile of fallen soot. It was surrounded by an unnecessary rusty iron fireguard. A bare boarded floor that might once have known of waltzing pairs and polish, but now scratched and broken. The windows at least, were provided with the soiled black curtaining to comply with the blackout requirements, wide open and introducing the constant Atlantic gales.

I was shown where my bed was. It was one of the low camp beds, as yet unmade. The mattress made up of three flat looking 'biscuits', brown, and as hard as wooden boards. There was one hard unbendable pillow, a couple of stiff canvas like sheets, and a couple of coarse blankets to complete the provision and promise of discomfort. "There", matron said. "That's your bed. I'll get someone to make it up for you". And that was that. "Oh… and tea will be at half past four". And duty done, she was gone.

Personal introductions were out of the question. We were expected to make our own arrangements for polite acquaintance. At her departure I was soon surrounded by the curious who wanted to know my name, where I came from, and the like. Not least, some details of what I might expect as a resident guest of Tabb's five star hotel. I was a little too overwhelmed by all the attention and a good deal too much information in the way of the 'horrific' 'who' to steer clear of, and 'who' might be sympathetically prone to 'creepers'. All of it important if one was to cope with the situation.

The truth is, that ninety percent of the inmates were evacuees. There were a few locals, but generally local parents knew better than to let their kids be sent there. Who were we to complain to in any case? We were hundreds of miles away from any help. There were also other restrictions laid on visits that ruled out swift communications anyway. Generally speaking, incarceration at Tabb's only lasted a matter of a few weeks, a pretty tough few weeks it is true, but by the time any complaint got back to base as it were, the patient was at home nursing their wounds, and Tabb's was best forgotten.

Except for most of us who experienced Tabb's, forgetting the experience might be easier said than done. It wasn't exactly a matter of discipline, but the lack of it might have been something that affected the patient less than it did the staff. It is possible (in fact probable), that the root problem was due to the fact that wartime staffing problems were to blame. It would be more than a shrewd guess to suggest that so called 'matron', would not have got a post in that role 'anywhere', let alone keep it for more than it took to discover the truth about her qualifications. In any case, Tabb's had to be at a very low degree of priority where nursing skills were concerned. I think the same principle applied to any post within the orbit of Tabb's responsibilities. The very building environment alone was testament enough to demonstrate this. Having said this, it would be unjust to suggest that it was all as bad as this and that all the staff were totally without feelings, but by the very nature of wartime restrictions and availability, even angels themselves would have been tested to the extreme.

True, there may have been some of us, the 'patients', who were well used to the rigours of 'rough living' and tended to be a trifle too difficult to handle under any circumstances. It wasn't quite a matter of 'jungle law'... one just had to acquire a primitive urge to survive some of the indignities most of us had to suffer.

Some notable staff members were rather too inclined to mete out their own brand of discipline in over enthusiastic doses. The idea presumably was to hasten a rapid cure-all of youthful exuberance and scabies alike. I couldn't have been the exception to the general rule. Whatever the treatment prescribed for me personally, seemed to be the main prescription for everybody. 'Saline' baths, sunlamps, and blue gentian artwork.

Baths twice daily and always barely warm enough for comfort. A thick and creamy infusion that smelt remarkably like pure tar, and rough towels. To say nothing of the 'nursing staff', whose duty it was to administer the 'punishment'. 'She' (I believe it was a 'she'), certainly wouldn't have graced the title of nurse, 'she' would have been better suited to have followed the occupation of 'Blacksmith'. Baths with 'her' in attendance were sheer terror and physical agony. Great hands as rough as sandpaper grasped slippery arms in vice like grips. 'She' found that failing a sure grip on flesh, or as a last resort, hair was a secure and convenient hand-hold. Once having secured a grip on 'something or anything', it then felt as though she used a scrub brush and rough floor cloth, especially in the most tender of places! (She may well have had some anti-male issues). Screaming and bellowing as she scrubbed and pummelled away, blissfully unaware of my cries of agony. "Keep still won't you…. Keep still will you".

Scrub, scrub, scrub, pummel, grasp, grip… suddenly to be hoisted unceremoniously out of the tub for the next part of the kill-or-cure treatment. The violent rub down with the nutmeg grater towel, finishing up 'red raw'. (All the scabs had gone of course, leaving behind red blotches in their place).

Meals…. There was a wartime source of wonder. We all knew about shortages, scarcity, and food rationing. Meals at home could be dreary enough but Tabb's Hotel catering arrangement and its diet sheet did not go in for ingenuity. Most mums did somehow manage to ring the changes to tempt the tastebuds. Tabb's worked solely on the basis of weight, bulk, calories, and nothing in between. At the appointed times for meals, we were divided into small groups of a dozen or so, in order to fit us into a small dining room that had obviously done service in the past more peaceful times for fewer guests than were catered for in its wartime role. Barely furnished except for a large square table, much battered and worn with the barest suggestion of polish remaining clinging on in patches here and there. Military type folding chairs that one tended to slip off of, or that threatened to fold up uninvited. There was a worn and lino'd floor covering, and everywhere was paintless and darkly rotting.

Breakfast…. Porridge (aptly named for its association), watery and lumpy, doled out in thick lumps, or cornflakes moistened with watery milk. No sugar. Brown bread and margarine, and what disgusting brown bread it was too! We all called it the 'rock of ages', heavy and coarse, gritty with un-milled wheat, sour tasting and stale. A few saucers of thinned down marmalade, weak tea poured ready milked from out of a large aluminium teapot, no sugar but evidently sweetened with saccharin. We were generally hungry enough to gulp down all we could when we could. The 'brown bread', disgusting as it was, tended to lay heavy on the stomach as it had to pass as satisfaction.

Dinner.... The everlasting memory that seems to block out any suggestion of any variation is pea soup. Not as the accepted description of normal pea soup. Dinnertime, a soup plate filled with it, together with boiled potatoes, a few scraps of carrot maybe, a hint of onion (doubtful). I remember cheap cut scrag end of mutton (more splintered bone than mutton), accompanied by 'brown bread'. I might be told differently. Might... that on Sundays it 'might' have been sliced beef. All I know, is that it is those two abiding recollections, 'brown bread' and 'pea soup', that were the staple diet.

Teatime.... Brown bread, a few dishes of watered down jam, a sticky fruitless currant bun, or a chunk of heavy 'eggless' sponge cake. Watery tea that tasted like the leftover from breakfast.

Supper.... Guess what? Brown bread milk sop (soaked in warm milk), a mug of cocoa as black and as milkless as 'Newgate's knocker', and as bitter.

Once (it must have been on the King's birthday), the early diners came back with the startling news that there had been real white bread. Wartime grey-white bread that is. It was only once though. Somebody must have forgotten to order the usual brown concrete, or it hadn't set in time for tea. After supper we were usually left an hour or so, with time to waste before camping the night in the derelict ballroom dormitory to toss uncomfortably half the night trying to find a softer spot on those frequently separating three mattress slabs. Listening for the rest of the night to the moans and groans of equally restless sleepers, disturbed by the yells and shouts of sleep talkers, seeing the sleepwalkers, and hearing the angry night attendants telling off the restless culprits for disturbing their hoped for peaceful night duty, and the never to be forgotten night of the 'Dippy visitation'.

The boy in the next bed to mine who was perhaps a year or two older than me (he was certainly bigger), complained early in the evening of a sore throat. Later, during the night, moaning and groaning and gasping for breath. The attendant came. High temperature. Call the doctor. All of us by now fully awake. The doctor arrived and took one look at his patient and quietly informed the night attendant… "Diphtheria…. Yes, yes. No doubt about it". There was panic. "Sorry, he can't be moved. Nobody must be moved for risk of spreading the infection".

All available hands were called to deal with the emergency. Hot water bottles, blankets… I heard it all. "Doctor, quick. Please". "Crisis. He can't breathe". "Nurse. Tube. Quickly now". He was choking. His rattling groans. The night lady attendant turned to me, "Go to sleep Johnnie". How could I? How long it went on, I do not now remember. Behind the temporary screens all was now suddenly quiet. No more choking. No more gasps for breath. I must have fallen asleep in spite of myself. When I woke it was daylight, and it was all quiet. The boy had gone. His bed was empty. Had he died? I do not know. Nobody said and nobody asked, but the ballroom was unnaturally quiet the next day.

Doctors and nurses came. We were not allowed out of the room and nobody, but the medical staff, were allowed into it. Everyone was swabbed for infections. Cleaners came and scrubbed floors and everything was washed and disinfected. All the bed linen and blankets etc., bundled up and changed. Those who hadn't been inoculated against diphtheria were injected (there were a few who had apparently escaped the mass inoculation carried out some few months previously). The boy in the next bed had been unfortunate, perhaps he hadn't been inoculated. Diphtheria was a killer. I hope he came through his crisis... I shall never know perhaps.

Chapter 27

Education, Academic & otherwise...
The Bathroom terrorist gets her 'comeuppance'!

I don't think that the education authorities actually forgot the important business of education altogether. We, the afflicted, might be temporarily released from the odious duty of school attendance. A small relief for some, I have no doubt.

I have a vague recollection that some provisions were made to occupy small groups at odd times in matters of great educational import. Occasionally, a few of the vaguely willing (but mostly unwilling) Tabb's wanderers, were gathered together to impart some essential educational necessities. I was never actually caught staring into space with nothing particular to do... except once. Having been taken off my guard against such an eventuality, I had usually managed to avoid confrontation with these useless mental exercises. The particular afternoon school session had been arranged without prior notice. Unfortunately, it seems, at a moment of hopeless distress on the part of the retired teacher brought in to bolster the educational morale, finding that she had not the slightest chance of imparting anything of lasting value, had long since given up trying.

So far, in this sorry tale, I have not mentioned the female population of concentration camp number one. They occupied the second floor and in good and proper order, to avoid possible suggestions of impropriety, there was very little communication between the sexes.

I might be taking too big a risk in pointing out that there wasn't very much intercourse between us. The scallywags on the first floor and the temptations of the second... except at mealtimes, and interesting enough the treatment room. Some efforts were obviously made to keep the genders apart but occasionally things seemed to go wrong and didn't go as planned. Tabb's boasted but two sunbeds, both in the same treatment room. Along with everyone else, I had been allocated sunlamp treatment... to be cooked on each side until crisp. That is where I discovered that the system frequently broke down and male and female found themselves in interesting company.

On one such occasion, I found that in order to preserve some kind of decorum in the situations, if I kept my eyes closed tight and pretended to be asleep, it didn't matter too much (I might have sneaked a sly look now and again). A lesson I had learnt from my first confrontation with the sunbed treatment, was that I had quietly contemplated a warm comforting snooze. The other bed not yet occupied... when all of a sudden, I was rudely awakened by a shy young lass of tender and obviously developing years who I noted, had removed her enveloping gown, and stood Eve like, ready to take her place on the sunbed when she espied me in nothing more than all my masculine glory gazing wide-eyed in wonder at this objective lesson. I had never been unaware of the usual essential gender differences so the revelation before me came as no great surprise but evidently she saw the matter in quite a different light. Of course, I was naturally embarrassed myself and tried to pretend that I didn't mind, and if she took the same attitude... she didn't! "No. No", she sobbed. "He is a boy". "I won't. I won't". "Now. Come, come. He is only a little boy. Be sensible girl now". I took the implied insult quite manfully. Anyway, by means of a generous assistance of sheer force, she was eventually deposited, complaining, onto the sunbed... subdued by hissed threats and dire consequences if she made too much fuss. "There", said a more considerate assistant. "Is that better"? Placing a tiny scrap of tissue paper over my manly dignity.

For reasons best known by nobody, it seems the poor girl had to endure her nakedness presumably on the basis that the idea of sunbed treatment is to get sunburnt all over, not to cover it all up. She spent the next half an hour sobbing. I hope it didn't cause her any lasting damage. I didn't mind it one bit, but then I suppose I had always been a little too precocious!

All in all, I suppose the situation did add a little something to my general education that I might not have acquired at Tabb's part time education facility due to the fact that biology was not part of the curriculum. Not officially anyway!

The Bathroom terrorist gets her 'comeuppance'!

Our particular antagonist 'nursing attendant', the terror of bath time repute, not only avenged herself on the luckless and powerless at bath times but she also stood out generally as one massive threat that put matron in the shade. Shouting and bawling at whatever she considered a digression from what she considered 'her' brand of good behaviour that is our complete silence and a stillness of non-presence. The fact that we were there at all was a matter of extreme irritation to her. Sarie Gamp (of Dickens fame) was never as cruel as our bath time terrorist could be. Her shouts could sometimes be delivered at the same time as vicious pinches, slaps, and pushes. She was hated above all else. As careless about her dress as she was about justice and caring... truly. Children can be deliberately troublesome, but how she managed to be engaged as a nursing assistant is beyond credence. True, wartime staff were not easy to come by and somebody had to do the job, better I suppose than nobody at all. It is possible that she was just doing a stint of compulsory labour either at Tabb's or some other black country munitions factory, or herding cows as a Land Army girl. I can well imagine her herding bullocks; she was perfectly suited. Whatever it was, it was evident that her main task in life was to make us as miserable as possible. Unhappy woman, she must have been.

Visiting was strictly forbidden, we were in 'isolation' and it meant what it said with no exceptions... except that I was due for a great surprise. On my bed one evening dreaming of nothing in particular, coming through the door of the ballroom, had it not been for the sudden silence, I would not have believed my eyes, was Dad, all smiles, and a broad dad grin.

"Hallo Johnnie. Surprised to see me"? Before I had found breath enough to answer him, he just laughed and said, "I bet you are. This is only a flying visit though". He had come all the way from London during one of his between jobs breaks to visit Lily and me, knowing that I was incarcerated in Tabb's trying to recuperate, or at any rate, merely trying to survive, only to discover that when he knocked at the front door as invited, and waited for the knock to be answered, he was promptly refused entry.

It had been our delightful 'fairy godmother', the bathroom terrorist, who had answered the knock and she had stood in his way, but she had not reckoned with dad's determination. In he came. He explained later that he had quietly let her know, "I've come all this way from London to be told by the likes of her that he was not allowed to see my son"? I don't actually think that there was the slightest trace of persuasion in the matter. He had walked in, or pushed in, and there was nothing she could do to stop him, and presumably induced somehow to show him the way because she had preceded his progress through the ballroom door. Her reluctance to do so was evident to us all.. muttering as she led dad to my bed. "I will have to report this, you won't get away with this Mr Insole", muttering and threatening for this invasion of her territorial right of domination. Grumbling at the far end of the room and taking it out on the innocent as usual.

He sat on my bed and I told him how we all hated her and her terrorist tactics. I thought I had spoken quietly but she must have had the ears of a wolf. From the far end of the ballroom she screamed, "I can hear you John Insole. I will speak to you later". Silly woman. That was the last straw for dad. He wasn't a big man, nor did he give the impression of aggression. He stood up from sitting on my bed and strode purposely towards the female dragon, backing her up against a convenient wall. Looking her straight in the eye, "You will not speak to him later. You and I are going to have a little chat first". With that, he marched her out of the ballroom to the approving cheers of all those who beheld this spectacle of a cringing wolf at bay. Returning a little later and alone and smiling, "You won't get any more trouble from her. If you do, just let me know about it". As if what he had done wasn't enough for us all, he asked if there was anything wanted. I had always wanted an encyclopaedia, so I thought 'here goes', so I said that is what I wanted. "Ah", he said. "That might not be so easy, but I'll try". I did eventually get volume one, that's all. I never got the rest. I still have it.

* * * * *

I had hoped for release and discharge from Tabb's soon. I had seen the doctor and he said that he was pleased with things, and I should be able to go home in a week or two, depending on if things continued to improve. Others too, were due for discharge but no, the ravages of 'scabies' persisted. I had one more horror to endure. Strangely, there were some odd things going on. Those who were apparently ready for discharge, for no apparent reason at, all broke out afresh with the complaint, until it was discovered it was... ME.

I have always had dry flaky skin. It seems that wherever I went, I left a trail of infected skin flakes behind me. Not only that, but a trail of re-infested unfortunate victims! There was nothing else for it but real and absolute isolation for me. Neither was I permitted to go anywhere where there was a possibility of a disastrous contact with anyone else. It was total isolation.

One of the ancient, and so far unused guest rooms along the corridor, was swept and dusted. A net hung at the window to make it a little more homely, and my camp bed moved into it. It was to be my prison for as long as it took to clear the infestation. Baths were out and blanket baths were in. Meals were taken in my prison, and worst of all a 'pot for the use of'. A few books were allowed but there was a very surprising turn of events. Our personal 'she-wolf', who had evidently been severely reprimanded and somewhat side-lined and demoted to duties in the background, had been personally given the responsibility to care for me. I understood perfectly that here was the opportunity for her to carry out a 'revenge', but she didn't. She had suddenly melted and did everything she could to keep me comfortable and cheerful. She found ways to find little treats for me. One of them was 'real white bread', and wonder of wonders, 'real butter'. I revelled in the privilege of benefits. She also chatted and told me of her home in Ireland (northern), and how much she missed her home etc. (Perhaps I understand better now why she hated her forced labour. It had never been a labour of love and she evidently hated every minute of it. Us, and everything about it). Suddenly, she was redeemed in my eyes. She wanted to get away from Tabb's no less than any one of us did.

I didn't altogether observe the isolation regulations. I'm afraid I did manage to sneak out of the room into the corridor a few times when there was nobody likely to be about. Usually at night. During the day there was always a lot of coming and going along the corridor.

The corridor windows overlooked the hotel's backyards. There were outbuilding and the kitchens. There was also an under the hotel garage that had been obviously taken over by a local undertaker. Generally, at night (dusk anyway), black limousines... hearses... ditto, were coming into the yard with coffins, and going out... ditto. Oh dear, I thought, in my moments of most rampant imagination. This was nothing more than a convenient way of disposing of us quietly. All the failures and the incurables like me, and I was to be the next... and it was only the bath time terrorists objective to fatten me up for the final end of it all. It was a fantasy that grew out of the dark nights as I lay trying to sleep, thinking of those coffins and their occupants who came up through the floorboards as misty ghosts to petrify me. I'd pull the blankets tighter around me and over my head so as not to see or be seen by them, and I would breathe as quietly as possible. Every creak and sound making me shake with fear, and the silence too. So isolated. So alone... and I dare not tell anyone of my distress. I had never been really scared of the dark before, or of silence, but I was then. Imagination invents terrors that do not exist, and they are so real, and not only in the young, but everything has to come to an end at some time. At last, I was clear. No more scabies. I could go home to Elmhurst. Auntie Hilda came for me.

Back at 'Elmhurst', I felt strangely guilty. I don't know what for, or why. I felt as though I had deliberately introduced some awful blight. I felt as if I had become the worst example of ingratitude to have brought them such concern and worries, not for my own problems but for their own wellbeing. I had been a risk and the scabies had become some awful crime committed because I shouldn't have caught it in the first place. I took it on myself that it must have been my fault. Unreasoned? Maybe it was. I felt the same back at Kehelland school. My granite doorstep came more into use as I drew further into myself.

I found changes at Elmhurst too. Lily who was into her thirteenth year, was finding things were getting difficult for her, and I expect everyone else as well. Lily had to move on. A place for her was found at Treswithian. She was not happy there at all.

The 'blitz' seemed to be over and done with, and Lily wanted to go home. She wrote home to tell dad what she wanted. Soon after, dad came on another flying visit to make the necessary arrangements for her return to London.

We walked out. I wanted to show dad the wonders of Hell's Mouth and the red-river path to Godrevy. He had his camera and some very rare and difficult to get, film (photos). As we walked, I knew that it was certain that Lily had made up her mind to go back to Wapping with him. He asked me, "Do you want to stay here"? I also knew that this would mean I would eventually go back to 'M' and Pop, and all the difficulties and virtual loneliness of Forest Gate, and that it would be the last I saw of Lily and dad, perhaps forever. "Or do you want to come home with Lily"? At that moment, it wasn't really a difficult question to answer, although there was a very strong 'pull' of Cornwall mixed in with a kind of vague feeling of filial loyalties to 'M' and 'P'... but... Wapping? It was really the first call on my filial feelings and the meanings of home. Bermondsey, Little Gran, and Uncle Robinson Crusoe were okay. Dagenham had a place and a meaning for me but then there was a Big Gran and Grandad, aunts, and uncle, who were real and permanent, and cousins who were real cousins. The place I wanted to be and where I really felt wanted. There was no hesitation in my reply. "Oh, yes please", and then a brief moment of fear. "But what am I going to say to..." and I could not give it the word 'mum'. I did not need to say it, his reaction was swift. "Tell her nothing. I will tell her if necessary". (He never did) And the matter was settled.

There was nothing more to be said. I didn't even have to tell Auntie Hilda and Unc' Charlie. Dad did the difficult bits for me. "John has decided to come home with Lily and me". It was done. I was close to tears for the awful brutality of the announcement and the finality of the decision, although I have to say now that it was the kind of situation that I was used to. I never knew where I would be from one day to the next. Dad was in a hurry to get back to London (I didn't know it then, but I learnt years later, that dad was a chemical engineer and had been engaged in important and very secret war work, but more of this later... The first next available train if possible... Hurried packings and difficult farewells.

As we walked away from Treswithian Downs and Elmhurst up the narrow lane to the main road into Camborne, I gathered handfuls of grass and wildflowers from the verge sides as a keepsake and a reminder. I listened again for the last time to the humming buzz of the singing telegraph wires that I had so often imagined were the muffled sounds of distant voices who spoke of mysteries and the secrets that I would never know, thinking at the same time of the wonder that these very wires stretched all the way back to Forest Gate. I could have phoned to GRA 3550 at any time, but I had not, nor had I wanted to or, as it turned out, I never did. A last look back at the diminishing group still waving goodbye at the back gate of Elmhurst until a bend in the lane was reached and we, and they, became part of both of our pasts and of our future memories. Filled as I was with the pent up excitement of going home, I felt like a long lost traveller glad at last to be coming home.

Chapter 28

Coming Home at Last – Evacuation Again – Guildford – (A leap forward in time)

The journey from Camborne to Paddington, if anything at all, seemed to take longer than our coming on the evacuation train. Not an unusual feature of wartime travel. Frequently, trains would be shunted into sidings out in the back of beyond somewhere to let essential wartime transports through. Troop trains, trains loaded with khaki army lorries, tanks, and military material. Our journey had been straightforward enough until we reached close to Saltash bridge. Even before we had reached the bridge with the arching span in sight, an air raid was in progress. The train shuddered to a sudden stop. The guns of Plymouth and the fleet in the Sound suddenly erupted in a crescendo of thunderous noise, blazing away at unseen targets above. The train had stopped almost at the crossing... and then 'they' came diving down. What a grandstand view we had. The sky filled with black and red streaked brown puffs of the anti-aircraft shell bursts. A black plume of trailing smoke snaked at the tail of one of the attacking planes as it fled. At least one of them probably never made it home! A screaming flight of hurricanes streaked over us. All over. The raiders chased away. There was no serious damage. Dad just laughed at my look of terror and excitement. The train cautiously crossed the bridge at a snail's pace.

There were no refreshments available on the train apart from a cup of tea, one small sugar cube each, and a few plain biscuits. Auntie Hilda had packed us a few sandwiches and surprise, surprise, a gorgeous pastie each. I saved mine to savour the anticipation for as long as I could until I could resist it no longer.

Paddington Station at last, looking very seedy in the unkempt fashion of the war times. The station was filled with khaki, air force blue and navy blue uniforms, red capped and holstered military police, and the civil police were equipped with steel helmets and gas packs and capes everywhere... checking papers and travel permits. There were piles of kitbags, backpacks and rifles and sergeants and corporals, enlisted and the conscripted. N.A.A.F.I and the Salvation Army (Sally Anne) tea and bun waggons dishing out the comforts in mugfuls and cheering smiles to the wearied travellers. Civilian passengers amongst the military wandered lost and bewildered waiting for trains that never came, or that seemed to go anywhere when they did. Sandbags were stacked in protective blast walls and conspicuously the damage already inflicted by the blitz, and noticeably a general tension that at any moment it could all begin again in another gut wrenching shrill siren warning and another slaughtering attack. Today... tonight... tomorrow... anytime.

True, there had not been a significant air raid for a couple of months (the only reason that dad had decided that it was safe for us to return home to London). Maybe it was because everybody else thought that the Luftwaffe had been sufficiently roughed up, or perhaps because it had exhausted itself, or London and all the other city targets throughout the UK, had shown their collective determination and their mettle. Or...? Or...?... but the threat was still there. Nobody at the time knew that the invasion and the blitz was off Hitler's menu for the time being. He had other fish to fry. Russia (and managed finally to get himself battered and fried in the process).

On the trip on the underground train from Paddington to Wapping station, there were the usual motley crowds of civilian passengers, but they were generally good humoured and cheerful. Everybody seemed to talk more freely with total strangers, supposedly a natural bond had built up because of the common hardships and the mutual dangers of the blitz. Every one of them (and us), had lost something or someone. Their homes and possessions. A friend or a neighbour. A cousin, or a boyfriend, or a girlfriend. Loved ones, or no one other single soul in particular. Mine was Derek, who had died together with all of his family. Who I knew I would never see again and found it impossible to understand why?

Londoners were normally gregarious and always full of ready cockney banter and humour. The situation (one must say) was the dire hourly… daily threat of extinction. Everybody shared the fears as well as the joys and the sorrows with each other and it made it easier to relate and share the burdens that may well have been their own on the morrow, and at the same time find something to smile about and to laugh at. One or two surface tracks on the journey revealed roofs denuded of slates and the bare roof trusses broken and often black and charred. Broken walls and window spaces leered at us as empty voids, frameless and glassless with flapping shreds of blasted curtains. Empty gaps where once there had been tall buildings, the tenements and the tiny workers houses now mere heaps of crushed and shattered bricks. Here and there were wisps of smoke curling from still smouldering cellars. Lily grasped my arm, "Oh look Johnnie. Look, it's terrible". Dad just laughed, not because he thought it was something to laugh about, but he knew we had not yet seen the worst.

We arrived at Wapping underground station. It was not like the Wapping underground station we had left on the evacuation train. I saw the sky from the bottom of the lift shaft. The lifts were not working but instead sat at the bottom of the shaft useless and broken. It was a long climb up to the street level. The very same original Brunel stairway circling the shaft looking a little more battered and littered with fragments of smashed debris and the grey gritty mortar dust of destruction that covered everywhere and everything. When we reached street level the old booking hall had gone, and a wooden shed had taken its place.

I was agog with the dramatic changes that had overtaken my Wapping. The massive wharves that fronted the river stood gauntly defiant, many of them burnt out hollow shells of jagged and twisted walls. I looked at it all in total dismay. It was the imagery all over again of the Hermitage Colonial wharf fire but multiplied a hundred times in a hundred different places. Piles of sodden and blackened wares spilled out of them. Heaps of tidily stacked mortar stained bricks salvaged for future emergency repairs. Lopsided loopholes, doors and platforms, their gates hanging precariously on twisted hinges closing off the emptiness behind them. Roofless buildings topped by black skeletal roof trusses open to the sky. Tortured steel beams, shattered floors like the floor I had seen full of jute sacked peanuts and my very special wharf-floor man. Half flights of barely supported concrete stairways rising up to the emptiness of nowhere. I stood transfixed with the floods of memories and the horrors of what I was seeing now... again. Dad just laughed. It was all one could do, laugh at it, and carry on with the fight.

Everywhere was still and silent. Not a horse and cart, or a lorry as I had remembered them. Not a movement save for the ever present pigeons and sparrows vainly searching in the sodden heaps for scraps still edible. Our way through the streets to Jackman House and Big Gran was met with patched windows and the same littering debris of demolition. The clearing up had begun in order to bring back some resemblance of normality. Roofs repaired and windows replaced. There had been little point in carrying out major repair during the height of the blitz, or to do any more than temporary and minimal weather proofing of roofs and windows. Tarpaulin patched roofs and light and waterproofed tared paper windows everywhere. Boarded up shop fronts in the Lane. Boarded up pubs. Those which had survived displaying the comforting information 'Business as usual', and just as frequently another sign declaring that sad information, 'Sorry, no beer'.

Watt's Street was no longer the street we remembered at its junction with the 'Lane'. Bombs had fallen in a line along it, and it was now just heaps and mounds of earth and deep craters filled with broken pipes curbs, paving slabs, and granite cobbles (I expect they are still buried there). Access was impossible into Jackman House except for a single file roped off wooden pedestrian walkway constructed over the craters. There had been a brick and concrete roofed shelter built in the grounds of Watt's Street buildings (a block of tenement flats), it was now a heap of smashed walls and concrete roof. It was thought there had been people, including children, sheltering in it... and then the bombs came.

Big Gran and Grandad were glad to see us. We were glad and relieved to see them too. Me especially, when so much else had changed around No.8 Jackman House. There they both were, just the same as they had ever been for me. Big Gran as round as she ever was, and grandad, cloth capped, and white silk scarfed as ever he had been too.

There were still his privets, petunias, and snapdragons blooming on the low parapet over the shop fronts in the Lane. The boxes a little more rotted and falling apart spilling black sooty earth around themselves, but they were an important part of my memories, and they were still there. Green and blooming, shedding an unusual brilliance in spite of a natural lack of Wapping colour and the effects of the blitz. The coal bunker in the passage, the ancient piano resting between the long absent parties and its clutter of dusty ornaments. Just as dusty as everything had always been. Nothing here had changed in spite of the chaos all around No.8 Jackman House. I was home at last and the journey had been long and wearily troubled.

The following day, dad took us on a tour of the devastation. The docks had died a premature and unnatural death. Very few ships were tied up to their accustomed home berths. Some ships still came in, mostly coastal traffic that had run the gauntlet of the Channel and the North Sea coasts. There was no longer any continental or international trade. What did manage to get through were diverted and docked and discharged at Liverpool, Bristol, or Cardiff. Anywhere further away out of reach of the Luftwaffe. The riverside wharves had all been mostly cleared of stored and stacked wares for their safety, apart from a few that struggled on in spite of the risks. Trade had virtually ceased, so in some economic sense; the blitz had achieved some dubious success.

We had only been home a few weeks or so... dad had gone off somewhere to work. Nobody knew where, or dared to ask him, but the very thing that everybody had thought was done with and was in the past, wasn't. The air raids. One auspicious night the warning sirens wailed out their stomach churning undulating threat. People had learned never to wait to see how things would turn out. Quickly, I was bundled out of a warm bed, there was no time to dress. A blanket wrapped around me, still half asleep. The searchlight beams, like fingers weaving in a synchronised dance across the sky, lit everything up. The guns opened up throwing countless shells towards the unseen threat. The barrage. An indescribable barrage of deafening proportions. Hundreds of guns firing at random. As we ran to the Gun Wharf shelter, a rain of lethal shrapnel fell around us in red hot steel torrents, clattering onto roofs, thudding, and bouncing off the pavements. We had to just run and hope for the best. Shrapnel killed outright, or severely maimed. At last, gasping for breath, we literally fell down the concrete stairs that led off from the old Gravel Lane level, down into the cavernous cellars of the massive wharf. Safe. Relatively safe that is! The bombs began to fall. 'Boom'! 'Bang'! 'Scream'! 'Thump'! Trembling cellar walls and floors, and the noise... penetrating even the massive walls and concrete of the wharf. Finding our allocated bunks, there was no chance of me, or any one of us, sleeping. Fear. Yes, shaking fear gripped me. The bunk I was allocated was the top bunk of three, close to the heavy concrete cellar ceiling. I lay there with no more than a foot of space above my head. I had a sudden vision of it all collapsing onto me and shuddered with renewed terror at the thought of such a death when all around me everyone was laughing and joking. Cards came out and a game set up. Groups of children dashing around playing hide and seek along the aisles of ranked bunk beds. Somebody was getting a boiler going for tea. All the while, the guns, and the bombs. Big Gran was telling me not to be worried. "It's only the guns you know, that's all. They will sort things out, you'll see. Tomorrow everything will be fine". Tomorrow couldn't come quick enough for me. The children were playing. Somebody got an accordion going and a sing song started up. I thought, if they don't care or are not afraid, it can't be as bad as I think it is. I mustn't be a coward. I began to feel a little calmer. One or two close ones fell, and my resolve wavered. How people went through fifty six plus nights of this, I just can't imagine.

For some unknown reason, apart from letting us know that the Luftwaffe were still capable of mounting another blitz whenever they wanted, they (the Luftwaffe) had decided to mount one of the heaviest raids on London of the whole war. It is said that a thousand sorties were flown in waves during the night, most bombers flying more than one sortie during the attack. The one saving feature is that it had not been concentrated on any specific target but had been scattered all over the whole of the London area at random, so the effect on any one area was fairly minimal. A constant rain all over London of high explosive and incendiary bombs. Whatever it had been, it had been a terrifying experience for me.

We had come home. Nobody had expected any more raids, especially of the same nature of those we had experienced the previous night which had only ended as dawn broke, but on the other hand, nobody was under any illusions that it couldn't happen again, or whether the unexpected raid had been the prelude to another blitz over the winter months. There was no longer any chance that the government would undertake yet another evacuation. Thousands and thousands of previously evacuated kids had made the trek homeward (in the unwise belief that the worst was over). Big Gran was not willing to take the risk. She 'asked about' to find us somewhere out of the danger zone. Docklands Wapping was still considered a prime target area. The vicar of St. Peter's Church, Fr. Young, apparently knew of two close neighbours in Guildford, Surrey, who might be willing to accept Lily and me as evacuees. Guildford was relatively close to home, only about twenty minutes on the train from Waterloo station but thought far enough away to be reasonably safe from possible air raids. Enquiries were made and back came the answer. "Certainly". Our bags were packed, and we were on our travels again, to strangers once again. (As it turned out, it was not to be the last either for me).

I was to be billeted with Mr & Mrs Mercer at 27, Newcross Road. Lily, a couple of houses along the row of terraced houses. Unfortunately, I cannot remember the neighbours name, but I do remember that it was with the wife and baby daughter of an absent soldier who was serving abroad. Mr & Mrs Mercer were an older couple with an older son who was I believe, also serving abroad. I never met him. They had another son who was about four years old who they called 'Mush' (I have no idea of his Christian name).

Mr Mercer worked at the Guildford Dennis factory that pre-war had produced lorries and particularly the iconic 20s-30s red fire engines, but during the war years it had only been army lorries and armoured vehicles. He never spoke of his work. At the time, very little in the way of civilian production went on in any industry. Every means of the national production had been turned over to essential war work, from making buttons for millions of military uniforms, to aircraft, tanks, lorries, guns, bullets, and ship building. Nothing else mattered. Whatever his job was, there was obviously very little money at the family's disposal. The houses in the terrace were typically Victorian two-up, two-down workers cottages. No bathroom. No kitchen. No inside toilet. The kitchen sink and gas cooker formed part of the back living room. An outside loo, and a narrow strip of garden, and the usual washhouse at the rear. The house and the homeliness of the billet was no less comfortably clean in spite of all its other deficiencies. It didn't matter. I was no less happy with my billeting arrangements.

I shared a back bedroom with another evacuee lad who, I am sorry to say, has also disappeared into the depths of an unrecallable memory and remains as one of the unnameable by me (a sad omission, isn't it?). In those unsettling times of forced movement and separations of most families from familiar homes and places, those around us sometimes passed us by as shadows across the normalities of awareness and fade and evaporate like a thin morning mist. The bedroom window overlooked the town of Guildford and the river valley, presenting an unrestricted view of the incomplete early stages of the new Guildford Cathedral construction. Construction began in 1936 but all building work had stopped at the declaration of the war. I was fascinated by the stark red brick block of what would become The Nave Crossing and the base of the planned tower. It dominated the distant sweep of the South Downs. It stood empty and forlornly abandoned, bare brick and naked concrete. I planned to go and see it close up for myself one day. As it stood, the R.A.F. used it for fighter pilot training and target practice. Spitfires constantly diving on it in pretend attacks, screeching over it, climbing and diving, twisting, and turning.

I did get there eventually with goodness only knows who. Whoever it was, I am sorry to say, has also faded out of my memory completely. Like so many of my oh so temporary companions. I rather fancy that this failing has much more to do with the fact nobody of those transitory years of mine were around long enough for firm recollections to be established. Strangely though, their faces and elements of their individual mannerisms have been retained. Their names and where to place them at a time and a place, have disappeared completely and totally beyond recall, and they have become mere shadows and unreality.

In spite of my lack of years, this view of the gaunt structure standing in its lonely and unadorned nakedness on its windy hill, was a strong focal point for me. Strangely. I felt rather than completely understood the mystery of the image which, in my mind, was neither a building or a ruin, marking a past or a future. All I can say is that every morning I woke and there it stood. A fixed and a permanent point in a very uncertain and troubled world. Not least my own personal troubled world! In fact, I was drawn and held in an awed fascination with the implications of the site and never felt happier than when I was finally able to wander alone around it amongst the few last remaining stacks of unlaid bricks and normal building site materials. Items waiting for the absent hands to return to place them in their allotted places. The bare grey concrete vaulted ceilings and openings of yet unframed and glassless windows and doorless doorways, and still more grey concrete steps and stairs leading to nowhere but an idea in the minds of the builders. The rickety wooden site hut, long since gone now and probably unremembered. It's rough boarded floor pitted and scuffed by cement stained hobnailed boots of bricklayers and mud caked labourers. In 1941, it also served the needs of those who came to wonder and to wander, as I did. Posters of artist impressions pinned to its rough boarded walls. Pictures and printed information about the building plans. Images of what the Cathedral would be like in the unsure future. A trestle table as rough boarded as the walls hid under white paper carefully pinned to its top, displayed the few paper thin, skimpy, wartime post cards and the only wartime discoloured leaflets available. Sometimes, there was a volunteer to assist and explain, and to collect the few pennies to add to the building fund. The cross, made of an ancient ship's timbers, stood alone, apart, facing towards the east. The potent shape a promise to the present and to the future generations to come. A stark declaration of that promise and intent. Even as the child that I was, I stood at its foot in the silence of the stilled and unworked site and wondered. Its awesome presence always drew me back.

A leap forward in time ....

I met my wife Margaret, in 1950 when I was doing my National Service in the R.A.F. as an unwilling participant in what I considered a waste of time and the years, but now, I am glad that I did them! Amongst the first tentative events of discovery in our developing relationship was a visit to Guildford and the New Cathedral... and there it stood. The same solid and firm sentinel. There have been many such visits over the years. We eventually married in 1954 (well, that is, I was persuaded in spite of the miseries of virtual poverty of prospects and the current difficulties of those lean years).

As the years unfolded, we brought our children with us (Peter, Susan & Jill), with the same intention to visit the Cathedral. We bought our bricks, so somewhere it is recorded unseen that we were all there. It would have been unthinkable if we had not stood where I had stood all those years before and not wondered as I had wondered.

The crypt too was one of those fixed points of focus for me, that had created those persistently strong images of place and meaningful presence in my memories. It was the only part of the building in 1941 that was recognisable as a place of purpose at that early stage of the building. Now, at this present time, on a recent return visit, looking down the very same, now unrecognisable, finished stairwell cordoned off by a forbidding red rope barrier saying, 'No Entry'... 75 years ago, I stared down the very same staircase of rude bare grey concrete walls and stairs that turned sharp left in its decent downward into the crypt. In the dim light there had been a carpenters bench, in 1941, still scattered round with woodchips and curling planed shavings left by the last craftsman, just as if gone home to lunch or to his supper at the workdays end and not yet returned. I knew about the existence of the present day crypt chapel in 1941 because it was the only area that had a doorway that could be opened and closed. Glazed windows at ground level and temporarily roofed over at the proposed church floor level in which had been stored various items. The usual building tools, spades, pickaxes, and the like, but in my time, 1941, empty and accessible for the curious like me.

Chapter 29

There's Always Something to Laugh About, After All!

On our return from Guildford, the most surprising thing to me was the humour.

Wapping people had always been of a cheerful disposition, smiling and impervious to the worst that life had always managed to throw at them. Any disaster, or any tragedy, sorrows, or hardships, had always drawn out of them a spontaneous reaction of discovering the 'funny side' of everything. Some might (who had no idea of the deep rooted reasons why) consider such humour as being callous and without sensitivity for the feelings of others, but not so. Wapping had always been a hard place in which to survive, and there was no point in dwelling on the shortcomings of their environment or their pecuniary circumstances. Unless one learned early in life to smile and laugh in the face of events that they had absolutely no way of avoiding... Disaster, tragedy, sorrow, not least the general poverty, was for them constantly a fact and the way of life. It had to be lived with somehow, or not survive at all.

The war time conditions, and the blitz was only regarded as an extension of conditions that one way or the other had existed for centuries. It was the same in principle if not in form.

Lily and I were treated to a whole torrent of funny and hilarious tales of the happenings and the doings during the blitz. Big Gran was an inveterate 'storyteller' generally laughing and crying at the same time as she told them. Seated as she would on a chair beside the 'peeyana', her ample form overflowing it, and rosy faced as she spoke. "D'yer know", she said. "During the blitz we used t' go down St John's wharf in the High Street t' shelter. One night it was foggy. Your Grandad sez t' me…", "Yer know Beat, it's so foggy I don't think there will be a raid t'night. Too foggy". "So, I sez t'im, le's go t' th' Ramsgit an' have a pint and go home an'ave a night in bed". Winking and laughing as she said it… (meaningly no doubt). "Well…", she continued. "We 'ad a pint or two, I s'pose. Didn't come away until closing. When we came out we couldn't see an inch wot with th' blackout an' it's bein so foggy. We got a bit lorst and couldn't see our way home. Suddenly, yer Grandad sez to me", "It's all right Beat, I've got hold of the park railings, we'll soon be 'ome now". "Well, we followed the railings and y' Grandad sez", "Ere Beat, it seems a long way", "But we kept going. A warden came along with his big torch and 'e sez", "Allo Beat an' Jack. Where are you's orf to"? "Going home", "I sez", "For a night in bed". "He laughed at us. Do you know what, we'd bin walking round and round the bandstand for an hour or more? Didn't get a night in bed after all. He took us back down to St Johns. The warning 'ad gone off".

There was always a funny side to every incident no matter how serious. Wapping people had always survived and laughed at their problems, it helped them to cope with their disadvantages. It struck me forcibly, having already experienced the losses myself. The untimely death of Derek along with everything else, I found it hard to smile or find anything to laugh about in such events… and there were Big Gran and Grandad. Uncle Jack of greengrocery fame, in fact everybody. There wasn't a sad face to be seen anywhere. Whether this was merely a sense of relief that the worst was over. The blitz seemed to have ended. Many had died. Friends and relatives homes and possessions had been destroyed. So many lives changed forever. Whether it was a relief or not, I can't say. I prefer to believe though that it was an expression of an inborn contempt for any sort of adversity, a natural quality and not just a feature of wartime Wapping. As I remembered it, humour always lurked beneath the surface, a grin always flickered at the corners of their mouths which would suddenly erupt into hearty mirth and a torrent of incorrigible cockney wit. Even so, I found it difficult to take it all in at first.

Dad was often away doing his bit for the war effort, frequently for weeks at a time. Sometimes he'd come home unexpectedly only to be off and away again within hours. Nobody knew where he had been or where he was going to be. Nobody dared ask because he would not say, nor what he had been doing. I did ask once where he had been and what he was doing. I got a very evasive answer. Sometimes he would give an answer that might have been the truth, but it was always more likely to have been anything else but, and he never told his story, ever. Even so, he did have his own stock of 'funny stories' to tell too. On one or two tours with him to view the destruction and dereliction, he explained as much as he knew of the incidents. He told me a story as we stood on Old Gravel Lane bridge to view the deserted dock. "When these wharves were burning", he said, "A fireman went out on one of the beams close to the lock over there…", pointing out the very place. "…to be able to get closer to the blaze and in a better position to direct his hose at the flames. He climbed up dragging a dry hose up behind him". "Rito". "He called his mates to give him some pressure. The pump thumped and the water shot out of his hose. Next minute…", he continued, "The fireman was flying through the air on the end of the hose and right into the lock. He wasn't going to let go of the hose and planed about in the lock like a speed boat. They hauled him out alright, a bit wet but he was OK". "I'm told…", he said, "… that he climbed straight back onto the same beam again and just carried on where he had left off". Laughing as he said it to us as if it were a great joke, and there it was again, the seriousness and the dangers the fireman had experienced were more than overruled and compensated by the 'funny side' of the incident. I wonder whether the victim had found it so funny at the time. I wouldn't mind betting a fiver to nothing, that he enjoyed the joke of it as much as everyone else did!

Dad wasn't finished yet. "This is where old (so and so)"... I forget the name. "... the warden had stood, in a sheltering doorway when a bomb exploded over there", pointing to where. It looked close to me. "He fell into the nearest shelter without a shred of his trousers left on him. They had been blown off of him in the blast, but all he kept saying was that he had lost his pea out of his whistle. It would have taken the pea out of my whistle; I can tell you"! If it had been only his trousers and his whistle the warden had lost. He had been very lucky. Dad said, "The warden hadn't stopped laughing about it since, himself", so even he had thought it was funny.

A lot of humour centred around poor old George Warner. He was the local barber whose original barber shop had been close to Grandad's fish and chip shop in the lane. He too had lost his shop in the slum clearances. He too had been offered a flat next door to Big Gran and Grandad in Jackman House, and a replacement shop on the corner of Watts Street. At least he could carry on his normal trade whereas Grandad could not.

During the war years he was an A.R.P. warden (probably the chief warden of his region). He carried out his duties very efficiently, some thought too efficiently. Fitted out in his duty navy blue boiler suit (Churchill's preferred wartime dress), belts and shoulder bag, service gas mask and cape, black steel helmet with the legend A.R.P. painted in large white letters. George was slightly portly, with just as slightly a tendency to Captain Mainwaring's (Dad's Army) pomposity. His tasks, apart from assisting in air raid emergencies, was to see that the local folk observed the blackout rules and regulations. He was very conscientious. Anyone careless about showing a chink of light would hear George's whistle blast and his irate shout, "Put that light out".

Everyone, the guilty and the innocent alike, would rush to check their blackout screens. People could be fined for the smallest infringement of the regulations. George, in his enthusiasm, had not been unknown to exercise his powers to see to it that the offenders were charged and dealt with by the majesty of the law. Many of his residents found that they had to explain to a magistrate that the light left on was by mistake and they were not enemy agents guiding the Luftwaffe bombers to their targets. Many were the blasts of George's whistle and the frequent bellowed warning, "Put that 'bleedin' light out".

George and his fellow wardens had their 'post' in one of the unoccupied flats on the ground floor of Jackman House. They only used one of the rooms and would sit for hours waiting for the call to action, or doing their required series of training information, or otherwise playing cards to while away the time (probably with a little light refreshment from various brown bottles) in between the usual routines for George to check that there were no lights showing in his manor.

Gran told the story of a red faced George puffing out a protest one morning as he shaved a bemused customer, that he had been 'done over' the night before. He declared that some 'bright spirit' had got into the post in the night through an unlocked window and had switched on a light in one of the unused rooms. "It must have been some joker from outside because there wasn't a bulb in the light fitting in that room and none of us wardens would have switched the light on because we don't use that room". "The someone had reported it to the 'nick', that there was a light showing at the wardens post in Jackman House". George and his mates had to explain to a disbelieving constable who had come to investigate the report, that it was a complete mystery to all and sundry. How the light came to be switched on, nobody could say. George was flabbergasted. For weeks afterwards, every time he was met on his rounds he was greeted with a whistle and a, "Put dat bleedin light out George". He was never going to be allowed to forget it. Still, to his everlasting credit, he did see the funny side of it himself and laughed along with the rest of them.

George's time would come though. Nobody takes too kindly to over officialdom. George was, it must be said, rather conscientious about his and everybody else's duties, and he let everybody know it, coming down heavily on those he caught neglecting them. No matter who it was, if he thought that his residents in _his_ sphere of influence were not coming up to scratch, they could expect a lecture on good wartime behaviour, not hesitating to put the offenders in extreme cases of neglect, up in front of the 'beak'.

During the blitz, he and his fellow wardens rose to the call and many acts of bravery were carried out, often in extreme danger to themselves. Many acts of selflessness and courage came out of the smoky Jackman House wardens post and the other posts too I expect! All of it unrecorded and gone without recognition. Such bravery on any other battlefield but on the dingy streets of Wapping and so many other places too, would have qualified for conspicuous bravery awards. On the night of the Watts Street stick of bombs that had fallen along the street, a brick and concrete shelter provided for the residents of Watts Street buildings had taken the full shock and blast and lay a heap of smashed walls and concrete. It was thought that people were trapped beneath the rubble and possibly children amongst them. George without hesitation 'went in' burrowing cautiously underneath the precariously balanced debris that at any second threatened to crush George and any buried victims. With bombs still crashing down all around them, the ground shaking beneath them, there was no time to think of the risks. It was too urgent to get in quickly and get the survivors out – fast. As I sat listening to Gran as she told it, thinking how brave George had been, I considered whether I would have been as brave. George was well built, as a matter of fact, he was a little over portly and past middle aged suppleness. With tears streaming down her face on recalling the ludicrous mental picture of events, she related it with evident relish. "You know what, he got stuck in the hole his self. They had to dig him out an'all".

That the victims might have been found to be beyond help anyway didn't enter into the 'funny side' of the tragedy. No one questioned George's bravery. Everyone admired him for his disregard for his own safety. That wasn't the point of the story. He was portly and found himself stuck in a hole… this raised the whole sad and tragic incident to the level of the hilarious. Funnily enough, George thought it was funny too and laughed along with everyone else.

* * * * *

Dad told us his own story too, that on Saturday 15th September 1940, he was at home on one of his infrequent 'breaks'. He said, "We had had one or two daylight raids, they had been going for the airfields mainly, but they hadn't amounted to much over London except the week before on the 7th of September when the docks first 'copped it'. Anyway…", he said. "I'd come home on the 15th and didn't give it much thought that there might be another raid like the week before. We'd been told that they had got a bloody nose over the week before and didn't want another one. I decided I would have a bath in the afternoon because I wanted to go out that evening. I ran the water an' as soon as I stepped into the bath the sirens went off. Blast! I thought, but I'll finish my bath. Well, the bombs started to drop almost before the sirens had stopped wailing. They were dropping so close that the buildings felt as if they were going to fall down. Everything spun and shook. Things were falling off the shelves. One bomb fell so close that I was physically bounced out of the bath and finished up a wet heap on the floor. Gran was shouting at me". "Quick Johnnie, get down to the shelter. Urry up". "All the time the bombs were falling". "Hurry up. We're going down now. Hurry. Hurry". "One of the ground floor flats of Jackman House had been converted into a shelter. The windows had been bricked up. Entrance doors had brick blast-baffle walls and the ceilings supported by a forest of heavy timber supports in case of the buildings collapse. It was damp smelling and dark but nevertheless a secure and safer feeling kind of place to be in". He said, "I thought I had better follow them as quickly as I could. I did not bother to dry myself so long as I managed to get my trousers on, and a couple of towels round me. I left the rest of my clothes on the floor. Unwashed and wet", he said, "I ran across the yards at the rear of the buildings. I looked up and saw lumps of concrete, bricks and debris falling out of the smoke blackened sky. The noise was incredible. A black curtain of smoke across the sky reflected the bomb flashes and the gunfire. Everything raining down. Shrapnel thudding down everywhere and glass flying. I don't know how I got over the yards to the shelter without being hit with something".

Big Gran took up the story. Looking for one solemn moment at the seriousness of the raid, shaking her head she declared, "Yes, it was bad that raid. Everywhere was ablaze. Jeez, I thought that we all had had it and we weren't going to get out of it. When he did get t' the shelter he was as white as my fresh washed sheets, just like he had seen 'Old Nick' his-self, but he did look so funny. We all had a good laugh. He was all wet and with just a little towel round his shoulders". "Ere John", "I sez t' him". "You've got yer trousers on back t' front and it ain't hiding much at the back. Your behind is showin". "In his confusion he hadn't noticed that he had put his trousers on back to front and unbuttoned". The wonder is that he even bothered with the trousers. The towels might have been enough for me. I might not have even bothered with them!

September 15th turned out to be quite a party with massed attacks in daylight on the East End dockland area that also continued through the following night. It also turned out to be the last daylight raid carried out on that scale by the Luftwaffe. There were too many over enthusiastic claims made of the numbers of 'downed' and 'definitely' destroyed enemy aircraft. It was said to have been 186. The truth was between 50 and 60 (allowing for some discrepancies). There might also have been considerable damages inflicted on those that did get back home after being mauled by the R.A.F. They _did_, however, get a bloody nose this time but then so did the East End. Poor old Wapping got a couple of black eyes to go with it.

What would anyone's first thoughts have been if the 'next one' could not only bounce one out of the bath but bounce one suddenly into the next world, washed, or unwashed. Wet trousered, or un-trousered.

* * * * *

What a whirl I was in. I spent the first few weeks back 'home' revisiting all those familiar places. I walked the walls, sniffed the perfumes still lingering through the myths of my imagination and the dungeon grating vents. I went on to the Shoreways, which were strangely quieter than I ever remembered them. The Tower and the Tower Wharf, looked again into the deep dark well of the Traitors Gate and I was remembering the story told by the bearded and moustached Yeoman Warder. I sat on the cannons and then ventured onto the beach. A real thorough journey of rediscovery and reaffirmation of my memories. Alone… I was always alone with my own thoughts.

The St John church had been burnt out and left as a blackened empty shell. The clock tower stood gaunt showing a timeless clock face toward the river. The old nursery school gutted and floorless and roofless. My friends, the statues, no longer stood in their niches. For aught I knew then, they had wandered away never to return. The little dark graveyard, still silently hiding behind its tall iron fence and padlocked gate, looking even more dismal and unkempt. Littered and broken gravestones scattered around in the tangled undergrowth demonstrated a morbid evidence that not even the dead had been allowed to rest in peace. A bomb had fallen amongst them and scattered their bones together with their memorials. Everything everywhere, battered, and bruised. Dereliction and total destruction. Patched up windows. Large gaps where once there were teeming streets of houses. Prussoms Street one vast empty space. The gas works no longer producing gas. The docks virtually empty of ships. One or two rusty old tramps that had run the gauntlet of the North Sea coast. A few maybe that had risked the Channel. The wonder is, that there were any ships at all.

Chapter 30

Isolation & Insulation

I had always, even as a very young child, recognised the 'atmospheric' peculiarities of my island home. Perhaps it had been because dad had infused me with the telling of his stories which always included the concept of Wapping's isolation from the rest of the East End. This isn't too surprising since pretty well every one of the islanders saw themselves as the cream of the East End London cockneys... always. One heard them speak of the 'outsiders' as being from foreign territories, no matter where. If one had to either get out of, or get into Wapping, one had to cross over a bridge, or water. Anywhere beyond the 'wall', or over a bridge was not Wapping.

Over the river, or as it was locally said, 'Over-th'-water', Southwark, and immediately facing Wapping's river front, Bermondsey, might as well have been an ocean away. Some Wapping dockies did work the 'Surrey Commercials' when the work was in short supply on the home quays. Grandad in his early years 'humped' deals of timber from ship to quay on his shoulders but rarely managed to find dock labour work in Wapping itself.

With the construction of the docks in Wapping, beginning with St Katharine's, it was the very first secure dock planned (but by no means the first completed because of the complexities involved), quickly followed by Wapping basin and soon after the London Dock complex including Hermitage and Shadwell basins. The separate dock companies soon discovered that there was a mutual advantage in linking the deep water basins by lock and canals, and further surrounding the whole with the massive construction of the 'Wall'. Wapping became at one stroke, an inland London island.

True, the massive East and West India companies had stolen a march on the development of the Port of London by completing their dock constructions further to the east some years earlier, on what was virtually open farmland and sparsely populated marshes... The Isle of Dogs. The area got this interesting name because it is reputed that King Charles kennelled his hunting dogs and bred the famed King Charles spaniels there. It is also thought that King Henry, the famous (or infamous) VIII, kept his packs of hounds there too. Anyway, because of the teeming slum situation existing on the muddy marsh of Wapping close up to the Tower, and the existence of the St Katharine's monastic hospice which had to be demolished, the completion of St Katharine's was delayed and was not finally opened until 1827. However, the Wapping marshes close up to the Tower moat, had been the first choice for a deep water secure basin to cope with the ever increasing volumes of international ship borne trade. It was also close to the city within its sphere of control, not least because there were already riverside quays and jetties fronting the marshes of Wapping that had been operating for generations, beginning (as excavations have revealed) the evidence for timber quays and jetties some dating (it is believed) from Roman times.

Now, as recorded history will bear me out, I am quite convinced that even before the development of the massive docking complex covering at least 50-60% of the whole marsh. There had always been a tradition with the majority of London's city dwellers that the marshes of Wapping were a no go area, peopled as it was by the wandering groups of London's disinherited criminal elements. Fagin like gangs of pickpockets, muggers, burglars, cutpurses, and cutthroats. Stealing and cheating a precarious living. There was no organised police force. The Lord Mayor and corporation had no authority beyond the confines of the city wall. Who then was to do anything about it other than to leave the area and its people alone to fester and, hopefully, rot away at its own pace and pleasure?

Wapping became an area that well deserved its reputation. Close up to the city boundaries it was an easy escape route. Wapping afforded swift and easy hiding placcs for thc bands of villains crowding thc busy city streets.

The massive undertaking of the digging and construction of the dock, basins, locks, and canals to be finally encircled and enclosed by the 'Wall' might have changed the area physically but somehow its reputation managed to survive. I have an easy justification for this view of the situation. The new docks still presented attractive opportunities for vice and criminal activity. Wandering seamen ashore with pockets full of pay. Cheap lodgings, brothels, pimps, and prostitutes. Ale houses and gin shops. Bands of roughnecks looking for easy pickings. Doubtful lodging houses. Not all of the traditional residents of the old marsh slum dwellings had disappeared overnight to set up their rookeries elsewhere. Some, no doubt, managed to get out of the hole they were previously in and found legitimate and paid work in the docks but for the majority there had been no need to change, or least of all had the opportunity to change, and certainly no desire to change their lifestyles. There were always the incidental opportunities to fleece, suck dry, or just simply rob the lost and all too often inebriated seamen rendered helpless and unable to help themselves. Many woke out of their stupor lying in a cold damp alley robbed and destitute. Even the very clothes they had been wearing stolen from off their backs.

There were still the easy thefts from the riverside quays and jetties from moored vessels in the upper pool waiting for a berth. Vice, theft, and violence was rife and ongoing in spite of all the attempts to curb the villainy and the losses.

Leading eventually to the setting up of the first waterborne police force in 1792 based on Wapping New Stairs. It hardly made a dent in the criminal activities of the desperate and the determined. The idea that Wapping was still a very dangerous place not only persisted but actually increased. Nobody, but nobody, would ever consider going into Wapping out of mere curiosity let alone sheer necessity. A tradition that I dare to say, continued right up to the eventual closures of the docks and I daresay it still does for those who are old enough to remember.

Charles Dickens though, apparently had no fears for his safety. Frequently wandering around Wapping to gather atmosphere for the scenery and the characterisation of individuals for his novels. Sam Weller was a 'recognisable' Wapping character if ever there was one. (Pickwick Papers). The Wapping workhouse (The Uncommercial Traveller) etc., etc., and Sairey Gamp and 'Quilp'(The Old Curiosity Shop). Isolation and insularity… a situation that suited the marooned islanders perfectly.

As far as isolation went, it was never too difficult to understand why. Quite apart from a reputation, even into the late 40s there was no public transport either into or out of Wapping apart from the East London underground 'rattler' from Shoreditch to New Cross on the south side of the river, so it was either 'Shank's Pony', or a couple of penny worth's on the rattler. Anyway, who would want to come to Wapping to wander around in its dark streets and dismal alleys and courts? One often heard it from outsiders that any unwise visitor who was considered a threat to the peace and tranquillity of the islanders could end up tipped over the nearest bridge rails, into the lock without the formality of the question, "Kin yer swim mate"? And if you can't, "Nar is der time ter larn"!

Whatever the state of things was prior to the 1930s regarding the villainous propensities of the locals, it has to be said that in spite of the huge expenditure of effort employed by the dock authorities and the dock police to curb the natural tendencies of the locals to help themselves because nobody else was likely to help them... It had always been the 'way' for Wapping men (and their spouses) to alleviate the local social deprivations. Poverty and deprivation were endemic and seemingly insoluble. The principal cause of this situation was wholly the fault of the 'casuality' in labour prospects.

The dock companies, in the early days of the dock, went into the enterprise completely convinced of the economic success of their investments for the future. 'Hey-Ho'... We have heard that story often enough since. Such was their confidence that they took on vast numbers of men on a full time and regular basis... but in due time... according to the old story... competition which resulted in the growth of 'over provision' of the available deep water berths, plus the virtually undisturbed riverside provision already well established, plus the unavoidable fact of shipping being what it was in those early days... principally sail.... there was no guarantee that any vessel would arrive at the expected time. Good winds, or foul weather might mean that vessels arrived in port either ten weeks early, or three months late, or frequently not at all. The result was that the port was either bursting at the seams with vessels moored in the upper and lower pools waiting for berths, or as frequently happened throughout the whole port complex, there were hundreds of unoccupied quays and jetties and ten thousand men stood idle. Next week though, the same ten thousand and ten thousand more, would still not have been enough to cope with the work available in the time limits required. A ship tied to a deep water berth cost ship owners too much in time and money. It didn't take the dock companies too long to realise this sobering fact. Hey presto! Overnight... "Sorry, not required, but if you come to the dock gate tomorrow there might be some work"... (and there might not)! A system that began in the mid-1800s and continued right up to the docks closures in the 1960s.

Wapping had been described as the 'poorest parish in London's East End' (Mahew's private survey of the East End)... probably, it was suggested, in the UK as a whole. Never mind the question of the alcohol abuse... that was a result, not a cause. Casuality and the uncertainties of regular paid employment, this was the main cause of Wapping's problems. However, Wapping men found the means to alleviate some of the constant and enduring consequences of poverty and want.

There had always been plenty of thieving going on in the docks. Many stratagems were employed to outwit the dock police (otherwise known as the 'Cabbige' locally). Very much in the tradition of their Wapping predecessors. Canned, bottled or any other goods that would not spoil by immersion were 'accidentally' knocked off jetties and ships at high tides to be collected from off the Shoreways during the hours of darkness at a convenient 'low tide'. There were even live sheep set unfortunately (and accidentally) adrift, to be fished out lower downstream. Sometimes, the unfortunate drowning of the equally unfortunate beast, did save someone the trouble of having to put it out of its misery. (I wonder if the dead sheep I saw on the shoreway was one that had been missed)?

Goods were spirited away on tugs and lighters to be shared out later. Bottles tucked down trouser legs. A story went the rounds of sewers used as entry to wharves at night when they were closed. One way or another, in spite of the heavy presence of the 'Cabbige', goods were 'liberated' somehow. Not many of the perpetrators were caught at it either. As the saying has it, 'Birds of a feather flock together'. Wapping men were 'to a man' members of a brotherhood of combination. It was the social cement that enabled them to survive.

Very little of the piracy was conducted for actual pecuniary gain, although this element had to exist. Boots and shoes, if they could not be acquired or liberated, had to be paid for. A little spare cash here and there helped to satisfy 'Nora Leech'. I daresay she never troubled anyone to ask where her dues had come from. I don't suppose she would have refused them if she had known that they had been the proceeds coming from out of the British and foreign bottling cellars (or in modern parlance) 'off the back of a lorry'. Everything though, found its way around Wapping. Practically everybody shared the bounty. All too often it was a case of accepting it or going without altogether. It was always a tough decision to make. Worried about feeding the kids… or…? What would you do? Let them starve, or cry themselves to sleep in hunger on moral grounds? I'll leave you to answer it yourself. I know what mine would be.

I remember tea, sugar, dried fruits, canned fruits and of course the ubiquitous bottles on Big Gran's coal cupboard lid at Christmas, or at other party times. Of course, I am not saying that they were all duty unpaid altogether, but…? And the question will remain unanswered. I have distinct memories too of various useful items going the rounds. Bags would be furtively accepted without comment or thanks and quickly disposed of in a cupboard or pantry, etc. The 'giver' would be a receiver at some other time.

Years ago, I read an account of a sorry story told by an individual who had inadvertently (indeed somewhat reluctantly) spent some unhappy time living in Wapping. In fact, the small family could be (and were) considered to be unwilling immigrants from other parts and therefore in Wapping's eyes they were 'foreigners'. That didn't really matter too much as far as Wapping folk were concerned, this sort of family immigration had always been a feature of the social order, but generally the only condition of acceptance within the ranks of the islanders was governed in the main on whether the 'visitors' were prepared to fit in or not. Most did, and managed to settle in, in a kind of unobserved and quiet manner but there were the exceptions. Evidently, this particular family moved into Wapping with their own ideas on how Wapping society should be conducted, evidently based on their own particular moral conceptions. In the end, Wapping managed to 'assist' this family in 'moving on'.

It was related by the good lady spouse herself. She said, "I was offered, and could not accept on moral grounds, a gift of what must have been 'stolen' goods. They went straight down the rubbish chute". There might have been a few of the more scrupulous individuals who might have taken the same attitude but in Wapping they were a very rare breed and certainly a silent one, who wisely kept quiet about their personal moral reservations. As my informant related, "The (fruit) was left with me but I couldn't touch them". The problem this caused was that she let it be known what she had done with them and spoke out openly in condemnation of the obvious theft to which sentiment, her 'hubby' fully approved and said so. The 'hubby' had found work in the wharves 'on the barrer'. The gang he was working with asked him to make the tea. He was told where to get it. On the way back with it he was arrested by the ever present 'Cabbige' and accused of 'theft' (he was in possession of the euphemistically 'borrowed' tea), charged with the offence and immediately sacked of course. He never worked in the docks again. The truth is, he was 'shopped' by the gang who sent him on the errand, innocently unaware of the set up. His erstwhile and unwise spouse went on to claim that his arrest and his dismissal was 'unjust'. "He was an honest man". Which indeed he was. Maybe it was a vicious thing to do, but then he didn't fit in and neither did his spouse. They were far too conscientious for Wapping realities and posed a danger to everyone, the guilty and the guiltless alike. They had to move on and there were no tears to see them go. It wasn't because Wapping men and their womenfolk were altogether incorrigible villains intent of fattening themselves and their wallets. This kind of stealing was all too often just enough to keep the wolves of hunger from gnawing at their kid's bellies. It was an established fact of the otherwise hard life in Wapping, that one accepted anything that was offered, and no questions asked about it. Nobody had any illusions about the source of these goods. They came infrequently enough as generally 'providential' manna from 'who knows where', and it was better not to know.

Whatever else one might think of this seemingly unholy and otherwise unsocial behaviour, Wapping society had been built on and only survived by a combination of shared interests. Nobody 'snitched', shopped, or let down their 'mates'. As if anyone would dare. If they did, they were finished in Wapping. Hence, our unfortunate victim of the institution of Wapping justice, a too finicky hubby of a too finicky missus. Wappingites never, never, never stole from, or harmed each other. They had to rely on the willingness of everyone to 'fit in' merely to survive. They certainly could not work without the support of each other. There was very little room for individual actions and contrary notions carried on for the individuals own sake. In its own way, it could be said to be a justifiable and definable Wapping social morality. It was this incidentally, that kept the social order together and functioning.

Chapter 31

A Strange Unexpected 11+ and a Stranger Outcome

By the end of 1941/42, it seemed as though the Luftwaffe were far too busy occupied in Russia and everywhere else to bother with these ungrateful islanders (Wapping and the UK both). They obviously couldn't spare the time and the energy to give us the attention that we had come to expect. In all fairness though, there had been a few air raids from time to time but nothing of any significance except to annoy folk generally. Most people heard the sirens and then hesitated for a moment or two to make the decision to run, or ignore it and carry on, or turn over and go back to sleep. It was always at night time of course, woken out of a blissful untroubled sleep and bundled up in whatever came to hand and a mad dash of two or three hundred yards down to the Gun Wharf shelter, lit on our way by the violent fireworks display of morale boosting, but otherwise useless expenditure of valuable anti-aircraft ammunitions aimed at one or two, and sometimes three enemy intruders who had already dropped their loads somewhere over the distant fields of Kent or Essex, and shoved off home as fast as their wings would carry them. Nuisance raids really, carried out merely to let us know that we were constantly in their thoughts and this limited activity was only a pause in the battle and things would liven up shortly and get back to normal. Not one of us could possibly know what surprises there were in store for us and what tomorrow might bring. However, it was felt safe enough for parents to let the kids come home. They began the trek homeward in their thousands, that is for those who had houses (and let's face it), those who still had families to come home to. The war had destroyed much more than just bricks and mortar.

We at Guildford, had somehow toughed it out. I had reached that magic time of 11 years old when we got educationally sorted and sieved out of existence according to the dictates of a sheer good fortune that one was having a good hair day or not… the iniquitous 11-plus.

Now, by all rights and factors in my short and chaotic time of life, I could already count up to at least a dozen schools which each I occupied for roughly a month or two duration. I had never really found the time to get settled anywhere, needless to say, most subjects were a bundle of bits and pieces of unconnected chaos. I wasn't by any means alone in this either. Wartime education was enough to blunt the brightest blades. Chaos is the best description and it affected everybody within the system.

I don't actually remember taking any kind of test or examination as such. The fact is that I barely remembered North St. Infants, Guildford, or was it junior? Beyond a vague recollection of being told that my next port of call was to be up amongst the 'big boys and girls' (or was it just boys?) at the fairly newly built and educationally prestigious school, Northmead, Grange Road, Stoughton…. Oh, and by the way, you have passed your 11-plus. I think there might be a long lost, or mislaid bit of paper somewhere that actually confirmed the fact. At the time I could not understand how I had managed to do something that I had no idea that I had undertaken, but still, nobody was inclined to dispute the verdicts of authority who ought to have been suitably qualified to know the facts. The question has to remain, was it a case of adequate mental excellence on my part, or the kindness and sympathy of somebody unknown? The only other solution I can think of, is that someone's adoring parents, who had been overconfident about an adorable capable son's abilities, had been very disappointed by the simple misfortune of an exam result being misplaced, or we had both forgotten to put our names in the right place? But then, knowing the state of the wartime conditions, probably the examiners couldn't read, or that somebody somewhere had decided to give me the benefit of the doubt. I think the truth is, that things like 11-plus examinations were decided 'at the time' in house as it were. I know I was always a little inclined to the romantic imaginative and always ready to 'tell the fantastic'. It all came down to the matter of bluff and huff... the truth is, in the end it might have been better for me if I had not passed a doubtful 11-plus at all. It might also have been a relief to me and everybody else that it turned out there wasn't a place available for me at whatever, or wherever Guildford Grammar School happened to be anyway.

Lily too had reached a similar magic age when a bigger more adult world beckoned. The school leaving age was then remarkably 14 years old and just as equally remarkable, this was still only a year beyond consent and choice, so it was back homeward once again with the equally satisfying benefit of a mutual consent and choice that a doubtful 11-plus might offer.

Finally, I arrived back in Wapping with this rather extraordinary piece of good fortune. An 11-plus, gratis somebody else's misfortune in missing out in the race for life and success, but what could one do with it? Dad and Big Gran decided between them that it ought to qualify me for 'something' rather than the usual, but the big question was 'what'?

Wapping was also Stepney, and Stepney Borough Council had already taken steps pre-war to replace grammar schools with a comprehensive scheme with the laudable purpose of eliminating the concept of privilege, wealth and selection. One of the first tentative steps towards a more egalitarian system of education.

Big Gran and Dad decided that my spurious qualification entitled me to a place at one of the central schools that had replaced grammar schools and where an 11-plus did not count. I was taken along to the nearest 'central school' to home. Myrdle Street. A little non-entity of a street, turning out of the Commercial Road, something like a mile or so from Jackman House, and I was offered to the unlucky headmaster as the best thing he had ever come across since... well, since last week when he accepted a young hopeful who could well have qualified to eventually cope with his own headmastership with lots of potential to spare. I had an 11-plus to prove my own stupendous capabilities!

I went on my first day with great apprehension of what to expect. I had seen some of the things that were expected of me. At the first interview the head asked me, "How far have you got with algebra"?... "Oh, I see... Well, never mind, I expect you will catch up. How are you with French"?... "Oh, dear... Well, that's a start I suppose. I daresay you will improve. You will do your best to catch up... won't you"? I promised I would try my best. "Alright, you may start on Monday next".

I was really terrified that I was about to be unmasked as the fraud that I felt I was and decided I would just have to bluff it out as best I could. On the following Monday, I discovered with considerable relief that he had no intention of starting me off in a situation that I was never going to cope with. In fact, I suspect that it was about a year later than I should have been enrolled at Myrdle Street, so I had to pick up from the bottom. Quite apart from this, I soon discovered that I had to compete with those who in my opinion, had already reached those dizzying heights of academic achievement even before they had arrived at Myrdle Street Central School. It was some comfort to my damaged pride for me to know that they probably had the advantage of an uninterrupted continuity. If I was going to catch up and do my best, I had a very long way to go.

The Inner London Education Authority, The London County Council, Stepney Borough Council and perhaps also the redundant Middlesex County Council, singly or all together, had done a sterling and everlasting work during the worst of the war years, attracting the best possible teaching staff available in order to keep up the highest possible standards. Teaching was not a reserved occupation. The best and the youngest were mostly in uniform or otherwise engaged in essential war work. Their task to attract the best, was possibly aided by the challenges offered to vocationally minded teachers to enter the war torn streets of the East End to give the best possible chance of a decent education to its war torn children.

I realise it now but not at the time, Myrdle Street Central was an exemplary example of the standards maintained as far as it was possible within the restraints imposed by the shortages of 'everything'. There was barely a detectable difference between the average grammar curriculum and what was provided by the 'centrals'. Every subject was taught albeit within the restrictions of qualified teaching availability. Advanced mathematics, languages, history, science, technical drawing, geometry, woodwork, metalwork, Latin, typing and shorthand, Greek history, the mythology, and philosophy. Somehow, it was all there but not in a bundle so that individuals had to take in the lot and finally choke on too large a meal, but each individual was assessed and encouraged in their strongest subjects and were allowed to concentrate on those. We were actually given our own choices in extracurricular subjects outside of the national requirements. It certainly helped me in certain respects. My own personal regrets are that I was not able to take full advantage of the possibilities and opportunities on offer. I was too far behind my peers, and I was struggling to catch up, never mind keep up. In the end, I almost gave up trying and withdrew into the safer world within myself.

Myrdle Street and much of Aldgate, Commercial Road and Whitechapel, covering a large area extending down towards the Thames to the very borders of Wapping itself, and towards east Smithfield, were predominantly Jewish. A large number of the school's intake were Jewish. If I gained anything at all from the school curriculum, I soon began to understand what Jewishness meant in a generally anti-semitic world, and an opportunity to draw on a potent experience of the past that had far reaching effects on my future social attitudes. However, I won't accept that the non-Jewish world of the East End was, or could have been, accused of being rabidly anti-semitic beyond an indefinable sense of misunderstanding and awareness of the culture differences which did create those areas of separation and misunderstanding for us, the relatively few, 'Goy' kids at Myrdle Street. It came down to something as simple as 'custard'. We found it difficult to 'swallow' the need for the school meals to observe the Kosher dietary laws. Milk and meat were never allowed to come into contact with each other. There had to be separate cooking utensils. Plates for this, and plates for that purpose. The main irritation for us 'Goy's' was apparently having to put up with the 'milkless' custard which we understood was 'Kosher'. For us, it wasn't custard at all, but a lemon flavoured opaque yellow sauce. "We want proper custard", was the cry sent up by us of the Kosher uninitiated, which almost caused a race riot amongst a generally peaceful pupil community. The headmaster had to intervene and do something about it. (He was not Jewish incidentally), so he invited the local Rabbi to come to the school to explain the kosher dietary laws to us. I personally, couldn't understand what all the fuss was about because I quite liked the unusual sauce anyway. The Rabbi was quite a jolly old boy. He made us laugh with typical Jewish anecdotes and jokes. It was all good fun. Out of it, I discovered that the Jews could always take jokes against themselves and just as often, telling them against themselves in the first place and enjoying them as much as we did. We 'Goy's' could always be relied on to dish it out, but all too often were not able to take it.

It wasn't all I learnt about Jewishness, which I turned into a very profitable side-line. I had palled up with a Jewish lad of about my own age. He and I shared a common disability... school! Both of us tailed more or less at about the same level of incompetence. In many ways we helped each other if only in the sense that we shared the same problem enemy.

David was a sensitive boy. Whatever his academic abilities might have been, or not been, somehow I had linked with him. His deep introspective brown eyes glowed with an inner smouldering. He had a slight tick of mouth which was more pronounced towards a stutter with trying to reach into matters that moved him. I saw that he was desperately trying to put words to his feelings, something we both separately shared. We talked of all things and everything. We spoke of the war, and of the Jews because he was a Jew and had heard some of the current rumours. Nobody could be absolutely sure whether these rumours about the unfolding tragedy inside Hitler's continent were true, or just propaganda. He had relatives in occupied Holland and worried endlessly about their rumoured fates. His personal family experience had been the escape from Holland of his elderly grandparents who had managed to get out just in time, leaving behind sons and daughter and their grandchildren. Thankfully, they never got to know the truth of what happened to them. David had a great investment in the outcome of the war. There were no illusions within the Jewish community what the outcome of a Nazi victory would mean for them. David and I made plans of what we would do if things came to the worst. We devised schemes of the most fantastic nature. Plans of retaliation, with bands of us hiding up in secret places to come out at night to fight such heroic battles. I still had an ache for vengeance over the violent death of Derek, killed with his whole family during the air raid in 1940. For me, David had become almost a reincarnation of Derek. Of the same race but at the same time separated by creed. He too had had the same kind of sensitivity. Probably, if I had been able then to put form to the concept, I cherished and valued David's friendship the more because of it... mild, and as sensitive as both of them had been, who would not hurt or harm a fly, would have fought like tigers.

His family were not very strict in the Kosher and the sabbath laws, but he wasn't allowed to go very far on Saturdays anyway. I could visit him though, but it was mainly to sit and talk, or to do indoor things. He had a sister who was a year or so older than himself who had the same sort of expressive eyes as he, plus a beautiful head of black hair that flowed over her shoulders in a glistening raven cascade. At the tender age of 14, or thereabouts, she was well formed in womanly proportions. Of course, I was hopelessly in love with her, but at the mid twelve year old period of manhood and still in knickerbockers, I felt dreadfully inadequate and a helpless candidate for her attention, let alone her interest, but then I was also made to be aware by nothing that suggested her aggressive disapproval, but only because of that impenetrable wall and the unbridgeable gulf of (race), but certainly of creed. Never mind, I felt some comfort in the fact that she was nevertheless, just as much a daughter of her own and her ancestors instincts, and she was perfectly aware of my helpless condition... In true female style, her smile of welcome and the side long 'catch-me-if-you-can', glance. When not observed, the hesitant peck on her smooth blooming cheek, warm with her blush. I hoped this meant more than it otherwise might have intended. Merely a token expression of hospitality. Her duty done, she retreated back into her own kind.

I naturally looked forward to and enjoyed these Saturday sabbath visits. Sometimes, I even shared the wonderfully evocative (Shobas) (sic) Friday meal with them. The seven branched candelabra, the salt, and the bread and Grandad intoning the Hebrew prayers. As far as I could be certain, I believe David's dad was away fighting in the Jewish Brigade somewhere in North Africa, but sometimes I felt the need to go out by myself to see what was happening in other mysterious necks of the wood. On one of these walks, I had set out from home early in the morning for a Hebrew sabbath walk through Cannon Street Road. I saw the usual sabbath Jewish folk standing at their doorsteps. I had often seen them and assumed that they were just taking a morning airing. On this particular morning though, I had been watched by a bearded and homburg hatted individual. He beckoned to me and asked, "Will you do something for me? It is the sabbath you see". I said, "Yes. What would you like me to do"? "Come", he replied, and taking me gently by the arm he led me into his house and through a darkened passage into an equally darkened living room. I could just about see the vague forms of his family sitting silently about. He asked me, "Will you please take down the blackout screens and draw back the curtains"? I wondered at first why he hadn't taken them down himself, but I did what he asked of me, revealing his wife, smiling sons, and daughters. The sons wearing the little skull caps that I knew were called the 'Koppel'. The girls with flowing uncombed hair.

He asked again, "Will you please light the gas under a metal plate on the gas cooker", on which stood pots containing prepared meals and water for boiling. I was directed to adjust the gas flame to his wife's satisfaction. Next, it was the electric lights to be switched on, or off. All this time whilst these requests were being carried out, his family were nodding gratefully and muttered thanks. It also occurred to me that although these had been simple tasks, the profuse thanks did not match the little effort required to fulfil them. I was also rather confused by the thought that I was being asked to break what they must have considered the unbreakable law of the almighty sabbath, but it was alright for me to commit such a terrible sin that they could not or would not. I rather felt as though they were apparently quite willing to condemn me to eternal perdition to save themselves unless they were already satisfied that we, the unbelieving, were condemned anyway. I could not work out the apparent contradiction and it lingered on my lips to ask the question. 'If it is not right for you to work on the sabbath, why is it alright for me'? But I didn't.

When I had finished these simple tasks, which took all of ten minutes, I asked, "Is there anything else you would like me to do for you"? I was assured, "No thank you. We are very pleased. Thank you". As I left to go on my way, I was handed a very generous bag of sweets since there could be no sabbath financial transactions for the services I had rendered. My attention was directed to two of three pennies on a sideboard, indicating that I might pick them up if I so wished, thus avoiding the problem of actually and physically handing me the money in payment. The sweets, of course, was not technically a 'payment' but a gift, and would I please come again next sabbath? "Would I"? I was in business.

The news obviously went the rounds of the local synagogue congregation, that there was a 'goy' boy who didn't mind risking the consequences of his mortal sinning by labouring on the sabbath. I worked up quite a substantial clientele whose tuppences, the bags of sweets, and other inducements, made a big difference to my weekly pocket money of one and six, or in other intelligible words, the present day grand sum of seven and a half pence. By comparison with today's values, two such clients willing to reward me with tuppence each, would nearly double my weekly ration of 'dosh', plus the bags of sweets that came my way which were rationed at four ounces per person per week, or a couple of Mars bars if one could get them. I was in the money 'big time'. I never bothered to ask if my 'clients' could spare them. Many of them were as poor as the synagogue Hebrew mice were reputed to be and I could not take the money offered but decided that I would restrict what I picked up on a principle, to a single penny or just a few sweets. Sometimes, a piece of strudel would do. Sometimes I would take nothing at all to the evident relief of all. I just hadn't the heart to abuse their generosity. I suppose it created an atmosphere of happiness and satisfaction all round.

Sometimes on my way to school through Cannon Street Road, or on my way home, I would drop by to say hello, and not infrequently was offered a piece of cake or sumptuous apple strudel. That was the best. Rich and cinnamon spicy, crisp, and sugary. Jewish mums were usually very good cooks!

* * * * *

Close by Myrdle Street on the opposite side of the Commercial Road, was Hessel Street. This was a small Jewish daily street market rather like Watney Street but on a much smaller scale with stalls both sides of the street. I liked to walk through it mainly on my way to school. It was 'kosher' of course. Barrels of pickled herrings stood on the pavements. Jars of 'rollmops' in the shops. I bought cherries in season with my sin-money. Cherries and plums in season. A few home grown Kentish apples and when not in season a few carrots were a good munch. Wartime provision was very limited. I was always popular when I brought my goodies in to school.

I watched the licenced kosher slaughterer kill chickens. They had to be fresh and blood free. Crates of squawking birds stood on the pavements, feathers flew up in clouds every time the crate was opened and yet another luckless bird met its doom. Their throats had to be slit and the lifeless bird put head down into a cone shaped funnel. There were a dozen or so of these mounted on a frame, their blood dripping away into buckets under the racks. It was all a bit too macabre for me, especially as the swift operation of dispatching the fowls was being carried on with such an apparent lack of concern for the suffering birds. I asked the question, "Does it hurt them"? It was met with some amusement, and the reply, "Oh, no son. They are quite dead the moment the knife cuts the jugular". They didn't look very dead to me. I wondered how they could be so sure of that since it was obvious to me that my rabbinical licenced informant had never had his throat cut to find out whether it hurt, or not. I wondered whether I ought to pass over the fruit as a silent protest, but the cherries looked so sweet and juicy that I forgot my scruples and carried off a pound of 'white hearts' offered at nine pennies per pound (four pence). I gave the luscious 'reds' a miss for that day, they reminded me too much of the blood.

I was naturally forbidden to leave the school premises during school times, but one or two of the older boys and girls would sneak off round the corner to get a sticky bun or two, from a bakers shop in New Road. They could often be induced, or rather more generally, bribed, to get a bun for us younger, or less courageous kids. One particular day, they arrived back in the school grounds and made the startling announcement that the baker was selling banana buns and they had some to prove it. It must be remembered that we had not seen or tasted a banana for years. For some of us, it was barely a distant and vague memory. Bananas, of course, were unobtainable. The result was amazing. Within seconds, the playground was empty of children with a penny or two to spare (which meant all of them), either begged, or borrowed in an emergency. Curiosity, anyway, was the spur of the moment and had caused the sudden exodus. Everybody had suddenly disappeared out of the school including me, and a queue half a mile long formed at the bakers shop. It turned out that the buns were not the real thing but only flavoured, but they were yellow and sugary, and smelt and tasted like bananas. They were hot from the ovens, and we wanted them.

It wasn't long before the teachers noticed that the school was empty of their charges. When they were called in after breaktime there were no kids in the playground to come in. The teachers, together with the headmaster, came to investigate and to sort things out. They gave up in the end and joined the queue. We all trouped happily back to school in time to be discharged in time for the dinner break.

There was a long lecture the next morning at assembly by the headmaster, but he had to agree on being asked by one of the bolder spirits, "That the buns had been very nice". Banana buns were on offer for a few weeks afterwards at the bakers but either because his precious 'unobtainable' flavouring had run out, or he had taken the hint that the novelty had worn off, he baked no more banana buns. We heard that he tried orange buns next, presumably in the hope of another bonanza, but we had worked out his 'con' and refused to be sucked in again.

Chapter 32

Petticoat Lane – Sunday Market

David had no qualms about Sunday outings. He suggested that we could go to Petticoat Lane Sunday market in Middlesex Street, Aldgate. We went but seeing the crowds in the street he shied off saying that there were 'pickpockets', and in any case, he said he didn't like crowds and was intimidated by them. It was also said of Petticoat Lane, that one could lose ones wallet at one end of the street and buy it back at the other. I daresay there were a few pickpockets however, seeing Petticoat Lane market so briefly on this Sunday morning had whetted my curiosity. I resolved to explore it on my own next time. Anyway, it was not only possible but frequently probable, to lose a companion in the crush. It was always wise to arrange where to meet in case one got separated. Everyone got separated and the only way to prevent it was to be tied together. The following Sunday I made my plans. I had no wallet to pinch, so that consideration did not bother me, but I did have a half crown piece and a few odd coins in loose change that I had come by in my sabbath activity of assisting the devoted. Finding a secure pocket that hadn't too many holes in it (sound pockets were a luxury of the past), every pocket of mine had holes in them as well as the backside of my reputedly hard wearing corduroy knickerbocker shorts. (long legged trousers were only a dream of the unforeseeable future), not just because of a shortage of the necessary coinage of the realm, but because of the natural endemic wartime condition of shortages on the one hand, and clothing coupons on the other. I wasn't due for a new pair for at least another year, so it was making do and mend (not incidentally, Big Gran's strong point), or try to ignore the embarrassments. Safety pins were a very useful commodity in urgent cases. I solved the security of the half-crown piece by twisting it in my 'hanky' held tightly in my hand and then thrust into the virtually bottomless pocket. A strategy I decided would foil the attempts of the most determined, or skilled pickpocket.

Petticoat Lane Sunday market was far more crowded than Watney Street ever hoped to be. The massed press of people had to be experienced to be believed. Being somewhat of a diminutive stature, I was constantly at risk of being unnoticed until it was too late to avoid being stepped on, but by dint of a shove and a wiggle around the legs of all shapes and sizes, I always managed to get to the front of the various groups who had come to a solid immovable halt whether they wanted to halt or not. I didn't mind because it allowed me to witness some things at leisure, like the 'Dutch auctions' (mock auctions), and even one, or two (untypical for Petticoat Lane), genuine auctions.

I laughed along with everyone else around me at the cockney patter of the market men selling tea sets, or dinner sets. A dozen plates fanned out up his arms like playing cards… and his inviting patter… "Cum on nar gells. This 'ere is the only last free (3) sets of 'em left. Nar den, do yerself a favour. There yer are gall, if yer likes it, give yer old man a promise an' you'll get it. I ain't a askin' a fiver fer dis 'ere set, wood cost yer twenty quid at 'Arrods up West, or not at 'Arry's of 'Ounsditch neither. Ere yer are den, las' free. Not a fiver, three pounds – too much den? Alrite, two pound den". (Whoever Harry of Houndsditch happened to be)?

There were no takers. "Thirty bob den". Still no takers. "Alright den, gis a pund – we'll finish up in th'workis like dis". "Two more lucky galls dere". "Wrap em up 'Arry for the lucky ladies". "Dat's it… you sir an' you m'am". Then, with hardly a pause, "Nar Den, nar wot abart dis ere 'Roy-al wooseter tea set". The crowd moved on and five minutes later another group. The same, "Last three sets left"… plus the hundred others under his stall. The three lucky purchasers, when they got home, discovered that the same service could have been bought any day of the week from the local ironmongers oil shop and general wares store anywhere, for fifteen shillings.

Then there was the 'jockey scales'. It's operator claimed he was the official 'weight master' at "Nu-markit an' Epsom darns. Weighin' der favrits' orf before der racis". He 'jockeyed' up his Petticoat Lane trade by guessing his customers weight before they stepped on the scale. The temptation was to prove him wrong in which case the punter got his tuppence fee back. He was rarely wrong. I never saw many tuppences refunded. His method was to feel the ladies arms 'Fer der sack o'decency", and the gents thighs, declaring, "Rito sir", putting the guessed weights onto the scale pan. "11 ston' five an' a 'arf punds". "Right sir, step up an' tak' a seat". Down would go the seat and balance slowly with the weighted pan at 11 stone, five and a half pounds. A little white card with the weight and date scrawled in pencil and the weight masters invitation, "Try us again nex' wik guv', but miss art on yer toast afore yer comes". "Cum on ladies, who's next den? Try us on. Guess yer weight for tuppence. I gets it wrong, it costs yer nuffink". "Don't be shy luv, you's had yer leg felt a time or two I spec's. I don't mind if yer hubby don't". A giggling lady stepped forward and offered her arm. "Oh, 'e do mind do 'e? Oh, only cos yer as got the tickles as yer? OK, yer arm'll do. Does yer want me to shart out yer weight, or does yer want t'kip it secret"? He whispered his guess. The scale balances and the lady stepped off smiling. To her great embarrassment he told her and everyone else in a loud voice adding, "Better leave it fer nine months afore yer comes again"! I wondered why he needed the scales if he got it right every time?

* * * * *

Further down the lane was the pitch of a quack medicine seller dressed in hobnailed boots and white coated. He had an anatomical dummy, an armless and legless torso which when dismantled showed all the internal organs in their proper places. He sold a concoction that was supposed to be able to cure every ailment, known and unknown. He demonstrated by references to the various parts and organs of the dummy, explaining that his mixture had been proved by the very latest in medical science to be an effective cure for 'everything'. His spiel included the explanation, "Ladies an' gen'lemen. Dis 'ere secret receipt 'as come darn to us from ancient times. Wot wus only available to th' royals, an now we's kin offer it t' the gen'ral public fer the fust time". He pattered on and on describing what his wonderful and miraculous mixture would do for the heart, lungs and the liver.... Incredible! Everyone laughed at his easy banter and his apology. "That becos o' decency, this 'ere model can't show, you know what, ladies and what you gents ain't sa shy about". He went on to say, "But I assure yer, that this 'ere helixher 'ill cure even that... that is if yer hubby ain't farned a cure fer it already". There were plenty of laughs at that, and a dozen more bottles of coloured water sold at a shilling a go on the strength of his audacity and the entertainment value alone (some might even have believed it all).

Next, and close by, was the 'strong man'. Barrel chested and muscle bound, who claimed that he owed his strength to the fact that his doting mother had fed him from birth on a daily quart of 'Mortlock's' sterilised milk, followed by a quart of Guinness. He let us into the secret that his mum... "Bless 'er blessed memory, ad of a purpose kipt 'im orf th' gin, cos every good mum knows what as 'ow gin ain't no good fer mums, or yunksters". He may have been getting a rake off from the grocer opposite his stand who was trying to sell off his over enthusiastic ordering of sterilised milk. He performed with chains wrapped around his neck, inviting four of the beefiest men from his audience to pull on the chains as hard as they could to try and throttle

Cambourne, Cornwall, Christmas 1940.

Lily, John. June and Rodney at Elmhurst, 1941. Me ready to fight the enemy with Rodneys popgun.

Me, Dad and Lily on the gate opposite Elmhurst, 1941.

Me on the gate opposite Elmhurst, 1941.

Red River path walk, Gwithian, 1941. Dad asked me if I wanted to stay or come home with Lily.

Destruction of bomb shelter at junction of Watts Street and Old Gravel Lane, 1940.

Petticoat Lane in the 1930's (c.Tower Hamlets).

"Hoi, Wotcher Doin' 'Ere?"

Lily – photo dated Aug 1944.

PLA Clinic, Wapping Dock Basin entrance.

What have they done to my pre-school nursery?

him, reminding them to stop pulling when he signalled. "Just in case they were about to succeed", and anyway, it proved beyond doubt, "That he could never be hanged", etc., etc. His repertoire included milder feats of strength. Bending six inch nails, "It corst me a ton in nails". Tearing up phone books. Bound in chains and padlocks and performing feats of escapology with much heaving and rolling in the gutter to free himself from strait jackets and sacks, sweating profusely and breathing heavily. These final feats completed, he announced, "Tha' ends me demonstration lidies an' gen'lemen, but cos I has ter pay out a big 'surance policy in case I does get strangled an' me old lidy an' me kids as'll starve, I 'ould 'preshiate a small contribution ter help us art a bit. Anyfing 'ould be welcum an' I thanks yer all". Pennies, half pennies, three penny bits and glints of small silver coins showered into his temporary ring. "Me next demonstration will be in a quarter of a 'our whin I gits me breff back". In his fist he had a bottle of sterilised milk, took a long gulp, and said a few more, "Thanks", and we all filtered away.

One of the best characters for me was 'Prince Monolulu'. He was a colourful tipster known throughout the length and breadth of the East End and further afield. An unconvincing coloured man dressed in the style of a supposed African chieftain. He claimed that he was a real prince of Ethiopian origins. I use the word 'unconvincing' because even I could see that he had rather confused his dress metaphors somewhat. He wore on his head, a headdress that was distinctly North American Red Indian in character. On his feet, a pair of black ankle boots such as most labouring working men wore, under a robe of a multi coloured sort. He also wore western style trousers and the usual collarless striped heavy cotton shirt and waistcoat. He was minus a few teeth and certainly of Caribbean African appearance. His open mouthed cry, "I gotta n'orse... I gotta n'orse", amused me. I thought he only needed a horse to ride off across the American plains like the current cowboy and Indian film shows at the Troxy in the last Saturday mornings 'tuppeny' flicks.

One bought a little envelope from him for sixpence. In it was written the name of the horse which he forecast was going to be the certain winner of such and such, a forthcoming race. He claimed that his skills of correct forecasts were derived from his ancient knowledge of witchcraft, descending down to him through his distant Ethiopian ancestors… King Label-igro-lobo, or something like it in any case. Anything 'like it', or 'unlike' it would do. A ruler somewhere in the deep uncharted jungles of darkest Africa, hence he was the legitimate heir to the throne. 'Prince Monolulu'. He had to be for there was no other contestant to the title. Apart from his Sunday visits to Petticoat Lane, he also went to the races at Epsom Down, Newmarket, and elsewhere. I was told that he was driven to the racecourses in his chauffer driven Rolls Royce. If it were true, he must have always made the right forecasts on his own behalf as well as the addition of thousands of the punters sixpences. His clever image building evidently convinced them that he really did have the secret to successful betting. Folk swore by those little sixpenny envelopes. Some of the forecasts much have been winners by the very law of averages. However, he was a very colourful character and widely known all over the East-West, North-South of London and further afield. The like of whom will never be seen or heard again, crying out, "I gotta n'orse. I gotta n'orse". Good luck to his memory, to his fortune and to his Rolls Royce.

There was another tipster. He wore a bowler hat in the style of a course bookmaker. He advertised himself as a successful punter, displaying printed cards with details of his recent winnings for the 'flat' season, and reputedly a successful punter in bets 'over the jumps'. 'Stake money, four shillings and sixpence - winnings of 300 pounds'. 'Stake money, five shillings for first, second and third each way accumulator winnings – 1,412 pounds, four and sixpence half penny'. All displayed on his cards to persuade investors that his envelope forecasts were the only genuine 100% certain winners. I thought that the image was rather overdone as he also had a trained budgerigar which, on a command, generally activated by the customary sixpence, would pull out a small envelope from a rack of hundreds of them. Anyone would do, in which magically and mysteriously, the name of the winning horse was written. The hopeful punters also invested the budgerigar with some mystic powers of pre-knowledge to draw out the right envelope with the right horse forecast, so the bowler hatted tipster claimed, and there was the evidence of his winnings to prove it printed on his display cards of reputed winnings. I puzzled over this 'mystery' for a long time. How did the bird do it? Until I realised what the con was. The mystery had held me on station for a long time, watching and listening as the customers opened their purchased envelopes. Sometimes a companion would ask him, "What's it say"? The answer always the same. Same horses, same race, same day, same time. I had got it... every envelope had the same forecast. If the horse did not win, it was put down to the 'budgie' having a bad day. Anyone could have got the same result by sticking a pin in the race card published in the Daily Mirror.

I tried telling one hopeful punter (probably hoping to cash in on my knowledge). "Hey, mister. I know what it is. The tips are all the same in those envelopes". Mr Bowler hat had been watching me. After the person I had spoken to had left, he laid a very threatening hand on my shoulder and bending down to look me very closely in the eye, he whispered, "If yer don't want yer effin ead kicked in, you'd better piss orf quick". I decided on the latter very smartly and gave him a wide berth ever after, at the same time remembering to keep my mouth shut in future.

I got home to Wapping safely in time for Sunday dinner with half a crown's worth of overpriced rubbish that nobody of the pickpocket fraternity had taken a fancy to. I often went to Petticoat Lane after that, seeing that my property had never been threatened and neither did the crowds frighten me, I felt (and was) perfectly safe and free to wander wherever the fancy took me. I could linger if I wanted to and laugh at the easy patter to my heart's content, quickly though, coming to the realisation that the 'spiel' was perfectly rehearsed and practiced, and rarely varied very much apart from the occasional impromptu remark said in true swift cockney wit and humour. I also went 'rarely' with Lily and an aunt or two. We always managed to get separated in the crush, so I usually finished up on my own anyway.

Tubby Isaac's & Jellied Eels

Anyone who remembers Petticoat Lane Sunday market as it was in its heyday, would find it unforgivable if I could pass by in these brief recollections and forget to mention the ever present daily establishment in permanency of Tubby Isaac's jellied eels stall, on the corner of the Aldgate end of Middlesex Street. Reputably established since jellied eels were invented (a statement that must not be taken as fact. It was an invention of my own because I honestly don't know how long he had been established* on that particular pitch. It seemed as if it had been there forever to me). Every morning, till late at night, in bright sunshine, moonlight, or just fog, naphthalene gas lamp flare illuminating the groups around the stall enjoying Tubby's renowned delicacy, jellied eels served in little white china bowls that nestled in the palm of the hand. Half a dozen small pieces of eel set in the jellied plain stock that the eels had been stewed in. Apparently, the jelly seems to be a bit off putting for some uninitiated folk, but a true delicacy even in its own right, peppered and with lashings of vinegar. Absolutely delicious! Tubby's jellied eel stall sold other shellfish delights too. Small saucers of cockles, pickled mussels and probably the ubiquitous gob stopping hard chew of a whelk. Chunks of bread (never slices – chunks), given gratis with the eels. The pavement littered with the eel bones.

* 1919

I always looked on it in envy, at the obviously well breeched customers sampling Tubby's 'acknowledged' jellied eels... but they never were cheap at any time which in itself, must have added something special to the taste.

Chapter 33

Cathedral Bells & The Tourist Trade

I have always been an inveterate wanderer, even in those early days living in Hermitage. I liked nothing better when Lily was at school, to amble off somewhere on my own to explore the goings on in the local manor, getting myself into all sorts of places that by rights, I shouldn't. The well-remembered Wapping wharf floor and my very special wharf man at the time, I understood perfectly that any door that was open was to let people like me come and go as they pleased. This was not an unreasonable assumption I suppose, seeing that nobody of our neighbourhood had ever locked their doors against me, or anyone else for that matter. Coupled with this natural order of things generally, I was an easy chatterbox, ready to expound to anyone willing to listen to any one of my usual fantasies that spring to mind. There might also have been a practiced element of 'charm factor skill' that had often got me out of difficulties, really because it was also a form of wheedling my way in sometimes. It had to work the other way too in order to wheedle my way out of awkward situations.

In the early 40s, and me looking forward to the first year of my teens and not being too closely subjected to restriction, a feature that was fairly normal for Wapping of the times, children were rarely kept on too short a leash at any time. As I said, it was always a case of survival. Life had always been tough. You either learned early to cope with it or...? Well, there was no alternative. I suppose modern terminology would be 'streetwise'. I'll go much further than that in Wapping's 'pre 40s era' case and call it 'lifewise'.

It was an easy transition for me to slip whatever bonds intended (if ever they were intended), I always managed to find an 'open door' somewhere and made full use of the offered opportunities. My curiosity of places and happenings was apparently insatiable. I just had to find out the 'ins and outs' of everything. I also found out that my curiosity very often drew out of those who were unwilling to be observed, the threatening observation. "Piss orf yer nosey sod". A response that was just as frequently expressed in far stronger terms (depending on the intimacy of the occasion).

A story that will bear the telling now, with no recriminations, even so, it is a perfect example of what I mean. Looking back now at the event, I ask myself, could I help it if my curiosity had been roused by a chance remark? True, it was way back in my Hermitage days but nevertheless, I must have thought it significant enough to have remembered it.

Sometimes, when I had been taken over to Bermondsey to 'Little Gran's', dad always came to collect me. Always late evening and frequently in the dark. He would carry me home most of the way high on his shoulders 'flying angels'. I never felt very safe crossing Tower Bridge perched so high up and my feet about the level of the bridge handrail. I thought, if he should trip now, I would be pitched headlong into the murky waters of the Thames racing below and swept out to sea. I always asked him to let me down to walk over the bridge. Nervousness apart, it was just as much an opportunity for me to dawdle along and take my time to wonder at it all. He didn't mind either, I think he liked to stop and enjoy a moment or two to view the scene himself. It suited us both.

We left the bridge approach by means of the stairs down into the dim cavern of St Katherines Way homeward bound to Hermitage, passing the darkened and silent wharves dimly lit by the streetlights. As we passed a darkened wharf gateway, I saw the vague forms of two persons pressed into the darkest recess of the gateway. Naturally, my curiosity was well and truly stirred. I asked, "What are they doing dad"? "Oh", he said. "I suppose they're looking through the keyhole". I puzzled over this for months afterwards because I never realised that the gate had a keyhole to look through. Anyway, in any case, I reasoned, what could they have seen in the dark? I just had to find out what those people could have found so interesting. Actually, my innate natural instincts were aroused. I think I knew what it was but wasn't too sure and wouldn't say it anyway, but it was a few years in the coming. It had to wait until one dark evening during one of my late evening homecomings of my lonely wanderings. It was getting darker and by pure chance I was passing the very same gateway of the keyhole mystery. I heard noises. This I had to see. Somebody was at that same keyhole again. Creeping up quietly, I peered into the dark gate recess... such noises... so that was it (as if I had ever believed the keyhole story)! Dad's version of the keyhole wasn't the same as what I had understood it to be but only provided to accommodate a very different kind of key! Unfortunately, my curiosity had somewhat caused me to overstay a doubtful welcome. Suddenly, the girl became aware of my spying eyes peering round the corner. I had overlooked the fact that whereas I could barely make out anything clearly in the dark shadows of the gate recess, whoever it was hidden in the gloom was looking towards the light of the street and no matter how little I was, I was obviously clearly to be seen. "George... George", the distressed maiden cried. "The feller... the bloke...". Too late, I'd seen enough in the minute or so of uninterrupted viewing. George rapidly 'readjusted his confusion' and turned to me with menace. I was transfixed and unable to move. Grabbing me, he hissed, "Yer nosey buggar. Wot cher doin a spyin on us fer"? He was shaking with evident frustration of being interrupted at a critical moment. I was equally shaking with the fear of his violent reaction. The girl came to both of our rescue. Flustered and worried, appealing to 'George' in a moment of urgency. "Don' George. He meant no harm". She evidently knew who I was.

"It's Johnnie Insole". I knew who she was too, but I am not telling now. Had I not been known, well, no harm would have been done beyond a bit of embarrassment for the worried girl, though the consequences might have been more serious. "No. No. George... Me dad, George, 'e'll kill me for this". Appealing to me she said, "Don' you say nuffink Johnnie, deres a lovey". I promised I wouldn't. I was very relieved that George had been pacified a little and had even managed to see the funny side of the whole thing. I was even more relieved to have solved the mystery of the 'keyhole' at last, as if I ever doubted. We all managed to learn the ins and outs of things somehow.

Into the early 40s, my lonely wanderings took me into every corner of the near city, visiting all the usual city tourist sites. Westminster Abbey. Trafalgar Square. Buckingham Palace. The Mall, and the parks, Piccadilly, and Soho. St Paul's Cathedral standing like a gaunt massive island isolated in a sea of wartime destruction. All round it there was nothing left, blitzed, and burnt. The rubble had been cleared away leaving exposed the deep cellars and basements of the buildings that had once stood there. St Paul's standing in its defiant isolation declaring, 'The enemy passed this way'. While it stood, it would be a symbol of the national defiance and determination.

Nowhere in the city was too far away from home. At the furthest, no more than two or three miles distance. In any case, a few pence out of my sabbath sin money paid for a ticket from Wapping underground on the rattler which took me anywhere I wanted to go.

For instance, dad liked his classical music, more often than not, tuning his smart modern press button wireless to listen to it, mainly BBC3. I liked it too. Music both stirring and peaceful, solemn, and cheerful.

The promenade concerts continued throughout the war years, moving from the Queens Hall to the Royal Albert Hall after the destruction of the former in the blitz. As it turned out, it finally became a far more iconic venue and continues to be so to this day. Dad and Lily went, I wanted to go as well but he thought I was too young, but this didn't deter me. I was determined that his decision, "When you are older", was not going to stop me. If I couldn't go with them, I decided I would go on my own. I made my plans.

Came the time, with five or six shillings in my pocket and a few pence allowed for my fare on the rattler, off I went. Much too early as it happened. When I arrived at the Albert Hall, the queues for the 'promenade' stretched all the way round the hall and half the way back round the hall again. This was not going to be as easy as I had thought. Anyway, I joined the queue and feeling that I needed a little bit of moral support, I made sure that I got close to anyone who seemed more likely to be friendly. I stood behind a couple and in my usual chatty way I got talking to them. I asked, "How much is it to go in"? I believe it was half a crown for the 'Promenade'. That was okay so far. From there it led on to me being questioned. "Are you alone"? "Yes". "Have you been here before"? "No". "Where do you come from"? I always made a big play of the fact that I came from the deep dark canyons of dockland Wapping. "Oh", was the surprised reply. "Do you like music"? "Oh yes...", I said, "... and I have always wanted to come to a concert". I have never been known for my stature, plus the uncomfortable fact of wartime shortages, we all looked as though we were something out of a rag bag rejected by the rag and bone man. To increase the woeful apparition of this 'Artful Dodger' looking kind of individual, I was still in those embarrassing corduroy knickerbockers (and knobbly kneed) minus its normal pockets. A corduroy battledress blouse type jacket to match, practically naked and holey at the backside. Coming from Wapping must have seemed about right to them. After all, there was the reputation to back it all up. Here was something unusual for them (who probably came out of the leafy suburbia of somewhere like Wimbledon or Wanstead). A little 'ragamuffin' who liked 'classical music'. The idea must have appealed to the young lady

384

as she remarked to her partner, "Oh, how nice. Shall we take him in with us"? In an appeal to her otherwise doubtful partner. The very last thing he wanted, I expect, but 'take me in' they did, not into the promenade but into the auditorium seats… and paid my entrance fee as well.

After the concert, I was treated to a sandwich and a 'cuppa' before we parted. It had been a wonderful experience and I was hooked, line-and-sinker, for ever after. An experience that I enjoyed time and time again.

There was something else I learnt in the process about vulnerable young persons, especially sweet looking young ladies. How it was possible with the right sort of 'charm' factor, to wheedle into their good books. Mind you, it didn't always work out the way I intended. I tried the same ploy once at a West End cinema, only to be rebuked and told to 'Piss orf an' git yer mum ter mend yer trasis", which I worked out must have been the essential difference between matters of 'snob culture' and entertainment. Classical music and entertainment seemed to be incompatible. It isn't, it just so happens that it seemed like that to me at the time, so it must only have been a cultural snobbery on my part that fortunately got lost somewhere down the years! I didn't say anything at home about my excursions, I didn't think that it would have been approved of. On the other hand, I didn't know whether it would be or not, so I thought that discretion was the best course. I said nothing.

I was very impressed with St Paul's Cathedral. The great dome on the inside aspect was spectacular. The great empty space, the paintings on its inner dome. I wondered; how did they manage it? How were they painted? The galleries and massive supportive pillars.

Outside the cathedral, all noise and bustle. Inside, cool, and quiet. The small noises of distant cathedral movements ringing in echoing sounds that seemed to go on and on until finally whispering away into a silence. During the war years, there were not many visitors of a strictly tourist nature. Although it stood bravely and apparently virtually unharmed, there had been considerable bomb damage. The eastern end of the church. The reredos and the High Altar destroyed. The side aisles boarded off. The north transept roof and the church floor broken through by a penetrating high explosive bomb. There was also a general air of wartime neglect due presumably to the lack of cleaning staff, those that might otherwise have filled the need were either away doing military service or redirected into essential war work. The cathedral looked dusty and smelt dusty. Together with its wartime scars, the grand organ could no longer be played. Severely damaged, it had to wait for the post war years before it could be repaired.

I paid my three pence entrance fee to the whispering and the stone galleries and climbed the long winding low stepped spiral staircase to the whispering gallery and listened to the whispered words sent around the gallery and marvelled at it. Still further upwards from there by the narrow twisting stair to the 'outside' stone gallery and the base of the mighty dome and the stunning views of the city, the Thames, and the bridges. In those days there wasn't any other city building higher than the stone gallery at two hundred feet above street level.

A verger (or as I have since been informed were at the time employed as 'cleaner guide'), sat at the top of the stairs at the stone gallery level and was very surprised to see a little titch-like individual like me appearing. He asked, "Are you alone"? "Yes", I said. "Oh", he replied. It was obvious that he seemed concerned. I'm sure he must also have felt somewhat for my safety. After all, there was a hundred foot drop from the gallery to the cathedral roof and nothing really to stop me or anyone else, if they were so inclined, to take the plunge (intended, or not). He decided that the best course of dealing with the problem was to escort me around the gallery, pointing out the places of interest as we went. There (in the typical and permanent fashion of the smoky times) was Tower Bridge and the smudge of Wapping beyond it to the east. To the west, Big Ben, and away in the misty distance, the hills of the Thames Valley to the south and the north.

He asked me the usual questions. Where do I come from? Why was I alone? In my usual style I was only too ready to explain where I came from and why this, and how that. In fact, we sat in his usual 'station' at the top of the stairs chatting for what seemed like hours. He, explaining much about the cathedral building and its history in typical guide manner. I asked the relevant questions. He asked my name and he told me his. "Mr Boston". Finally, it had come to the gallery closing time. I said I would come again. He offered the information, "If you do, if you ask for me, anyone will tell you where I am. I could be anywhere in the building". I often went after that introduction. Sometimes, Mr Boston would be on duty in the crypt at the stone gallery or in a dozen various other places. Very soon, all the black cassocked verger-cum-cleaner-cum guide staff got used to me.

I do not know what Mr Boston's exact position was in the cathedral hierarchy, but he did seem to have some authority. Quite apart from the fact that he also seemed to have free access through any locked door. At his waist, he always carried a big bunch of keys, and nobody seemed to give him any instruction or direction. There was the odd occasion when he instructed and directed others. My assumption was that he was in some sort of authoritative position. Years later (many years later), on enquiry to find out some more about him, I was told that all the records of that period had been destroyed so my enquiry ended at that point, but then, if there is anyone out there who can tell me more of where he came from and what became of him, please do. Any member of family or friends. Anything about him. He never mentioned a word about himself except his name, Mr (just mister) Boston. No Christian name, and significantly that he had been 'rejected' as unfit for military service and that he felt badly about it.

In spite of his obvious reluctance (for whatever reason he chose to remain fairly anonymous) he was always ready to satisfy all my questions about the whole building. Its history. The destruction of the 'old St Paul's' in the great fire of London of 1666. The construction of the present cathedral. He showed me the wooden model Wren had produced to promote his proposals for the building. I saw the 'library' and the 'Deans' office. Once or twice, when he was on duty at the stone gallery, after closing time and the few remaining visitors had been accounted for, he would take me up to the Golden Gallery set at the base of the lantern atop the dome. From there, climbed the companionway-like ladders up to the cage under the ball and cross. The highest point of all if one does not take into consideration the fact that it is also possible to get up into the ball itself, but the top rung of the ladder into the cage was as far as I would have wanted to go. I looked up and saw into the dark ball interior. I already felt a strong tinge of fear because of the height and a realisation that the whole mass of the cathedral was beneath me and was supporting... just me. I stood almost at the top rung of the ladder and saw the whole 360 degree sweep of the City of London below my feet and far beyond. To the east and home, I saw again in wonder, the teeming river, and the few 'wartime' ships. The tall cranes stood as silent monuments to a crippled port. Around the cathedral the full extent of the destruction and the lonely isolation of its remarkable survival when everything around it perished. I stood at the peak and felt the pride of my place and being a part of that very same symbol of defiance. Above me, the empty sky laced with scudding clouds. Below me, the ever present hum of traffic and movement. The relatively few cars (by today's reckoning) and the iconic red London buses. Tiny dots of pedestrians crawling like insects busily about their daily occupations, bent either on a drudging labour or in search of pleasure. Sometimes on our descent back to the church floor and normality, he would explain the construction of the outer dome and how it was formed and supported by the massive oaken timbers. He walked with me around the brick built cone that supported the lantern (as he explained, "The whole 700 tons of it"). We stepped very carefully along the narrow, barely more than a foot wide, two boarded 'catwalks'. Quite a risky thing to do at any age and daring enough on Mr Boston's part, to say the least. I felt a bit shaky and nervous but at the same time immensely proud of the privilege of doing something not available to the general public. Maybe it might not have been allowed by anyone in higher authority if they had been aware of the risks he had taken.

Mr Boston seemed to me to have a 'carte blanche' over any decisions about it all. There was nobody to say 'no' to it anyway. Between us and the cathedral floor, there was nobody else but a great empty space. At other times, he showed me the 'chain' circling the 'drum' on which the whole dome structure is supported, put in place after it was discovered a slight movement of the whole cathedral slipping towards the Thames. In the course of measuring things, the true centre line from the top of the dome and the centre of the church floor, was six inches out of plumb. At the same time, in order to save costs, it was found Wren had filled the four major crossing piers with rubble. This had to be solidified by pumping liquified cement 'grout' into them. An operation that needed urgent attention (and months to complete), considering that the four piers had to support between them a massive ten thousand tons of lead, brick, stone, and London's pride. He showed me the monuments and who they recorded. Nelson's and Wren's tombs in the crypt. At the time, in the forties, Wellington's cast iron funeral chariot was kept in the crypt. I suppose it is now rusting away quietly somewhere else. Mr Boston took me over the upper side aisles ceilings and explained the construction of the saucer domes held in their places by the key stones and nothing else. Everything he knew he imparted to me, but the best was yet to come though.

September 1942 through October, November, and December into 1943, things were beginning to look much better on the war front. Rommel, and the Afrika Korps, had been brought to a standstill on his march to the Nile by Montgomery and the eighth army. 'The Dessert Rats' dug in and went on the offensive at a little Egyptian desert village called El Alamein, and the Afrika Korps and Rommel were now in full retreat all the way back to where they began in the first place. The back of the Afrika Korps had been finally broken after months of a seesaw advance and retreat battle fought out in desert sands of North Africa, and the Nazi campaign to drive the British out of the Mediterranean theatre altogether and deprive Britain of her main source of oil from the Middle East also, the inevitable disastrous loss of the Suez Canal, had failed.

Finally, the Afrika Korps and its unwilling Italian allies who hadn't wanted to go to war anyway, marched together into captivity, 150,000/200,000 of them. As if the victory of El Alamein had not been national euphoria enough, Paulus and the German sixth army became surrounded and trapped at Stalingrad and a whole army of a quarter of a million were annihilated and wiped off the enemies strength, shocks from which the Nazi war machine never recovered and the Nazi Empire visibly shrank. Like most kids of the times, I had a map of Europe and followed the progress of the advances and the retreats with little flags on pins. Suddenly, it was very apparent that the little red flags with the black crosses were slowly being squeezed into an ever decreasing encirclement. In typical Churchillian fashion, he summarised the whole situation of the victory of El Alamein by declaring, "This is not the end, it is not even the beginning of the end, but it is perhaps the end of the beginning". There was no longer any risk of a Nazi invasion and the church bells were permitted to ring out their message of relief. The banning of church bells was lifted entirely dating from Easter Sunday 1943.

One of Mr Boston's responsibilities was to ring the 'chimes' on Sunday mornings. The removal of the restrictions on the ringing of the church bells wasn't a problem, it was finding the people to ring them. The war time conscription of men had depleted the availability of experienced bellringers. The St Paul's congregation was fortunate to have a fairly large pool of 'ringers' and was able to maintain a regular full twelve bell peal on one Sunday in every month (and on special occasions). As I remember it now, the remaining Sunday's had to be 'chimed', that is the bells were not 'swung', but struck by fixed hammers and Mr Boston seemed to be the only member of the cathedral staff who could do it. (There might have been others I didn't know about. All I do know is he always did it)! He asked me to meet him at the main west doors at ten o'clock. I knew I would be there if I had waited all night.

Just inside the north aisle entrance is a tall double door to the clock tower. It was always locked (and probably still is). He found an enormous key on his bunch and opened the door. I saw for the first time the high tower wide cavern that forms the base of the clock tower. It rises about 50-60 feet from the floor level to ceiling, about a third of the full height of the whole tower. Around the walls spiralled the 'geometric staircase' in a long low spiral mounting up the towers walls. The public do not get to see this wonder which is a pity because it is so beautiful. The staircase handrails were wrought iron and gilded. In the centre of the cavern hung the clock weights. In the silence, I heard the clock's mechanism pacing out the seconds. Mr Boston pointed out the few pennies on the weights placed there to regulate the clock's pace. One taken off or put on, could make the difference in the days of telling of the time. We climbed the stairs to yet another door leading off of a little staircase landing atop the stairs. We crossed the nave west gallery situated over the main west door to reach the 'bell tower'. Up a short narrow circular stair from off the south upper aisle, and finally into the belfry.

It was not yet time for Mr Boston to ring the chime so there was time to spare to show me the bell loft and the peal of the twelve bells. It was then that he explained that a chime is when a bell is struck when stationary with hammers and he pointed out to me the mechanism to do this from the belfry by means of separate cables, and the peal is when the bells are swung. He told me that the full peal of the twelve bells is the heaviest in the Empire. The smallest and lightest as I remember it, being the thirty hundred weight (1½ tons), the heaviest 'Big Tom' at 63 hundredweight (3 tonnes 153 kilo).

The chime was rung from a console set on a wall of the belfry over a little low dais rather like a pulpit. From the console, thin cords led upwards and disappeared through the belfry ceiling into the bell loft. Mr B' mounted the dais and began to play the chime, pulling in an ordered sequence on the cords mounted in a frame (rather like a harp). I was suddenly amazed at the loudness of the bells in the loft above and marvelled that it was because of one man plucking those thin cords which could produce such a noise. He told me that it was quite safe to climb back into the loft to watch the chime hammers strike the bells but that it was something that must never be done while a full peal is being rung. It hadn't been unknown for the swinging bell clappers to break off to fly off in all directions. The great volume of sound that greeted me in the loft, standing not more than a dozen feet away from the stationary humming and vibrating bells, was terrific and very exciting. I peeped... well, actually I stood, where I knew I could have been seen from the street and the cathedral forecourt, but then I was proud and not yet thirteen years old until a few months hence.

It was nearly time for the five minute bell to be rung. Mr Boston had asked me to be back in the belfry because he wanted to show me how the 3 ton bell was swung. In any case, it was unsafe to be in the loft with a swung bell and the risk of a flying clapper. "Just watch me this time", he said. "Maybe one day I will let you ring it yourself". I wasn't too sure about that but then... maybe if he let me try one of the chime cords. It looked quite complicated and what a mess it would be if I got it wrong, but for now, "Just watch me, I will teach you how to ring it".

After this, I was back again many Sunday mornings. Eventually, he said he thought I was ready to ring the 'five minute' bell. I was very nervous. With my feet firmly clamped into leather loops fixed to the floor, he began, "Slow pulls on the bell rope now". I had a lump in my throat with the anxiety of doing it just right. I was going to be in trouble if it wasn't, I had been _severely_ warned. "If the bell goes over the top of its swing, let the rope go. Do not... repeat... do not try to stop it. Bell ringers have been killed trying to stop a 'wild bell'. If the bell goes over the top of its swing at the top of the bell wheel, it will keep on going round and round in a full circle winding the bell rope on the wheel. The only thing that would stop the ringer hanging onto the rope would be the belfry ceiling thirty feet above and certain death". A warning indeed!

With my feet strapped to the floor, "Take hold of the rope now, the way I showed you. Pull down slowly... gently now. Not too hard, not too far. That's it". I was surprised how lightly I had to pull on the rope. "Then...", he continued, "... let the rope rise with the return swing. When it stops rising pull down on it again just a little harder this time". "That's it. That's it. That's right. Get the rhythm of its swing. Feel the rhythm of the swing". The rope sally slipped through my light grasp. "Squeeze it as it goes through to control the pace. That's it. Keep it going, you're doing fine". Faster and faster the bell rope rose and fell. Gentle pulls on the down rope, tighter grips on the sally on the up, I felt the burn on my hands as it went through. He could teach me no more; I was on my own now. He just kept saying to me, "Feel what the bell is doing, pull an' check, pull an' check".

Forty feet above my head the bell was rising in its wider swings. I measured its pace. Just gentle pulls now to keep it going... higher and higher. The descending rope coiled at my feet. The bell must now be getting near to the top of its ring, I could feel it through the rope. I let it rise and a pause, let it fall and held it there for a fraction of a second. Another gentle pull on the rope and suddenly... the first strike! The monster a hundred and more times my own weight was speaking. "Careful now", Mr B' was warning. "Hold it there. Hold it just there". One pull on the down rope now that was too hard and the bell would begin a wild wheeling in a full circle casting off its hammer as it spun, winding its rope on its wheel, dragging an unwary 'ringer' with it and a death blow on the belfry ceiling, but I had got it under control. I was its master, and it was doing my own bidding. One fatal slip now and it would be my killer. 63 hundredweight of swinging bonze tethered to a five and a half stone little boy. It was straining to go over but I had got it. The higher it swung, the louder the strikes. I wanted it to speak. I wanted it to shout. It was mine and I possessed it. Checking its swings, the rope 'sally' now whizzing through my hands. A gentle squeeze on the 'sally' and a gentle pull and hold him. A swing and a strike on the up. A swing and a strike. Swing and a strike… I had his rhythm; I was in control. The hot rope and the 'sally' whizzing through my hands… wonderful… just wonderful! I had 'dared' it and won. Thinking as I rang, the bells voice can be heard all over the city of London, and if the wind was in the right direction it might even be heard in Wapping!

I was shouting as I rang… laughing and shouting. "This is me. It's me. Can you hear me"? Mr Boston was shouting and laughing with me, but didn't he take a risk. I was glad that he had. I was very lucky and very proud. I wrote my name on the belfry wall with a stub of pencil, I daresay it has been painted over by now. I claim to be the 'youngest' and the 'lightest' bell ringer EVER in the belfry of St Paul's Cathedral. I was barely thirteen and weighed five and a half stone. (I only knew that because I had recently been weighed on the Petticoat Lane jockey scale).

On my way home, I felt like asking everyone I met whether they had heard me. "Did you hear it? It was me. It was me", because I… just me, had given the bell a voice. From the moment of the very first strike it had welled up inside of me. "This is me. Can you hear me? It's me".

The H.E. bomb that had struck the north transept roof exploded in the upper aisle destroying a large area of the transept roof and ceiling. The debris (which consisted entirely of Portland stone) crashing down, broke through to the crypt. Both the north transept and the underlying crypt had been boarded off to prevent public access because of the huge hole in the church floor. Mr Boston told me that he had been on duty the night that it had happened, during his frequent stints of fire watch and air raid precaution duties. He showed me a small partitioned off area in the crypt close to one of the main piers. It wasn't very much bigger than a cupboard with just enough space for a low camp bed. He said, "If there was no raid in progress, it was possible to get a few hours sleep". These night fire watch duties were obligatory as well as a normal days work before and often the day following, so a few hours' sleep if there was no emergency was important. He told me that on more than one occasion he had had very little sleep for several days at a time. The little partitioned cubicle was just a few feet away from where the transept ceiling and the church floor had crashed through into the crypt. He said, "It made quite a mess of the camp bed but fortunately neither I, nor anyone else, was in it at the time. I was on the roof at the time, dealing with incendiaries". On the night of the blitz great fire of London, he had been on duty. He, and the A.R.P. and the cathedral staff and volunteers, dealt with 75 firebombs on the roofs. Most of them hadn't penetrated the roof and some of them were extinguished by the melting lead. Churchill had said, "The cathedral must be saved". The disastrous destruction of Coventry cathedral was still very raw in people's minds. The loss of St Paul's would have been another crippling blow to morale. If it were possible, everything that could be done had to be done. There could have been nothing short of a miraculous intervention. If it had been 75 H.E. bombs that had been dropped and not incendiaries… even so, if the firebombs had penetrated, it would have meant the total destruction of the cathedral. Anyway, it had been saved by the men and the women volunteers who braved and risked their own lives and who stood their ground against the onslaught of fire and blast, openly exposed. They bared their chests to confront and confound the nation's enemy as well as their own fears, and it was only because of that bravery and determination that St Paul's still stood, defiant as the symbol of a nation's resistance and defiance.

The debris had been cleared away in the crypt but there was still a pile of broken chairs, kept I believe, because they were not too badly damaged and might be repairable. In the back bookrest of one of them, I found a small scrap of hastily cut paper. I still have it. It was a prayer for protection against air raids.

A Prayer for Protection Against Air Raids

Almighty and most merciful God,

Who dwellest not in temples made with hands: Be Thou the guardian, we beseech Thee, of our churches and our homes; keep this Thy House in peace and safety; and grant that all who worship here may find their refuge under the shadow of Thy wings, and serve Thee with a quiet mind; through Jesus Christ our Lord.

Amen.

The tourist trade

I spent quite a lot of my spare time at the Cathedral (some of it should have been spent elsewhere, at Myrdle Street School for instance) getting to know more about the building. Its history and its building, it's monuments and so on. I read avidly Harrison Ainsworth's novel 'Old St Paul's' to 'bone' up a bit on my real lack of topographical history. All this, together with my lonely wanderings about the capital (and my inveterate nosey curiosity), I built up a fair knowledge of the places of interest. I knew where they were and how to get to them.

By the late 1943 and beyond, the city was full of American airmen of the eighth air force based in East Anglia. They came to the capital in droves in off duty times to see the sights mainly (and sample other delights on offer probably). Not that there was very much in the way of diversion apart from…? I think trade was fairly brisk in some areas?!! I met groups of them in the cathedral and offered to 'show them around' and explain some things to them. There were no official guides as such, so nobody minded. I did not actually mind either because at the end of these impromptu 'tours', they were always extremely grateful and generous. They were generally very open and made something of a fuss of me. Mind you, I did tend to wave the Union Jack a bit. Perhaps, thinking about it now, I might also have been a shade 'impolite' at times, reminding them, "America. Ah yes, you might have skyscrapers and cowboys, but this is big history. Thousands of years of it. The Romans and Saxons, and the Danes. Kings and queens etc." In hindsight, it was not nice perhaps, coming from a thirteen/fourteen year old titch like me, and a 'ragamuffin' to boot. It could have been a bit insulting, but they always took it onboard very well and seemed very impressed with my nationalistic enthusiasm. Well, it could have been otherwise. A cap was always passed round with profuse thanks. I don't think they had caught on to the equivalent values between pounds, shillings and pence too well compared to dollars. There were never 'coppers' in the hat but always silver shillings, florins and half crowns.

Not infrequently, I was asked how to get to other places of interest as well. "Where is so and so"? And so on. I sometimes offered to show them where and how to get there. I was often taken to these places in taxis. Sometimes treated to meals. Some of the requests were not always cultural either but I knew the score. I knew where to find what they were looking for. I understood the coded and mostly embarrassed euphemisms and usually indirect references connected to the 'right sort of bars'. Really, I hadn't the faintest idea what or where a 'right sort of bar' might be found but guessed that somewhere like Soho was the most likely place to find it. The best thing to do was to get them there and then leave them to sort the rest out for themselves but not before a little more appreciation found its way into a cap though.

I was just as keen to show them the 'other' side of London's glories too. A few of them, I found, were reasonably well informed about London's dockland role and a history based mainly on Dickensian descriptions. Dickens has always been a very popular author in America. Fortunately, I had a liking for his novels myself and had read as many of them as I could get my nose into. They seemed to be interested in the Jack the Ripper kind of places too, where it all happened etc. All of this was my kind of territory. Of course, I was only too happy to tell them, "I come from Wapping". (My 'spiel' was well practiced) "It's the dockland area, and I live with my Big Gran an' Grandad, an' I have a sister, Lily. Dad works away on important war work". "Oh, and here's a little something for your Grandma". I am ashamed to say that she never got it. In any case, I never told 'anyone' about my 'tourist' enterprise. I was rich beyond my wildest dreams what with my tourist trade and my regular sabbath sin money. It was something that I did not want to explain away. However, I claim to be a wartime pioneer of the post war tourist guide industry. I hope they do as well now as I did then. Some weeks I had as much as three/four pounds at my disposal. Any man, any ordinary working man who earned as much in any week in those days could count himself as being reasonably well paid.

Unfortunately, it couldn't last forever, and it didn't. Thinking about it all now, and remembering those pink faced young men, most of them not many years my senior, I often wonder now, how many of them died in the violent skies over Germany and elsewhere, thousands of miles from home. I hope I did something to cheer them on their way to whatever destiny lay in store for them. Belated thanks to them too, and their fortunate survivors.

Chapter 34

Who's for Funny Ideas? – Bits & Pieces – Politics and a Return Unopposed

Amidst all this heady excitement, I still had my trials on a daily basis. Trying to catch up in my usual carthorse fashion with my racehorse friends at Myrdle Street central, never quite making it to the finishing post, always at least thirty furlongs behind the front runners. I had though, found another friend who limped along with me more or less together but even he, I noticed, sometimes forged ahead leaving me trailing a few paces behind.

He was 'bookish'… so was I, but my preferred reading matter did not seem to match what was required to help me in the current school curriculum. If it was into Shakespeare at the time, I was bound to be into Dickens. I was always bound to be into something else. Perhaps it was something to do with the inherent rebel in me that determined my own course of discovery. I worked consistently according to the dictates of what I thought was important to me at the time, to be absorbed at my own pace and along the fixed lines of my own agendas. The truth is, that I was a mite too undisciplined to subscribe to whatever others determined for me. I know now that my awkward attitudes made things worse for me than they might otherwise have been. I might have gone a little further than I did if I had been prepared to knuckle down more into the relevant serious schoolwork. The reasons, I suppose, had as much to do with the fact that I actually gave up trying to catch up. My contemporaries were always ahead and out of sight. It might have had something to do with the situation that I found myself in. Beginning early on, it was too full of so many contrasting circumstances that were so marked and so intriguingly different, and far too often too temporary.

Interestingly, the memories of these times for me, are on the one hand sharply focused as distinct visual events and yet on the other hand, appear like passing shadows briefly glimpsed before disappearing into the mists of time, a condition that applied more to those that peopled those places and events. They became the nameless part of both the place and the event. Somehow the event and the place remained with me and those that peopled them became the shadows. The nameless figures drifting across the mind. Names are such a problem for me. I can fix the image of the shadow but not the name. In a sense, my memories are peopled with ghosts but nevertheless, these ghostly images in the mind _are_ very real people co-existent with the reality of the memory. David, my Myrdle Street friend... I cannot say 'companion' in a true sense of its meaning, was Jewish, and in many ways reminded me of Derek both in appearance and manner. Perhaps I was drawn to him for this very reason.

There was also (I understand it now but could not have done so at the time), an indefinable otherworldliness about him that appealed to my sense of the mysterious. If there was any companionship it existed mainly in the understanding that we shared similar interests. We were moved by the same influences in a kind of joint admission of inspiration that reached beyond his Jewishness, creed, or race. In a sense, we were able to enter into each other's culture in our own personalities without considering them as barriers to communication. The things we shared were neither Jewish or Christian, or race or colour. His music was my music, and this alone puts it as simply as I can explain it.

* * * * *

In our Hermitage days, Lily and I never neglected the obligatory Sunday visiting to our 'Little Gran'ma Wrighton', who lived in Bermondsey. It just meant that we had to travel a little further and venture over the borders of Wapping into foreign territories. We had to cross 'Tower Bridge', so it seemed a bit like going overseas.

Because she lived in Guinness' Trust buildings in Snowsfields, I always expected to actually see snow. "Not in the summer, silly", Lily would remind me. I never remember seeing it in the winter either, so I naturally worked it out that Lily had got it all wrong, because I might have got it all wrong too did not count! Little Gran had rather a missionary turn of mind with evangelistic inclinations. I rather suspect that I had been a candidate to be evangelised. Our visits on Sunday mornings usually coincided with her attendance at 'Arthur's Mission Hall', a mission that I believe had affiliations with The City of London mission. We were often 'shown off' there. Little Gran lost no opportunity to secure my earthly wellbeing and a guarantee for my soul of a place in heaven, which I was assured was mine for the asking. I was probably an ideal candidate for sanctification as I didn't want to upset her by asking too many awkward unanswerable questions. They lingered on my lips all the time, so I went along with it as manfully as I could. The big unanswerable question over the whole issue, was that it seemed that I had to die first in order to qualify for a place in heaven. I wasn't too keen to do that, not yet anyway. I reasoned it out that if I leaped at the idea of an instant chance of admission… I'd finish up dead, so like all good men and true, I put off the decision and left it there for the time being to be sorted out later.

The meetings were alright. We sang choruses… well, others did. I mimed where I could and coughed and sniffed where I couldn't! The visiting mission speaker on one particular occasion was a Mr Waller. It was he, who later gave me the red clothed Bible in which mum scored out my name and Bermondsey address when I lived at Forest Gate. I think he must have been in league with Gran. He had his eye on me.

He knew who I was and where I came from. He was going to tell us a story about God's house. I was very interested because I was very curious about such things. I wondered if Mr Waller did his Sunday visiting duties like everyone else and had been to God's house, and that this was why he knew where it was and what it looked like. He began, "Boys and girls. We have a little visitor here with us today and he comes from Wapping. Wouldn't it be nice for us all to say, Hello Johnnie, it's nice to have you with us today, and welcome"? A tired and bored chorus of, "Ello's", rounded that one off nicely. He continued, "I'm going to tell you about God's house, and I am going to ask Johnnie to help me out". 'Help', I thought. It's me that needs the help. I don't know a thing about God's house. I knew lots about 74 Hermitage Wall, but nobody wanted to hear about that, but being a little on the extrovert side of shyness, I willingly complied. Mr Waller set me up on a chair at the front… (I wouldn't have been seen otherwise), my head normally barely came up to the chairs seat. He placed his hand on my head. "Now, boys and girls", he began. "Here we have little Johnny. He comes from Wapping". Now, that statement of fact set me apart from the rest of his audience for a start. Everybody knew what Wapping's reputation was all about, probably including the kids. Most of their dads had to find work in the docks but it was recognised as a fact of life that few Bermondsey dads ever found work in Wapping, not if Wapping men knew about it, he would soon find himself swimming for his life in the murky waters of a convenient lock. Mr Waller went on to reassure them that although I came from Wapping, they were all safe from any violent outburst on my part, "But…", he reminded us, "… like all the children everywhere, we are all God's children, and I am going to use Johnnie as a living example of God's house". That's good, I thought. It's going to be a 'living example'. I'm not going to have to die first! There was more to come though. He continued, "God doesn't want us to wander around in darkness shut out from God's love and care for us forever, do we"? Well, I understood that part of it. 74 Hermitage Wall was pretty dark most of the time. So far so good, this demonstration was working out okay and I was beginning to get to grips with the idea. Profound shakes of the heads and the worried, "Nooo's", from his duly concerned congregation, including my own, voiced in sympathy for the sentiment of the moment. After all, nobody wants to be alone and in darkness. Do they? The only problem I saw with this was the implication seemed to be because I came from those dark and violent regions of 'the island' over the water where the Godless cannibals dwelt, so I was the worst kind of outcast, like some primitive savage in the darkest jungles.

I wanted to know what God's house looked like anyway, so I shut up. He began to get to the nitty gritty. His hot hand still on my head. Referring to my hair, "And here is his roof. It's just like a thatch". Most of us hadn't the foggiest idea what a thatch was but never mind, the simile 'roof' had to do. Pointing to my eyes, "And here are his windows", and my mouth, "Here is his front door". I was getting his drift fairly quickly, but I could also see that by his present rate of progress it was going to be a long time before he got to the ground floor and the scullery, the wash boiler and the brown earthenware butlers sink. I didn't want him to forget a very important feature that confirmed my house was complete. I thought I had better remind him to mention it, "And I 'ave got a tap too". Mr Waller had gone suddenly very quiet. The children were beginning to titter. Mr Waller had taken a moment too long to grasp my meaning and lost control of the whole thing. My peers had been much quicker off the mark. They knew what I had meant. So… that was the end of that little story which was a great pity because I would have liked to have heard the rest of it. Mr Waller recovered his composure, "And now we will sing some choruses". I was no wiser about God's house than when the story had begun.

Little Gran, who played the piano just like mum, mysteriously by ear for the mission and the Sunday school, had witnessed the event, afterwards chuckling and telling me, "Serves him right, he shouldn't have said that you were a little Wapping outcast. He didn't mean it", she said, but couldn't continue speaking because she had burst into a gale of laugher. I suppose it was a bit funny, but every proper house had to have a water tap didn't it, but then I suppose Mr Waller learnt an important lesson himself never to use a little boy from Wapping to demonstrate God's house ever again.

* * * * *

It would be far too fanciful an idea on my part to suggest that Wapping's social order had not been influenced by the developing twentieth century's concept of social change. Of course, there were 'outside influences' but the same driving necessities that had chased the Salvation Army out had never changed. Not one of the islanders wanted to reject anything that would benefit the peace and the comfort of life. If it didn't, or it threatened the finely balanced social equilibrium, there was enough already to contend with without having to espouse 'funny ideas'.

The collected instinctive wisdom soon sorted out the facts from the fictions, and the best place for the fiction was over the bridge rails and into the murky waters. Put simply (at any rate for Wapping men), it was a case of being prepared to exchange their trousers for a better pair but not what held them up. The realities of life in Wapping were generally unavoidably impossible to hide behind a Mrs Grundy's type snow white lace curtain and her aspidistra. Even for the comparatively young, including myself, the basic facts of life and the mysteries of sex itself, were together not the great unknowable's. Anyone who might have had the notion to 'con' us with silly stories about storks and gooseberry bushes would depart embarrassed and probably shocked.

* * * * *

George, of keyhole notoriety, would be told, "Rite son. You's 'ad th' fruits. You's made yer bed, nar you 'ad better lie on it", the same for his partner but it was never, never, never a case of a Mr & Mrs Grundy's door barred to either of them. If George ever wanted to work in the docks again, he had better lie on the bed of his own making and feel comfortable in it. There might have been a few exceptions to convention, but it usually always worked out well enough. If it didn't, then the best remedy was to 'move on'.

On a visit once to 'somewhere' (I was very young when it happened and I suppose thought to be too young to notice anything strange about the visit and out of order), I was taken to Pop's mother's house at Manor Park. I know now I got a bit bored and wanted to play out with some of the local children who were playing in the street. In my eyes at any rate, her house was rather posh, set in a typically Victorian kind of suburban street avenue with privet hedges and monkey puzzle trees in the front gardens. "Yes, alright", said the Teutonic matriarch, but went on to warn me, "But you are not to play with...", (I forgot the name). No explanations were offered to me as to why I shouldn't play with him, but his peers let me into his secret. "He has got a naughty name", one of them explained. "My dad says he is a bastard", said another. Very nice wasn't it! It put me into a dilemma. I couldn't understand why I shouldn't play with him, he looked alright to me. I cannot claim that the significance had dawned on me right away, but it had registered long enough to be thought through in its worst context years later.

Such attitudes (I honestly believe) couldn't and didn't exist in Wapping. That is not to say that because of this there was no moral criticism of illicit extra or premarital activity, but it only went as far as, 'it is done, there is no mending the situation'. Get on with it. True, it was always a case of 'or else', or accept the consequences, usually extreme in default of the only adequate remedial behaviour. Marry her or run as fast as you can. So much for the Manor Park 'funny ideas'. Manor Park were welcome to them! Outright promiscuity was another matter. There would naturally be strong objection and possibly ostracism toward the guilty.

Chapter 35

Street Girl

Prostitution... ah well? Who can say? The same kind of censure would apply. The very idea that any Wapping girl (well, any girl), could sink so low, would have been unthinkable. Sex, for its own sake on the other hand, one looked the other way and thought their own thoughts. My own father's reaction and attitude all those years ago in answer to my question, "What are they doing Dad"? And his facetious reply (laughingly) said, "Oh. they're looking through the keyhole", meant exactly what his reply had implied. Prostitution though, was a very different matter.

Everybody old enough to understand knew about such things, including me. There were no known specific areas of activity locally, but I was told that one didn't have to travel too far to be able to find it if one was so inclined.

In my early teens, wandering about as usual, on one occasion coming homeward from somewhere or other, I was coming through Pennington Street which more or less followed the Wapping borders marked out by the ever present Dock Wall and the highway. The whole area between Pennington Street and the Highway had been a tight crowded warren of little alley like streets before the blitz.

In the thirties, the L.L.C had begun the process of slum clearance, and a new block of flats like Jackman House had been partly built when the declaration of war had stopped all building work except for a large brick and concrete roofed shelter that occupied part of the site and stood then in stark solitary isolation, as if floating in an ocean of empty desolation. I had to take time out in my homeward march to have a closer look at it. It had evidently been used during the blitz because it was still equipped with the standard stretcher-like three tiered bunk beds. It was very dark in there and it smelt damp (but then every shelter smelt of decay and damp due to a serious lack of ventilation)... Well! Actually, in most cases none at all... I had my torch. Everybody carried a torch in those times because of the total blackout regulations. Close by the entrance, as well as the usual heap of rubbish, my torch beam revealed a liberal scattering of 'condoms'. We knew them as 'French letters'. Some of them obviously very dried up and others in various states of freshness. It was immediately obvious to me that the shelter was being used by a 'working girl' and on a regular basis. Well, the shelter _was_ rather isolated and convenient, so anything going on was less likely to be seen. My curiosity was really well and truly roused. I was going to have to check this out!

It was obvious to me that it was going to be a case of timing that was the deciding element. I decided that it would be unlikely to be carried out during daylight hours, so it was going to be a late evening or dusk vigil if I was going to witness any activity at all, and mostly at weekends too. I made my plans.

I was almost on the point of giving up after several attempts to get it right. I knew that the shelter had been used at times when I hadn't been around, for the obvious reason the fresher evidence remained, when suddenly one evening, I got lucky. Just as it had turned from dusk into the blackout darkness, I saw a glimmer of a torch beam lighting a weaving way as somebody picked their way across the bomb site debris, and best of all heading in the direction of the shelter. As it came closer I could make out that it was a couple. A male and a female. They went into the shelter. I quietly made my way as close as I could to the blast baffled entrance and at the same time, keeping myself ready to retreat pretty smartly in an emergency. By the time that I had arrived at a convenient place, I was close enough to hear everything. I heard voices. The girl was giving her client the benefit of instruction, quietly but distinct enough for me to identify her words. "No kissing please sir", and something that sounded like an appeal for her general comfort, and a grunted unconvincing male assurance of compliance with her 'innocent' maidenly request for this level of consideration. There were several minutes of relative silence broken by a few 'urgencies' and a final 'grunt' which even at my state of sexual inexperience, I understood to mean... finis, followed quickly by an angry outburst from a disappointed client that five minutes of a promised hour had been provided and fifty five were missing in the bargain. "Where the eff were you"? He shouted. "I want my money back, you bitch, or else", etc., etc.

The confrontation between client and provider must have ended in the girl returning his contribution to the agreement, and I thought it was the appropriate moment to move out of view and away from a possible confrontation with an angry 'punter' bent on revenge, I slipped as quietly as I could round the back of the shelter. There wasn't very much in the way of cover, or a hiding place anywhere in the vast empty bombed out site of Pennington Street. I thought it was best for me to stay out of sight until things had calmed down and they had gone their separate ways to mine. The gent stormed off still hurling curses at the girl. She did not make an appearance until he was well out of range. I wasn't worried about her from a violence point of view, but still wary of any awkward reactions on her part for what I had heard, she was obviously very distressed and frightened and still sobbing.

I have to admit that I felt a certain sympathetic softness which in some ways was not befitting the nature of the event, and out of the gloom I gave her another shock by enquiring as gently as I could, "Are you alright luv"? "Oh gawd, where did you come from"? She shakily replied. I had to tell her that I had heard it all and at the same time tried to reassure her. "It's alright, I don't mean you harm. I was just passing and saw", etc. Anything that came quickly to mind to cover my own embarrassments. The last thing I wanted was for her to think that I was nothing more than a sneak and something worse than awful, which is what I thought I was. "Has he gone now"? She asked. "Yes", I said. I now had the time to see her better in the dim light of my torch. She looked so young. She _was_ young. I asked her how old she was. I was quite shocked to learn that she said she was sixteen. Not just sixteen, but as she said it, "Nearly sixteen", compared to my nearly 14. "Will you walk with me a little way"? She pleaded. "There's a dear. It's only a little way near Leman Street. I don't want to meet up wiv 'im again"? "Yes", I said. "I will walk with you".

As we walked, I explained again that I had seen them go into the shelter and I had been curious to know why. "Well…", she said with a definite trace of annoyance. "… now, you do know why, don't cher"? It wasn't just said in a tone that betrayed a conscience or embarrassment, but clearly an annoyance that I had witnessed her downfall. She plied her trade openly enough though! We talked very little to begin with. She was constantly looking over her shoulder to check whether we were being followed by her angry client bent on revenge. I wasn't too comfortable either with the idea of getting involved with something that might turn nasty but as usual, it was quiet everywhere. Not a soul out and about in the enfolding darkness around us that had hidden them and were not seen, just as we too were hidden.

Slowly, as she became more calmly aware that I meant her no real harm and was sympathetic towards her present plight, she spoke more openly about herself especially about what I had seen and heard. "Taint th'fust time it's 'appened, I kin tell yer", she said. "I alwus gives them their money back. Could git nasty if I didn't. I ain't got no 'minder'. Anyway, wot's a li'l feller like yo's doin' wanderin' about for"? I never said anything because I didn't want to explain why. "Oh", she said. "Are you's lookin' about fer a gel then 'an' all"? I didn't answer that either. She must have thought about it… "Nar", she said. The one enquiring look at me and my shaking head had confirmed her suspicions. "Nar", she said again. "I don't s'pose yous ever 'ad a gell... have yer"? "I mean really". I didn't answer those questions either. One enquiring look at me was enough to confirm the story of my sexual status without a word spoken on my part. There was another extended interval of silence between us that bespoke my confusion and her consideration of what should come next in our conversation. She broke the silence... I could think of nothing to say.

As we walked, my unusual and unlooked for companion took my arm in hers and pulling me closer to herself in a tight grip, she reassured me. "Don't worry luvie, I ain't goin' ter eat yer". She must have noticed my natural nervousness, not least the struggle I was having to keep up and managing her noticeable slight advantage in leg length. She asked me again, "Come on luvie, you kin tell me. Yu ain't ever 'ad a gell, like what I mean, have yer"? I knew exactly what she meant. "No, I haven't". Another extended silence until she had obviously thought about my answer. Then, "Thanks fer tonight luv. You're a nice boy, not like me. I ain't a nice gell like I should be". We stopped momentarily. I looked at her and saw the tears in her eyes. She bit her lips on her struggled words, heaving a deep felt sigh and said, "I don't want to be a bad girl, but we ain't got a lot o' money, me, mum an' me three little brothers. Me an' me younger sister. Mum can't work, she ain't well. Me dad's in Africa. Don't hear nuffink from 'im. Might be dead I s'pose. I don't know". "Uncle 'elps out a bit. Well, 'e ain't uncle really, you know, just fer a bit of company I s'pose. A warm bed an' breakfast like. Comes when he's randy. Leaves something on the mantel piece for mum. I woke up one night to find him in bed with me. It was okay I s'pose. Well, nice really! Mum knew, she said it was alright an' gave me some 'rubbers' in case of accidents. I 'ave to 'elp out you see. It's a few easy quid. Not bad fer wot I like doin', is it, but I don't want to be a bad gell really. All I want is a nice fella an' all. Get a nice house an' a few kids maybe". I didn't know what to do or say, and how to properly deal with this developing embarrassing situation. I offered her the few remaining coins in my pocket, but she wouldn't take them. "Oh, no luv", she said. "I don't want cher money fer nuffink. I don't want cher money fer sumffink, nor neither". She stood close up to me and looking straight at me and in a firmly held enquiry into my avoiding eyes and said what I had been expecting. "If you wantster… you know what I mean, you wantser ave me, you can now, if you do, or any time. I don't want nuffink from you… just you and me like". I stood stock still and could not utter a word in reply. Because I couldn't answer her she helped me out by saying, "Alright luv. I understand. I am going home now, but thanks again. Thanks". She took my hand and squeezed it to remind me. "But remember me. The offer stands anytime". I just nodded. "Right, thanks". We turned away from each other, she in her own direction and me in mine, and with that we parted forever. She toward her uncertain future and me towards mine.

I often think of it now and wonder. I knew she wasn't a nice girl in an accepted moral sense, but I had detected even then, a latent kindness of temperament and her warm hearted softness in spite of her trade (whether a description like 'trade' can be said of what she was driven to do). Her mum, "Not well". Her brothers and sisters, "I has to help out a bit". As far as I could see in the dim light of my torch, I could see the freshness of a young face as yet unmarked. Pale grey eyed with the soft look of pleading in their innocence also spoke as clearly to me even as she said it. "I don't want to be a bad girl. All I want is a nice fella, a nice house and a few kids maybe".

As I see it now, a mere girl in years marked out by her circumstance and misfortunes for an awful future driven by a desperate necessity. I hope not. "I just wants to mak' it good", she had said. Well, I hope she did.

I never saw her again. I was drawn back to the shelter several times, perhaps in the hope of seeing her again… perhaps? (also, for the best).

It was evident that she had either changed her ways, or her location because the risks were too high… or, again?… or…? I shall never know.

* * * * *

Me being born in Dagenham apparently didn't automatically deny me my birth right inheritance as a fully accepted member of Wapping society. However, there might have been a grace-and-favour element in this because of Grandad and Big Gran, and quite a few other members of the Wapping Insole clan. A fairly close genetic family member I spoke to once, who might have been otherwise overlooked because through an unfortunate matter of marriages through a couple of generations, he had lost the name. To make the situation a little more complicated, he had also moved away from the real sphere of influence… Wapping itself. Anyway, he told me that the tradition with his branch of the family down through the female line, believed that the Insoles of Wapping were regarded as the island's equivalent of the 'mafia' (which might fit the islanders reputation anyway).

I wished that I had known this during my time. I might have made a bit more capital out of it, but I think this idea is a long way from the truth beyond the undeniable fact that some members of the clan happened to be shopkeepers, or in some influential position in employment. If for no other reason than they had broken the cycle of casual dock work as a sole means of survival, and it carried with it a 'kudos' which marked the family out as the exception to the general rule… enviable perhaps, but surely not malignant. Some years ago now, speaking to an elderly Wapping lady (long since with her island ancestors), she reminisced. "Aunt Beat, yer Gran'ma", she said. "She were a real lady wiv them 'ats wot she wore, an' them smart black dresses an' her glubs up t' 'er elbers… an' yer Gran'dad orf up th' lane in a carriage an' pair orf t'der races". I think that this will say enough as far as a 'mafia' comparison is concerned!

My going to a reputedly 'Jewish' school though, was a totally different matter. What is more, it was a school outside of the island. This caused me endless trouble with my peers. In the first place, Myrdle Street Central was not specifically a Jewish school although most kids (if not a large majority) were Jewish. It made no difference me trying to point this out. The fact is that it was still a school 'outside' and therefore suspect in their eyes, and therefore unacceptably 'foreign'. Consequently, I was lumped along with it as suspect. Before I say another word, I have to make it absolutely clear that the islanders attitudes were nothing to do with race, creed, or colour. They were attitudes that were born purely from considerations of self-preservation. Quite simply, survival DID mean the fittest, fit enough to keep the little they had for themselves. The same principle did not just apply to the Jewish community, but to anybody and everything 'outside', whether they be Jewish, Muslim, Christian, Hindu, or nothing in particular. Neither was colour an issue.

The issue of me going outside of Wapping to a 'Jewish School' was an issue that was going to be sorted out in the best traditions of Wapping justice, based entirely on the trials by fist and valour, strength, and loyalty.

Most of my friends accepted me on my face value, maybe with some reservations of their own, so long as it did not stretch their Wapping loyalties too far. On the other hand, there was one particular lad who had made it his own personal duty to 'sort me out'. Reports had filtered down the local telegraph that he was out to get me for no other reason that I know of, other than the known fact of Myrdle Street. They knew nothing of my Hebrew sabbath sin money. It might have been another nail in my intended coffin if anyone had. The goliath that I had been singled out to face happened to be the dominant warrior of a certain tribal group whose territory covered the whole area of Riverside Mansions, an area which just about qualified as the real Wapping merely because it was slap bang on the most eastern boundary between the real Wapping and Shadwell. Not one of his tribal gang dared to contradict him and wisely avoided any confrontation with him. I had the distinct feeling that I was going inexorably defenceless to the slaughter. I feel a little queasy about having to admit at this late stage, that I tended towards the company of the girls about town. I also have to say in my own defence, that it wasn't because I was particularly 'girlish' in a known sense. I had noticed that I had gained a little protection from female company having noticed that boys generally liked to be on their best behaviour when girls were around, frequently trying to enlist me to curry a little favouritism on their behalf. A sort of go-between desire and embarrassments, some of which intervention, I usually turned generally to my own account.

My major problems usually began when inadvertently, I was exposed and alone. Coming home from school for instance, was definitely risky. I had heard on the jungle telegraph that there were mutterings in the camp of my antagonist that the warriors were becoming impatient that, "This little 'effer', who wint te a Jew's school an' as got te be put darn, once an'fer all". Danny's authority was beginning to suffer from my very necessary strategy of avoidance. It had become a case of 'cat and mouse'. Unfortunately for me, I was the mouse. It became a battle of wits rather than of brawn. Where size and muscle were concerned, I was definitely at a serious disadvantage. Everybody anticipated the inevitable outcome. Lamb chops for dinner and I was to become the sacrificial lamb for the slaughter.

He made the first move knowing that I could not get back home without crossing Old Gravel Lane bridge. He had no difficulty in setting up his ambush on the bridge itself. He was there waiting… on his own. He obviously didn't think he needed any help to 'sort me out'. This is it, I thought. The muddy brown waters of the lock looked so threatening. I could not retreat anywhere. I was going to have to face up to this now, I had no choice, but Danny was in no hurry. He didn't want to get it sorted too quickly; it was after all the psychological bit that he was intent on enjoying. He greeted me with great civility (considering his real motives). "Hello", he said. "Wot cher got there then"? Pointing to a few books that I carried. "Just books", I shakily confirmed. "Jews' books, ain't dey". He asked, but didn't wait for my answer, he had already lost interest in them. "Yer goes t' a Jews' school don't cher" (which was the problem for him) and not the books. I hoped that I might talk my way out of the developing problem. "It isn't a Jewish school, it's for anybody. There are some other boys from Wapping that go there as well as me". "Yeah, I know. Thems go ter a Jews' school an all". The implication was of course, that he didn't approve of that fact either. "I sez yer goes t' a Jews' school th' same as them does… got it"? I had got it in one. He left me strolling away whistling as he went to indicate that his word was law in his manor, as I would get to know soon enough for myself.

On the whole, there was no real antagonism towards the Jewish community so long as they kept themselves to themselves. A good many Wappingites worked for them and with them and might even associate with them on a friendly basis. The explanation for what seemed like Wapping's antagonism and the oft heard 'no Jews down Wapping' comment, was purely political. Wapping people were no more anti-Semite than they were anti-themselves. They didn't actually want to live in Wapping, much less wanted Wapping men's jobs (nobody blamed them for that). Who would? It was all about politics.

The old Stepney Borough Council was dominated by the old type socialists. Of course, Wapping was in the forefront of the red march. Some of the best and ablest, left wing councillors came out of the murky depths of the island. Far too many to enumerate with the exception of one gentleman in particular, he was of Irish extraction. A Roman Catholic… and a Sullivan. Councillor Sullivan dominated Stepney Borough Council. The local joke about that was that the initials carved over the council office door, S.B.C. meant Sullivan Brothers and Cousins, not Stepney Borough Council. He never denied that all the chairmen and women of the committees, and for that matter, all the officers were 'to a man'. His man. He was also a member of St Patrick's Church in Greenbank.

It wasn't a rare sight to see on Wapping's R.C. procession days, at least a dozen or two dignitaries of the council on parade behind the drum and fife band. Not only was the island Catholic dominated, so was the Borough Council. Everything was set up to last the millennium. It was unshakable power, or so it seemed.

Something seemed to go wrong though. To begin with, the Roman Catholics were being challenged in the council chamber. There were a lot of Jewish constituents in the East End and Stepney numbered a great many of them. It wasn't long before they woke up to the fact that democracy, being open to all citizens entitled to the vote, meant that they too could play their part in local affairs, so they put up their own candidates and captured their own wards on the Jewish vote. They were all left wing socialists, and they did not threaten the politics of the chamber, but Sullivan and his trusty cohorts were slowly losing their grip. Sullivan was fearful that the power he held could fall and the island's influence over policy could be lost if something weren't done about it. Hence the election cry, "No Jews down Wapping". He could not argue against their politics. They were the same as his own (and probably more left wing), but ancient fears that had always gripped Wappingites... 'Outsiders', who happened in this case to be Jewish, was subtly used (as it happened, not so subtly either), to discourage any political Hebrew adventurist from chancing his arm in order to dislodge Sullivan from his power base. Out went the clarion call, 'No Jews down Wapping'.

There had been a rumour that an alternative candidate for the St George's Ward had been suggested that would have effectively removed Sullivan from the council chamber altogether. As things stood, nothing was ever done unless Sullivan approved of it. There were of course, many an able Jewish socialist councillor capable of replacing him as council leader and they had just the man for the job. In the end, nothing came of it, so it must remain forever just a rumour because I prefer to believe that nobody from 'outside' would have stood a chance of being elected by a Wapping St George's ward. Plus, the interesting fact that Wapping's reputation was well known as being violently inhospitable to any unwelcome stranger. I think this kind of risk had more to do with the proposed candidates decision not to fight the seat than any political considerations. He would, after all, have had to canvas the area, deal with the local residents and take a walk around the Borough ward. He probably got as far as 'A bridge', took one look into the dark waters just waiting to close over his head, and his enthusiasm suddenly evaporated. Sullivan was welcome to it!

At the following election, Sullivan triumphantly found that he had been returned unopposed having successfully persuaded the majority of his council colleagues that he was still the best man to lead the party and the council. Still, it had done no lasting harm to raise the war cry, 'No Jews down Wapping'. After all, it had proved to be the best defence of his own and Wapping's political interests for the present as well as for the future. Hopefully, for the next thousand years.

The same forces drove my less than friendly antagonist, Danny. In his eyes, I had been no less of a threat… a thin edge of a wedge. As he saw me walking back home over the bridge he actually saw a long line of strangers following behind. My head had to be cut off, and quickly. That is once he had extracted as much pleasure as he could out of the cat and mouse game he was playing with me. I was always careful to make sure that any expedition around the hometown always included girls. I felt relatively safe when they were around, having noticed that the boys generally respected their presence. (There must have been an element of chivalry mixed up in there somewhere). We were exploring the wide open and extensive bomb site of Prusom Street. It had been totally wiped out as a community in its own right in the blitz. It was my favoured place of archaeological artifacts of the recent history of the site. Pots, plates, cups, and saucers came to light, mostly broken and sometimes twisted and blackened by fire. Once, I found the half burned remains of an incendiary bomb complete with its tail fin. I took it to school and gave it to our science teacher. He said it ought to be handed into the police, or the local A.R.P. post for disposal. An incendiary bomb mainly consists of a pure magnesium body that when ignited burns with a fierce white hot blaze, but I have a suspicion that he never handed it in either because strangely, I noticed that one or two of his class experiments included fragments of magnesium. I can only guess where he got the magnesium from. I asked him whether I could have the tail fin as a souvenir as a bit of a reward for letting him do what was legally necessary to do, and he said, "Oh no, you can't have it... I... er... I handed it all in". Oh yeah, I thought. I bet you didn't!

On another occasion, we found a half buried battered album of ancient photos. Very wet, but miraculously the photos in between the limp pages were still recognisable. I took it home with the intention of trying to find if any of the people recorded were known and perhaps returned to their family. Enquiries were made and the album displayed in the local Post Office. After some time, and when nobody had claimed ownership, it was returned to me. I looked at the photographs long and hard, wondering who were these people? Where are they now? Who did the album belong to? They turned out to be unanswerable questions. They might as well have remained buried undiscovered and forgotten forever. There was never anything of any great intrinsic value found. Prusom Street people had never owned anything of any great intrinsic value.

I had my head down an old manhole trying to determine the direction of the broken pipes. My companions all knew of the feud between Danny and myself. One of them whispered a warning to me to hide. Telling me with some evident anxiety, "Ere cums Dannie,

Johnny. E's on his own d'ough. P'raps 'e wont see yer if yer hide".
None of us were convinced by these hopes. Danny was well known for
revenge at his own convenience and always when there was an admiring
audience. We had inadvertently strayed onto his own territory. There
was no point in a joint defensive effort, Danny would have picked them
all off separately one at a time. Danny was never deterred by numbers,
the bigger the audience to witness his supremacy, the better. We were
trespassers on his patch, that was all the excuse he needed. No doubt
the internal telegraph had warned him of my presence. He came alone,
confident that he could sort out this minor matter without any help.
All he needed were the witnesses of my final downfall.

He strolled confidently towards us. Some of the more timid were
making rapid plans to quietly depart the scene of possible bloodshed.
Others, not wanting to get involved with the likes of Danny, pretending
that they had nothing to do with the group that included me. I knew
that my time had come. Danny had decided that his time had come to
'sort me out'. Coming straight for me and ignoring everyone else, with
real venom, he spat out his opening barrage. "I got yer now yer littul
twat. Yer got yer gells wiv yer yu effin big pansy"? I stood transfixed.
Danny, I suddenly realised close up, was at least six inches over my head
and probably twice my weight. Close up he looked too much to me like
the proverbial 'barn door'. There was going to be no parley. His fists
clenched and eyes that declared his intention fixed on me like a tiger
stalking its prey. The girls were naturally keen to see what the outcome
of this affray was going to be. I rather fancy that it was going to be
'admiration' for the victor, and motherly nursing for the vanquished...
me obviously. Suddenly, out of the mists of time, came Uncle Bob's
advice offered to me all those years ago. "Never mind the bumps and
bruises. Take it all. Never turn yer back. Put up a good show then win,
or lose, you'll make friends on him". I never could imagine Danny as
a bosom friend, but my dander was up. Those weeks of torment at the
hands of this raging bully. The sneering gibes and the taunts rose up

in me and it was going to be 'survival', or 'die'. I stood on the kerb of the road to give me some height. I was not going to retreat. He came close up to me putting his face close to mine. Instinct. Self-protection. Survival... Now, get in first. My fist formed a tight clenched knot of repressed anger directed towards this unmitigated bully.

From somewhere around the region of my knees, like a coiled spring acting with a will of its own, with everything I had behind it, up came my fist. 'Crack'. The pain of contact shot through me but it had connected 'smack' on the button of his confidently protruding chin. Down he went like a crumpled wet sack not knowing what had hit him. What is more, he stayed down for what seemed to me to be a worrying length of time, obviously trying to work out where he was. He staggered up onto his feet but obviously stunned and in no state to be able to continue. For a brief moment he was trying to stand upright, then he went down again to sit shaking his head and muttering. "Taint fair you effin littul snide. I weren't ready", but I had been ready hadn't I. He would have hit me first without an apology. I paid him out in the same coin, and he hadn't liked it. He staggered off, offering his usual threats. "You's jest wait 'ere. I'se comin' back wiv my friends, den you's 'll see then". We waited, but he never came back.

The news went round like a dry grass fire. Little Johnnie Insole who had stood over his vanquished enemy and had invited him to 'come on then, let's finish it'. I don't remember saying such a thing. I must have been maddened by the unexpected success. The bully had been vanquished. I revelled in the limelight for months afterwards. I certainly wouldn't have wanted another confrontation with him. I hoped he felt the same way. If he didn't there might have been a very different outcome, but I was never troubled with Danny or anyone else for that matter after that.

Finally, the question remained unanswered of what should be done with the photo album? I decided that the only proper and decent thing to do would be to rebury it where it had been found. It seems a macabre thing to do now, but we performed a kind of burial service over it. I had the awful feeling that it was more than just symbolic. A feeling that stays with me even now.

Most of my contemporaries at Myrdle Street, to say the least, were totally and absolutely 'socialist' (no less than their parents were). Many were the lively discussions, although it must also be said that there were very few contentious opponents to the general thrust, or the propositions under consideration.

Both David and I, were usually to be found in amongst the most vocal of the band of 'cheerleaders'. I never actually noticed it at the time, but these mostly impromptu dissertations frequently arose out of the lessons in the general curriculum and the teachers themselves entered into them. In fact, it might have been more likely that it was they who generated the topics in the first place! Thinking about it now, I would have to say that this kind of teacher initiation was never blatantly political on the surface and somewhat restrained but nevertheless delivered within an historical educational framework. Whatever the justification might have been for the blatant political content, it was obviously slanted by what were evidently socialistic views of their own. They may have been taking some risks of a politically motivated censure that would have put them outside the generally accepted demands for teaching standards of impartiality of opinion.

Prior to the 1930s there had been a conservative M.P. for Stepney but beyond those years it would have been difficult to find a Jewish constituent who would vote conservative (or, at any rate, admit to doing such a thing). Let's face it, pretty well every national European 'pogroms' of antisemitism had risen out of the nationalistic politics of extreme right wing conservative attitudes but then, as for the risks that our teachers might have been taking, as far as these Myrdle Street discussions were concerned, nobody was ever likely to complain about a lack of impartiality. Not in the politically left wing hotbed of Stepney. However, it was not because Jewish voters were rabidly communist, but on the other hand they might have been more staunchly left wing than labour tended to be in those days (or, as some would say, as nearly communist in principle if not in practice). Frankly, in a typically British manner, it could be said that in most social issues there wasn't very much in the area of 'practice' separating the two parties.

In those dramatic and unsettled days of social change of the 1930s, Danny Frankel finally won the seat for Labour and managed to lose it post war to Phil Paratin who fought the seat on a straight communist ticket on the back of the Jewish vote because it was claimed that Frankel had seldom visited the constituency during the war years of tory coalition, but perhaps more significantly, he had neglected the Jewish interest both at home and internationally. Although, it is fair to add, the Jewish community of the East End, considered themselves as essentially English/British, seeing that they were all of the majority who could rightly claim by virtue of 1st-2nd generations birth rights and in many cases, several generations more. Even so, they also generally maintained either Dutch, Polish, or Russian Jewish traditions. All of them had originated as European refugee immigrants. Unfortunately, though, they did manage to present a concept of several separate nationals within a nation. I believe this factor alone was a major factor for the kind of antisemitism I personally experienced in my ways around the borough. Another aspect of this kind of distrust was generally held populist opinion that the Jews were (every one of them) fabulously wealthy. A view though that was totally misguided. A walk around the parish that I knew would soon reveal the opposite reality. On the other hand, they did and still do have, a latent talent for business and economic wisdom, added to which is the undoubted element of most Jewish parents to ensure that their progeny entered into the professions like the law, accountancy, banking, medicine, music, science, teaching, the arts and entertainments, politics included, and if all of this was not possible, opened shops and organised the means of supply and manufacture. Driven, I am certain, by the fact that these strengths seemed to offer the best defence against oppression and discrimination. If there had been any realistic evidence for the Nazi claims of a worldwide Jewish conspiracy and world and economic domination, it may well have emanated from out of this erroneous concept.

We all wanted changes whether Jew or gentile. In those rare moments of togetherness, we all agreed that we faced the common foe. It was no individual. No particular organisation. No political concept, race or creed. Just the system that allowed such discrimination to flourish. Such poverty and deprivation that we saw around us every day. Such ignorance and simple misunderstandings. We all wanted changes encapsulating the simple virtues of fairness and the common good. A heady concept for everyone and yet for me, one that was expressed in one very simple idea. 'From each, according to ability, to each, according to need'. 'SIC'. Ex 'Clause 4' (Labour Party constitution).

I joined the Y.C.L. (Young Communist League). I was never a too enthusiastic member of the group. I think my membership was more to do with an ongoing search for answers on my part. I was certainly sympathetic with the members general political aims but on the other hand, could never be persuaded to get involved in the more active workings of the group such as leaflet distribution and 'illegal' fly posting which was mainly carried out in the dark hours of the blackout. All over Stepney one saw the evidence of this activity. Every morning the white circle and lightning flash symbol, together with the slogan 'second front now' meaning of course, the promised and long overdue invasion of Nazi occupied Europe to relieve the pressure on the Russian front who were suffering terribly.

At those times there was a huge surge of sympathy for the U.S.S.R. The United Soviet Socialist Republic, which had suffered a huge sacrifice of Russian blood in breaking the back of the Nazi advance at Stalingrad. Stalin, the ex-devil incarnate (justifiable) enemy number one, had been resurrected as the benign 'Uncle Joe'.

The airwaves of the B.B.C. were filled with the stirring tear rending sobs of the current hit of those times 'Lovely Russian Rose', 'Where the River Volga Flows', etc. The stirring peals of 'Addinsell's Warsaw Concerto rang out. Huge propaganda symbols now discarded in the dustbin of an embarrassed history. The tide of North Africa Nazi advance of Rommel's 'Afrika Korps' had been turned at El Alamein and the Nazi's never returned at Stalingrad. The retreat was on. It had been a long hard struggle to march forward and a longer and harder way to go before the end.

Chapter 36

A Step Back in Time - Battle of Cable Street – October 8th, 1936

I was just four months through my fifth year. There had been troubles and social disturbances already throughout the 1920s and early 30s that had signalled the coming of the dreadful second world war of the 1940s. Industrial disturbances. The 20s general strike and the social unrest, not least troubles generated by the B.U.F. (British Union of Fascists) and the Mosley Marches through the most sensitive areas of the East End which were intended to imitate the deranged examples of their Berlin mentors. The Jews and a mythical Jewish conspiracy of world domination were the target of the cause of every ill and the world's troubles, and the Jews were to be attacked on any or no pretext at all, by the League of British Fascist thugs led by Sir Oswald Mosley and his demented black shirted brutes. I was to witness for myself how true this description turned out to be. The horrific truth!

I have few recollections about the circumstances in which I found myself aloft high up on Dad's shoulders at Gardiner's Corner, Aldgate East, beyond the fact of recent information is that Dad and his younger brother Bob, had probably inadvertently decided that they would add their own vocal protests to the proposed Mosley march. There had already been an outcry of protest about the B.U.F's intention to organise the march planned to start from Mint Street, and from there through Mansell, or Leman Street to Aldgate and Whitechapel Road and on through Whitechapel, a densely

Jewish populated area. There was naturally a serious threat to the peace resulting in a petition to the Home Office to ban the march altogether, which failed on the basis of a right to protest and free speech and freedoms etc.

Anyway, there I was, hoisted high above the gathering crowds. We had travelled from Wapping underground on the 'rattler', and I very distinctly remember we had joined a rowdy and boisterous crowded train for the two station trip to Whitechapel. The majority of those in the crowded carriage were obviously the black shirted thugs, just like those I had seen on news reels shown at the cinema and in newspaper pictures, who were then rampaging across Germany. Every one of them armed with clubs and staves and obviously prepared to use them. I was terrified. I expect that Dad and Uncle Bob were already wondering whether it had been a good idea to bring me with them, but I was told eventually that dad had said, "This is history in the making" and he wanted me to, "Witness it".

The train emptied at Whitechapel station, and we were pushed forward. I have a very clear image of being hemmed in by a group of black shirted red faces looking up at me with menacing grins. I saw a raised club and its enraged threat of violence. I remember waiting for the anticipated blow that never came, clinging onto dad with all my strength and rolling myself into the smallest possible ball and screaming in my five year old terror. Everything else blotted out. There had also been a train journey to Aldgate or Aldgate East from Whitechapel. What I do remember is emerging onto the street level to be confronted by a noisy shouting swaying crowd. I remember a rank of stationary tramcars at Gardiners' Corner, Aldgate, and mounted police trying to push the crowds back to allow the Mosley marchers through to Whitechapel Road and on through Whitechapel.

The thing that stands out in my memory is the swinging batons of the mounted police and the big brown horses being ridden sideways into an unyielding crowd of protestors trying to push them aside. The same thing was happening at Cable Street at the same time, and also at Gardiners' Corner.

They shall not pass…

We were pushed back into a shop doorway by a friendly enough policeman saying, "Please. Step back now sir" but nevertheless firmly, and from my lofty high point perched on dad's shoulders, I saw the running battles being fought out in isolated groups composed of the anti-march protestors, the police and the Mosley inspired fascists. The police trying to force a way through for the fascist march. The police had no friends amongst the massed anti-march protestors!

Stones and missiles rained down. The shouting and the crash of breaking glass of shop windows being smashed. Lorries carrying the stiff upright bodies of the fascists sitting like stuffed shop window dummies on the open flatbed lorries that had been stopped by the sheer numbers of the crowds. They weren't going anywhere. I watched as one of the lorries dismounted its cargo of black shirted thugs to join in with the police baton charge in trying to clear a way for them to retreat rather than to continue to attempt an orderly march. They never got back onto the lorry but were unceremoniously pushed into the revengeful crowd determined that "THEY SHALL NOT PASS". I saw them being dragged from virtually under the hooves of the stumbling police horses. Blooded, most of them, and left to stagger away as best they could. Most of them were not shouting so loudly then as they retreated with their miserable tails tucked between their cowards' legs. The demented bullies who had been so keen to shed the blood of the innocent had discovered the bitter taste of defeat rather than the triumphal one they had expected and at the same time had discovered that East Enders, whether they were Jewish, Protestant, or Catholic, or nothing more than just East

Enders, were not going to take it lying down and were quite prepared to shed more of the blood of the guilty bullying aggressors than their own.

Chapter 37

Doodlebugs – June 6th, 1944 – 'Overlord'

The invasion of Europe had begun. There was great excitement. Big Gran woke me early. Grandad had got up earlier as usual and had switched the wireless on as usual for the morning news. I heard him shouting to Big Gran (which was unusual). "Beat. Beat. The invasion has started". The BBC news reader was still repeating the brief announcement. "This morning, the allied forces, supported by...", etc., etc. Mentions of Normandy.... The bulletin was necessarily brief and short of detail at that time barely past dawn, and the invasion not yet more than an hour or two since an allied foot had stepped unchallenged and unsecured onto the Normandy beaches. Nobody at this early hour could have known what the outcome would be and whether the boasted Europe fortress wall would prove to be the defeat of the invasion. (We know the answers now).

Around Jackman House came the excited sounds of the unaccustomed early risers suddenly precipitated into an excited wakefulness. Nobody was going to sleep on undisturbed now. People running along the balconies and the knocking at doors. The news being shouted up and down the lane. Everything was on an early move. The exciting news spreading like a grass fire. Everybody wanted to be the first to tell the next person the marvellous news. I personally, leaped quickly out of bed and bounced around trying to get dressed and out onto the street. Dashing up and down the stairs, knocking at doors and getting into the mood of excitement. I might even have been a little too enthused and a bit of a nuisance to those who already knew and were taking the news with something a little too much like disinterested calmness for my own satisfaction. Surely, I thought, this could never end in defeat. It must be the end now. Maybe, just maybe? (I understand now) that it could only have been that this calmness I sensed, was the outward expression of everyone's fear of a possible (and probable) failure. You see, everybody had anticipated such an event. Everybody could see with their own eyes the enormous preparations for it. London itself was filled with stocks and stores, vehicles parked and stacked (and that not too inconspicuously either). One particularly large empty bombed site on the Aldgate end of Commercial Road was filled with loaded army lorries parked bonnet to tailboard. There might have been close to a hundred of them. Just before June 6th they all disappeared overnight. The city was full of uniforms, British, American, Canadian, French, Polish and Dutch, and as always a babble of languages. I had watched along the Wapping river Shoreways the conversion of dozens of Thames flat hulled lighters being converted into bow-ramped landing barges. I can't help thinking now that the troops who were landed in them must have experienced a wild trip from ship to shore in a rough sea. Flat hulled Thames lighters had never been designed as seaworthy vessels. Every one of them too, had gone a week or two before D-Day. We all knew what they were for and where they were going to finish up, on a French beach somewhere, it was just a question of when, and for everyone except a chosen few, where?

There hadn't been any significant air raids for a long time. They did visit us from time to time. Perhaps one or two aircraft manned by either exceptionally brave or on the other hand, exceptionally stupefied airmen. These raids could almost be said to have been suicide efforts. By this time, the night-time air defences had been improved so much that intruders rarely came and got away unscathed or undamaged, and frequently not at all. When these raids did occur, there was always a lot of antiaircraft gunfire. A lot of noise and often of very short duration.

430

Maybe one or two bombs were dropped, scattered here and there and no particular damage done. After one of these raids, out and looking for shrapnel, or at that time the long strips of 'window', long strips of foil 6-10mm wide, silver on one side and matt black on the other (the defence against the radar), on my usually 'dragged' walk to school (Myrdle Street), there was yet another bomb crater right in the middle of the vast empty bomb site of Pennington Street, so most of the few bombs dropped actually went unnoticed and probably unrecorded.

We rarely went to the Gunwharf shelter now. More often than not it was a case of before we had got halfway there, having been dragged out of a warm bed, we were on the yawning and weary stagger back home again because the 'all clear' had sounded. Sometimes though (I think it had something to do with a sixth sense that had warned the 'blitz people') there was a feeling of really something threatening this time.

There had been a raid or two, or at the very least it had been nothing more than just a 'warning' sounded... and nothing happened. The 'blitz-wise' seemed to know instinctively when it was just a warning and they just turned over and went back to sleep again, but this time Gran roused me with a tensioned, "Come on Johnnie. Wake up. We had better get down to the shelter quickly". The nearest to home was just across the 'yards' to No.8. A ground floor flat which had been bricked up and reinforced with heavy beams. It had not been used very much lately during the later years of 1944 but on this occasion, strangely, everyone seemed to have responded to their own 'sixth sense' and the shelter was crowded, including the now wide awake children dashing around in a night-time frolic, purely in memory of those long lost and overdue party nights.

For some unknown reason, this particular raid had dragged on a lot longer than had become the usual course of events when there might be a deafening crescendo of heavy gunfire. Now and again, there were the normal recognisable throbbing sounds of high flying German aircraft engines and the sky crisscrossed by searchlight beams and the sparkling flashes of the antiaircraft shells exploding above us. Suddenly, one of the planes had been caught in a web-like choreographed triangle of searchlight beams and it was desperately trying to weave, climb and dive out of the glaring grip of the fatal lights following its every move. Suddenly, there was an increased crescendo of the 'heavies', a concentrated barrage of gunfire, and the illuminated dot was surrounded by shell bursts. A hit and a red flash. The stricken plane turned and twisted and began a red streaked spiralling fall. Zig-zagging this way and that way on its doomed decent. We cheered and hoorayed as it fell. One of my watching companions shouted, "We's got th' bastid. Wow! Dinnant it go down… Wham", and another cheer. "Where did it go down, d'yer think"? It would be talked about for a while… then forgotten.

I could not get out of my mind the images of what must have been the flaming desperations of the doomed airmen, knowing as they must have realised the certainty of a death finally in the crumpled and exploding metal remains. For me, at the time, yes, I knew they were Germans and enemies intent on delivering destruction and death, but surely like everyone else during those desperate years, they too must have constantly felt the presence of a violent and painful death just as we also felt the constant presence of a sudden loss of relations, friends, and homes.

I cheered along with my companions and at the same time, I could not overcome the feelings of horror. The thoughts of the burning and crushing of living flesh. I can't now, and I still shudder at the thoughts. I still wonder if any of the doomed airmen got out alive.

June 13, 1944

Barely weeks after the Normandy invasion and a long hard struggle to secure the beachhead, the combined allied forces slowly began a painfully hard fought battle to deepen and widen the beachhead. It began to be seen that the balance of decision had been made in favour of success. The vaunted 'Atlantic Wall' might have caused a reversal of fortunes but for a fantasy in the mind of a lunatic. Even so, we found ourselves dragged out of bed once again. The warning sirens had sent out their awful stomach churning forecasts of terror and we found ourselves back in the Jackman House ground floor shelter again.

The Blitz sixth sense had come into operation again. We took up a hopefully temporary residence in the Jackman House shelter on the advice to stay put, obtained by that miraculous sense which was determined to keep us out of the warm comforting folds of bed and an embracing peaceful sleep. Partly, it has to be said, there were no provision of those three tiered bunk beds in the Jackman House shelter, so it was a case of either taking the risk of possible extinction, or…. I'm getting ahead of myself, so I had better explain:

There had been no 'all clear' sounded after an hour or so, during which hour there had been an occasional flurry of gunfire off somewhere in the distance. A few brief hesitant searchlights switched on and after a short hesitant search for… nothing… another hour passed and still no 'all clear'. Then suddenly, we all heard it approaching. First the distant gunfire to herald its coming, then closer and louder. An A.R.P. man always stood at the shelter entrance during raids in case of an emergency and to be there to keep things in order. The shelterers suddenly became 'fearfully' silenced by a strange staccato roaring guttural throb as it (the something) passed over… then silence. Not many seconds later, an almighty earth shaking explosion. The attendant A.R.P. warden came into the shelter full of excited and shocked excitement to tell us, "I saw it go over low down", he said. "It must have been a crashing enemy plane. There was smoke and flames at its tail. Never seen anything like it before. Gone down hereabouts, close somewhere. I'd better go back to the 'post', we might be needed somewhere", and off he went. He was very soon back to tell us some incredible news. George Warner would know of course! "They are sending over unmanned flying bombs. We have been warned about them and we have been expecting them". There was stunned silence in the shelter. Now we knew why there had been no all clear siren sounded. He went on to tell us, "These things could come over 24 hours of the day at any time, any day. My advice...", he said, "... is to get sorted out with your usual allocated wharf shelters". For us, it would have to be back to our allocated three tier bunk beds in the Gunwharf cellar shelter.

The first salvos of the rocket bombardment had begun, and we did not know it then but only when the bombardment finished. There would be no 'all clear' siren sounded. For the rest of that night, we heard them going over one after another to fall, and the explosions, some far away and some closer. The unmanned indiscriminate and, for that matter, the unknowing destroyer. The 'Doodlebugs'. Buzz bombs. The V1, had arrived.

The Nazi's had unleashed their secret revenge weapon, the V1, in a desperate attempt to reply to the invasion of Normandy and hopefully to stave off an inevitable defeat but in Hitler's revenge maddened way, he ordered them to be aimed at completely the wrong target. London maybe, if the invasion bridgehead had been the target, it might have caused a great many more problems and the possible disruption of supplying the huge logistics of the invasion effort, possibly bringing about a completely different outcome.

The big question on everyone's lips was, "What now"? We couldn't sit all day in the ground floor Jackman House shelter 24 hours of the day, every day waiting for an all clear. It was impossible to think of getting back to bed that night. Big Gran and Grandad decided that the best option was to take George Warner's advice and take up an (as it turned out to be) almost permanent nightly address at the 'Gun'. Our bedding was still there, and presumably ready. Probably a little dampish but better a dampish bed for a night's rest than to risk an unending sleep of eternity. The sooner the better if our A.R.P. comforter was to be believed. "Once thems 'as got our range", he said, "Them's Doodles could come over in their thousands". They did actually, but luckily not all together and equally fortunately, not all successfully and on target. Many were knocked out of the sky by gunfire or blown out of the sky by our battle hardened 'Battle of Britain' pilots. Sometimes tipped over by our skilful (and courageous) aerobatic fighter pilots by getting the fighters wingtip under the Buzz bomb's wingtip and flipping it over. (I actually saw this tactic happen over the Thames estuary).

Finally, and not until the launch sites had been overrun, it was recorded that four thousand (and a few hundred more perhaps) had been launched and most of them fell and exploded harmlessly but alas, far too many reached London and with terrible results. The Gunwharf shelter though was still open for business in spite of the fact that there hadn't been customers through its doors for many a month previously. When we did arrive, extremely tired and grumpy, it was looking very unused and smelling of damp bedding still on most of the bunks. There was a cold feeling of abandonment about it although the facility had been well enough maintained because one never knew. Neither we, nor the 'authorities', could be sure whether the shelter would ever be needed again. It was clean with that smell of having been closed up and the cellar air heavy with a staleness mixed up with the copious use of scrubbing and disinfectant.

There wasn't many of us in there on the first night of the first recognised 'Doodlebug' bombardment, even so, a sleep was almost out of the question. As if these rampant and troublesome disturbances were not enough to keep me and everyone else awake, some of the more wakeful shelterers set up an impromptu concert party and had resolved to sing the remains of the night away. I began to wonder whether the Gunwharf shelter precaution had been a good idea. There were, it is true, quite a few rumbles and whomps of explosions and just as often noisy eruption of heavy antiaircraft gunfire, mostly though away in the distance, close enough at times now and then, but then one never knew. Then, on the other hand, I thought, if it's right, as commonly said, that one never hears the one that has your name on it, then at any moment I could be buried under the massive wharf and concrete floors just above my head. There were also stories of people buried under debris (like the Forest Gate cellar shelter) who could be drowned in a flooded cellar or were gassed by broken gas mains. I lay on the top bunk worrying and considering how much weight these fragile steel bunks could hold up, and ridiculously wishing that I was on the bottom bunkbed instead of the top one, and conversely, it was always somebody else 'getting it'. One never knew though. Maybe the next? Then again, one would never know if it did! These were the thoughts and questions that grabbed my troubled imagination. Ideas that had been gathered together from many remembered conversations of the times, gathered together also with that other kind of fatalistic attitude that it is never, never going to happen to me but always to someone else! Perhaps, in the end it had been the only way to cope with the ever constant, ever realistic daily threat of sudden death. One never knew, did one?

Within the restrictions of faulty recollections, I am convinced that the usual 'all clear' never did sound. For that matter, I don't think there were any 'warning' sirens either. There was no point. One just had to accept that the new situation was not governed by the 'norm' of definable periods of an air raid when attacking aircraft either came over singly, or en-mass and generally departed or hopefully, not at all. These unmanned flying bombs however, broke all the normal rules of engagement of the blitz experience. These things generally came singly, one or two, or maybe several. One after another in one long continuous barrage at any time, or all times of the day. Every day, week after week. It could have disrupted everyday life entirely. Shutting shops, offices, factories. Stopping trains, busses. Closing cinemas and sports meetings etc., etc., but there again, these things, life itself, could not stop for 24hrs a day, seven days a week.

There was nothing else for it but to just carry on, ignore it and hope for the best. All of the schools remained open. I have no doubts whatsoever (particularly in London, of course) that every other member of the school age London generation of the times, like me, will also remember sitting or doing whatever activity in a normal school life, when suddenly hearing that awful gut wrenching deep throbbing indescribable Ramjet propulsion engine of the 'Doodlebugs' approaching or flying overhead, feeling again, the stomach churning pause in whatever we were doing. The look on everyone's face as every eye turned upwards to travel the unseen path of the bomb flying on to threaten everyone else. The somebody else, and not me. Most times they just flew on by accompanied by the inevitable light ack-ack gunfire. At other times, the tensions frozen by a sudden spluttering dead stop cut out of the Ramjet engines... and the 'blast count' began on everyone's lips... 1, 2, 3, 4... on to 14, 15... and then the ground shaking explosion, fifteen seconds being the usual maximum glide time interval before the end of the count. They usually travelled at about four hundred miles an hour with probably a range of about a maximum of 100 miles.

Truthfully, it didn't take most of us too long to test the generally held belief, 'if you can hear it, you're safe. If not, it won't matter whether you heard it or not'. It really got to the point in everyone's way of dealing with it, to simply somehow instinctively, on a basis of once heard, just ignore it as best you can and get on with whatever you were doing. "There goes another. Wonder who got it this time", then carry on.

Occasionally, there would be a relatively unexpected, unanticipated huge school shaking 'thump' and a rolling thunderous 'whoomph', clearly indicating the immediate direction of the 'incident' and to feel the instinctive and dreadful moment of panic from those who lived in that direction. It might have been their own street that had 'got it' this time. Their own parents. Their own brothers and sisters, friends, or neighbours. Their own houses. One never knew. It was always going to be the somebody else though, not me. Just a moment or two of shocked silence and the teachers urgent, "Okay, everybody. Calm down now". Sometimes though, these events had been rather closer to home. Too close, when the head on the next day would come into the classroom 'silently' with just a nod to the teacher and just as silently walk to an absent classmates place, emptying the desk of its contents of schoolbooks and personal possessions. No announcements. No explanations of why, just the disturbing sense of the headmaster's feelings that he had failed to overcome, knowing that the classmate would not be coming back to school.... So did we.

It might have been just a case of 'bombed out' and moved away... or not, but always the knowing 'whisperer' would usually know the reason why. There never were any official announcements of casualties whether fatal or not. In fact, nothing reported in the press at all. The idea was to give the enemy no information about where the missiles were falling. Only false reports to give the impression that they always fell miles off the intended (more than hopeful target), to encourage the aimers to change their calculations. The Doodles were hopelessly erratic anyway. It was always a random hit or a miss. It might or might not hit somewhere in London, or nowhere at all!

No information was ever given. Not official, not by anyone. Not by the teachers, just "Okay, calm down now and get on with your lessons". Carry on regardless. The moment has passed. Today? Tomorrow? Who knows? One never knew. The one comforting thing for me though, was to be extra careful that nothing, however revealing, incriminating, or otherwise, should be left in my desk to be cleared by others tomorrow… well, if not incriminating, possibly embarrassing, or something sensitive and personal that I would not like to be generally known and giggled about. I quietly removed the evidence and scattered the bits and pieces into the dustbin of emotions. Unrequited. Buried them out of sight just as we had buried the photo album of Prusom Street to moulder and to return to dust.

There has always been that strange human phenomenon which determines that if ever there is an accident anywhere, or men anywhere digging holes in the ground, one can always guarantee that if there happened to be a hundred curious souls anywhere within walking distance of a mile or two of the 'incidents', one could be sure that the same hundred would gather to 'gawp' at the accident or stand for hours watching the hole get deeper. For no apparent reason other than the one who stood beside him for at least an hour before he had arrived, could still offer no explanation for doing so upon being asked the obvious question, "What's happening? Why are they digging that hole"? One could expect a hundred different answers which exactly matched your own instincts in direct correspondence to the number of people gathered to watch the hole being dug. It is the only explanation possible why most folks cannot resist the natural instincts to go an' 'ave a look at the unexpected, unusual and the dramatic. Might I suggest, these Doodlebug incidents could have had something to do with the unnatural method of pilotless rocket and random means of delivering death and destruction. It did not seem to equate with the ancient rules of human knightly engagement, face to face with one's enemy, lance to lance, sword to sword… Spitfire pilot to an equal enemy.

Whenever I surveyed the usual heaps of rubble and broken debris that had destroyed whole streets and closely knit communities, I was always struck by the impossible to answer thoughts of whether the individual that had pressed the firing trigger had ever thought about the consequences. I don't suppose now that he would have given it very much thought, any more than the bomber crews of the 'Lancaster's' hovering over the stricken cities of Hamburg, Essen and Cologne, gave it any other thought except revenge. I think I understood this only too well. I had a personal score to settle over the premature and violent death of Derek, which but for an unexpected twist of the fatal decision on my part, I might have shared with him.

We had taken up a more or less permanent nightly residence at the Gun Wharf shelter. It was obviously the best possible safe option for the nightly visitations. As far as the same kind of risks during the days are concerned, there was nothing else for it but to just carry on. 'Business as usual'. It is impossible for me to say now that I wasn't scared and troubled by the constant threat of extinction. It could happen anywhere. At school. At home. Just out walking. On a bus. On a train. Even the otherwise safe shelter of the mighty Gun Wharf might not resist the monstrous shock of a Doodle explosion. Again, and again, we sat at school simply doing our work.

On one dramatic occasion there was no advance warning. Not a sound. No gunfire. Nothing unusual, but this time... suddenly, an unheralded ear splitting thunderous crash! The building shook violently. Strangely, even in my shock, I stupidly watched a light pendant with its typical green shade swinging. Just momentarily a brief hesitation of shocked silence. This one, close... far too close. Everyone looking at each other in a sort of dazed shocked state. Within very few minutes there were fire engines, ambulances, and the emergency services. Bells clanging, racing to the incident. No matter... back to work again. We saw brown smoke drifting across the sky. "Alright now, calm down now" Mr Pace, the form teacher insisted. "Let's get back to work". He didn't look very calm and 'alright' himself. We became very blasé about the whole business of Doodlebugs, Buzz bombs or flying bombs. They all meant the same thing.

Wapping, fortunately, by comparison with the blitz in the 40s, was relatively spared buzz bomb incidents. (There wasn't much left to destroy anyway). A couple of Doodles fell close enough to be called local incidents. One of them, it must have been earlyish in the morning, and a rude awakening for us slumbering Gun Wharf shelterers. Several of the younger compliment, including me, decided instantly that we would 'go an' 'ave look'. We had been told that it had exploded on the Shoreways of the Metropolitan Wharf at New Crane Stairs out of Wapping Wall, not much further away from the 'Gun' than about 150 yards. This we had to see. There wasn't any need to get dressed. Nobody undressed for bed at the 'Gun' apart from boots and shoes, quite apart from considerations of privacy, one never knew when one might have to make a hurried exit. Big Gran told us of an experience she and Grandad had had during the blitz (which demonstrated the point). "We used to shelter at St Johns Wharf out of the High Street during the blitz", she said. "One night the High Street was ablaze from one end to the other. There was no way that we could get out and the wharf could have gone up in flames and us with it. The High Street was blocked in both directions from end to end. There was no way out of the wharf except by a couple of tide tossed flat hulled lighters tied up to the jetty, reached by equally tide tossed ladders. A very risky thing to do. There was about a hundred of us in the shelter to transfer one at a time down the ladder into the lighter. We were landed further down river towards Shadwell". It was situations like this that decided whether we undressed or not. Nobody undressed and neither had we. It was not the done thing at the Gun.

When we arrived at the site not long after the incident, it was said to have exploded on the shoreway at the high tide. The tide was still at the full, and not yet turned, but poised stationary at the state of the flow just on the point of turning to the ebb. There was no obvious damage to the wharf or the jetty that we could see. The only evidence of the incident was that the motionless tide was covered over a considerable area with a drifting mat of white feathers and dead pigeons. The high wharves at the riverside were the natural roosting places for Wapping's flocks of pigeons. I suppose that they were as like the ledges and crags populated by their rock dove ancestors, plus the added advantage of a ready food supply of spilled grains.

The blast of the explosion had utterly cleared the whole roost along a hundred yards of the riverside. There wasn't a live bird to be seen anywhere. There must have been hundreds of them killed and beginning a swift funeral journey on a falling tide down to the sea. I don't think I was alone at that moment as we stood on the stairs landing who felt the same as I did as I saw it. The innocence of the pigeons was the same as for people. At that striking moment it didn't seem to me to make any difference, it was the pointless death of innocence of everything that really mattered.

Another of these 'must go an' 'ave a look' incidents, clipped Wapping's highway borders at Shadwell. It had fallen close to a block of L.C.C. (London County Council) flats just like Jackman House, completely blasting them out. I don't know whether there had been any injuries or fatalities. I believe there were none. Hopefully, they had all wisely taken up their nightly residence, like us, at their own local shelters. As soon as we could we were compelled by that innate curiosity to 'go an' 'ave a look'. When we got there the flats were still being cleared of the tenants belongings. It was being carried out by the civil defence authorities because no tenant was allowed back into the building for obvious safety reasons of possible severe structural damage.

Quite a crowd of the curious, including us, gathered together as well as the considerable ranks of anxious tenants. Piles of their possessions in the street. Void glassless windows with scraps of torn and tattered curtains hanging in shreds. Glass and doorframes, window frames, bricks, roof tiles, blast crumpled items and debris scattered, littering everywhere, crunching underfoot. Beds and chairs. Bundles of bedding, mats, and lino. Suddenly, a lady close by us yelled out, "'Ere, that barstid as got me'wirelis"(radio). A man was hurrying away with what the good lady claimed to be her much prized 'wireless' tucked under his arm. (There were a few shameless looters with absolutely no conscience). Some of the crowd did not wait for a judicial enquiry about the ownership of the disputed wireless. He was dealt with there and then quite deliberately and methodically. The attending police just stood by and watched. They didn't like looters either! He was pounced upon, not by a dozen screaming women, oh no! It was a relatively drawn out affair with first one or two fierce matrons who could definitely vouch for the fact that the precious 'wirelis' was their neighbour's wireless. Kicking, punching, and scratching, he could do nothing to defend himself except to submit to this torrent of rough justice. When they had exhausted themselves, another pair took over, and the next, and the next. Between them they ripped off his clothing item by item until he was a near naked bloody mess in the gutter. The police just stood and watched it all. Finally, they just picked him up and called him in their report 'a casualty of the incident'. If there was still a spark of life left in him, he would be charged with the serious offence of looting. His assailants, however, would not be charged with ABH or GBH, manslaughter, or outright murder. Nobody had seen a thing!

During our enforced bed and breakfast residence of the Gun (minus the breakfast), somehow things seemed to fall into a regular routine. Sleep was always a problem. There were always the disturbing sounds of restless shelterers coughs and the grunting stiff movements. Staggering noisy journeys to the night chemical toilets in the semi-dark of the dimmed lighting. Now and again, the thumping vibrations of yet another doodle explosion somewhere. Late comings and goings in and out of the shelter for all sorts of reasonable purposes, official and otherwise, accompanied by the annoyed shelterers grumbled comments, "Kin yer make a bit less noise mate. We's all tryin ter git a bit o' sleep ere".

Occasional regular visits by an A.R.P. warden who, according to official regulations, was duty bound to let everybody know he was carrying it out to the letter by making sure that he woke everybody up in the process. Then, there was always something special happening that guaranteed that everyone was woken up. I suppose, the fact that generally there were usually about sixty or seventy shelterees trying desperately to at least, "Git a bit o' sleep". Many of them just gave up in the end and took the risks of sleeping at home, so much so, that the numbers of shelterers gradually got fewer and fewer. On one night in particular, somebody came into the shelter. I was just about conscious, and he made straight to our tier of bunks and shook Gran quietly saying, "It's alright mum, it's me". I was suddenly wide awake. It was Dad, come home for one of his getting rarer short visits. As usual, he came home suddenly and unannounced. Nobody ever knew when he was likely to turn up, often for just a matter of hours and away again just as suddenly. Never more than a couple of weekend days, neither would he say where he was or where he was going, or what he was doing while he was away. Sometimes he was gone for weeks. He never wrote to tell us where he was. If it was necessary to contact him for any reason (it had to be urgent or not at all), we were to leave a message with his normal (nominal) employer, Frasers. Sometimes we got an answer but not from him directly, and there he was, out of the blue. We were all awake now. Gran struggled off of her bottom bunk. "It's my Johnnie. He's come home", in a loud enough manner to wake everybody.

Of course, everybody knew Johnnie Insole. They knew, or certainly generally thought they knew, that he was doing something rather special. He was always smartly dressed in his dapper Savile Row tailored suits and a collar and tie and carrying a bulky briefcase. I had a sneak into it once when I shouldn't and saw what I shouldn't have been seeing. Sheaves of notes that consisted of numbers. Not one word to identify it. Pieces of technical drawing, again, with not a word but only numbers that meant nothing to me or anyone else. Obviously, pieces cut from larger plans so that it would be unintelligible to anyone who ought not to see them. His leather case pass with the gold embossed crown and portcullis. W/D stamped on the shiny leather case - Ministry of Supply.

Very rarely, and so rarely that I absorbed and remembered everything he said. Sometimes he would speak about (the unspeakable). I asked him once, "Where have you been Dad"? and got an answer, "I've been working in Cambridge, and guess what"? He said. "I met up with Cousin Dougie Insole. He was captaining the Cambridge University cricket team playing on Parker's Piece, an inter-university match I think. I took a break from work to watch the game. We had a little chat to catch up with the news". This was a good opportunity to ask another question. "What were you doing in Cambridge then"? I got an answer, "Oh", he said, probably taken off guard for a brief moment. "Oh… er… erecting pectin tanks for Chivers jam factory". That was it. No more to be said on the subject. On another brief moment he volunteered the information. "We dug out tunnels under a mountain and set up a factory underground". Nothing about what for or why. "Just for reservoirs and drainage", as an afterthought.

Dad's brother, Uncle Bob, like dad was of military age and had been called up for conscripted service in the army. Dad though, was a highly qualified chemical engineer and was in a reserved occupation. He had to serve in his profession, he had no choice in the matter. He did his bit, nevertheless. At another time, he volunteered a snippet of information that he had been working in Nottingham for 'John Players', "Sorting out the cigarette machines for them", and he brought back with him several cans of fifty very special cigarettes. 'Perfectos Finos (or something like it). At a time when one had to get lucky enough to get hold of a decent packet of cigarettes, he explained,

"You can't buy these cigarettes. They're made specially for government offices, the palace, embassies and foreign 'big-wigs'". Good enough reason I suppose for a distraction from the war effort. The cigarettes _were_ good. I pinched a couple just to try them, naturally!

And there he was, turning up unexpectedly at the Gun Wharf shelter at something like two/three hours after midnight... and everyone was awake, there was no getting back to sleep now. He explained that he had had to walk most of the way from Paddington because there had been problems of bomb damage. I expect he managed to find a little refreshment on his way home. Somebody offered to make tea to help the matter along. The shelter was reasonably provided with the means of a small corner set aside and a sort of primitive catering area set up. To complement the arrangements, some handy individual had knocked up a fairly decent table and a couple of rough timbered benches to sit at, frequently used for other recreations other than eating. Cards usually, or just sitting around chatting. Tea made, Dad, Gran, and as many who could be accommodated at the table sat around it. The conversation turned on the present state of things. People were getting fed up with the present situation. Somebody asked Dad (as if he could have known the answer), "When is this all going to end Johnnie"? And Dad didn't answer immediately but after a pause of about half a minute or so, he just laid a forearm on the table and sticking his thumb upright, thought for a moment and then calmly said, "I don't know. All I can say at this moment is..." (a moment or two of hesitation) and then, "Never mind these flying bombs. We expect that there may be other types of rockets coming over soon... but 'he' (meaning the collective enemy) doesn't know what is going to hit him. We have been working on an explosive that is so powerful that a piece the size of my thumbnail would blow Wapping to pieces... and Berlin". Suddenly, the shelterers who were sat around the table leapt into a torrent of questions. "What"? "When"? "How"? Dad was silent. "Come on Johnnie, you can tell us". Johnnie Insole of course would know the answers.

Dad must have realised that he had said too much of the forbidden subject and stood up quickly and said, "I don't know. I really don't know. I'm sorry, but I'm done in and I am going home to bed". He left the shelter without saying another word. Gran decided to go with him. Grandad and I stayed to listen to a babble of the repeated conversation going the rounds of the shelter and with that, everybody was asking the same questions, including me. By the time we got back to No. 8 in the morning, Dad had already left and gone to 'wherever' he was mysteriously going to, not to be heard from or seen, until the next time he came home weeks later. Shortly afterwards, the shelterers had the answer to at least one of Dad's predictions about the "Other types of rockets coming over".

The V2 rocket bombardment began. They simply arrived unannounced out of a clear sky unseen and unheard. Just a sudden terrific explosion and sudden devastation and a huge crater. The shelterers at 'Gun' could not quite go along with the governments explanations that these events were caused by broken gas mains… well, gas explosions? The object of explaining it this way must have been to prevent wholesale public panic. They had no need for such caution, it was just something else that we had to get used to. For me personally, there were still a good many things to be got used to, but perhaps that might be another story. In the meantime (and probably time to draw this one to a close) I began it with the simple object of recording events as much for my own satisfaction and to bring together the story of my early experiences of Wapping and what it was all about, and what a story it has turned out to be. I had always 'felt' in some sort of strange way that this part of my life (on reflection) began to reveal how much those experiences had played their part in creating the person I am. (Some might think for the worse rather than for the better)! The truth is that I was never parted

447

from it and I never left it. It was always there. Perhaps in the end it is nothing more remarkable than the fact it is in the blood, just as instinct and genetics are, maybe even hormones?

Chapter 38

Were there really two Wappings? - R.C's v Anglo's – 'Blues and the Whites' 1999

Several years ago now, on one of my visits, I stood talking to a resident Wapping octogenarian friend. We were recounting the 'once upon a time's'. The used to be's... how things were. A wide range of conversation. He suddenly surprised me. "Wappin 'yer know is really two Wappin's". From where we stood on the corner of Prusom Street in the 'Lane' pointing to Green Bank on the other side of the 'Lane' towards the Tower and the west, he said, "People 'ere abouts used to say that's darn Wappin 'tween the bridges". He went on to explain himself. "I think it was two wards. Funny ain't it. This 'ere way...", pointing down Prusom Street and towards the East, "... is St Georges", and then pointing to Greenbank towards the west, "That's another ward I think. I s'pose it was all Wapping though ain't it"? I thought that what he was wanting to say was that it didn't really matter what polling station one voted at, and he was trying to explain it. To be honest, I understood what he meant but I let him speak on. "Yer know's abart the Catholics an' the protestants I suppose"? "Yes", I said. "That was a lot of the problems wasn't it"? After a long pause, he replied, "Well, don't think that it was really. Funny thing that is... Catholic boys married Protestant girls... an' the other way round o'course". Let's face it", he said, "Makes no diff'rence in bed, do it. Same as mine an' the same as your'n, ain't it"? He laughed at his own joke adding, "Least ways I dinnant find any difference". The implication was clear enough. Neither did he say whether he was Catholic or Protestant.

There was nothing to choose between them anyway. Wise old man. He continued, "I was talkin' abart the two Wappin's, weren't I"? He had lost the thread of his conversation and carried on about something different. "When these new buildings was put up in the thirties, or was it the twenties? Me and th' misses an' the kids, they was young then, 'moved into one of the flats. The old house we were in got pulled down. You know what? An old girl what lived down Prusom sez to me, "It's all rite for you's darn' Wapping way, you's got 'lectric lights now, ain't cher"? Well, some of them only 'ad gas yer see. Some only had oil lamps. They had th' gas but pennies for the meter wasn't so easy to come by. Most times oil was cheaper but then going t'bed early in the dark can turn out to be a lot dearer in the end, ain't it? Anyway, some of us were better orf than some of the others. The docks yer see. Not always a lot of work, even then. If yer can get it". But he hadn't finished yet. "I was telling yer... two Wappin's weren't it? Wasn't nuffing too bad y'see. It weren't like it were once. Real bad things then. Lots of fight an' troubles when I were a young boy... not yesterday I can tell yer. I remember some of it meself... me dad 'specially. It was hard for 'im I 'expects. We always had bread on the table though. Yer Gran's fish and chips was always a treat, not dear either. It were the Catholics an' the Protestants. I s'pose even in th' docks an all. Usually if there was a job goin', the first question you'd be asked is, are you Catholic or Protestant? Daft weren't it. The Catholics was the Blues, and the others was th' Whites. Labourers, on the barrers an th' like. That's what. Usually the R.C's got the jobs. It dinant get any better any time, really. Funny that, ain't it? Takes a bit o' workin' out, don't it? In the end though, they helped each other out. Funny that, ain't it"? Our own Uncle, greengrocer Jack Insole was a practicing R. Catholic but none of us took any notice of that... it is funny, isn't it?

He had a lot more to say to me. He continued. "The Blues 'adn't got it all though. The St Peters boys, and the gals, who went to St Peters School, them city gents what had given a lot of money for it, used to take thems that had a bit o' brain an' gave 'em a good education. Them made it good. Still have the reunions yer know. They ain't forgot neither and it ain't one or two neither. I can tell yer a few what 'ad surprise yer". "Whatever", he said. "It was good darn 'ere, weren't it? Didn't want no truck with nosey people what wanted to stick their oar in. What did they know about it"? To make the point, there was something else he thought that would explain the whole question. He began, "I didn't work much in the dock, only when I was a kid for a while. Had enough of that an' all. Hows-ever…", he said. "I got a job in the Red Lion Brewery. They said it were the oldest working brewery in the country where Matilda House is now. I got work in th' warehouse. It used to be on the Wharf on the Shoreways at Hermitage where they stored the barley, the malt, an' hops for the beer, you see. It was brought up the river on the Thames barges. The blokes what used to work there were always pissed. Big bellies an' all. A quart a day was alright. We were allowed that, but it was more like a quart an hour for some of 'em. I didn't drink much but I just watched for the guv'ners ter give 'em the wink and all that. Well, about that old warehouse. It was all wooden beams and knocked about. Been there a few hundred years I think. Well, plenty of dusty old cobwebs, I can tell yer. It had been built into the new wharves in the 1800s and nobody knew it was there. Now, that there Dickens Inn, what is in St Kat's now, when they pulled down the wharves they found the old ware'us I had worked in. I could have told them it was there, cobwebs an' all. Do you know what they did? They moved it all in one go, inch by inch, into St Kath's, tarted it up a bit as a pub and called it Dickens Inn. Dickens Inn, my arse! What had it got to do with Dickens? Nothink! Still, I s'pose that blokes is still getting pissed in it. Got rid of the effin cobwebs and all, ain't it". He finished, "I ain't sorry the docks is gone neither. No effin good for nobody". He went on his way and I on mine. Regretfully, I did not get his name, now he is just another of those ghosts of Wapping's past.

Epilogue: 1

Musings Sat on a Low Brick Wall – R.I.P and an Obituary – 1940s

I liked nothing better than to go out in Wapping's blacked out and darkened streets. It always seemed to me at those times, it was those moments when an openness and the silence of the countryside had crept back in the dark to reclaim for itself a few hours of supremacy.

Just occasionally, voices, sometimes close by, sometimes far off. Maybe laughter. The late night children at their nocturnal games which I might have otherwise joined. Sometimes angry voices but more frequently a brief chorus of merriment as a door into an otherwise indiscernible blacked out pub was opened and quickly closed again, allowing a cloud of light and sound to drift into the dark street, finally to drift away as a low echo reflected back again as if trying to re-join the pub's happy warmth and enjoyments.

There was no heavy and noisy traffic, just that unaccustomed silence pierced now and again by a rolling echo of a ship's siren departing from its berth on a night tide going down stream. The answering 'pipe' of an incoming vessel.

The darkness and an unaccustomed clear dark blue sky. Not a light anywhere to reveal that the broad cities of London, Southwark, and Westminster were together spread out beneath its brilliant star studded vault.

Around Jackman House, fronting a narrow strip of hopeful grass a few feet wide, there was a low brick wall. Pre-war it had been mounted by an iron fence. It had been requisitioned and melted down to help the war effort, ultimately to be showered back onto us as anti-aircraft shell shrapnel I suspected. I used to sit on it in the dark to think my own thoughts and dream my own dreams. What did all this mean for me? What place in the scheme of things did I fit in? Spending time to evaluate and to put into some kind of manageable perspective all that had passed me by. Well, I didn't know when? From the beginning I suppose, but then I was conscious that there was something inexplicable. Strange, yet somehow beautiful that needed expression going on.

This strange place... no one could ever claim that its usual work-a-day aspects were ever likely to be a source to inspire thoughts of an artistic nature, although perhaps I _had_ seen something remarkable as Lily and I stood a while on 'Tunnel Pier' with Grandad. Those other clear and well defined memories too, Hermitage, alive and vital, thronged with characters and character. The closeness and the belonging. The sadness, the humours... and the partings.

As I sat all alone and yet never really feeling alone, surrounded as I was always aware of those constant companions, my rough, tough, ruddy faced brawny 'Wharf Man'... I thought of him standing before me in the darkness of my thoughts. His hands on his hips and looking down at me again. "Hoi... wotcher doin' 'ere den"? Tell me Mr Wharf Man, I didn't really know. What was I doing there? Like so many others, he was no longer there to tell me but as I sat on my low wall, I distinctly heard him laugh his laugh.

Somehow, in some mysterious ways, I had always felt and known of a driving force of compulsion. When Dad came to Cornwall to bring Lily home, even before he had asked the question, "Do you want to come home with Lily to Wapping, or do you want to stay here, go back to Forest Gate"? I had already made up my mind. It had to be, go back home to Wapping. As I sat on my particular 'low wall', I knew it was where I should be. In the darkness, sat on my 'low wall', summoning back again the myriad scenes and the million memories that had drawn me back. In the silence and the deep shadows of the streets nestling under the contrasting brightness of the star lit skies, lone people stumbled out of the gloom and passed me by unaware that I watched their faltering ways guided by the small spots of light shed by their shaded torches and wondered, do they feel like I do about this strange virtual manmade island home? Do they have memories like mine? I knew that I had 'seen' the 'something' on Wapping pier with Grandad and Lily. I wanted to 'see' it again and again. It was all around me and always had been!

No one who ever visited Wapping in those days would expect such a strange and somewhat claustrophobic and often dreary place, to be the source of mystery and inspiration. An overgrown and unkempt dilapidated graveyard, locked and padlocked, hiding a mysterious past. Shielding the shadowy ghosts that I saw wandering in the tangled undergrowth. As a child I saw them. I knew that they were watching me as I passed by, daring me to look and be terrified, defying them in my determination not to look. As I sat on the 'low wall' I saw them and had no fear of them, or the hobgoblins and fairies tapping at the St John's pre-school nursery window, or the secret panel on the wooden carved stairway. The entrance to tunnels that led all the way to the Tower... Traitors Gate, Dead Man's Hole, and the Tower Beach. St Katherine's Dock bell in the mornings and crowds waiting at the dock gates hoping to be 'took on' for the days' work. The P.L.A. remedial nursery... Pier Head, and Wapping Old Stairs... The Shoreways and rubbish, drowned cats and dogs and the stinking dead sheep. Ships and lighters... tugs and Thames barges... and on... and on. Tumbling through my mind and demanding to be noticed and recalled.

Epilogue: 2

The Present

My family, who I expect I managed to bore to distraction a time or two, will tell you that my Wapping story had simmered within me for as long as they were old enough to listen to my tales. Ninety years on, my feelings and that which had generated them has not changed and never will. The truth is, that emotionally I have always been a Wapping boy, whatever my circumstances have been or might be, in whatever future that is left to me.

I began this chronical with the question; 'Whereabouts in London do you come from'? Perhaps a shorter explanation could have just as easily explained the 'Hoi... wot cher doin 'ere, and why"? Without the necessity to undertake the laborious two fingered exercise it became; I could have just mentioned the simple fact that I am proud to call myself a Wapping boy and leave it at that. It would not have been enough, because I also carry a burden of responsibility to set on record a story which is less about myself and much more a story about a real community, of a real place, a real society that existed in time and space. Had existed and is no more.

Real people that are no more, sadly, whose like will never be seen again. Just as finally as I had searched the vast open space of Prusom Street, looking for the evidence of homes and habitations that had once stood there, even then, at fourteen years old, I felt myself moved by an awareness of the living past. I held the sodden stained photo album in my hands and the images revealed page by page were only the ghosts of the people that had lived there. I have a duty to erect a monument to their memory. Later we reburied them with no witnesses... reverently... and left them to return to the ashes of the homes they had once occupied.

The London dock complex and Wapping basin. The Hermitage, the smallest, the pier head entrance to the dock have been filled in for the benefit of future archaeologists to dig out again and wonder about. St Katherine's dock however, being in a tucked up closeness with the Tower, has escaped that particular fate but only supposedly for the sake of a euphemism described as 'preservation'. The most that anyone who actually knew the old dock would be able to say about that is that it is only a 'preserved' hole in the ground with some genuine Thames water in it. If, 'preservation' had been the real intention, it has been nothing short of a devious vandalism upgraded by the high sounding name of St Katherine's Yacht Marina... (Haven)? Well, that's honest I suppose. Its proximity to the Tower and the City did lend itself to a kind of 'Disneyland' tourist attraction with added benefit of somewhere for the privileged to moor their expensive yachts. In fairness though, it is always difficult to balance necessity against 'preservation'. If for no other reason but its historical values, it should have been preserved as it stood. Future generations will not know anything about its real past from what it reveals now.

Never mind the eco-blitz that has been fought over the dockland area as a whole, those that had lived close by St Katherine's, in particular those who had worked the dock (including my own brother in law, Jack), couldn't recognise it. Obliteration not 'preservation', surely? In its heyday it was certainly not glamorous. Definitely not spick and span, sparkling with fresh paint of pastel shades, all a-glitter with yacht hulls of brilliant white. Quite the opposite.

Closely enclosed by massive wharves and high gated walls, dirty and dusty in a work-a-day fashion, the dock basin itself was never seen from the 'outside'. Now and then, one caught a fragmentary glimpse of the untidy quays through an open gate revealing a dock basin filled with grubby rust covered vessels, straddled over by the tall grey steel latticed cranes, smoke grimed tugs and battered steel hulled lighters. Tar and rope bales, boxes, and barrels. The smells of tea, coffee and wines and spirits and leather. An acrid smell of smoke and the hot ships sides. Ivory too. St Katherine's was the world centre for the import and export of ivory. Shouting men, whirling cranes, and screaming rope. None of these things of course could be preserved, neither could the dock in its functional state.

Let no one fool you though, that it has been preserved. All that remains now is a tinsel confection. A toy town harbour and part-time sailors playing at ships. The truth is that there was never any intention to 'preserve' the dock, only to maintain a 'reserve' of privilege, counted in the end… echoing a fundamental truth. An economic bulldozer is finally more powerful and irresistible than any other machine that mankind may devise.

Visitors

Visitors 'darn Wapping' way today may safely visit now but will not see the same Wapping that Lily and I saw or feel what we felt of its past hundred or more years life of the docks, or know of those who had lived in Hermitage before us into the thirties and beyond into an uncertain future.

Hermitage as we knew it has gone completely. Where there used to be those close packed houses just like No.74 Hermitage Wall, and mostly just as dilapidated, held together as a community with a mixture of small dock related businesses and shops strung along the narrow cobbled streets and further enclosed by the tall wharves at the riverside and the ever present dock wall on the other, imprisoning everything and everyone in their tight embrace. Many of the Blitz broken and burnt out wharves have been demolished, those remaining have been converted into smart apartments and luxury penthouses. The girdered walkways no longer leap across the street. The lock entrances of the Pier Head, Hermitage and Wapping Basins have been filled in. The swing bridges are gone, and the basins built upon. Many sections of the ever dominant Dock Wall have been brought low. Wapping is no longer regarded as a manmade inland island (which in any case was always an isolationist idea that suited the islanders' interests to believe, rather than as fact). The old Hermitage people have gone too. Rubbish no longer lies on the Shoreways and the children who played on them have gone, swept away on an irresistible tide of their own unknowable futures.

The river now flows by as long vistas of clean waters. The wealthy are returning, perhaps caught by a still lingering aspect of the place drawn by a hint of a romantic past. The old Hermitage residents would have liked it better if the wharves and the new houses had been converted and built for themselves!

The now 'infamous' and defunct 'News of the World' printing press, built on the Western Dock, precisely on the site of the vanished quays at which in the 'old days' vessels discharged cargos of newsprint destined for the London newsprint presses. Some of those vessels had been the tall clipper like ships I had seen coming through the Pier Head entrance in the early thirties.

The new tenants may feel some nostalgia for the past. They might think there is a romance about the history of the place. If the dirt and the sweat of hard labour for the rewards of mere pitiless pence, and the uncertainties of work experienced by the Wapping dock workers on a daily basis can be called romantic, then Hermitage and the whole of Wapping was the most romantic place on earth. On the other hand, perhaps it is only because Wapping has now become the up and coming new Chelsea. Whatever the reasons for their new tenancies,

I have to tell them that their new homes and the streets surrounding them are filled with the ghosts of a vibrant and stable community whose richness of character they have no hope of ever achieving. No financial consideration or social status will ever buy them that. They may, however, feel some humility because of this. I hope so.

In the end, all that can be reasonably hoped for is that when they look upon the river scenes from stairways that still exist, or from windows that were once busy loopholes, perhaps the very same loophole at which I watched from my hot stacked jute sacked perch, the fat hollow looking ship at the jetty being unloaded, there might be a fleeting thought for my 'rough, tough wharf man', and for the countless un-nameable men who passed that way before him to sweat at an endless labour, day in and week out, year in and year out. Think of them and be humbled. Maybe at the same time, listen to the ghostly echoes of the teeming river's dockland sounds, glimpsing misty shadows of the long ago departed ships that are never to return to their berths on the empty waters. You will never be able to get the 'feel' of these things in such a fleeting moment of an imagination in one such tiny fragment as if seen through a momentary chink in time and place itself. These present times, and the changes that have come with them, had to come.

Some were glad to see it go, others were sad. No one would want to see again a return to the bad and the "Its good darn 'ere ain't it"? days, or the criminal system of casual labour with its daily insult at the dock gates to decide who would get a day's work on offer and 'cross the chain', or who did not. No one but their landlords would want to see standing again those pestilent houses and those derelict tenement blocks like Royal Jubilee Buildings (and there were others like it) rise from out of the dust, the ashes, and the rubble of the past.

Even so, I know with absolute confidence and conviction that Wappingites themselves, wherever they have been scattered, indeed the very few who still remain in the old place surrounded by their memories, they will know of it and yearn for a return of, "It's good darn 'ere ain't it". When we ourselves have gone, who will be left to remember?

Rest in peace!

Epilogue: 3

Lily's Singing

Lily had always had a good singing voice. At Verney Gardens in Dagenham we did have a piano and Mum could knock a tune or two out of it 'by ear'. Lily and I had been coerced into learning our party songs. Well, actually I had been coerced into learning a terrible version of tonelessness. I wasn't at all impressed with the idea of singing, even I was aware that I sounded about as tuneful as an average frog at mating time, but I had to do it.

Mum. Whatever else one could have said about things in general, and it wasn't about her musical talents, but it could have been everything about her 'middling-class' aspirations, 'keeping up with the Jones's' and all that. In the current vernacular of the times, it was said to be 'all peeyaners', net curtains, aspidistras (with the choice additive) and no knickers, but in the more genteel modern parlance 'a little bit of bling'… 'getting it over' ones neighbours, is definitely not a new age of enlightenment in normal social behaviour.

Lily did not need encouragement. She just sang naturally.

Dad. His smart new up to the minute modern press button radio, it was his pride and joy. It also offered Lily the opportunity to sing along with the entertainment stars of the times. Lily could match any of them in an almost perfect mimicry of tone and voice, from soprano to contralto.

461

Lily had started work in the 1940s at the 'Minories' (Middlesex) Street (otherwise known as Petticoat Lane). 'Real' tailoring as opposed to machining, for tuppence a dozen piecework. Recently I watched a TV program about wartime work in the factories and there was a scene of factory girls singing along with the rhythm of the machines. It immediately reminded me of something Lily had told me about her own wartime experiences. It connected with me and in my own mind's image I saw her singing instead and heard her too! She had told me, "We used to sing along with our workmates", she said. "Although I often found myself singing solo... and I got told off because everybody stopped work to listen to me, but they said that I could do a 'turn' at an inhouse organised lunchtime concert instead". Dad took up the story because he had been invited to the concert. He said, "Lily had the top spot. They announced her... "And now we have our very own Lily Insole", and she came out on stage singing, everybody in the audience cheering and singing along with her. It did not take long before she was spotted by a visiting guest, a local Jewish BBC comedian 'Issy-Bonn' and she was duly auditioned by the BBC". I believe it was for a regular appearance on the BBC sponsored daily 'Workers Playtime' lunchtime concerts, which were designed as morale booster concerts to let the world and especially the enemy, know that we could still sing 'and let the world go by'. She claimed that she had 'muffed' the audition and didn't get the spot. She didn't 'muff' it at all. The truth was more likely that the spot had already been given to somebody else (known) who had to go through the normal process of selections. Unfortunately, Lily had been the sacrificial lamb but in the process, what the BBC found was that Lily had very good prospects for her voice capabilities, so what they offered her was to take up a program of voice training instead and to read music 'by ear' was never going to be good enough, but this would have meant that it was 'full time' and residential and she would have had to live away from home. The big problem with this arrangement was that Lily was not yet 16 and still regarded as a juvenile. In those enlightened times one was still a juvenile until one was 21. Moreover, there was no one with legal authority for her. Mum had unofficially disappeared over the horizon and Dad was more often than not enlisted, seconded, or otherwise engaged on War Department – Ministry of Supply projects all over the UK. As far as I know, Lily didn't even have anything like a permanent address except perhaps No.8 Jackman House. To all intents and purposes, she was virtually homeless. She and Dad had stayed on at 26 Verney Gardens, for far too long, rubbing along somehow until Dad had to move back home to Wapping, but No.8 Jackman House only had two bedrooms and nowhere for Lily except a bed space here, there, and anywhere, with willing (and not so willing) cousins, friends, or distant relatives.

I never realised what this must have meant for her at the time. I feel very guilty now that I ever complained about my own personal misfortunes and uncertainties, but then we were both victims of a circumstance not of our own making. As she once remarked to me in later years, "It is a wonder that we didn't go wrong, John". My reply came straight off the top of my head. "Well, didn't we? I suppose things could have been better". Lily rarely spoke about her past but in the end, for me, Lily's 'singing still', and I cherish the memory. There was one special moment. It was usually Saturday mornings and Lily always came to No. 8 then, and with Dad's super up-to-the-minute-press-button radio playing as usual and Lily singing along with it, I went out onto the balcony and saw the neighbours running along the other balconies overlooking the back yards and knocking on doors and calling out, "Lily's singing. Lily's singing". She came out onto the balcony, still singing, and suddenly there was an impromptu concert. Her audience would not let her go. Lily was singing.

The outcome of the audition was that Lily could not take up the offer. There were the natural concerns within the family with the idea of her being away somewhere (out there) alone. On the other hand, the BBC would not, or even could not, take the responsibility for her. The result was that Lily insisted to the last that she had 'muffed' the audition. I think that she had been really keen to 'give it a go'. No one can possibly know now, how, or what, she had felt about yet another disappointment in her life. All I do know is that she retreated deeper into herself and never sang another note. It must have run very deep indeed.

Well Lil', wherever you are, even if it is only in my memory (maybe others might remember too), it will always be "Lily's singing". As I said, "Things might have been better".

Epilogue: 4

For Dad too... Things Might Have Been better.

John Williams Insole. Born 1904. Wapping.... Wapping 1939.

Dad would have been of military age like his younger brother, Bob (My fighting 'kick 'em in the balls' instructor). He had to answer to the general 'call up' and spent 4-5 war years on the West African Gold Coast protecting... well, something!

On the other hand, Dad was a qualified chemical engineer. He never said so, but he was, and he was enlisted in a reserved occupational status and thereafter served the national interest on the industrial front. Something that he never ever spoke about except for one or two 'off the cuff' events that we now know were devious answers that just managed to say something close to the truth and at the same time hid the truth behind it. He was always away somewhere. We never knew where, or what for. Sometimes he would arrive home unexpectedly for a few hours, "Just passing through on the way to somewhere else", and then he was gone again. Sometimes away for weeks on end. At other times, maybe for a weekend, "A few leave days". If Big Gran needed to speak to him (it had to be urgent), the arrangement was through a contact number through his nominal employer... that is 'Frasers', who would relay a message to 'someone' 'somewhere unknown'. Sometimes, there was no reply for weeks and then it was never Dad himself. Never a direct call from him. Maybe he would just turn up himself instead.

Even then, I noticed that he never carried any luggage, only a battered sort of briefcase.

During my imprisonment at Stalag No.1, Tabbs Hotel, Redruth, when he just turned up in the evening, I asked him then, "Did you come on the train from Paddington"? He surprised me by telling me, "No, I came through the Severn Tunnel", and then went on to tell me about it, 'The Tunnel'. That is when I asked him, "Why"? He merely said, "Oh, I was working near Cardiff". That's all. Nothing else. We had to wait many many years after for the answer to my question. Well... that is only a speculation answer, and it wasn't near Cardiff at all, or probably not.

1942/43

Back home in Jackman House, I sneaked a peep into his briefcase. There were papers in it that on a swift glance showed that there was not a word anywhere to identify anything but lists of numbers and symbols. Other pieces of tech' drawings, again with no words only numbers and drawings just like the London underground railway map. I say pieces, because they were obviously from larger drawings that had been cut into pieces and none of them in his briefcase matched together. His slide rules and a couple of micrometers and his pass. A smooth thick brown shiny leather card case with gold embossed Crown and Portcullis marked W.D. Ministry of Supply, and his photo. In my hands I held his identity authority. I read quickly 'give named bearer without hinder'. I dare not read any more and quickly put everything back. Knowing I had done something terribly wrong, I had visions of firing squads and 'shot at dawn'. Later, I saw for myself what the pass could do.

We were travelling together from Waterloo to Guildford. I went with him to the booking office. I saw him push his shiny card case over to the clerk and just said, "Two. Guildford". The clerk just looked at the card and the photo, reached for a form and said, "Sign here please Mr Insole", and she issued the tickets. In the train I asked him, "Did you have to pay the fare"? "Oh, yes", he said. "The firm pay it for me", and then he went on to explain. "The 'firm' I am working for have to pay Frasers £75.00 a week compensation for me being seconded to the other firm", or 'firms'. (I think now that the other 'firm' might well have been the government. Speculation of course)!

On another occasion, I dared to ask him, "Where have you been Dad"? "Oh", he said. "Cambridge" and went on to explain. "And guess what? I met up with Cousin Dougie Insole. He was captaining the university team and they were playing on 'Parker's' an inter-university match. I had an afternoon to spare. We met up and had a good chat about this and that". That's all he said. I dared ask another question. "What were you doing in Cambridge"? "Oh, erecting 'pectin' tanks for Chivers Jams". We discovered post war, many years later, that 'Pectin' was the cover name for the chemical weapons program.

At another time, he created yet another mystery. Cigarettes. He came home briefly with several cans, packs of 50 cigarettes. 'John Players – Perfectos Finos'. He said, "I've been working at Players in Nottingham. These are top quality, can't buy them anywhere. They are made for the palace and government embassies and the like". During the war years, of all things, cigarettes weren't easy to get. Short supply of course, especially the best brands. Usually, "One packet only, sir", unless of course one knew someone who knew somebody else who might get some next week if you had the right sort of money. That is several cans of 50 very special 'fags'. "Sorting out their machines". In the middle of the war? No way! For 'Spitfires' maybe. The palace and Westminster? Well, no doubt!

As I said, those wartime mysteries had troubled me somewhat. My mind, being like young minds the world over, generally deals in fantasy. I suppose though, on reflection, there must have been around me at the time many others who wondered about Dad's 'comings and goings'. Dapper suited in his Saville Row suits and briefcase. Obviously, someone important. He would know the answers. Speaking to him and recalling the Gun Wharf incident and the shelterers question, "When is all this going to end Johnnie"? And his reply, it had to wait a few years until it became clear what he had meant. Personally, I think that he had said too much 'in his cups' than he had intended. The question had to be what *did* he know? That question also had to wait until... sometime around 2002.

Up until then, Dad had managed first to survive, and secondly to remain silent about what he was up to during the war years (and after the war years apparently). On one of our infrequent visits to him at home, we arrived at a time when he was 'resting in bed' later than usual. "Go up and talk to him John. He'll like that". I did. It struck me that at last it was going to be an opportunity for me to be able to talk to him alone about... well, about the things that had never been spoken of.

Our conversation centred around the usual salutations of general matters of health and such like, and with a little prompting, eventually he spoke of 'the past' and told me that he felt guilty about us all, saying, "Perhaps I could have done more". "Such as what"? I asked. "Well, perhaps I could have kept things, and us, together. Maybe a flat", "Oh", I replied. "That would have been nice wouldn't it. A nice thought Dad, but who was going to look after us? Lily was eight and I was five. Not only that but you were never at home, working away on goodness knows what mysterious doings". He considered for a moment and finally just nodded. "Yes, I think you are right. Never mind, there's nothing we can do about it now. I think it was tough on all of us". I answered him, "Yes it was, but one way or another we came through somehow, but there is no need for you to feel guilty. There was nothing you could do". There was a long pause while I considered my next move. "Oh, yes", I said. "That brings me to ask, what were you up to during the war"? He drew a blanket up over his face and said, "I'm scared. John, I don't want to talk about it. Anyway, it's nothing to be proud of. I don't want to talk about it". "OK", I said. "Is it because you signed the 'Official Secrets Act'? Because if it is, then all I can say is, so did I because of my elected work in local government, so anything you can tell me I can't repeat can I? In any case Dad, I don't suppose there is anything you can tell me now that isn't already out there". "That's as maybe", he said. "Just the same, it isn't all out there and I can't talk about it". It might have been left there at an end, but I was sure that he would talk, so I reminded him of what I already knew. I told him, "In (my son) Peter's research, he had come across the meaning of 'Pectin'. It's the cover name for the chemical weapons program isn't it"? "Oh", he said. "Yes". And also, "That story about digging under a mountain for reservoirs and drains lark, you told me about. That was at Rhydymwyn, North Wales, wasn't it? To do with Tube Alloys, not drains and reservoirs. The cover name for atomic weapons research and development. You were working on that too, weren't you"? He just nodded. There was a long pause. I wondered whether the conversation had come to an end there but suddenly, he sat up and said quite bluntly, "Yes, but don't let anyone ever tell you that the Americans developed and built the 'Bomb'. They didn't. It was ALL British technology". He went on further to tell me, "In fact, we had enriched enough uranium for the first three (bombs). One for the test, one destined for Hiroshima, and one for Nagasaki. We had even worked out how to trigger the things. They were ready to be built by the end of 1943 (note the date), but we had nowhere to test it, or the money, or the manpower to carry on. We knew the Germans were working on it. Do you remember that raid we did on the heavy water plant in Norway? It was totally unnecessary, but we wanted them to believe they were on the right track, and we wanted to keep them on it. We knew they would be fiddling for years down the heavy water route, by us knocking out the plant we hoped they would think that we thought it was important enough to disrupt it. Well, we could not go any further, so we sent everything to the States. The lot. They had nothing! We even chose the targets. They wanted to go for Tokyo. 20 million people, and we said no. They had carried out the first test and it had worked. When they dropped the Hiroshima one, I thought, oh my God, what have we done. Terrible, terrible bloody things. I am ashamed that I had any part in it". After a long pause there were other questions I wanted answers to. I broke the silence. "Well, come on Dad, we might as well clear up one or two other questions while we are about it. Those cigarettes, 'Perfectos Finos' you brought home from Nottingham and John Player's. That was all about 'cellulose acetate, wasn't it? Used in cigarette filters. It is also a neutron marker. We found out on the net. Players had tons of the stuff and also the machines for making just the right sort of filter to filter out the enriched uranium. Weapons grade uranium. Something perhaps that you were responsible for"? He just nodded.

Interestingly, later we visited the site at Rhydymwyn, and our willing guide said, "Everybody working here thought that what went on in Building 45 was 'making filters for the use of' that's all". (Dad's John Player's filters)? Also, interestingly, it struck me on our visit that things about security were quite loose at Rhydymwyn, in a sense that they had shown the factory workers a film about the chemical weapons activity at Rhydymwyn. Not something that ought to have been so widely and openly talked about, surely? Which Dad also mentioned... "We had 15/20,000 tons of mustard gas and we warned the Germans that if ever they used the stuff on us or caused a whiff of mustard to be released by enemy action, then we would drench Berlin and Germany in retaliation. A perfect umbrella under which to carry out 'Tube Alloys' unhindered. Rhydymwyn was never bombed, not because they didn't know what went on there... chemical weapons, that's all".

Dad's visit to the Gun Wharf shelter in the early hours of the morning. "Really", I reminded him, "I don't think that you should have said as much as you did". "I know", he said. "I worried about it for a long time. I had been threatened you know, with serious 'consequences' if I talked 'out of place' about anything we were doing, where we were doing it, or what for. I slipped up badly didn't I? Still, I got away with it, luckily".

Well Dad, whether I should have said all this now I don't know, but it is only for the best intentions. Perhaps just to clear up a few misunderstanding about the important British role in the whole framework of nuclear physics and its consequences. The bomb. After all, it was Rutherford who had succeeded in 'splitting' the atom at Manchester University in 1919... the rest is history.

Dad managed to survive beyond his century and very nearly made it to his 101st. Amongst his few remaining papers we found a letter addressed to him at the Atomic Weapons Research Establishment, Aldermaston, in 1962, so he was still involved somehow. The worst of it for me, was that at the time, I protested on the 'outside' while he was on the 'inside' helping to build the 'bloody things'. I had no idea. Thanks Dad! Anyway, he did have a conscience. He did feel that it was "nothing to feel proud of". If for nothing else, I hope he rests in peace at last. I had nothing to forgive him for, nor did anyone else. He merely did his duty like millions of others like him.

Recently, speaking to friends just returned from an Australian trip, the conversation skirted around the subject of Botany Bay. My friend said, "Oh, yes. I've got something to tell you about that. I was walking around Sydney on my own. You know how it is. It was hot and sticky. I thought I'd have a drop of Aussie coolant. I stood up at the bar next to an Aussie feller and we got talking, as you do. He asked me, "From back of the old country are you"? "Yes", I said. "On a bit of a holiday", and what with this and that, you know how it goes, we got around to exchanging names. For a moment I was a bit stunned. He said his name was Insole. I remembered what you had told me, that if ever I came across an Insole anywhere in the world, it had to be a relative.

"Well, I'll be damned", I said. "That's a coincidence. I have a friend and neighbour back home, he is an Insole too and comes from the East End of London, from Wapping". I didn't get very far in telling him anything else, he interrupted me. "Well, I be 'effed'! I know about that lot. I ought to, I've done me ancestry and all that. They were mostly fishermen out of Barking Creek. Well, I'll be stoned! The other lot finished up as something big. Coal mine owners in the Rhondda, in Wales. Tough on us ain't it cobber? Finished up here. Me Great Grandad won a free ticket to the Botany Resort". He said, "Got done for a little bit of river piracy, or something". He was lucky I s'pose. He could have got the (drop) and I would not be here boozing with you if he had".

"It was my turn to be stunned. Oh great! What a coincidence". I asked my friend if he got his address or phone number? "That's just it matey, I was so surprised I completely forgot to ask him for it. Sorry".

That's a shame, it would have been a very interesting contact. I would have liked to continue the conversation. Well, as Grandad had said, "If you meet up with an Insole anywhere in the world, buy him a pint because he's a relative". So, if you are about, somewhere out there, get in touch. I owe you a pint (or my heirs will). My address may be found from my publisher (if ever this is published).